TRANSNATIONAL CRIME
IN THE AMERICAS

TRANSNATIONAL CRIME IN THE AMERICAS

An Inter-American Dialogue Book

Tom Farer, Editor

ROUTLEDGE
New York & London

Published in 1999 by
Routledge
29 West 35th Street
New York, NY 10001

Published in Great Britain in 1999 by
Routledge
11 New Fetter Lane
London EC4P 4EE

Printed in the United States of America on acid-free paper

Design: Jack Donner

Library of Congress Cataloging-in-Publication Data

Transnational crime in the Americas : an inter-American dialogue book
    / edited by Tom Farer.
            p.   cm.
    ISBN 0–415–92300–X (cloth).   —   ISBN 0–415–92301–8 (pbk.)
    1. Transnational crime.   I. Farer, Tom. J.
HV6252.T72   1999
364.1'35'097—dc21   99–17455
                                                       CIP

For Kieran and Paola,
at the beginning of their great journey

CONTENTS

ACKNOWLEDGMENTS

Without the unstinting support of Peter Hakim and Michael Shifter, respectively President and Senior Fellow of the Inter-American Dialogue, the inquiry that culminates with this book would not have advanced beyond the rudimentary ideas I brought to them three years ago. They helped me identify the central issues the other authors and I have tried to tackle, and provided me with an enormously congenial institutional home. This is the second book I have done under the Dialogue's aegis. I hope it will not be the last. In a capital city filled with think tanks dedicated to defending one or another dogma, the Dialogue is rare in its readiness to support inquiry wherever it may lead, whether in terms of diagnosis or prescription. Implicitly it defends the proposition that hard heads are required to advance the purposes of soft hearts. In addition to Peter and Michael, I want to thank other persons associated with the Dialogue for their assistance at different points in the project, and particularly to mention Abby Horn and Jennifer Burrell.

I want also to thank my fellow authors. An integrated collective work requires from each participant a certain subordination of the ego which is not very common among busy and successful experts. To some degree they must indulge the editor's preoccupations and tolerate his genial harassments. Working with this splendid group of scholars has reminded me that team sports offer distinctive pleasures.

Shortly after the beginning of this project I moved to Denver University to assume the deanship of its Graduate School of International Studies. Given the relentless demands on any academic administrator in this market-driven age, I would have found it extraordinarily difficult to complete my own contribution to this collective effort were I not blessed by having Elizabeth Parmalee as my research assistant. I owe her profound thanks for hauling me to the finish line while completing her doctoral work, helping to manage a nonprofit organization, and being a wonderful wife and mother. Whenever I began to think I was intolerably busy, Elizabeth would unknowingly restore my sense of proportion.

—*Tom Farer*

PREFACE

Transnational crime poses a significant threat to democratic governance in the Americas. Yet, despite the manifest importance of the phenomenon, its implications are poorly understood. There has been little systematic effort to fathom the full dimensions of transnational crime in the hemisphere—its effects not only on governmental institutions, but also on the rule of law, social conditions, and economic performance. To the extent policy prescriptions have been put forward, they have tended to be sweeping and lacking in a careful analysis of concrete situations and the availability of resources—financial, human, and institutional.

This volume seeks to fill that void, and to serve as a valued source of information and analysis on transnational crime in the Americas. Tom Farer, dean of the Graduate School of International Studies at the University of Denver, came to the Inter-American Dialogue with the idea for the project a few years ago. Farer, who had successfully directed a previous Dialogue project on changing notions of sovereignty in the Americas, was particularly well equipped for this challenging enterprise. Known for his rare mix of imagination and rigor, and his impressive versatility, Farer skillfully conceptualized the effort and worked closely with the Dialogue to identify and assemble a high-quality group of policy analysts from Latin America, the United States, and Europe. His direction was superb.

Farer reviewed and commented on all of the chapters, which in most cases went through a number of drafts. The contributions also benefited substantially from an intensive, two-day workshop in July 1997 in San José, Costa Rica, which brought together all of the authors and a diverse group of first-rate analysts and practitioners from Central America. The Dialogue is grateful to the Faculty of Latin American Social Sciences (FLACSO) for its collaboration in organizing a public session, where some of the preliminary ideas and recommendations of the project were presented and discussed. We very much appreciate the generous support provided by the Swedish International Development Agency (SIDA) for this meeting.

Many others also deserve credit for their role in this project. Dialogue program associate Jane Marcus effectively coordinated the effort from the outset; her successor, Abby Horn, skillfully organized the San José meeting and made sure the project moved forward. And Dialogue program assistant Jennifer Burrell performed a variety of invaluable tasks that finishing such a volume entails.

The Inter-American Dialogue's research and publications are designed to improve the quality of public debate and decision-making on key issues in Western Hemisphere affairs. The Dialogue is both a forum for sustained exchange among leaders and an independent, nonpartisan center for policy analysis on U.S.-Latin American economic and political relations. The Dialogue's one hundred members—from the United States, Canada, Latin America, and the Caribbean—include prominent political, business, labor, academic, media, military, and religious leaders. At periodic plenary sessions, members analyze key hemispheric issues and formulate recommendations for policy and action. The Dialogue presents its findings in comprehensive reports circulated throughout the Americas. Its research agenda focuses on four broad themes: democratic governance, inter-American cooperation, economic integration, and social equity.

—*Michael Shifter*
Senior Fellow
Inter-American Dialogue

INTRODUCTION

President Bill Clinton helped trigger this book. For at an early point in his administration, he began to include transnational[1] organized crime in his mantra of threats to the national security both of the United States and of respectable countries generally. Unlike, for instance, the proliferation of weapons of mass destruction and even global warming, this issue did not have any real history on the agenda of national concern either in the U.S. or any of its major allies other than Italy, which was mainly concerned with the activities of the mafia at home. Yet, unlike certain other candidates for the post-cold war agenda, organized criminal activity across national boundaries had been around in one form or another for a long time; indeed, perceived as smuggling, it was downright ancient. One wondered: How could it suddenly have become such a grave menace . . . assuming it had? Assisting in the book's insemination were those writers like Claire Sterling and think tanks like Washington's Center for Strategic and International Studies that produced books and conferences announcing in apocalyptic terms an explosion of organized criminality across national frontiers. Having faced down the Comintern, were we now beginning a new twilight struggle, this time with a "Crimintern" (to borrow Tom Naylor's ironic analogy)?

Alongside the big claims were the huge figures that regularly found their way into articles in papers of record, figures like the one hundred to four hundred billion dollars of annual revenues imputed to the drug trade alone. Assuming these evident guesstimates were anywhere near accurate, what did they in fact describe? If it were nothing more than the total of all retail transactions between a legion of street-corner dealers and millions of consumers, that was one thing. If, on the other hand, it represented the cumulative disposable income of a small number of major producers, shippers, and wholesalers, that was quite another. For in the latter case, it could be translated into stunning economic and political power.

The ease of translation and of counteraction by established governments was bound to vary with crime's organizational structure. Was respectable society confronting a few large, tightly knit criminal hierarchies exercising cartel-like power to exclude competitors and shape prices, hierarchies capable of coordinating grand strategies of political infiltration and paramilitary intimidation both at their original domestic bases and abroad? If so, they could be seen virtually as alternative governments in many parts of the world, the equivalent, almost, of belligerent states. Huge cartels might at first glance seem peculiarly dangerous. But their very size and hierarchy would make them vulnerable to precise identification and decapitation: even on the most paranoid view of their financial and military assets, they were hardly in a position to challenge the United States and its allies in a head-to-head competition for power.

If, on the other hand, the political economy of illicit goods and services was closer to a free market than a cartel, a market with many and rapidly changing players, the players being rather small nuclei that contracted out many enterprise functions and extemporized alliances both at home and abroad, the resulting policy problem would appear both less forbidding and more intractable.

In trying to imagine the content of a prudent policy response to transnational criminal activity, other questions occurred to me. One was the relationship between criminal activity and the licit economy seen both as a structure of supply and demand and the venue of respectable actors. How closely were they intertwined? For instance, was organized crime largely parasitic, simply an added cost of doing business, or did it provide goods and service covertly demanded by respectable actors albeit prohibited by states? If the latter were true, then crime would prove a Hydra: cut off one head and another would appear to reap the hyperprofits that result when demand is strong and the risk of fulfilling it high.

Deep integration of the licit and illicit economies, if it existed, would pose additional problems for strategists of crime suppression. A priori, it would then seem difficult to war against one without collateral damage to the other. Defoliation by aerial spraying, for instance, is not an exact science. In trying to destroy fields of poppies or coca, one might easily destroy legitimate crops, as well as create public health hazards for peasants toiling, eating, and drinking in the targeted fields. And suppose part of the licit economy depended on income generated by the illicit, was not the sudden loss of that income bound to be traumatic? Strategy would need to account for the breadth of the trauma and the costs of recovery.

Everyone concerned with organized crime seemed to agree that a key element in any suppression strategy was an attack on the laundering of its proceeds. Could that attack be pressed home without close monitoring and increased regulation of international financial transactions and without tearing rents in the veil of secrecy woven by beneficiaries of the huge offshore economy, including the Fortune 500 and the superrich? And could it be done without producing serious rifts among the Western states who, by their acts and acquiescences, had fostered the climate of confidentiality, the tax havens, and the other features of that economy?

These were among the prominent questions for which the existing literature did not appear to have adequate answers. At least that was my view and the view of my colleagues at the Inter-American Dialogue. Providing answers, however provisional, (or at the very least better hypotheses) was one purpose for launching the scholarly collaboration that culminates in this book. The ultimate purpose, of course, was to illuminate and assess, in light of the data and analysis assembled by our authors, the policy options available to the United States and to all countries concerned with transnational organized crime.

While organized crime is a global phenomenon, nowhere—with the exception of the former states of the Soviet Empire—has its salience been as high as in the Americas and nowhere else has it so complicated interstate relations. Although Western Hemisphere criminal activity has other dimensions, for foreign-policy purposes it is essentially coterminous with the drug trade. By emphasizing supply rather than demand, that is by making interdiction rather than treatment and other domestic measures the centerpiece of U.S. response to drugs, the United States has made the drug issue a central element of its relations with many Latin American and Caribbean countries. In some cases, most notably Colombia, Panama, and Bolivia, drug policy drives everything else. In others, for instance Mexico, it regularly threatens to do so, whatever the cost to both parties.

While seeking to destroy the trade rather than trying mainly to mitigate its consequences, Washington has found a new rationale for training and arming military forces in Latin America with dubious records for respecting human rights. Coincidentally, it has induced their concentration on internal security issues, an orientation that in the past has encouraged military intervention in national politics. In the manner of a not entirely benevolent hegemon, it has arrogated to itself the right first to decide which countries are making the appropriate level of effort to suppress the production and export of forbidden drugs and then to determine the allocation and size of rewards and punishments. And on occasion it has violated the territorial integrity of Latin neighbors—whether openly and massively as when it invaded Panama in order to arrest General Manuel Noriega—or clandestinely, as when it hired Mexican police officers to kidnap a doctor suspected of complicity in the torture-murder of a U.S. drug agent. It may fairly be said, then, that the organized drug trade has induced U.S. behavior not entirely compatible with strengthening hemispheric cooperation, fostering human rights, and increasing respect for international norms.

As a working hypothesis, it seemed reasonable to assume that the prominence imparted to transnational organized crime by U.S. drug politics distorts understanding and thereby deranges policy. Drug politics could easily end up as the tail wagging the global strategy of response to transnational organized crime. In an effort to contain that risk, the first six chapters of this volume attempt a global response to the questions enumerated above. We look generally at the organized crime phenomenon: its incidence, functions, severity, and morphology. In addition, we assess its relative importance among candidates for the national security agenda, dissect its connection to the offshore economy, and compare U.S. and European perceptions and responses. Only then do we turn to the Americas. There we pursue the phenomenon through detailed case studies that seek to illuminate etiologies and morphologies of organized crime, to assess the role of organized crime in the politics and economies of various states, to clarify the relationship between the licit and illicit economy, and to expose the consequences of anticrime strategies. Finally, in the volume's concluding chapter, I attempt to elaborate the policy implications of the preceding edifice of data and analysis.

Neither this nor any other book can be the last word on the subject. Our collective hope and belief, however, is that we have advanced the dialogue.

—*Tom Farer*

NOTES

1. In connection with organized criminal enterprises, pundits, scholars, and politicians use "transnational" and "international" either interchangeably or indiscriminately. If that is an offence, I too should plead guilty. Either seems to be acceptably connotative. On balance, largely because the word "international" has long been associated with relations between governments, I slightly prefer the word "transnational" in referring to the activities of these non-state actors. They are reminders that nongovernmental organization (NGO in the contemporary idiom) is not a precise synonym for virtue and that international civil society, being a society, is not uniformly virtuous. Transnational criminal organizations might be seen as NGOs with attitude and bayonets.

TRANSNATIONAL ORGANIZED CRIME: AN OVERVIEW

1

Rensselaer W. Lee III

INTRODUCTION

Recent transformations in the global economy and in international political alignments have been a boon to the criminal underworld. Capitalizing on increased cross-border flows of goods, money, and people, criminal organizations have expanded their territorial reach and augmented their wealth and power relative to national governments. This development has spawned various direct and indirect threats to U.S. national interests. On the one hand, the new face of organized crime introduces new uncertainties into the international political environment, complicating U.S. relations with a number of foreign governments. For example, powerful narcotics constituencies increasingly influence electoral processes, challenge the political status quo by seeking de facto political representation, and undermine the rule of law in a number of Latin American and Asian states. In postcommunist countries, violence, corruption, and predatory behavior associated with emergent *mafiya* formations possibly complicate the transition to free markets and the development of stable democratic systems. On the other hand, organized crime's business lines—such as extortion rackets and trafficking in weapons, drugs, or (potentially) fissile nuclear materials—are themselves a threat to public safety and the health of populations. The devastating social and human consequences associated with drug consumption in the United States represent an obvious case in point.

The contours of the new international crime threat are in certain respects diffuse and ill-defined. Organized crime itself is an elusive phenomenon. Most definitions include at least three characteristics—continuity of operations, practice of corruption, and a capability to inflict violence. Some include Weberian attributes such as a hierarchical structure, clear division of labor, and prescribed organizational codes and taboos.[1] Within the global criminal archipelago, some forms of entrepreneurship approximate traditional models of organized crime, even resembling formal organizations in certain operational aspects. Yet some organized and continuous criminal activity—cocaine wholesaling within the United States (a multibillion-dollar business), for example—involves very little interaction with the authorities; criminals simply find it more advantageous to operate in the shadows without resorting to violence or corruption.[2] Likewise, much of the heavy lifting in international illegal commerce, from heroin trafficking to the smuggling of radioactive material and counterfeit money, is done by ad hoc criminal coalitions with few apparent resources, little formal structure, and uncertain connections with the political or official upperworld. Such groups commonly coalesce for one or two deals, divide up the proceeds and then disband.

Still, the concept of organized crime retains analytic and practical significance for this discussion. Traditional organized crime is a consequential force in much of the modern world, especially in fractured states with weak central government (the situation in much of Latin America and Asia) and in countries undergoing difficult economic and political transformations (the situation in the former Soviet Union). In such cases crime groups have been able to accumulate significant wealth and to protect their businesses by nourishing connections with the political authorities or by coercing and intimidating them. At the same time, modern organized crime, capitalizing on trends in the global economy (reduced border and customs controls, increased rapid technological change, and the like), is acquiring transnational characteristics. Organizations that maintain permanent representation ("cells") outside their home countries, enjoy corrupt relationships with foreign leaders, forge strategic alliances with criminal counterparts abroad, and penetrate the legitimate economics of other states are by definition transnational. Such transnational criminal arrangements represent difficult targets for law enforcement systems of nation-states. Criminals can exploit asymmetries in national legal or regulatory regimes to avoid detection or prosecution. Partnerships among different criminal entities with different comparative marketing strengths could vastly accelerate international trafficking in weapons, narcotics, and other dangerous materials.

U.S. international crime-fighting strategy as it has emerged in recent years comprises two related but distinct imperatives. The primary imperative is to limit the availability of criminal goods and services that are legally proscribed or injurious to society.

In the narcotics field the standard fare of supply reduction measures includes eradicating coca and opium fields, destroying processing laboratories, and seizing illicit drugs en route to the United States. An additional imperative, one that has acquired increasing prominence in the 1990s, is to attack and disrupt large aggregations of criminal power. In practice this has meant breaking up so-called cocaine cartels, immobilizing their top leaders, and severing drug traffickers' links to the legal economy and to the power structure. The new ideology of crime-fighting portrays international organized crime, including narcotics trafficking, as a threat to cherished values such as national sovereignty, democracy, and legitimate economic progress. Some observers view global crime as a kind of successor menace to monolithic world communism. For example, the late writer Claire Sterling referred to a "planet-wide criminal consortium" that came into being when the Soviet Union collapsed and that threatens "the integrity and even the survival of democratic governments in America, Europe, everywhere."[3]

Counterorganization is emerging increasingly as a rationale and justification for U.S. crime-fighting efforts overseas. (This is evident, for example, in the Drug Enforcement Administration's "kingpin" strategy that targets the heads of major cocaine-trafficking families in Colombia, and in the renaming of the State Department's Bureau of International Narcotics Matters as the Bureau of International Narcotics Matters and Law Enforcement Affairs.) One reason is that counterorganization has shown tangible results, at least in Colombia—consider, for example, the virtual destruction of the notorious Medellín cartel in the early 1990s, the more recent incapacitation of the Cali cartel leadership, and the successful prosecution of high-level Colombian officials and politicians for corrupt links to the Cali mob. On the other hand, supply reduction has been an unmitigated failure, at least as judged by trends in the U.S. marketplace. Per gram prices of cocaine and heroin dropped by approximately two-thirds between 1981 and 1996, while purity of these drugs increased respectively by 44 percent and 83 percent, according to the U.S. drug czar's office.[4] Whatever the benefits for Colombia, the apparent demise of the traditional cartel structure has not reduced the availability of cocaine on U.S. streets. A related reason is that onslaughts against malevolent criminal entities and their ties to power—though not without risk—have a certain basic legitimacy with publics and governments. Measures that are most likely to stop drug flows, on the other hand—such as sealing large extensions of the U.S.–Mexican border or conducting a massive aerial blitz against Andean cocaine crops—affect the livelihood of large populations and are probably infeasible politically. From a domestic U.S. perspective, though, reducing the drug supply is the principal significant justification for U.S. counternarcotics programs overseas; most Americans understandably are likely to care less about protecting the integrity of Colombian or Mexican democratic institutions (if this is what is at stake) than about getting psychoactive substances off America's streets.

Furthermore, U.S. concerns over organized crime in its national and transnational dimensions are partly attributable to the demise of Soviet communism and to post-Soviet "mission creep" of national security elements of the federal government. As an artifact of U.S. post-cold-war consciousness, the threat is sometimes overblown or misinterpreted. Some qualifications and corrections are in order here. For example, current U.S. security doctrine routinely depicts drug-trafficking organizations as threats to democratic institutions, especially in the Western Hemisphere. Yet all important drug-producing and -exporting states in the hemisphere have functioning democratic systems, so that proposition requires some analytical refinement. The illicit drug trade has financed authoritarian regimes—that of Luis García Meza in Bolivia in 1980–1981 and of Manuel

Noriega in Panama in the mid- and late 1980s—yet production of cocaine and the drug transit traffic respectively in Bolivia and Panama flourished and even expanded after these dictators departed from the scene.

Modern narco-elites in Latin America, in fact, behave politically very much like traditional economic elites. They fund political campaigns (often spreading contributions among opposing candidates), sponsor party-building and get-out-the-vote activities, and lobby legislatures for passage of laws favorable to narcotics business interests. Narco-businessmen are the principal or the sole source of funding for election contests in some regions, so their activities probably serve to increase the overall level of political participation. Interestingly, a recent (1997) State Department report asserts that large trafficking organizations "in many ways" represent "a greater threat to democratic government than most insurgent movements," but this is typical Washington hyperbole.[5] To be sure, the ability of drug dealers to influence electoral outcomes and to corrupt public officials, legislators, and judges can undermine public confidence in democratic institutions and processes. However, such a threat is long-term and diffuse, whereas in countries torn by civil war (in Colombia, for example, the main guerrilla groups control an estimated 20 to 40 percent of the nation's territory), the insurgent challenge is immediate and substantial.

The tendency toward threat inflation is also apparent in much U.S. commentary on crime trends in the former Soviet Union. "Roughly two-thirds of Russia's economy is under the sway of crime syndicates," says a recent (1997) report by Washington's Center for Strategic and International Studies (CSIS). "Russia is in danger of evolving into a criminal-syndicalist state," says the CSIS report. The fusion of criminal capital with the state bureaucracy has created "virtually a full-fledged kleptocracy," says Benjamin Gilman, chairman of the U.S. House International Relations Committee.[6] But if organized crime is as ubiquitous as these writers suggest, the concept loses much of its organizational shape. Instead of defining violent and lawless subgroups, it begins to encompass much of the Russian state and society. For example, the so-called shadow economy in Russia is indeed large, accounting for some 20 to 40 percent of the country's gross domestic product, according to different estimates. Yet most of this share consists of legal production and commercial activity unregistered and hence untaxed rather than traditional *mafiya* pursuits (drugs, extortion, weapons trafficking, and the like).[7]

Furthermore, artificial biases inflate Western assessments of Russian organized crime. What are considered serious crimes and punishable corrupt behavior in Western countries are not necessarily considered so in the East. For example, the rules concerning the privatization of state assets in Russia are murky at best and are widely flaunted. According to investigative news reports, Moscow Mayor Yuriy Luzhkov, a possible presidential contender, benefited directly from the sale of municipal property to the prominent real estate firm "Most" (Bridge) in the city.[8] Prime Minister Victor Chernomyrdin, until May 1992 the chief executive of the state natural gas company, Gazprom, reportedly ended up with 1 percent of the company's stock after it was privatized—an equity holding worth a minimum of $1.2 billion and possibly as much as $7 billion.

(This egregious windfall led a former Yeltsin National Security Council member, Yuriy Skokov, to label the premier "the chief mafioso in the country.").[9] Obviously Chernomyrdin, Luzhkov, and countless other officials reaped rewards from opportunism during the breakup of the Soviet system and afterward; yet to label these senior political leaders criminals is pointless—for better or worse, they represent the state of the system in Russia today.

Such caveats and concerns aside, organized crime and transnational crime clearly merit an important place on the agenda of international concern. The juxtaposition of powerful crime organizations and weak states poses subtle threats to government authority and legitimacy, and to the operation of free markets in these countries. Moreover, organized crime historically has tended to exploit, manipulate, and exacerbate conditions of economic dislocation and political upheaval. In addition, the transnational operations of the criminal underworld augment the supply of illicit products and services that have dangerous, if not lethal, ramifications for human societies everywhere. (The latter proposition is explained via comparative analyses of two illegal businesses that this writer knows well—drug trafficking and the smuggling of nuclear materials.)

Still, transnational crime is far from being a satisfactory substitute for world communism. The fight against this phenomenon in its various manifestations confronts the United States and the international community generally with some painful choices. Such dilemmas have been especially apparent in the area of counternarcotics policy, where the proverbial ax can cut both ways. It is now painfully apparent to U.S. policymakers that the production, sale, and export of narcotics are closely interwoven with the economies and political systems of many countries. These activities are an important source of foreign exchange, income, and employment in the affected states. Criminals' episodic positive contributions in certain areas—for example, delivering social services to impoverished peasants and slum dwellers and contributing to local security and counterinsurgency operations (in Colombia and Peru)—underscore the complexity of these linkages. Quite obviously, counterstrategies have to be coupled with care.

For instance, military intervention against the cocaine cartels or stiff economic sanctions against a host government could actually create public sympathy and support for criminal groups, while materially weakening the capacity of the government to defend itself against them. Aggressive campaigns to eradicate drug crops can generate peasant support for antigovernment insurgent movements (and actually have done so in Colombia and Peru) and may impoverish countries with disastrous human or developmental consequences. Even financial strategies, such as freezing traffickers' assets or blacklisting their commercial ventures, can hurt legitimate business interests in some drug-torn countries (or, in the case of Mexico, can inflict collateral damage on the U.S. economy); obviously such measures need to be carefully fine-tuned to inflict minimal damage on the wider economy. The larger point, though, is that the so-called war against drugs in this hemisphere is subject to a multitude of compromises and constraints that practically vitiate the effectiveness of antidrug efforts, especially those focusing on curtailing the supply of these dangerous substances.

THREATS

"Institutional" Threats

Organized crime in the post-cold-war era presents an array of complex and novel challenges to United States security interests. Traditionally a domestic concern in a handful of countries (such as the United States, Italy, and Japan), organized crime's increased scale of operations, territorial reach, and destructiveness potentially threaten the stability of the international order. The threat has several dimensions. First, massive changes in the global economy—stemming from disintegration of hostile power blocs, technological advances in transportation and communications, and diminished government controls over flows of goods, services, and money—have fundamentally changed the context in which organized crime operates. Increased legal commerce provides a handy cover and justification for the movement of illegal merchandise and cash proceeds. As a result, criminal organizations have been able to globalize their operations, to position themselves in new markets, and to expand the range of their illicit activities.

A second dimension is closely related to the first. Largely as a result of expanded transnational activities, criminal organizations have been able to accumulate wealth and power on a scale that rivals or surpasses the resources available to the state and potentially impairs the legitimacy and effective functioning of governments, although this is not necessarily the criminals' intent. In some Latin American countries, narco-business income is so large relative to key economic variables that it could easily alter a country's path of economic and political development. In Colombia and Mexico, the taint of criminal funds has already compromised top political echelons, permeated legal economies, and in the view of some observers, undermined the moral basis of the state. In countries of the former Soviet bloc, that is, countries transitioning from authoritarian to democratic rule and from statist to open economies, *mafiya* structures (some of which are almost coterminous with the state bureaucracy) are associated with rampant corruption and profiteering in central government institutions—the cabinet, the legislature, the economic ministries, the security services, the military—and with massive illegal exports of capital from Russia. Partial criminalization of economic and political life has doubtless weakened public support for privatization and democratic reform in Russia and other newly independent states (NIS), although the reformers still command majoritarian support in Russia.

A crucial question concerns the political agendas of organized criminal formations—their intentions vis-à-vis the state authority and the exercise of institutional power. Generally speaking, criminal mafias are not philosophically antigovernment, antidemocratic, or anticapitalist and certain of their activities may even widen democratic political participation, as already noted. (In this respect they can be distinguished from guerrillas or terrorist groups that seek to overthrow governments and radically overhaul society.) But in order to conduct their illicit business and to insure against an effective repression from the state (if not now, then in the future), they wage war against institutions arguably vital to the health of democratic systems—strong judiciaries, transparent political parties, laws that effectively circumscribe illegal activities and punish wrong-doing, and authority structures that are impermeable to corruption. Organized crime could be accused of seeking to debilitate those parts of the political system that are impediments to its activities while preserving those aspects—such as voting and elections—that are useful. Like modern corporations, *mafiyas* may support a range of candidates for public office to guarantee a reservoir of support in incoming administrations.

Furthermore, criminals' strategy tends to favor the decentralization of state power to make it more penetrable. In some parts of the world, the criminal underworld has supported or even sponsored political challenges of varying seriousness to central government authority. In Colombia, for example, narcotics traffickers and paramilitary organizations schemed to create a separate "Department of the Middle Magdalena" (a trafficking stronghold) in the early 1990s. The Medellín kingpin Pablo Escobar launched a quasi-separatist movement, Antioquia Rebelde (Antioquia in Rebellion—Antioquia is the department of which Medellín is the capital) in 1993 as a final gesture of defiance against the Bogotá government. Italian organized crime has historically favored a devolution of power and, according to a recent assessment, would welcome the prospect of an Italy split into three independent federations. And in Russia mafia gangs and local political bosses in Yekaterinburg repeatedly crafted a scheme to set up an "independent republic" of the Urals in the early 1990s.[10]

Also, organized criminals, like legal economic groups, seek a measure of influence over a nation's principal institutions and its political leaders. The result has been perverse and persistent corruption that has affected the workings of government at all levels. Of particular concern are criminals' efforts to control points of entry into the political system (documented in Colombia, Mexico, Italy, and elsewhere) by undermining and manipulating elections to high public office. As noted, the criminals' main interest is usually to ensure access to the winning candidate rather than to favor a particular party platform; however, their interventions may distort outcomes and diminish the validity of the democratic process.

A classic case in point was the 1994 presidential election in Colombia, in which Ernesto Samper's campaign managers obtained a generous donation of $6 million from the leaders of the Cali cartel. According to Samper's then-campaign treasurer, the candidate himself approved the arrangement, and even promised as a quid pro quo to respect the rights of traffickers and to grant them lenient surrender terms if and when he assumed the presidency.[11] The opposing candidate, Andrés Pastrana, was also approached with a contribution offer (the size of the proposed donation is not known) from the Cali mob, but reportedly refused the offer. The large influx of cartel funds—used to cover media advertising, party rallies, and various vote-buying activities—possibly meant the difference between victory and defeat for Samper. The two candidates were in a virtual dead heat after the first round of the election, but Samper edged out a victory by a razor-thin margin of less than 2 percent of the votes cast in the second round.

The presence of a large organized crime sector also increases the threat of violence against state institutions and the political class. Recall, for example, the fearful terrorist campaigns of Sicily's Cosa Nostra and the Medellín cartel—exemplified in the murders of high-level officials and politicians, the destructive bombing attacks, and (in Colombia) the kidnappings of members of elite families. The exercise of violence, like the practice of corruption, is designed to weaken the political will of the authorities and to reduce law enforcement pressure on criminal organizations and leaders. For example, the political protection strategy of Bolivia's cocaine-trafficking organizations and Colombia's Cali cartel relied almost exclusively on delivering bribes and favors to power holders ("We don't kill judges or ministers; we buy them," Cali leader Gilberto Rodríguez Orejuela reportedly said on one occasion.).[12] Nevertheless, even "peaceful" crime formations can resort to violence if beneficiaries of criminals' largesse renege on their promises, or the consortia's ramified net of political and institutional connections comes under attack by reform-minded governments.

Latent Political Threats

As noted above, organized crime can coexist successfully with nation-states and democratic systems, but its activities nonetheless also create stress within the existing political order. Under certain circumstances, such activities can contribute to a breakdown of the system. One danger is that criminal enterprises or parts of them will merge with and reinforce existing civil conflicts or separatist tendencies. For example, the international traffic in drugs and arms has been associated with partial disintegration or airtight breakup of nation-states such as Burma and Afghanistan, and with festering internal wars in Colombia and Peru. In Burma, Khun Sa's Shan United Army (SUA)—nominally an insurgent force seeking political independence from Burma—controlled significant territory along the Thai-Burmese border. At one time, the SUA transported and refined approximately 80 percent of the opium produced in the Golden Triangle.[13] (In 1996 Khun Sa reached a peace accord with the Burmese government and surrendered under favorable terms; the SUA was dismantled.) In Colombia and Peru, antigovernment "narco-guerrillas" tax production and shipments of narcotics to further their stated objectives of toppling the government and introducing socialism. In Colombia, insurgent groups' earnings from the cocaine and opium trade range from $400 million to $500 million per year, according to a 1998 Colombian government estimate, which leads many Colombian observers to believe that the guerrillas constitute a drug "cartel" in their own right.[14] At the same time, alliances of cocaine traffickers, rightist paramilitary forces, and rural landholders set up their own "antisubversion" bastions in parts of the country that are weakly controlled by the government.

In Russia, organized crime has contributed to centrifugal political trends (recall the political project of an "independent republic" of the Urals) and to the breakdown of law and order in certain regions. Currently the biggest single threat to Moscow's control derives from the breakaway Chechen state in the Caucasus, which successfully fought the Russian army to a standstill in 1994–1996. (The Russians and the Chechens reached a cease-fire agreement in 1996 that did nothing to resolve Chechnya's status.) The Chechen state survives largely because of dona-tions from ethnic Chechen criminal organizations operating in other parts of Rus-sia, and the republic itself has been a haven for criminal activities ranging from heroin refining and trafficking to the smuggling of weapons and nuclear-related materials. Elsewhere in Russia, criminal groups are entrenched even in the Urals, where they pose a possible threat to central government control over the country's most sensitive nuclear enterprises, and in the Russian Far East, where they impede government plans to manage and develop the resources of that vast region.

A second type of threat is almost a mirror image of the former: that flagrant lawlessness and criminal threats to the legitimacy or integrity of governments will provoke a citizens' backlash of sorts—facilitating the growth of extremist or authoritarian movements that promise to reestablish order and fairness. The Cuban Revolution of 1959 owed its success largely to the collusive and degrading relationship between the American mafia and the Cuban power structures in the 1940s and 1950s. The conversion of Cuba into a tourist mecca for cocaine, pros-titution, and gambling, and the criminals' penetration of many sectors of the Cuban economy did much to delegitimize the Batista regime, offering a conve-nient political pathway for Fidel Castro's rise to power.[15] (Ironically, both drug trafficking and prostitution today are on the rise in Cuba, reflecting the decay of the Castroist order and an increasingly pervasive capitalist ethic on the island.) Similarly, in postcommunist Russia, rising lawlessness and corruption generate feelings of nostalgia for authoritarian government and state control, especially among older Russians. The political significance of the law-and-order issue is dif-ficult to gauge so far. The potential popularity of General Alexander Lebed (seen by some as an authoritarian figure), secretary of the Russian Security Council during 1996, doubtless derives from his strong public stance against crime and corruption and from several tough anticrime measures he sponsored while in office. (Lebed was ousted by Yeltsin in late 1996.) Nevertheless, establishment reformist leaders also cite the danger of organized crime to the Russian state; President Yeltsin himself in 1994 reportedly described Russia as a "superpower of crime" and "the biggest mafia state in the world."[16] Since the criminalization issue has been co-opted by both sides of the authoritarian and reformist divide, it loses much of its political salience. No doubt, intensified criminal activities fanned the discontent that produced ultranationalist Vladimir Zhirinovsky's electoral success in the December 1993 parliamentary elections, when his "Lib-eral Democratic" Party won 23 percent of the Russian vote. Zhirinovsky's plat-form included "on the spot execution of criminal gang leaders by firing squads" and seizure of criminal assets to finance a reduction of government budget deficits. (Other aspects of Zhirinovsky's program doubtless appealed to the Russ-ian voters. For example, the candidate favored restoring Russian sovereignty over Finland and Alaska. One of his more charming schemes involved setting up giant fans in northwestern Russia to blow radioactive waste over the Baltic countries). Fortunately, the Liberal Democrat Party lost half of its electoral strength in the 1995, Duma elections although another antireform party, the Communists, increased its share of the vote from 12 to 23 percent.

Latent Economic Threats

Observers disagree over the magnitude and even the direction of the effect of organized crime on economic growth. Indeed, the evidence is mixed. Ostensibly, criminals' activities in the economic sphere (in contrast to their forays into the political system) produce some positive effects—increased employment, infusions of foreign exchange, and widened income opportunities for poor people. Spending by narco-traffickers in South America irrigates industries, such as real estate and construction, and stimulates local commerce. Profits of organized crime and drug trafficking invested in legitimate businesses contribute measurably to the local economy. Yet the direct economic costs associated with a large organized crime sector can also be significant. Weak law enforcement, violence against businessmen and bankers, and pervasive official corruption scare away investment and jeopardize a country's economic future. Foreign direct investment, excluding portfolio investment, in crime-ridden Russia in the period 1991–1996 was twenty-two times less than investment in China ($7 billion compared to $156 billion), although Russia is twice as large and twice as wealthy (in per capita income terms) as China.[17] The same factors encourage illegal capital flight from Russia, estimated at $50 to $150 billion since 1991. Criminal racketeering represents another obstacle to growth; the president of Russia's Free Economic Society (an entrepreneurial association), Vladimir Ispravnikov, estimates that enterprises' protection payments to various criminal structures hike prices of goods and services by an average of 30 percent, clearly dampening consumption and harming normal economic activity.[18]

In addition, organized crime creates indirect economic costs. Successful illegal businesses have a tendency to displace legal economic activity. In Russia, according to recent estimates, the so-called shadow economy, which partly includes the businesses of organized crime, doubled in size between 1994 and 1996, while the formal economy slid by 10 percent.[19] In the Andean case, narco-dollars flooding Andean economies stimulate booms in certain economic sectors such as construction and real estate; yet the resulting overvaluation of domestic currencies discourages legal manufacturing by making imports cheaper and exports dearer. Contraband purchased with drug dollars has the same effect. The danger is that over time a country will lose its ability to produce tradables and become dependent on illegal exports.

Meanwhile the debate goes on. Francisco Thoumi, for example, argues the case for the parasitic model of the recent drug industry in Colombia. He cites an interesting statistic that from the late 1970s to the early 1990s, a period roughly paralleling the ascendancy of the Medellín cartel, the Colombian economy grew an average of 30 percent more slowly each year than from the mid-1960s to 1971. Seemingly, the crime economy depressed the growth of the formal sector of the economy. However, other factors—government mismanagement, low raw materials prices, activities of predatory guerrilla groups, and foreign competition in critical industries (such as textiles)—also affected economic performance. Moreover, the violence associated with the Medellín cartel may have been more off-putting to investment growth than the business of cocaine per se. A completely different take on the issue of cocaine's economic effects was argued by two Harvard scholars, Mario de Franco and Ricardo Godoy, in a 1991 study. They contended, writing about Bolivia, that "cocaine production confers unambiguous benefits to the nation. A 10 percent increase in cocaine production raises GDP by 2 percent and lowers unemployment by 6 percent."[20] The effects of cocaine production and trafficking on South American economies are probably both positive and negative, which no doubt explains why Andean leaders are afraid to attack the industry at its roots.

Threats—Outputs

Organized crime's various direct or implied institutional threats are more a domestic than a foreign-policy concern. The United States has largely contained or marginalized its organized crime problem. Certainly the American mafia lacks the clout and connections that it had in the 1930s and 1940s, and various successor underworld groups (Colombian, Mexican, Dominican, and the like) generally prefer to minimize interactions with upperworld agencies—cops, politicians, and the like. Furthermore, even a very large illegal business such as narcotics (which, according to the drug czar's office, yields $62 billion annually in total sales) represents a trivial part of the $7 trillion legitimate U.S. economy. Thus, drug dealers' ability to shape U.S. economic or political institutions is minuscule, although it is vast in Latin America and other parts of the world.

Certain activities (illegal businesses) of transnational criminal groups, though, represent a visible or potential danger to U.S. society. One such threat is drugs, or rather addiction to drugs, which correlates with high public health costs, with high incidences of gang behavior, property crime, homicide, and with a general deterioration of family and community life. The drug czar's office estimates that the "social costs" of drug abuse, mostly crime-related costs, amount to $67 billion per year.[21] Prohibitionist regimes designed to prevent the sale and use of drugs are also costly (and probably need to be reappraised), but the theory behind such regimes is fairly straightforward—that psychoactive substances are harmful and addictive, and that consumption of them undermines social stability.

Certain other products circulated by transnational criminals—such as exotic weaponry, explosives, nerve gas, toxic chemicals, and nuclear materials—are unambiguously dangerous to human societies, although (unlike drugs) the dangers tend to be episodic or futuristic. The smuggling of nuclear materials, for example, barely touches the United States, although it is a fairly visible problem in Europe. While most of the nuclear materials peddled internationally qualify as radioactive junk that cannot be used to fashion nuclear weapons, certain beta- and gamma-radiation sources such as cesium-137, cobalt-60, and strontium-90 pose very significant environmental hazards. Also, in today's world, the possibility of significant leakages of fissile materials (highly enriched uranium and plutonium) and weapon components into world markets cannot be ruled out.

Materials and components could easily be smuggled to the United States by criminal conspiracies or terrorist groups and assembled to make a bomb.

BACKGROUND AND TRENDS

Actors

Virtually no country is free from organized crime and almost every country has produced criminals who belong to or work for such groups. Nonetheless, eight countries have brought forth the largest and strongest of such organizations: the United States (the American mafia or Cosa Nostra, which has also long operated in Canada); Mexico (the Juárez, Tijuana, Guadalajara, and Gulf cartels); Colombia (the Medellín and Cali cartels); Italy (the Sicilian mafia or Cosa Nostra, the Calabrian 'Ndrangheta, the Neapolitan Camorra, and the Sacra Corona Unita of Apulia), the former Soviet Union (hundreds of Russian and various Caucasian *mafiyas*), Turkey (a dozen or so Turco-Kurdish clans), Hong Kong-Taiwan (the six Triads) and Japan (the Boryokudan, more usually called the Yakuza). Of these, the Colombians, the Sicilians, and the Chinese are generally considered the best organized, the most ubiquitous, and the most powerful. Recently, however, Russian organized crime has begun to rival these in power and global reach; according to CIA director John Deutch, some two hundred large *mafiya* groups conduct extensive criminal operations throughout Russia and around the world.

While they are smaller, criminal organizations based in Korea, the Philippines, Thailand, Burma, Pakistan, Israel, Albania, Nigeria, and Jamaica have also begun to cause serious worry for law enforcement officials. All of these criminal organizations engage in the smuggling and sale of controlled substances and illegal drugs. But they also profit from other crimes such as smuggling illegal immigrants; white slavery; murder-for-hire; protection rackets and extortion; loan sharking; currency and document counterfeiting; money laundering; arms trafficking; vehicle theft; pillaging of financial institutions; and the pirating of properties protected by trademarks and copyrights—all activities that do direct and serious damage to American interests.[22]

Wide agreement exists that organized crime poses subtle threats to national integrity and democratic institutions, corrodes and degrades the international business environment, and threatens Western visions of a good society. Yet the precise character and contours of the phenomenon remain unclear. As suggested above, groups differ significantly along such dimensions as size, wealth, internal structure and cohesion, core activities, and international links. For instance, Colombian organizations concentrate on one product line—drugs—while most other crime groups engage in a range of illegal activities. The Yakuza and the American Cosa Nostra derive most of their earnings from domestic activities, whereas Colombian traffickers' profits depend almost entirely on international sales. Also, modern criminal enterprises do not necessarily conform to traditional models of organized crime that emphasize such attributes as hierarchy, continuity of operation, and corrupt ties to governments. Much harmful criminal activity is carried out by flexible, loosely structured systems that expand or contract in accordance with changing opportunities and risks. Some groups are venture-specific: perpetrators come together to commit a crime, divide up the profits (if any), and then disperse. Such a pattern is characteristic of Chinese heroin groups and many nuclear-smuggling networks in former East-bloc states. In the United States, computer crime that costs U.S. companies an estimated $10 billion per year is generally perpetrated by small teams of digital "hitmen" or by isolated talented hackers. Vast organizational resources, elaborate hierarchical arrangements, and coteries of compliant government officials are not prerequisites for serious crimes—including actions that can cause great damage to the planet.

Finally, conceptions of organized crime as composed narrowly of underworld figures with criminal records (Latin American or Sicilian Cosa Nostra bosses or Russian "thieves in the law") also fail the reality test. Modern criminal offenders are as likely to come from the upperworld as from the underworld. In post-Soviet states, for example, leaders of crime syndicates can be bureaucrats, managers, former black marketeers, KGB, military officers, or even teachers. Journalist Stephen Handelman writes that of eighty leading criminals in Moscow identified by the Russian Ministry of Internal Affairs in 1993, most had occupations listed in police files as "industrial manager" or "business director."[23] Some types of Russian "establishment" crime have grave international implications. For instance, ranking military officers' illegal or gray-market sales of weapons and equipment such as AK-47s, armored vehicles, MiG aircraft, and toxic chemical agents are a prominent security concern in troubled areas of Eurasia. Former KGB officers were linked to the trafficking of radioactive materials in Europe in the early 1990s, and reports have surfaced that Russia's Foreign Intelligence Service masterminded a plutonium smuggling episode in Germany in 1994. A so-called "Moscow Narcotics Group" comprised of former KGB officers has exploited former intelligence assets to develop a worldwide heroin-trafficking and money-laundering network. Part of the group's heroin supplies originated in a modern pharmaceutical-chemical laboratory located in Chechnya. (This operation was reputedly shut down in January 1995 following Russia's invasion of the breakaway republic.)[24] Reputedly the group is collaborating with criminal organizations in Colombia, Italy, and Mexico in various drug distribution schemes. Finally, both Russian customs officials and foreign visitors to Russia report that senior managers of Russian nuclear enterprises have tried to sell radioactive materials illegally through networks of commercial contacts and scientists abroad. In sum, the extraordinary diversity of criminal actors operating in the world today requires more comprehensive and sophisticated definitions of organized crime than now exist.

Preconditions

A number of different factors have led to the recent growth of international organized crime. The collapse of the Soviet empire and the reintroduction of capitalism in China have removed cold-war barriers to business but also to criminal activity. Expanding worldwide financial and market systems have increased the magnitude and frequency with which people, goods, and money move across national frontiers. For example, the volume of U.S. merchandise trade grew 1,300 percent from 1970 to 1994, more than twice as fast as U.S. gross domestic product. As of the mid-1990s more than 250 million people, 75 million cars, 3 million trucks, and 500,000 rail cars cross the U.S.–Mexican border each year. The sheer volume of such movements and transactions allows much criminal enterprise, including smuggling and money laundering, to go undetected.

Regionwide lowering of barriers to trade and financing, the establishment of a free-trade area in North America (NAFTA), and the ongoing lowering of customs and passport controls in Europe have also provided unintended opportunities for the spread of criminality in the guise of legitimate business. For example, Peter Andreas notes that cocaine traffickers have established factories, warehouses, and trading companies or fronts in Mexico in anticipation of the boom in cross-border commerce under NAFTA.[25] In former Warsaw-Pact states, porous frontiers and newly convertible currencies have increased the attractiveness to international criminals of local markets for drugs and other illicit substances. Drug addiction is soaring in most of these states. At the same time, the demise of Communism and the dilution of state power in these countries have diminished resources available to law enforcement and security agencies; also, democratization has placed new constraints on their agencies' operations. As a result of such trends, organized crime in its various product lines—among them drug trafficking, counterfeiting, dealing in stolen cars and art objects, arms smuggling, and commerce in illegal aliens and human body parts—is flourishing in post-Communist states.

Perhaps the greatest beneficiary of these global economic shifts and political realignments has been the illicit drug trade, which is both booming and evolving in new directions. The traffic in narcotics, manipulated by powerful transnational actors with supporting casts of domestic entrepreneurs, today generates total revenues of up to $400 billion annually, according to United Nations estimates. The most dynamic recent growth has been in opium production, which has almost doubled since 1987, according to State Department figures.[26] Significant new opium cultivation has appeared in Colombia, Venezuela, Vietnam, China, and post-Soviet Central Asia. Colombia, traditionally a "cocaine" country, now supplies a majority of the heroin consumed in the United States, according to the Drug Enforcement Administration. China is now an important transit country for Burmese heroin; also, entrepreneurial North Koreans are entering the heroin business, perhaps with the backing of the Pyongyang government. Poland, China, Russia, Azerbaijan, Mexico, and the Baltic States are emerging as important producers and exporters of sophisticated amphetamine drugs. Demand for cocaine, though stabilizing in the United States, is soaring in Western Europe; moreover entrepreneurial criminals are increasingly peddling cocaine and heroin to consumers in Eastern Europe and Russia.

Finally, organized crime—like many modern corporations—has developed new strategies and structural arrangements to compete more effectively in the international market place. That is, organized crime has become truly transnational as opposed to a mere assortment of national organizations with arms-length trading relations. This new phenomenon is difficult to define precisely. What can be said, however, is that they share the following key characteristics.

Establishment of Affiliates or "Cells" Abroad
Like multinational corporations, major crime groups have stationed permanent representatives abroad to handle the organization's main businesses. For instance, until the U.S.–Colombian crackdown on the Cali cartel in 1995–1996, Cali-based trafficking organizations maintained networks of importers and distributors in most major U.S. (and some European) cities; these trafficking agents worked under tight operational supervision of the "head office" in Cali. (Every dollar and every kilogram had to be accounted for and every customer for the merchandise required prior approval from Cali.) Cali's distribution networks in the United States have since been cut back, but Mexican trafficking organizations are now establishing cells in many U.S. cities to handle cocaine distribution. In Germany, the federal police have identified sixty-eight Italian crime cells, many with ties to Italy's four major criminal formations, which engage in weapons and drug dealing, trafficking in stolen cars, and money laundering throughout the country.

Corrupt Relations with Foreign Leaders
Perhaps the clearest examples are in the Western Hemisphere, where crime and degradation associated with the South American cocaine industry have metastasized to Central America and the Caribbean. Over the past decade, Colombia's cocaine cartels have reached beyond their home base to cultivate ties with political leaders and top-level officials in a number of Central American and Caribbean countries: for example, Panama, the Bahamas, Antigua, the Turks and Caicos Islands, and even communist Cuba. The aim has been to enhance cocaine logistics and money flows—for instance, to obtain landing and refueling facilities, docking facilities, storage sites, permission to operate cocaine laboratories, and various financial and money-laundering services. Colombia organizations are even rumored to have contributed funds to the 1994 presidential campaigns of Ernesto Perez Baladeres in Panama and Ernesto Zedillo in Mexico. Like organized crime itself, the taint of political corruption is acquiring a distinctly international flavor.

Transnational Strategic Alliances
Like multinational cooperation, criminal organizations increasingly seek partners abroad to maximize market opportunities, improve logistics, and reduce business exposure. Often this means relying on a foreign partner's smuggling or money laundering networks and superior knowledge of local conditions (including corrupt connections to law enforcement). Archetypal examples of such cooperation include Colombia's umbrella agreements with Italian crime syndicates to sell cocaine in Italy and Central Europe. These arrangements address such issues

as terms of delivery, payment schedules, prices, and market development. Italian police have recorded discussions between the Sicilian mafia and the Cali cartel regarding formation of a dedicated infrastructure of front companies to manage large-volume flows of narcotics and banknotes. Similarly, the Cali cartel has reached agreements with Mexican traffickers whose knowledge of the U.S. border and access to top Mexican police and judicial officials represent invaluable smuggling assets. Such ties extend even to former Warsaw Pact states, where the Cali cartel has cooperated with former Czech intelligence officers, Polish businessmen, and assorted Russian criminals to open nontraditional land and sea routes to ship cocaine to Western Europe.[27] Finally, the Sicilian mafia and other transnational groups have established a variety of money laundering arrangements with Russian crime syndicates: these involve converting dollars to rubles and rubles back to dollars, and also swapping dirty money for Russian weapons, raw materials, and real estate.[28]

An even more astounding instance of Russian-Colombian criminal collaboration detailed in a recent *Washington Post* investigative report concerned international transfers of advanced weaponry. According to a 1997 federal indictment, a Russian émigré group based in Miami had arranged the sale of at least two Soviet-made helicopters to representatives of the Cali cartel. The negotiations for the sale were conducted at "Porky's," a Miami nightclub owned by one of the criminals. Furthermore, U.S. officials interviewed by the *Post* say that the discussions had included a proposal by the Russians to provide the cartel with a diesel-powered submarine from the Russian naval base at Kronstadt (in the Gulf of Finland) at a price of $5 million. The price also included the services of a crew of twenty for one year. The submarine would have been an important adjunct to the cartel's smuggling operation; however, the Cali representative backed out of the deal, "apparently feeling such an enterprise was too ambitious," in the newspaper's words.[29]

Legitimate Investments in Foreign Countries
Organized crime groups are increasingly deploying financial assets outside their host milieux, to hide criminal proceeds from the authorities, and to facilitate business operations and (in some cases) to enhance their legitimacy locally. Examples are legion: mafia expert Alison Jamieson reports that the Sicilian Cuntrera-Caruana clan maintains a wine bar, an antique business, and a travel agency in the United Kingdom as covers for importation of cannabis from Kashmir and heroin from Thailand. Similarly, a leader of the Campania (Naples)-based Camorra group owns five container companies in Marseille to facilitate the Camorra's cigarette- and heroin-smuggling ventures.[30] Cali organizations established an agricultural import-export firm in Prague and a "Polish-Latin American club" in Krakow (which employed three Colombians from Bogotá), both as fronts for cocaine-trafficking. Investment decisions sometimes serve long-term and diffuse strategic purposes, such as making inroads into legitimate economic and political establishments.[31] For example, in 1993 Italian agents of the Cuntrera-Caruana clan were exploring the possibility of investing in the German steel industry. The Italian Ministry of Interior reported in the same year that Cal-

abria's 'Ndrangheta were preparing to purchase a bank, a chemical plant, and a steel works in St. Petersburg for $2-billion-worth of rubles through a complex financial transaction involving banks in Switzerland, Luxembourg, and Germany.[32]

SPOTLIGHT ON ILLEGAL BUSINESSES

Introduction

Criminal enterprises manifest a broad range of organizational forms. At one extreme, such vehicles comprise tightly organized and continuous operations resembling, with due provision for illegality of operations, the pattern of modern corporations. (A difference is that criminal organizations are likely to maintain fewer "in-house" professionals, such as lawyers, accountants, and shippers, preferring to contract such services as needed.) At the other extreme, they comprise fluid, nonhierarchical systems of criminal entrepreneurs who work together for the duration of one or a few crimes. Archetypal examples of the first pattern are Colombia's cocaine-exporting organizations—perhaps the most successful and wealthiest criminal groups operating in the international arena today. Examples of the second are the visible nuclear smuggling networks identified in former Communist states in the 1990s (the visible trade, though, obscures organized crime's apparently increasing participation in high-value smuggling operations, a chilling new development to be discussed below).

Drug Trafficking

The Colombian Cocaine "Cartels"
The business of exporting cocaine was once upon a time a relatively simple affair. Cocaine was produced in makeshift laboratories with rudimentary technology; some of these operations were located in private homes on the outskirts of major cities. Human courier "mules" smuggled small quantities of cocaine—a few grams or a few pounds in luggage as personal effects. Trafficking organizations were typically simple in structure, comprising a Colombian buyer, a smuggler-courier, and a point of contact in the United States, who received the merchandise and sold it to a U.S. wholesaler.

Growing U.S. demand for cocaine in the early and mid-1980s precipitated major logistical and organizational changes in the Colombian cocaine industry. Production and transport were revolutionized. The "mule" system was superseded by fleets of light aircraft that could carry loads of 500 to 1,000 kilograms of cocaine. By the 1990s, traffickers were using merchant shipping, cargo jet aircraft, and semisubmersible vessels to export multiton loads of cocaine to foreign markets. Export routes, developed with extreme care, required the complex coordination of many activities: air, sea, and overhead transport; aircraft refueling and maintenance; loading and unloading and storage of drugs; delivery of bribes to appropriate officials in transit countries; and—in recent years—intensive collaboration with trafficking organizations in these countries. Traffickers, especially those associated with the Medellín coalition, also sought to realize economies of scale in production. Huge cocaine laboratories, some the size of industrial factories, were set up in remote jungle and plain regions; some of these plants were equipped with chemical recycling facilities that permitted the use of the same batches of chemicals several times in processing.[33]

As the cocaine traffic expanded, the industry became specialized and hierarchically organized. By the late 1980s, an integrated and efficient international marketing structure had developed: trafficking organizations per se comprised principally top leaders, senior managers, and their staffs; these "core" organizations conducted the entire range of trafficking functions, working through layers of subcontractors and freelancers who provided key specialized services, including refining, smuggling, distribution, money laundering, and enforcement. The organizations did not attempt to restrict supply and prop up wholesale cocaine prices (which dropped by 60 to 80 percent during the 1980s). Yet sophisticated patterns of collaboration developed among these organizations, albeit usually on a regional basis. The groups co-financed and co-insured large shipments of cocaine, pooled information on law enforcement activities (such as planned raids against major leaders), developed joint counterintelligence and counterenforcement strategies, and collaborated to improve their bargaining positions vis-à-vis the state. In Cali, according to a *Miami Herald* report, major drug kingpins each contributed $200,000 per month to maintain a joint intelligence-gathering operation; much of the money went to bribe police, army officials, and politicians. Similarly, Cali leaders such as the Rodríguez Orejuela brothers, José Santa Cruz Londoño, Helmer Herrera Buitrago, and Juan Carlos Ramírez reportedly established a common $8-million fund to influence the outcomes of the 1994 presidential and congressional election campaigns.[34] Also, in the 1980s and early 1990s, leaders of the Medellín and Cali cartels negotiated as a group with the Colombian government in an effort to obtain collective judicial benefits such as sentence reductions, an end to extradition, and even amnesty for their crimes.

The core groups established elaborate networks of importers and regional distributors in the United States. In New York City, for example, Cali organizations reportedly maintained ten to twelve marketing subsidiaries, or "cells," each comprising ten to twelve salaried employees who earned anywhere from $2,000 to $20,000 per month. Cell directors reported directly to the home office in Cali, where the directors made all key decisions on the cell's activities—they set prices, determined the amounts of cocaine to be sold, and approved prospective buyers. This cell structure, which benefited from a large Colombian resident population in the United States, allowed Cali-based exporters to obtain per-kilogram cocaine prices two to three times higher than those realized by selling to a U.S. wholesaler at the point of entry. Trends in the industry dictated forward integration. At the beginning of the 1980s, cocaine dealers could realize a gross income of $40 million and a net income of perhaps $38 million (a 95 percent profit rate!) just by delivering a ton of cocaine to first-level wholesalers in the United States. By the beginning of the 1990s, lower cocaine prices and the necessity of shipping the drug via more complex and expensive routes (the result of stronger U.S. air and maritime interdiction efforts) had reduced smuggling profits to 50 percent or less of earnings. (However, such profits were still enormous compared to those in most legitimate economic activity.)

The cartels were, nominally at least, associations of independent entrepreneurs. No formal superstructures existed to coordinate activities, marshal resources, and resolve disputes. In practice, however, important kingpins performed a coordinating role. Cali leader Gilberto Rodríguez, for example, enjoyed a so-called *poder de convocatoria*—power of assembly—that allowed him among other things to negotiate with the Colombian government on behalf of other Cali figures. Pablo Escobar exercised enough clout within the Medellín constellation of trafficking organizations to exact "war taxes" from his colleagues to pursue a vindictive vendetta against the Colombian state in 1989–1993.[35] More formalized arrangements have existed elsewhere. The Sicilian mafia and the American Cosa Nostra maintained ruling "commissions"—in effect, underworld governments above the individual organizations or families. The commissions regulated joint ventures between families, enforced property rights, allocated territory, approved the initiation of new members, and controlled the use of violence. Collective political decisions made by the Commission of the Sicilian Cosa Nostra range from the (uncharacteristic) transfer of support to Socialist and Radical Party candidates in the 1987 general elections to the assassinations of magistrates Giovanni Falcone and Paolo Borsellino and of Sicilian political figure Salvo Lima during 1992.[36]

In the cases mentioned above (and in significant criminal groupings elsewhere), the "underworld government" function exists principally to maximize business risks and to develop a common strategy vis-à-vis upperworld governments. The threat surely does not relate to the possibility of price-fixing for illegal goods and services, but rather to the potential for a coordinated challenge to state power and authority. Furthermore, the ability of organizations to establish working transnational links—Colombian with Sicilian and Mexicans, Sicilians with Americans, Colombians and Sicilians with Russians—allows them to move criminal goods and assets around the globe with increasing impunity. Concerted efforts by the international community to break up large criminal aggregates, to destroy "underworld governments," and to disrupt transnational alliances among criminal groups thus would seem to be essential attributes of a modern crime control strategy.

The Different Faces of the Nuclear Smuggling Business

Russia has been described as a third-world country with a first-rate nuclear capability. The country has more than ten thousand strategic and tactical nuclear weapons and almost seven hundred tons of fissile uranium and plutonium stored outside of weapons. It has about the same GNP as the Netherlands with ten times the population. The passing of the Communist dictatorship has left a power vacuum at the center, possibly endangering Russian's ability to monitor and control arsenals of weapons of mass destruction as well as technologies and components used in manufacturing such weaponry.

A compelling manifestation of those problems has been the soaring illegal traffic in radioactive isotopes and other nuclear materials that originates principally in nuclear complexes in former Soviet states. To be sure, the traffic appears to follow a dynamic different from that of conventional criminal businesses. For example, evidence of a true black market for nuclear materials is difficult to establish. Most stolen material qualifies as radioactive junk—posing environmental hazards, perhaps, but not useful for making nuclear weapons in the classic sense of the term. Few actual sales of nuclear contraband have been recorded in the former Soviet Union (FSU) or in the West. Indeed, buyers, when they surface, usually turn out to be undercover police, security officials, or journalists cooperating with the police. Traditionally, important organizations and players in the Russian and international criminal underworlds have shown little interest in procuring or brokering radioactive substances. This is not because crime groups practice gang taboos or patriotic self-restraint but because organized crime's core businesses—such as narcotics, extortion, bank fraud, and raw-materials smuggling—offer fewer risks and a superior cash flow picture. Amateur criminals (for example, ill-paid nuclear workers, small metals traders, and opportunistic businessmen) thus predominate in the supply chain for nuclear materials and components and determine its specific organizational character.

Yet the nuclear traffic is not exactly innocuous. In at least fifteen cases in the 1990s, authorities in Western Europe of the former Soviet Union have confiscated quantities of plutonium or highly enriched uranium that could be used to make nuclear weapons. In one highly publicized incident, a Colombian national, Justiniano Torres Benitez, smuggled almost a pound of plutonium in a suitcase aboard a Lufthansa flight from Moscow to Munich in August 1994. Another high-profile case was the seizure of nearly 3 kilograms of 87-percent pure uranium-235 in Prague in December of that year and the arrest of a Czech physicist and several co-conspirators who had arranged the delivery of the material from Russia.[37]

Furthermore, there exists the frightening possibility that finished nuclear weapons are actually available on the black market. In August of this year, a pair of Lithuanian nationals were sentenced in Miami for trying to sell forty antiaircraft missiles to undercover U.S. agents posing as members of a Colombian drug cartel. In videotaped discussions with the agents, the Lithuanians also mentioned that they could procure a tactical nuclear weapon and smuggle it into the United States if the "Colombians" had any interest. The Lithuanians gave the name of a St. Petersburg company that could help arrange the deal—a company that allegedly was staffed by former KGB operatives and that had connections to the Russian Academy of Sciences. Were the Lithuanians just scam artists—of which there are a great many in the nuclear black market? Or did they really have the connections and the wherewithal to supply a nuclear device? One does not know for sure.[38]

All signs indicate that controls within the Russian nuclear establishment are in a horrible state of decay. Perhaps the most serious problem is the growth of a privatization mentality within the nuclear complex. Economic reform has meant a license to steal. This has resulted in broad systemic corruption and a variety of insider threats and conspiracies. The archetypal nuclear criminal in Russia is not a lowly worker (although workers account for many of the minor thefts from enterprises), but rather someone with clear "establishment" links—a plant director, a chief engineer, a government official, or a military officer.

To mention some examples in the 1990s: in Murmansk, officers of Russia's Northern Fleet orchestrated a major theft of several kilograms of highly enriched uranium; they simply broke into a padlocked storehouse and made off with submarine fuel rods containing the material. The director and senior managers of a Sverdlovsk weapons plant and several officials of the Ministry of Atomic Energy stand accused of illegally exporting $23-million-worth of radioactive materials to the West. (Fortunately, these were medical isotopes, not fissile materials, according to Russian newspaper reports.) A British engineer visiting a top-secret defense plant in Sverdlovsk in connection with a consulting assignment on nuclear environmental problems was asked by his hosts, including the plant's director and two local government officials, to arrange certification by a European laboratory for samples of weapons-grade plutonium; the apparent idea was to obtain documentation that would facilitate sales of this material to unnamed international buyers.[39]

Indeed, conditions in the nuclear complex may be even worse than they appear. A highly placed Russian source in the Russian Academy of Sciences who works closely with nuclear and dual-use technologies apprised this writer of a bizarre scheme to import uranium concentrate from Kazakhstan, enrich it in Russian plants equipped with isotope separation capabilities, and then export the product via smuggling routes leading across southern Russia and Azerbaijan. The uranium enrichment services are contracted by Islamic, principally Chechen, criminal groups that hold previously negotiated arrangements with final buyers outside of Russia. Some tens of kilograms of weapons-grade uranium leaked out of Russia in this fashion during the mid-1990s, according to the scientist, most of it destined for Iran, Pakistan, and Middle Eastern countries that maintain clandestine nuclear-weapons programs. Obviously diversion on such a scale, if this is indeed occurring, would require the active collaboration or at least the acquiescence of senior nuclear-plant managers, and possibly of Russian government officials as well.[40]

Finally, criminal proliferation of nuclear materials increases the likelihood of devastating actions by terrorist groups or criminal extortionists. Even if traffic in weapons-grade or weapons-usable materials is successfully contained, widespread availability of toxic radioactive materials such as cesium-137, cobalt-60, and strontium-90 is in itself worrisome. Even ordinary reactor waste can be a weapon in the hands of terrorists. A terrorist might fashion a dispersal device combining conventional explosives with, say, cobalt-60 or plutonium oxide and contaminate a wide area. Certain powdered radioactive substances introduced into a ventilation system of an office building or hospital could create massive fatalities. The question is whether the terrorist group in question can accomplish its aims most effectively with a nuclear device, with conventional explosives, or with chemical or biological weapons.

Fortunately, there are few examples of nuclear terrorism to date. Recall, however, that in late 1995 a Chechen military commander Shamil Basayev arranged the burial and the subsequent discovery (by a Russian news team) of a canister of cesium-137 in Moscow's Izmailovsky Park. At the time the Chechen leader threatened to turn Moscow into an "eternal desert" from radioactive waste. Economic desperation can even lead to terrorist-type episodes. Captain Mikhail Kulik, an investigator for the Northern Fleet prosecutor's offer, recounts such a case involving a worker at a repair facility for nuclear submarines. After not being paid for a few months, the worker decided to post a notice on the bulletin board of the plant threatening to blow up a workshop containing two reactors. Though he was caught, the incident could be a harbinger of worse things to come.[41]

Other Strategic Threats

Nuclear smuggling is not the sole criminal proliferation threat emanating from the former Soviet Union. The deteriorating condition of its military-industrial complex has also increased the role of illegal transfers of toxic chemical and biological agents and technologies for making them. Such transfers, in fact, have already occurred, alarmingly with the apparent complicity of high-ranking Russian officials. In 1995, for example, General Anatoliy Kuntsevitch was dismissed for having "masterminded" the clandestine shipment of 800 kilograms of nerve-gas processors to Syria in 1993. In the same year, according to two Moscow investigative journalists, then-secretary of the Russian Security Council and First Deputy Prime Minister Oleg Lobov sold the know-how to produce sarin, a nerve gas, to the fanatical Aum Shinrikyo sect in Japan for $100,000. In March 1995, Aum Shinrikyo released sarin on a packed Tokyo subway during rush hour, killing twelve people and hospitalizing at least seven hundred. Aum also acquired an MI-17 military helicopter from Russia, intending to use it to disseminate toxic agents over Japanese cities; a corrupt Russian parliamentarian reportedly helped expedite the shipment of the helicopter to Japan via Azerbaijan.[42] International crimes of this magnitude, like the smuggling of weapons-usable uranium or plutonium, are infrequent occurrences (they do not exact the visible and continuing toll on societies that drugs do); nevertheless, their implications for the security and stability of nation-states are enormous.

ORGANIZED CRIME AND THE POLITICAL ORDER

Organized crime's threat to the political order is subtle and insidious rather than direct and overt. Unlike terrorists or guerrillas who operate more or less outside the system and who seek radical political change, criminals usually seek to manipulate the system from within. Indeed, well-organized groups conduct their businesses with the protection and sometimes the active support of governments. Collusive ties between government and criminals are manifested in a number of ways. The most basic, of course, is the nexus of criminal money and functions of government. Corruption may be systemic, focused on influencing key officials, opinion leaders, politicians, or legislators. The aim here is to protect the integrity of the organization and its leaders and to promote legislation favorable to criminal interests, and in general to ensure a crime-friendly environment. In Colombia, for example, cocaine-trafficking groups successfully lobbied (and also threatened) legislators to secure a provision in the 1991 Colombian constitution outlawing the extradition of Colombian nationals to the United States.

On an operational level, corrupted law enforcement officials allow individual illegal transactions (such as drug processing or shipments) to proceed unhindered. Officials provide their criminal clients with advance warning of government raids and dragnets and sometimes with active protection against competitors. In Mexico, the country's most powerful drug kingpin, the late Amado Carrillo Fuentes, had enlisted top generals—including a career army officer appointed to Mexico's National Institute to Combat Drugs in December 1996—to pursue a rival drug coalition dominated by the Arellano Felix brothers. (The officer, General Jesus Gutierrez Rebollo, was arrested in early 1997.) In Colombia, a case in point was the conspicuous failure of the government to arrest Pablo Escobar for many years, despite a series of encirclement campaigns conducted by thousands of soldiers and elite police troops. As a former Escobar associate remarked, "half of those who work for the government are protecting him while the other half are pursuing him." (Escobar was finally tracked down and killed by police in December 1993, ten years after he became a fugitive in Colombia. Escobar's main rivals, the leaders of the Cali cartel, provided intelligence information to the government that facilitated the search for Escobar and the ultimate dismantling of the Cali cartel.[43]) Similarly, judges and police officials on traffickers' payrolls make a mockery of the criminal justice system. Again in Colombia, henchmen of the Medellín cartel reportedly offered judges trying drug cases "plomo o plata" (lead or silver)—a bullet if they convicted, money if they let the trafficker go free. Not surprisingly most judges chose the latter option. The Cali cartel's technique was somewhat more refined, relying on massive bribery of power holders and power seekers. Recent events in Colombia are suggestive of the dimensions of the problem. As of this writing, at least twelve Colombian legislators, as well as an attorney general and a defense minister, have been jailed for accepting money and favors from Cali traffickers in the 1994 elections. Santiago Medina, Samper's campaign manager, believes that at least seventy congressmen were elected with funds provided by the cartel. As noted, Samper himself is widely accused of complicity in soliciting donations for his campaign, although he was exonerated by the Lower House of Congress in an overwhelming vote (111 to 43) in June 1996.

In some cases, government officials became active participants in criminal ventures. In Peru, for example, military commanders serving in the Upper Huallaga Valley obligingly helped local drug dealers build clandestine airstrips and also permitted the transport of cocaine in military helicopters.[44] In Colombia, a recent investigation disclosed the existence of a "Blue cartel" of at least ten military officers operating within the Colombian air force. In a November 1995 incident in Mexico's Baja California Sur, Mexican Federal Judicial Police unloaded a jet loaded with Cali cartel cocaine and made off with the drugs, worth an estimated $100 million in the U.S. market.[45] In another smuggling operation in the Mexican state of Quintana Roo, police commanders reportedly were "coordinating the drug shipments" while "the staff chemist at the local office of the federal attorney general was employed by the traffickers to analyze the purity of the cocaine."[46] In Russia, as already noted, senior government officials appear to have masterminded the illegal shipments of chemical weapons technologies and components to foreign buyers during 1993.

Official tolerance of criminal activity is another form of collusion. One reason derives from criminals' economic clout in some societies. Take, for example, the Andean countries in South America. Cocaine is the region's largest export (in fact it is Latin America's second-largest export after petroleum). Cocaine accounts for approximately 3 to 4 percent of the gross domestic product of Peru and Bolivia, and at least 8 percent of Colombia's. The cocaine industry employs 450,000 to 500,000 Andeans directly in farming, processing, transport, security, and money handling operations.[47] Legions of others earn a living by providing goods and services essential to the industry. Andean governments are reluctant to launch a frontal attack against a lucrative industry that is an important source of revenue and employment. Real or perceived threats such as violent retaliation from drug lords, a foreign exchange crisis, an economic downturn in narco-dependent industries (such as construction and retail trades), upsurges in guerrilla violence, and migration of hordes of dispossessed coca farmers to Lima, La Paz, and Bogotá largely explain governments' inaction on the drug front.

A complicating factor is that narcotics organizations have taken over functions normally reserved to the state, especially in such areas as social welfare and (ironically) maintenance of law and order. In Mexico, Colombia, Bolivia, and Peru traffickers have devoted large sums to community development projects (such as roads, schools, and housing). Such activities have expanded drug capos' bases of political support among poor communities that governments were unable to reach. In Colombia and to a lesser extent Peru, paramilitary organizations financed by drug dealers supplanted a weak central government in providing local security against predatory guerrilla groups.[48] In Russia also, organized crime provides many of the services that citizens expect from states, including employment, protection of commercial businesses, collection of debts, various welfare activities, and support for scientific research. According to Stephen Handelman, one St. Petersburg mobster, Anatoliy Vladimirov, made a large donation to an impoverished astronomy research institute in that city, in return for which grateful scientists decided to name an obscure star "Anvlad" after their benefactor.[49] Obviously, narco-traffickers' intrusion into areas of the state and the law imparts a new and ominous dimension to their activities.

Acquiescence sometimes verges on active collusion. That is, governments (or parts of governments such as military or intelligence organizations) employ criminals to accomplish specific political objectives. Examples of such partnerships are legion. During the Second World War, the U.S. Office of Naval Intelligence (ONI) formed understandings with both the American and Sicilian mafias to help undermine the Fascist regime in southern Italy. Also, U.S. authorities co-opted the American mafia to help screen out German saboteurs from among longshoremen working on the docks of the port of New York. In Southeast Asia during the 1950s and 1960s, the CIA provided financial and logistical support for various anti-Communist armies that supported themselves principally from the traffic in opium and heroin. Also in the early 1960s, the CIA sought the assistance of American mobsters Johnny Rosselli and Sam Giancana in carrying out an assassination plot against Cuban leader Fidel Castro. In China, Generalissimo Chiang Kai-shek relied on the notorious Green Gang, a Shanghai Triad group, to conduct a massacre of his erstwhile Communist allies during the Northern Expedition in 1927. In the early 1990s, the Peking government seemed prepared to cooperate with Triad groups in Hong Kong to undermine or demoralize the democratic government of that colony. "As for organizations like the Triads in Hong Kong," said the head of China's Public Security Bureau in April 1993, "as long as these people are patriotic, as long as they are concerned with Hong Kong's prosperity and stability, we should work with them." In Colombia in the 1980s and 1990s, the army has formed tacit countersubversion alliances with rightist paramilitary groups, some of which are funded partly or largely by wealthy narco-traffickers; in certain instances, the army has provided training, weapons, and even intelligence support for these private military bands. All of this is not to say that governments and criminals are natural allies. Yet such opportunistic manifestations of collaboration against outside threats to the status quo underscore the complex systemic and parastatal ramifications of the organized crime phenomenon.[50]

Legitimate economic elites have also enjoyed collusive relationships with criminals. The Ford Motor Company used American organized crime figures as strikebreakers in the 1920s and 1930s. The elaborate apparatus of offshore banks, shady lawyers, and anonymous corporations in Panama and the Caribbean obviously benefits the criminal underworld, but it was created largely by upperworld business leaders anxious to avoid regulations, reduce taxes, and maintain corporate secrecy.

DEALING WITH ORGANIZED CRIME

Introduction

Organized crime and transnational crime in their various manifestations pose a number of challenges to modern nation-states and to the international system. Those discussed above include organized and unorganized diversions of strategic nuclear materials, a booming global trade in narcotics, the potential symbiosis of organized criminality and separatist or insurgent movements, and the subtly corrosive effects of a large criminal sector on democratic institutions and processes, especially in weak developing states. The threat to democracy is not always clearly defined—criminals' political agendas tend to be hidden and focused on themselves (on issues of immunity or judicial leniency, for example). Nevertheless, the corruption and violent behavior associated with criminal elites impairs the mechanism of government and (possibly) damages a country's prospects for successful political and economic development.

Given these concerns, governments need to develop more effective counter-measures against transnational criminal actors. Certain obvious prescriptions include improving cross-national police cooperation (especially East-West cooperation), sharing intelligence on criminals and crimes-in-progress, rationalizing and harmonizing national laws against serious criminal offenses, and increasing transparency in the international financial system. The United States and its Western partners must work to strengthen the administration of justice in states where defense mechanisms against drug-sponsored corruption and violence are weak. Helping governments to target, seize, and administer assets belonging to criminal figures is an essential aspect of "counterorganization" strategy. Such policy tools as the annual drug certification process in the United States, if applied fairly (which it is not), can spotlight problems of high-level corruption in drug-source countries and impel their governments to take countermeasures.

Countercrime initiatives must also be tailored to the specifics of illegal businesses. Much so-called economic crime in Russia, for instance, can be eliminated by rationalizing tax codes and export control regulations; current confiscatory tax schedules strangle business productivity and encourage unhealthy collusion between businessmen and underworld figures to evade taxes. Fighting narcotics businesses requires breaking up large criminal cartels that export illicit drugs and also wiping out the cultivation and refining of these substances in some countries. (An alternative strategy that would diminish the attractiveness of such businesses to criminal groups is simply to decriminalize or legalize the production and sale of drugs.) Measures to combat nuclear smuggling—a particularly virulent threat to international stability—are relatively straightforward: preventative measures include technical assistance to increase safeguards at vulnerable nuclear facilities in former Soviet states, economic forms of assistance to improve the livelihood of poorly paid (or unpaid) nuclear workers, and programs to retrain weapons scientists to work in civilian occupations. A second line of defense is containment—improving the ability of law enforcement to detect and intercept stolen nuclear materials and nuclear contraband crossing national frontiers. In Russia, where only 25 percent of the frontier posts are equipped with working radiation monitors, the issue of containment acquires particular urgency. Fortunately, U.S. counterproliferation programs in former Soviet states are proceeding on all these fronts, albeit with woefully inadequate funding. (Such programs received roughly $120 million in total funding in FY 1997 compared to $450 million allocated to the international war against drugs.)

Yet the fight against transnational criminal enterprises faces an uphill battle in many respects. One major obstacle is the sheer difficulty of interdicting cross-border movements of drugs and other forms of contraband. Reference has been made to the expanding global legal market for legal goods and services that creates a ready pipeline for the smuggling of illicit goods. The overall (1996) U.S.–Mexican trade volume of $130 billion, the hundreds of millions of legal border crossings each year, and both countries' vested interest in the expansion of the North American Free Trade Agreement (NAFTA) have created an almost impossible situation for law enforcement. For example, U.S. customs officials are able to subject only 25 percent of the 3.5 million commercial vehicles entering the United States from Mexico annually to a "narcotics enforcement examination." Yet a single conveyance is capable of transporting tons of narcotics in just one border crossing "while easily blending in with legitimate trucks." Unfortunately the border has become a veritable sieve for drugs. Recent law enforcement estimates suggest that Mexican traffickers are delivering between five and seven tons of narcotics—including cocaine, marijuana, heroin, and methamphetamines—to the United States *each day*.[51]

Furthermore, traffickers are consistently improving and diversifying smuggling methods to adopt to changing law enforcement conditions. For example, nuclear smugglers appear to be making less use of European transshipment routes, where the chances of detection are relatively high, while moving shipments of materials through southern Russia and Central Asia, where border controls are almost nonexistent. Increased U.S. interdiction pressure in the Caribbean in the early 1990s resulted in a relocation of cocaine-trafficking routes to the U.S.–Mexican border. Furthermore, the sheer variety of vehicles that modern smugglers use to move bulk cocaine shipments—cargo jets, merchant shipping, tractor trailers, camouflaged small boats, and (in Colombia) specially produced semisubmersible vessels—represent a daunting challenge to law enforcement.

Adaptable smugglers, porous borders, and high-volume legal trade flows vastly diminish the chances of successful supply reduction, whether focused on drugs or on other illegal activities. U.S. authorities are able to seize perhaps 10 to 25 percent of the drugs entering the United States each year. By the same token, a determined effort by a criminal conspiracy or terrorist group to introduce a nuclear device or the materials and components for making one into this country would stand a very high chance of success.

Other reservations concern the expressed U.S. policy of breaking up large criminal organizations and severing criminals' links to power and to the economic system (the "corrupting power of the drug lords," and so forth). Colombia has been virtually the sole laboratory for such counterorganization policies in the 1990s. The United States is afraid to compel Mexico to crack down on its trafficking organizations or to take unilateral steps against such organizations because of the special nature of the U.S.–Mexican relationship (the common 2,000-mile border, NAFTA, Mexican sovereignty concerns, and so on). And there are practical limits to U.S. power. The United States and other Western nations can do little to counter the widening influence of organized crime over state institutions in Russia and other NIS countries, even though such influence poses clear and direct, as well as indirect, threats to Western security.

In addition, counterorganization strategies can in certain circumstances be destabilizing—subtly affecting power relationships in a country to the disadvantage of its legally constituted government. In Colombia, for instance, U.S.–Colombian efforts to dismantle the Medellín and Cali cartels—while valuable from a number of perspectives—may inadvertently have worked to the advantage of Colombia's Marxist guerrilla groups, which have fought for years to wrest a larger share of drug action from traffickers. In balance-of-power terms, weaker trafficking organizations are less able to defend their ranches, laboratories, and trafficking routes against guerrilla attacks, which means that they are forced to pay out an increased share of their profits in "war taxes" to guerrillas. Furthermore, a number of guerrilla fronts are apparently actively entering the cocaine trade as producers, at least at upstream levels (cultivating and intermediate processing). Some sources, in fact, refer to Colombia's FARC as the "third cartel"—an exaggeration perhaps, but suggestive of the insurgents' increasing penetration of the drug trade.[52]

Finally, with respect to the drug trade at least, transnational criminal enterprises produce some economic benefits for some countries. In Latin America, for example, much evidence suggests that illicit drug businesses bring in foreign exchange, create new legal businesses and jobs, and raise income for hundreds of thousands of low-income farmers. Countermeasures against drugs can jeopardize other important values such as stability and economic prosperity. Government assaults on rural coca production in Peru and Colombia, for example, threaten the economies of entire regions and generate widespread unrest. A further result is to cement alliances between coca-growing campesinos and antigovernment guerrilla groups.[53]

Short-term economic disruption can also accompany offensives against narcotics kingpins. Following a crackdown on the Cali cartel, unemployment in Cali, Colombia's third-largest city, rose from 9 to 15 percent between mid-1995 and mid-1996. During the same period, real estate prices collapsed, retail sales dropped to a fraction of 1995 levels, and private investment in the city came to a virtual halt. The Colombian economy grew almost 60 percent more slowly in 1996 than in 1995, although factors other than drugs partly explain this much weaker performance.[54]

This same line of argument is reflected in a recent article by Thomas Naylor, "From Underworld to Underground" in *Crime, Law and Social Change*. Naylor poses the question of what would happen if the policies in North America were mostly successful in shutting down the activities of Jamaican *ganga* (marijuana) gangs. Ostensibly a serious crime problem would have been eliminated; yet, as Naylor notes:

> The story does not stop there. Deprived of a market, large numbers of Jamaican *ganga* farmers, many of them refugees from the previous collapses of bauxite mining and sugar cultivation, would be driven out of business. They would move en masse into the urban slums, swelling an already enormous problem of urban crime that threatens the country's social stability as well as

tourism, by far the most important source of legal foreign exchange. They would also emigrate abroad in increasing numbers, joining the ranks of illegal aliens in North American cities and, along with them, the manpower of the exiled "posses" who would compensate for the loss of *ganga* profit by putting more energy into "crack" and extortion. Meanwhile, back in Jamaica, banks drained of liquidity would cut back loans to legitimate businesses, and the country's exchange reserves would be depleted sufficiently for it to drastically reduce imports of capital equipment necessary for economic growth. Under the circumstances, Jamaica's often less-than-enthusiastic response to North American concerns over *ganga* trafficking [becomes] considerably easier to understand."[55]

The argument should not be pushed too far. Narcotics supplier countries experience important economic costs as well as benefits (for example, overvalued local currencies, a depressed legal export sector, competition from cheap imports and contraband). Furthermore, as Colombian economist Eduardo Sarmiento notes, the elimination of cocaine would produce "a temporary drop in economic activity and income levels" but would also facilitate policies for expansion of manufactured exports and for import substitution, "giving greater dynamism to the economy."[56] Still, the uncertain overall short- and long-term effects of the narcotics traffic on national economies creates ambivalence toward the drug trade, and weakens the resolve of government in dealing with it. Governments seem willing to contain the more obvious types of sociopolitical dangers from drug dealing (such as narco-terrorism or high-level corruption). At the same time, they are inclined to try to capture the economic benefits of a lucrative illegal industry—for instance, by offering incentives to repatriate illegal capital ("tax amnesties") or by relaxing foreign-exchange restrictions. Governments' willingness to collude with drug dealers on the economic front obviously complicates the development of a successful counternarcotics strategy in this hemisphere.

Lessons of the Drug War

America's so-called war against drugs in the 1980s and 1990s has been a conspicuous foreign-policy fiasco. Since 1981 the U.S. government has spent approximately $23 billion on various source-country and border-control programs aimed at reducing inflows of foreign illicit drugs into the country. Yet drugs, such as cocaine and heroin, are cheaper and more readily available in U.S. domestic markets than they were at the beginning of the 1980s.[57] In addition, as a 1997 report by a Council on Foreign Relations Task Force notes, U.S. programs "have done little more than rearrange the map of drug production and trafficking."[58] Two extremely undesirable shifts in the configuration of the international drug market can be noted. One is that Colombia, which produced almost no heroin in the 1980s, now supplies most of the heroin market in the northeastern United States, according to the U.S. Drug Enforcement Administration (DEA). Also, the DEA reports that almost two-thirds of the heroin seized in the United States in

1996 originated in Colombia.[59] The second is that Mexican crime networks have capitalized on the weakness of the Colombian cartels to carve out a larger share of Latin American cocaine exports and of cocaine wholesale markets in the United States at the Colombians' expense. Mexican organizations have eclipsed Cali cartel groups as the preeminent distributors of cocaine in the West Coast and in major Midwestern cities such as Chicago, Houston, Denver, and Dallas.[60] As a result, Mexico's narco-wealth has increased dramatically. Much of this money returns to Mexico, bringing in foreign exchange, creating new businesses and jobs, and raising income for tens of thousands of low-income families. Some of it is invested in the legitimate economy—for example, trucking and freight companies, race tracks, banks, natural-gas companies, the dairy industry, the tourism industry, and some public services such as schools, clinics, and amusement parks. In other words, traffickers have been able to entrench themselves in an economy that, unlike Colombia's, has extensive links with the United States (annual U.S.–Mexican trade is about $130 billion, almost 20 times our trade with Colombia). A related development has been the spread of drug-related corruption to most of the country's elite institutions—the military, the police, the attorney general's office, Congress, and the state governors. Also, the stain of corruption has reached out to federal and local agencies on the U.S. side of the southwestern border, so the problem is no longer confined just to Mexico.

Unfortunately, Washington's response to the growing Mexican drug connection has been awkward and ambivalent. The intent apparently is to "manage the issue" to prevent it from threatening the development of trade and investment ties with Mexico. This has produced glaring inconsistencies in policy. For example, in February 1997, for the second straight year, the administration decertified Colombia as an ally in the war against drugs largely because of the scandals surrounding the 1994 election campaign and because of Samper's insistence on remaining in office. Yet the administration gave full certification to Mexico in both years, despite what the State Department calls "persistent corruption at all levels of government."[61] The U.S. State Department has revoked entry visas of top Colombian politicians, including Samper, for alleged ties to the drug business. Yet to my knowledge no such action has been taken against Mexican politicians in office who have received donations from drug dealers. The U.S. Treasury Department's Office of Foreign Assets Control has identified more than one hundred "specially designated narcotics trafficking" companies that are linked to leaders of the Cali cartel and their relatives. U.S. companies and citizens are prohibited from doing business with these entities. But no such inventory exists (publicly, at least) of Mexican trafficker-owned enterprises that operate along the 2000-mile border between the United States and Mexico—sometimes on both sides of the border—and that serve as conduits for the movements of drugs, drug money, and other types of contraband.[62] No doubt U.S. policymakers fear that a crackdown on Mexican drug smugglers—for example, freezing their American assets and preventing trafficker-owned enterprises from doing business in the United States—could have repercussions for Mexican exports and for the economy, which is intertwined with Mexico's along the border. Meanwhile Washington's rhetoric about Mexico stresses cooperation, mutual respect, sharing "a common integrated vision," whereas U.S. commentary on Colombia emphasizes the problems in the relationship and tends to be condemnatory.[63]

Furthermore, while Colombia has served as a kind of social laboratory for U.S. countertrafficking and cartel-busting activities, U.S. law enforcement and intelligence agencies have not nearly the same freedom of action in Mexico. The ability of the Mexican government to successfully confront and dismantle the Mexican drug cartels on its own cannot be taken for granted.

Such dismal realities suggest the need for a reappraisal of U.S. counternarcotics policies and goals. To be sure, such policies have produced visible successes, such as weakening the traditional Colombian cartels and disrupting some of their ties to the political establishment. Yet they have obviously failed to stop the drug trade and have created problems of their own in some countries—unrest and violence among rural dwellers, increased guerrilla inroads into the drug trade, and economic displacement and downturns in some locations. Also, U.S. preoccupation with dismembering Colombia's drug mafias has produced a shift of criminal power and resources to Mexico, where, it seems, the counterorganization strategies of the U.S. government can be implemented only on a restricted scale, if at all.

What, then, is to be done about international drug control? The United States can probably continue almost indefinitely to "muddle through" on drugs; however, many U.S. and Latin American observers believe that repression of the drug trade, at least as practiced to date, has failed, and that different policy directions need to be considered. Several such alternatives are outlined below. One bizarre idea that has received some attention in Latin America is to achieve reductions in narcotics exports through negotiations and accords with drug chieftains themselves. A second is to refocus federal antidrug resources to emphasize supply reduction rather than demand reduction (which would mean scrapping many international programs). A third is to relax drug abuse and control laws and, ultimately, to move from prohibition to regulation of presently illegal narcotics for which demand is apparently insatiable. All of these options are flawed, in this writer's opinion, but these shortcomings must be balanced against the irrationalities, inconsistencies, and perversely harmful effects of current supply-side policies.

The Negotiations Option
The idea of negotiations with drug criminals has some appeal in Latin America, especially in 'Colombia, because repressive solutions have not worked well, and because frontal assaults against trafficking organizations carry high political and economic costs. The Colombian government has conducted direct (face-to-face) and indirect negotiations with cocaine kingpins from 1984 through the mid-1990s. In such narco-dialogues, traffickers have offered to surrender to justice, dismantle their operations, and turn over trafficking assets and related information to the government. Also, Pablo Escobar and other Medellín kingpins offered in the early 1990s to end their violent confrontation with the Colombian state. Concessions sought from the government have included (at different times)

amnesty or immunity from prosecution, judicial leniency, guarantees against extradition, and the chance for reintegration into Colombian society. In Mexico, a leading trafficker, the late Amado Carrillo Fuentes, made a more brazen (perhaps tongue-in-cheek) proposal: he promised to "act like a businessman and not like a criminal," and not to sell drugs in Mexico if the government would give him a free head in pursuing his narcotics trafficking activities (see Table 1.1).

In Colombia, in 1994 the leaders of the Cali cartel offered to implement a plan to reduce cocaine exports from Colombia by 60 percent in return for lenient treatment (meaning short jail sentences or house arrest). An important question is whether the Cali dons were capable of controlling or influencing directly a sufficiently large percentage of Colombia's refining and exporting capacity to accomplish such a reduction. Much recent information suggests that the Colombian cocaine industry as a whole is more decentralized and balkanized than it was in the 1980s. "There are many cartels," Cali leader Gilberto Rodríguez noted in a 1994 statement.[64] Yet drug kingpins may possess considerable leverage vis-à-vis lower-level operators—for example, they can discontinue purchasing of products or services, or simply withhold protection from laboratories, transport companies, distribution cells, laundering operations, and other key trafficking entities. Whether traffickers would be willing to exercise such powers or to divulge valuable information on the inner workings of their cocaine enterprises is, of course, an empirical question—information that fingered colleagues, associates, and subordinates, for instance, would likely expose the Cali leaders to lethal reprisals from fellow traffickers.

Table 1.1 Amado Carrillo's Proposal for a Peace Plan with the Mexican Government January 1997

What Carrillo wants from the government:
- To be allowed to pursue his business
- Guaranteed peace for his family
- To keep 50 percent of his possessions

What he offers the government in return:
- To help put an end to nonorganized drug trafficking
- To act like a businessman, not like a criminal
- To not sell drugs in Mexico
- To sell drugs outside the country; that is, in the United States and Europe
- To bring dollars into Mexico in order to help its economy
- To act neither violently nor in defiance

If this is not accepted, he will transfer his offer, with its benefits, to another country.

Source: A confidential military computer file obtained in July by the Mexican newsweekly *Proceso*, published in *Harper's Magazine*, October 1997, 14.

In any event, in Colombia, negotiations with traffickers proved useless as a tool of counternarcotics policy. By and large, surrendering drug traffickers did not go out of their way to cooperate with the authorities. Indeed, Medellín kingpin Pablo Escobar and several Cali traffickers turned themselves in under favorable plea-bargain arrangements, but continued to run their businesses from jail. In this respect the Colombian authorities proved to be inept negotiators. However, the Colombians' principal aim in conducting such narco-dialogues was probably to reach an accommodation that would reduce societal violence in Colombia—not to achieve a reduction in the cocaine trade per se. Viewed as a conflict-resolution mechanism, negotiations probably helped to rein in the Medellín mafia and to prevent outbreaks of disruptive violence from other traffickers; yet the government paid a steep price in terms of lost prestige and legitimacy and diminished leverage vis-à-vis the country's powerful criminal sector.[65]

Demand Reduction
A third option is to reconfigure drug policy by closing down most overseas programs and redirecting resources from interdiction and domestic law enforcement to "demand reduction" programs. This might save some money in the short term, and certainly funds for prevention and treatment (which now account for only one-third of the federal drug-control budget) need to be increased. But prevention and treatment are not a panacea and are not necessarily effective against the hard-core users who account for the bulk of consumption of cocaine and heroin. Also, the U.S. international image might suffer by pulling out of the Andes and other drug-torn areas and leaving the field to national governments and to traffickers. In addition, U.S. narcotics assistance programs might be considered a counterweight of sorts to the economic and political power of drug kingpins, even if they do not do much to stop the drugs themselves. Still, investment in demand reduction, especially treatment, may be a relatively cost-effective way to cut drug consumption. A 1994 RAND study found that $34 million invested in treatment reduced cocaine use as much as $783 million spent on overseas counternarcotics programs or $366 million spent on interdiction.[66]

Legalization
Legalization also represents a widely discussed policy option. Possibly a distinction can be made between "legalizable" crimes (such as drugs or gambling) and criminal activity that is simply too dangerous to society to merit a legalization or decriminalization approach (such as extortion, international financial fraud, or smuggling of advanced weaponry and nuclear materials). On the drug front, legalization commands a measure of support in both producing and consuming countries and in certain respects represents an attractive, if risky, alternative to current policies.

Advocates, of course, argue that legalization—by removing black-market incentives to produce, smuggle, and distribute drugs—could undercut the economic power of the narcotics mafias and, in turn, reduce criminality and corruption associated with the drug trade. Some 80 to 90 percent of the estimated $8 to $10 billion of gross annual earnings of Colombia's cocaine multinationals comprises value-added in smuggling and distribution. In this sense, legalization is the ultimate counterorganization strategy. A legalization strategy would help beleaguered Third-World governments to better cope with assorted threats to national sovereignty and integrity posed by different participants in the drug trade. As things stand, any group that controls a piece of the drug action can buy weaponry, occupy part of the national territory, and contest the authority of the government or—alternatively—buy immunity from elements of state apparatus.

Legalization's downside is that it would almost certainly increase drug addiction and related public health costs in the major consuming countries (and possibly in the major producing areas as well), although proponents of legalization argue that such increases would be temporary. More importantly, malevolent organizations that now traffic in drugs would not necessarily cease to exist because their main product no longer commanded huge returns. (In organization theory this phenomenon is called the *succession of goals*. A textbook legal example was the shifting of the March of Dimes's mission to prevention of birth defects after the discovery of a vaccine for polio.) Similarly, when Prohibition was repealed in the United States the criminal organizations that had flourished from peddling bootleg whiskey simply expanded into new areas, such as extortion, gambling, loan sharking, murder-for-hire, and of course, drugs. (A critical problem is that criminals develop new lifestyles, expectations, and obligations from their illegal occupations). Similarly, legalization might drive the multinational drug cartels into equally dangerous or more dangerous criminal pursuits such as smuggling weapons or nuclear materials, or producing and shipping container-loads of expertly engraved counterfeit U.S. currency.

Another argument for legalization, one often articulated in the Andean countries, is that governments could earn significant revenues by taxing legal narcotics businesses. However, if narcotics entered the stream of legitimate commerce, the United States—having access to the most advanced plant genetics, agricultural technology, and processing methods—would probably emerge as the world's most efficient producer of illicit drugs. That is, Third-World producers would have a difficult time competing with the United States. A country such as Colombia, which has a strong "comparative advantage" in drug refining and smuggling, would be especially unlikely to benefit under such a scheme. Of course, the United States might charitably consent to a system of export quotas for Andean cocaine-producing states.

The advantages of legalization thus are uncertain, though counterarguments also require qualification. For instance, the succession-of-goals problem is not unique to legalization. Successful international campaigns to wipe out drug crops or to limit consumption of illicit drugs also would shift criminal power and resources to other illegal businesses. The likely extent of such transference, though, is open to question since drugs are more easily produced and sold than most other criminal commodities. More serious reservations about deregulation and legalization relate to anticipated substantial increases in consumption and in associated public health costs. Possibly, the costs of increased consumption might be offset partly by "the gains achieved from making some form of drug abuse safer and from reducing much of the crime associated with the black market for illegal drugs."[67] Also, legalization supporters argue that savings in criminal costs that now account for the bulk of the federal budget can be passed on in the form of expanded and more effective drug-prevention and treatment programs. Still, legalization faces an uphill battle politically—most Americans recoil at the idea of making cocaine, heroin, and methamphetamine as available commercially as, say, alcohol or tobacco products, and indeed the health risks of such a permissive regime would be considerable.

The broader issue, though, is the need for change in current U.S. drug policy that is wasteful and unproductive by any standard. Radical departures from this policy, especially in its international dimensions, need to be explored and assessed. Governments should support research that identifies potential costs, benefits, and trade-offs of different counternarcotics policies and different regulatory regimes. Such an exercise would rationalize America's overall anticrime effort and also free resources to target transnational crime threats that present a clear and present danger to international stability.

NOTES

1. For a comparison of definitions of organized crime by the FBI and the Russian Ministry of Internal Affairs, see Center for Strategic and International Studies (CSIS), *Russian Organized Crime* (Washington, D.C.: CSIS, 1997), 24–25. See also Patricia Rawlinson, "Russian Organized Crime: A Brief History," in *Russian Organized Crime: The New Threat?* ed. Phil Williams (London: Frank Cass, 1997), 29–32; A. I. Gurov, *Organizovannaya Prestupnost'—Ne Mif a Realnost'* (Moscow: Znaniye, 1992), 18–45.

2. For an excellent statement on this point, see Petrus C. VanDuyne, "Organized Crime, Corruption, and Power," *Crime, Law, and Social Change* 20, no. 3 (1996–1997), 201–6.

3. Claire Sterling, *Thieves' World* (New York: Simon and Schuster, 1994), 13–14.

4. White House, Office of National Drug Control Policy (ONDCP), *The National Drug Control Strategy, 1997. Budget Summary* (Washington, D.C.: ONDCP, 1997), 240.

5. U.S. Department of State, *International Narcotics Control Strategy Report*, Washington, D.C., Mar. 1997, 6.

6. CSIS, *Russian Organized Crime*, 2, 15. Admittedly, CSIS also quotes statements by Boris Yeltsin, Yuriy Luzhkov, and other Russian leaders that appear to support the "criminalization" argument.

7. See, for example, V. O. Ispravnikov and V. V. Kulikov, *Tenevaya Ekonomika v Rossii: Inoi Put i Tretya Sila*, Moscow, Rossiiskii Ekonomicheskii Zhurnal, Fond za Ekonomicheskaya Gramonost', 1997), 28–32.

8. Stephen Handelman, *Comrade Criminal: Russia's New Mafia* (New Haven: Yale University Press, 1995), 145–46.

9. Peter Reddaway, "Scandal Dogs Russia's Rising Star," *The Washington Post*, 20 Aug. 1995, C3.

10. On these points see the following sources: Patrick Clawson and Rensselaer W. Lee III, *The Andean Cocaine Industry* (New York: St. Martin's Press, 1996), 114, 190. Handelman. *Comrade Criminal*, 111. Alison Jamieson, "Mafia and Institutional Power in Italy," *International Relations* (London, 1994), 2, 23. The mafia has episodically supported an independent political status for Sicily. For instance, mafia representation discussed the possibility of Sicilian independence with high-ranking U.S.

officials after the Allied invasion of Sicily in 1943. Alfred McCoy, *The Politics of Heroin: CIA Complicity in the Global Drug Trade* (Brooklyn, NY: Lawrence Hill Books, 1991), 363–64.

11. Santiago Medina Serna, *La Verdad Sobre Las Mentiras* (Bogotá: Planeta, 1997), 110.
12. Clawson and Lee, *The Andean Cocaine Industry*, 57.
13. McCoy, *The Politics of Heroin*, 414.
14. María Cristina Caballero, "La guerilla billionaria" *Cambio-16*, 6 Jul. 1998, 28–31. According to the report, the guerillas earn another $500 million plus from extortion and kidnapping; in effect, they constitute multiline criminal enterprises.
15. Perhaps the best source on the mafia's symbiosis with the power structure and inequities associated with privatization in pre-Castro times is a recent Cuban study: Enrique Cirules, *El Imperio de la Havana* (Havana: Casa de las Americas, 1993).
16. *CSIS Russian Organized Crime*, 2, 69.
17. Telephone interviews conducted by author U.S. Department of Commerce; U.S.: China Business Council, 10–11 Jun. 1997.
18. Louise Shelley, "The Price Tag of Russia's Organized Crime," *Transition* 8, no. 1, Feb. 1997, 7–8; Tatyana Boikova, "Criminal Structures in the Economy," *Delovoi Mir*, 16 Jul. 1996, 4.
19. *Tenevaya Ekonomika v Rossii*, 32; and U.S. Agency for International Development. "Maintaining Country Progress in Central and Eastern Europe and the Newly Independent States," Washington, D.C., Sept. 1997, 30.
20. Francisco Thoumi, *Economic Politics of Narcotraffic* (Bogotá: Tercer Mundo, 1994), 56–57. Mario de Franco and Ricardo Godoy, "The Economic Consequences of Cocaine Production in Bolivia: Historical, Local, and Macroeconomic Consequences" (Cambridge: Harvard University, 2 Aug. 1991), 20.
21. Office of National Drug Control Policy (ONDCP), "Reducing Drug Abuse in America," ONDCP, Washington, D.C., Oct. 1997, 14–15.
22. Rensselaer W. Lee III and Brian Sullivan, "International Crime," in Institute for National Strategic Studies, National Defense University, *1997 Strategic Assessment* (Washington, D.C.: U.S. Government Printing Office, 1997), 197–208.
23. Handelman. *Comrade Criminal*, 70.
24. "Ivan Ivanov," *International Narcotics Trafficking and the Former USSR* (Moscow: Feliks Research Group, Feb. 1995), 40, 49–50, 76.
25. Peter Andreas, "U.S.–Mexico: Open Markets, Closed Border," *Foreign Policy* no. 103 (Summer 1996), 57.
26. U.S. Department of State, *International Narcotics Control Strategy Report* (Washington, D.C., 1997), 24–25.
27. Rensselaer W. Lee III and Scott Macdonald, "Drugs in the East," *Foreign Policy* no. 9–10 (Spring 1993), 100–1.
28. Alison Jamieson, "Transnational Italian Organized Crime," *Transnational Organized Crime* 1, no. 2, 165–66.
29. Douglas Farah, "Russian Mob, Drug Cartels Joining Forces," *The Washington Post*, 29 Sept. 1997, A1, A16.
30. Jamieson, "Transnational Italian Organized Crime," 151–65.
31. Janusz Stostak, et al., "The Godfather's Shadow," *Express Wieczorny* (Warsaw), 2–8 May 1996, 3.
32. Alison Jamieson, "Mafia and Institutional Power,"19.
33. Clawson and Lee, *The Andean Cocaine Industry*, 38.
34. Ibid., 40.
35. Ibid., 48.
36. Jamieson, "Mafia and Institutional Power," 8–9. The shift of votes was meant as a "warning" to the Christian Democratic Party that the mafia wanted better judicial treatment during the ongoing "Maxi-Trial" in Palermo.

37. Rensselaer W. Lee III, *Smuggling Armageddon: The Nuclear Black Market in the Former Soviet Union and Europe* (New York: St. Martin's Press, 1998), 73–109.
38. Stephen Handelman. "Let's Make a Deal," *The Toronto Star*, 5 Apr., 1998 (Electric Media).
39. Lee, *Smuggling Armageddon*, 129–35.
40. Ibid.
41. Mikhail Kulik, "Raskryto Yeshcho Odno Yadernoye Khishcheniye," *Yaderny Kontrol'* (Nov. 1995), 5.
42. On these points see the following sources: Leonid Krutakov and Ivan Kadutin, "Seko Asahara's Russian Trail," *Passport* (Moscow), no. 5 (1997), 27–29. (The authors are correspondents for *Izvestiya*.) U.S. Army War College, Center for Strategic Leadership, *Report of the Executive Seminar on Special Material Smuggling* (Carlisle Barracks, PA, Sept. 1996), 27–3.1 (Remarks by Jonathan Tucker).
43. Rensselaer W. Lee III, "Colombia's Cocaine Syndicates," in *War on Drugs: Studies in the Failure of U.S. Drug Policy*, ed. Alfred McCoy and Alan Block (Boulder, CO: Westview Press, 1992), 109. Clawson and Lee, *The Andean Cocaine Industry*, 115.
44. Tim Golden, "U.S. Officials Say Mexican Military Aids Drug Traffic," *The New York Times* (26 Mar. 1998), A1.
45. Council on Foreign Relations, *Rethinking International Drug Control*, Task Force Report (New York: Council on Foreign Relations, 1997), 22.
46. Sam Dillon and Tim Golden, "Drug Inquiry into a Governor Tests Mexico's New Politics," *The New York Times*, 26 Nov. 1998, A1, A6.
47. On these points see Clawson and Lee, *The Andean Cocaine Industry*, chap. 1, 18–30.
48. Ibid., 48–49, 184–91.
49. Handelman, *Comrade Criminal*, 58.
50. Lee and Sullivan, "International Crime," 205. McCoy, *The Politics of Heroin*, 162–92, 300–6. Seymour Hersh, *The Dark Side of Camelot* (New York: Little-Brown, 1992), 162–68. Frederic Dannen, "Partners in Crime: China's Bonds with Hong Kong's Underworld," *The New Republic*, 14 and 21 Jul. 1997, 18–26. Clawson and Lee, *The Andean Cocaine Industry*, 186–92.
51. John Ward Anderson and William Branigan, "Flood of Contraband Hard to Stop," *The Washington Post*, 2 Nov. 1997, 1. Office of National Drug Control Policy (ONDCP), "Enhanced Truck Inspections," *Report to Congress* (Washington, D.C.: ONDCP, 1997), 6.
52. Remarks by Alejandro Reyes at U.S. State Department briefing for the U.S. Ambassador to Colombia Curtis Kamman, Systems Planning Corporation, Rosslyn, VA, 17 Dec. 1997. Clawson and Lee, *The Andean Cocaine Industry*, 179. For an excellent analysis of the FARC's new inroads into the drug trade, see Major Luis Alberto Villamarin, *El Cartel de las FARC* (Bogotá: Ediciones El Faraon, 1996), 1–245. Another reason for the increase in guerrilla earnings has been the 50-plus percent increase in Colombian coca cultivation since 1994. Much of the new cultivation is located in remote areas of southern and eastern Colombia controlled by the FARC.
53. Clawson and Lee, *The Andean Cocaine Industry*, 217–18.
54. Ibid., 206–7. "Political and Economic Outlook 1997," *Colombia Foreign Investment*, no. 13, Apr.–Jun. 1997, 6.
55. R. T. Naylor, "From Underworld to Underground," *Crime, Law and Social Change* 24, no. 2, 1995–96, 83.
56. Carlos Arrieta et al., *Narcotrafico en Colombia* (Bogotá: Tercer Mundo, 1990), 93.
57. ONDCP, *The National Drug Control Strategy 1997: Budget Summary* (Washington, D.C.: ONDCP, 1997), 22, 240. ONDCP. *The National Drug Control Strategy 1996: Program Resources and Evaluation* (Washington, D.C.: ONDCP), 312.
58. Council on Foreign Relations Task Force report, 4.
59. U.S. Department of State, *International Narcotics Control Strategy: Report*, Washing-

ton, D.C., March 1997, 89. National Narcotics Intelligence Consumers' Committee (NNICC), *The NNICC Report 1996* (Washington, D.C.: DEA, July 1997), 28–30.

60. Douglas Farah and Molly Moore, "Mexican Drug Traffickers Eclipse Colombian Cartels," *The Washington Post*, 30 Mar. 1997, A1, A18. *The NNICC Report*, 6.

61. U.S. State Department, *International Narcotics Control Strategy Report*, Washington, D.C., Mar. 1997, 140.

62. Office of Foreign Assets Control, "Specially Designated Nationals and Blocked Persons," 15 Dec. 1997, 1–48.

63. See for example the Joint U.S.–Mexican Government Report, *U.S./Mexico Bi-National Drug Threat Assessment*, Washington, D.C., May 1997, i, ii, 1–2.

64. Letter to Juan Lozano, *El Tiempo*, 7 Nov. 1997, A-6.

65. For detailed discussion of these issues, see Clawson and Lee, *The Andean Cocaine Industry*, chap. 4, 90–127.

66. Council on Foreign Relations, *Rethinking Drug Control*, 33.

67. Paul Stares, *Global Habit* (Washington, D.C.: Brookings Institution, 1996), 110.

INTERNATIONAL ORGANIZED CRIME, NATIONAL SECURITY, AND THE "MARKET STATE"

2

Gregory F. Treverton

The question is not whether international organized crime is bad. It is. Nor is the question whether the United States, government officials and private citizens alike, ought to worry about it. They should. The form of organized crime represented by drug trafficking has been on the security agenda. Now, trafficking plus economic integration and Communism's disintegration create a new threat, one that puts the governance of key countries, like Russia, at risk and seems a menace stretching inside U.S. borders. Still, the issue is whether organized crime amounts to a threat to *national security*—not in the cold war's expansive meaning, when virtually anything sought by any interest group, from highways to student loans got "national security" attached to it, but rather in an old-fashioned sense of posing a palpable threat to the nation's territorial integrity, economic well-being, or core institutions.

The provisional answer is "probably not." Crime will be a nuisance, one that will put pressure on U.S. institutions and practices, but it is not a serious threat. That answer is, however, less interesting than the vast changes wrought on the various meanings of security by the cold war's end, changes which demand that, in order to make sense of the world and to adopt sensible policies, one distinguishes between purposive threats and "threats without threateners"—what are sometimes called *systemic threats*. With that distinction in hand, I turn more specifically to international organized crime now occurring amidst, and partly feeding off, the transformation of international politics. The Westphalian notions of state sovereignty are passing away, replaced by economics as the driver of international politics: enter the "market state."

THINKING ABOUT NATIONAL SECURITY: THE THIRD TRANSITION

The bombing of the federal building in Oklahoma City drove home security's split personality.[1] The split is suggested by our language: security has both "international" and "social" as common modifiers. On one hand, the all-encompasing cold-war use of "security"—almost exclusively in terms of a threat based beyond our borders—now seems a period piece. Yet because the Soviet Union, armed with nuclear weapons, could threaten America's very existence, there was a certain logic to defining security by reference to abstract, if terrifying, threats located abroad.

Oklahoma City reminds Americans that most of the time—even during the cold war—a person's sense of security has a distinctly local character, definable in terms of whether one can be assured of work and walk the local streets in safety (or do business with government without fear of more than frustrating delay).

The point of departure for thinking about national security today, a point stressed in a volume I edited with Graham Allison, *Rethinking America's Security*,[2] is that this is America's third postwar transition this century, one at least as portentous as those after World Wars I and II. As background to just how much has changed, it is worth considering the main features of the cold-war definition of security:

"Stun" Value
It almost goes without saying that the Soviet threat, symbolized by nuclear terror, had a stun value that is not true of today's concerns. Terrorism may have a comparable effect, when a World Trade Center or Oklahoma City occurs, but the stun is isolated. It does not provide a comparable catalyst for politics or policy.

Priority to a Perceived Military and Alien Threat to Our Nation's Security
In the last transition, Americans decided—not quickly or easily but in the end decisively—that containing Communism, above all in Europe, was more important than concentrating on the domestic economy, circling the wagons in the Western Hemisphere, pursuing the notion of world order embodied in the UN Charter, or some other overriding objective. The nation came to a strategic proposition: X is more important than Y or Z.

A Global Threat to Be Countered Globally
In many respects, the cold war seems exceptional in American history. Security was defined expansively to include not just the United States, which, after all, never was at physical risk save for nuclear weapons, and not just America's treaty allies and friends, but also, sometimes, something uneasily described as the "free world."

Unifying Threat
The father of nuclear strategy, Bernard Brodie, observed that nuclear war would unite in death all Russians—men, women, children, and the KGB. The same was true of Americans. While in fact African Americans and other minorities did a

disproportionate amount of the dying in actual combat, *in principle* nuclear terror did not discriminate.

Responses Relatively Cheap
In 1945, America held half the world's economic product. It was relatively unconcerned about the negative effects of that economic activity, like pollution or resource depletion. The combination gave the last transition a simplicity this one will not have. Then, responding to the Soviet threat was relatively cheap. To be sure, American citizens suffered the terror of nuclear weapons and the tax burden of armament—high for defense, but for Americans the overall tax burden was moderate by comparison to almost all other developed countries—but otherwise were not much affected. The threat, if terrifying, remained mostly abstract. Americans did not meet Russians on the field of battle.

None of these features is self-evidently the case today. Then, national conceptions and politics reflected the primacy of external security. Budgeting gave pride of place to money for defense; domestic spending paid the compliment by adding "national defense" as a modifier for education or highway programs. Now, that hierarchy is doubly destroyed: not only is X no longer self-evidently more important than Y but also X and Y themselves are not useful descriptions. "Foreign" and "domestic" are so intertwined as to be unhelpful categories.

For instance, the proposition that domestic well-being, if not security, can no longer be isolated from trends abroad is widely given lip service. But it has no agreed policy content. Does it mean that, with no Soviet Union, America can bargain harder for economic advantage? But if so, with whom, and for what? The global processes afoot mean poor countries are no "threat," despite wild rhetoric to the contrary: virtually all of America's sophisticated manufactured imports come from rich countries, for instance.

Does that suggest hard bargaining with rich countries? If so, for what? So long as domestic patterns of savings and consumption do not change, reducing America's trade deficit with Japan only means increasing it with someone else. And it takes no crusty conservative to fret that governments will bargain on behalf of "sunset" industries, not sunrise. After all, no one lobbies on behalf of employees whose jobs have not yet been created or are multiplying faster than skilled workers can be found to fill them.[3] So the Clinton administration wound up, despite better intentions, twisting Japanese arms over automobiles.

Should the causation then be reversed, with concerns abroad seen as consequences of failures at home—to cut the deficit or improve education or infrastructure? These arguments make more sense. But they sweep aside broader unease about exactly where the international economy is heading. That unease is reflected in the paradox of current U.S. attitudes—lingering fear of the future at a time of prosperity.

In that sense, the cold war's ending also marked the end of relatively familiar international economic terrain. Why, for instance, should hot flows of international finance, huge but still small by comparison to national economies, push the United States toward higher interest rates it does not need or inflation it cannot afford? More structurally, how important is a residual U.S. security umbrella over Europe and Asia, not to keep them closed to aggressors but rather open to international commerce?

The fact of economic interdependence makes any too-close analogizing with older American history suspect, but it is possible the United States will again shrink the perimeter of its interests. That much was suggested by the United States' long standoffishness with regard to Yugoslavia's civil war. The perimeter might be a North American economic area. Or the United States might try to square diminished grasp with undiminished reach. That might require real partnership with other nations, something for which the Gulf War coalition provided a foretaste.[4]

Or the definition may be more selective, with some traditional real estate, like Yugoslavia, slipping beyond the pale of America's interest, with others, like Kuwait, for combinations of new and old reasons, remaining solidly entrenched near the perceived core of national interests. It is hard to predict what will occur in this connection. Environmental issues like global warming might drive attention to distant lands now barely on the radar screen of popular concern.

Today's security concerns are not all unifying, responding to them will not be comparably cheap, and the burden of response may be visibly unequal. When recent polls show 75 percent of all Californians but only 30 percent of "leaders" placing immigration atop the public agenda, it is tempting to dismiss the difference as ignorance. Yet immigration may be a threat to some Americans, to their sense of position, if not their livelihoods, even as it is a boon to others. The connection between security's external and local meanings is in question during this transition. The question is a reminder that while one marvels (or recoils) at how much the cold war's end has changed the world, it has changed Americans more.

THE WORLD OF 2010

Predicting the detailed state of the world a decade or two hence is fool's play. Yet 2010's major powers are tolerably clear. So are the global processes that will shape 2010, if not how those processes will play out.

Global Military Power
In aggregate military terms the United States is indeed the sole superpower. That state of affairs will change, if at all, only close to 2010, conceivably by a Russian resurgence but more possibly by the emergence of an Asian peer, most probably China.

Political and Economic Power
The United States, Japan, Europe, Russia, and China will shape 2010's world. There is uncertainty about the last two, and room for arguments at the margin about whether, say, India or Brazil might reach the list.

Dispersion of Power
If nation-states are not about to go away, then power is dispersing, both above and below them. States are challenged from above and below. From above, not

even the United States is any longer a large enough unit to stay in the first rank economically on its own; autarky equals poverty, as India, China, and the Soviet Union all found in their different ways. States have been forced to cede power to regional trade groupings, like NAFTA, or to international institutions like the International Monetary Fund (IMF) or the World Trade Organization (WTO). They also must open themselves to wider economic forces they may be able to affect but cannot control. The Asian nations discovered this in spades.

From below, bankers, criminals, terrorists, and drug traffickers all act around and through states. They become forces in their own right, challenging state power from beneath. National leaders are still held accountable, yet their control of events is fading.

It is critical, however, to be clear about cause and effect. Public commentary links Rwanda, Haiti, Somalia, and Bosnia as "failed states," where governance has all but collapsed under the weight of poverty, population, crime, and disease.[5] Yet on closer inspection only Somalia and, more provisionally, Haiti fit the label. In Bosnia, the problem was not weak states but surprisingly strong ones that, alas, wished to occupy the same geography. And Rwanda seemed an old, and old-fashioned, civil war.

Rather, diminutioning of state power is best conceived along a continuum. At one end lie the industrial democracies. Hardly any of them, however, fully exercise all the attributes of state power—witness the lawlessness of America's inner cities. Somalia is perhaps at the other. In between, the most obvious partial failures are territorial—for instance, Peru ceding control of much of its territory to Sendero Luminoso in the 1980s. But the more arresting partial failures of state capacity are probably not uncontrolled territory, but unmet expectations on the part of citizens. So, too, the global processes afoot are tolerably clear if their end points are not.

Economics
Interdependence is becoming real, with dizzying speed, so that distances matter less. Already, for instance, southern California's highest-value exports move by air; even higher-value exports—ideas, software, movies—move by ether, almost instantly. The future lies not with Radio Free Europe but with the Internet. Colleagues, whether academic researchers or members of a criminal gang, can cooperate almost as easily between Santa Monica and Singapore as between Cali and Bogotá. In one sense, the process is integrating. In another, however—and more tentatively, for the data are not yet in—the gap between haves and have-nots is growing, both among societies and within them.

In one respect, though, geography still matters. Of economic factors, one, human capital—that is, people—does not move freely. They may move more freely than governments would like—impelled in normal times by economics, the desire for a better life elsewhere, and in abnormal times by war—but they are still controlled. Geography still matters, and human flows between neighbors have become if anything more important, especially if the neighbors are, like the United States and Mexico, rich and slow-growing in native population, on the one side, poor and populous on the other. States' efforts at control may be largely illusory, but those efforts continue to be made in strenuously purposive ways that are not for goods or capital.

Rising Belief in the Immaterial

Former Yugoslavia and the Islamic revival seem, tentatively, two sides of the same coin. Partly in alienation from processes of global integration, peoples are seeking forms of transcendental association. They seek to differentiate "us" from "them." One side is the quest of ethnic kin for smaller units, often for states of their own. This is not just a result of the death of the Soviet Union's deadening hand. It has existed, arguably, since the French Revolution and coincides, intriguingly, with the Industrial Revolution. Borders are now in question.

The obverse is the rise of belief in the immaterial. Put crudely, men and women don't lay down their lives for the free market; if they ever did for Marxism, that was long ago. The loss of community in modernizing societies may propel the search for something in which to believe; the anomie of being marginalized may sharpen the search. Today, it is religion that most visibly provides such a purpose. But it is not beyond imagining that by 2010 other transcendental belief systems will arise.

Technological Revolution

Communications make it possible, for instance, for drug traffickers to encrypt their communications, or for would-be Haitian boat people to learn within a day what fraction of their predecessors have been screened into the United States.

More broadly, this period of technology, as opposed to the first generation after World War II, seems to be contributing to growing disparities in income. The premium on knowledge is high; poor countries (or poor citizens of rich ones) cannot use cheap, unskilled labor to create a niche.[6] For nations, the lesson is that of their endowments, only one really matters—the quality of their people.

Changing Demographics

Over time, enormous disparities in north-south growth rates will sharpen emigration pressures. More imminently, youth "bulges"—cohorts much too large to be integrated in the job force—hint at instability in key developing countries, Egypt and Turkey for instance.

Environmental Concerns

These too are chronic, not acute, but imagine what two Chernobyls within a year would do to the international agenda.

OLD THREATS AND NEW

For some developments that emerge from these processes, the old-fashioned language of threat is appropriate.

Rogue States

The nation-state is not about to go away. Pronouncements of its demise are, to paraphrase Twain, premature. Indeed, recent events have demonstrated how awkward it can be for the United States and its partners to deal with rogue states, even ones with but a fraction of America's military power. North Korea, Iraq, and Iran top today's list. No doubt 2010's list will be different, but the characteristics of those on it will be much the same: alienated from the political, ideological, or territorial status quo, consequently ready to challenge the basic norms of global order, and determined, relatively cohesive, and advanced enough to aspire to dangerous weaponry.

For these threats our existing armory—both real and conceptual—is more or less apt. Deterrence and its means are relevant. Yet notice that the United States fought Desert Storm, the cold war's European war transplanted to Arabia's sands, with an eye on the bond markets: it passed the tin cup afterward, lest the war's cost increase the American deficit. And the instruments for dealing with most possible rogues—whether blocking North Korea's path to nuclear weapons or preventing Russia's slide to autocratic enmity—are not strictly military. They are more political and economic.

Terrorism

The World Trade Center bombing was a reminder of American vulnerability. So, in another way, was Oklahoma City. If there is good news, then it is not much better than the bad. It is that technology has not yet dramatically broadened the menu of terror weapons. The principal exception is the Soviet Union's collapse, which risks the diffusion of nuclear bombs, materials, or know-how. Each day brings fresh tales of would-be deals in nuclear materials. So far the large seizures have not been bomb-grade, and the bomb-grade seizures haven't been large. Many have been "stings." Yet that real materials have been stung is hardly reassuring.

The bad news is that terrorists have long had plenty of violent wherewithal. The basic design of atomic weapons hasn't been a secret for a long time, so building one for terrorists is a fissile material and engineering problem. More ominously, the Tokyo subway gassings underscore that lethal chemical weapons have been and are within reach of almost any terrorist group. So are biological ones.

If terrorists have not used atomic or biological terror, that is probably because they haven't needed to do so. "Conventional" explosives have been more than enough damage for their purposes.

If anything is new, it may be motivation, a point hinted at in the World Trade Center and Oklahoma City bombings. Most previous terrorists have been rational, if extreme; they have sought specific political ends. Thus, they have had to reveal their role, opening the possibility of retaliation against them or their state sponsors.

Future terrorists, however, might be anomic, their terror pure revenge, their behavior beyond calculations of deterrence and retaliation. The globe has seen their kind before. Because the United States is both the prime defender of the existing order and the premier evangelist for its secular, liberal ideological underpinnings, it will be the "Great Satan," the target of choice for these avengers. But few places are strangers to terrorism; yesterday's sponsors of terror may be tomorrow's targets.

For other developments, however, the old language misleads. These developments can be thought of as *threats without threateners*. If they are a threat, then the threat results from the cumulative effect of actions taken for other reasons, not from intent that is purposive and hostile. Those who burn the Amazon rain forests or try to immigrate here, or even those who traffic in drugs to the United States, do not necessarily wish Americans harm; they simply want to survive or get rich. *Their* self-interest becomes an American's threat. They differ sharply from the cold war's nominal threat. These *threats without threateners* are:

1. *Chronic and long-term, not acute and short-term.* Human beings, with their adrenaline systems, are optimized to deal with acute threats, like war, not with chronic problems whose causes are today but whose consequences are tomorrow or the day after. We are galvanized by the stun effect. We do better at fighting wars than at maintaining New York's bridges.
2. *Not necessarily "zero sum" in the way traditional threats were.* In war, we think, one state's loss is another's gain. By contrast, action against environmental degradation can produce gains for all. But notice the limits of this difference: the United States and the Soviet Union were military competitors, even adversaries, but they shared an interest in not blowing the planet up. By about the mid-1960s that positive-sum dimension came to outweigh the zero-sum competition in their nuclear relations.

By the same token, while states may all stand to gain if environmental problems are addressed, they will still be competitors over who pays and how much. The cutting down of the Amazon forest is almost a pure loss for most of humankind; it is not, however, for those who do the cutting. And the familiar incentives to free riding will obtain: it is in both of our interests that there be rules to govern international economic interchange, but if you play by the rules and I can cheat a little, I get the benefit of both the rules and my cheating. Indeed, the more others play by the rules, the greater the incentive for me to cheat. That is true for economic exchanges. It is also true for environmental control, where states, regions, or individuals could have both the benefits of, say, cleaner seas and the economic gains if they cheated a little. It may also be true for some aspects of law enforcement.

And these *threats without threateners:*

3. *May not be reversible.* The effects of wars, after all, were reversible within a generation or two. Not so, perhaps, for global warming.
4. *May be less susceptible to unilateral approaches than traditional security issues.* During the cold war, the United States felt impelled to make alliances and other such arrangements, in economics as well as security, but Americans still felt many of the levers of their security were in their hands. That seems less so for many of the "new" issues. In that sense, the United States is coming to be less different from other nations than it was.
5. *May lie beyond the domain of government.* If national security was a government monopoly during the cold war, then that is much less true of newer

challenges, where many of the levers are in the hands of companies or private citizens.

6. *May be neither so cheap or so unifying as traditional security threats.* Addressing some "new" problems may, by contrast, require Americans—or at least some of them—to drive less or work harder or otherwise change their behavior in more than trivial ways.

THE RISE OF THE "MARKET STATE"[7]

What lies behind both old threats and new, and the uneasy interplay of the two, is a transformation of international politics. To overstate only slightly, the primary drivers of international politics are economic, yet our habits of thought and our institutions remain powerfully conditioned by the cold war's focus on interstate relations and the balance of power. That transformation is often mentioned, but its implications are far-reaching. They are yet to be apprehended. To be sure, traditional issues among states remain, but they too are conditioned by the economic context. Witness the Russian debate over NATO's impending enlargement eastward: that debate is intense but almost entirely among specialists inside the Russian "ring road." For most Russians, polls show, the real issues are much closer to home, in their economic situations and how Russia's insertion into the global economy bears on them.

Yet our existing armory—both conceptual and policy—is rooted in the traditional image of international politics. There is thus a mismatch between what drives international issues and how they are addressed. Take immigration as an example. War aside, what drives immigration is almost entirely economic—the push of desire for a better life and the pull of interests of powerful groups in the receiving states. Yet policy approaches to it derive from the older vision of international politics, one dominated by notions of border controls, citizenship, and sovereignty. There the mismatch is almost total.

As the traditional politics of interstate rivalries cedes place to the global market, governments lose unique attributes of their power. Armies and territory count for less, and the critical "levers," many of which used to be in the hands of government, pass to the private sector. Americans retain, though not for long, the fiction that the Federal Reserve sets U.S. interest rates. In fact, the German Bundesbank is as important, and both pale by comparison to private transactions. During 1983–1988, the ratio of public to private flows of capital to the poorer countries averaged just under 2:1; over the course of 1989–1995, the ratio switched to almost 5:1 in favor of *private* flows.[8]

In today's relentless competition, the market respects neither the borders nor the icons of the traditional Westphalian state. It does not care whether the worker is Filipino or American, Chinese or German, man or woman, homosexual or military veteran. If the person can do the job, he or she is rewarded, and if not, not. "Made in America" is not a label of interest to the market because the citizen as consumer has become indifferent to the national appeal. Nor are national cultural symbols of interest except as marketing devices: ask any American who has

traveled and seen sweatshirts with "random English" on the front, or, more striking still, ventured to ask a foreigner wearing a Harvard T-shirt which class she
was in and received only a blank stare in return.

In these circumstances, American politicians and their colleagues abroad get
blamed for what they cannot control. In the United States, the ambivalence about
the market state is manifested in complaints that the government has not done its
part in educating citizens or preparing them for global competition. And so Mr.
Clinton sometimes behaves not as president but as mayor of the United States,
speaking of education and law enforcement, worthy subjects over which he has
almost no authority.

It is worth stretching for three more far-reaching implications, for they bear
directly on international organized crime:

The Market State Devalues International Organization
At a minimum, international institutions are orthogonal to the market since
those institutions are creatures of states, based on notions of state sovereignty.
This applies to NATO as well as to the United Nations. It leaves international economic institutions, like the World Bank or the WTO, in a tenuous middle
ground. On the one hand, they may be less devalued by the market state than are
international political or security institutions, for they have value as rule setters
for international commerce. Markets require legal frameworks that make the
behavior of other actors relatively predictable.

Yet, on the other hand, not only are most governmental institutions swamped
by private international transactions—what the IMF or World Bank does is more
and more overshadowed by private capital flows—but the status of those institutions is itself open to question or change, for they too are creatures of governments, not of the forces that drive international politics. To overstate only
slightly, the World Bank has moved from an earlier role as the giver of assistance
provided by governments to that of convener of major international banks.

To Some Extent, Law is Also Devalued by the Market State
After all, law itself is rooted in the traditional state. And so, at a minimum, the
legitimacy of law in its current form is more and more questioned. As a sovereign, Charles V could simply order a criminal's head chopped off. Bill Clinton
can hardly come close. He could sign and the Senate could ratify a treaty ban-
ning chemical weapons which contains provision for challenge inspections by
other states of suspected private production facilities in the United States, but
neither he nor the Senate could promise to deliver on that promise. They could
only promise to try.

More to the point for international crime, as the market state erodes distinctions between citizens and noncitizens, older notions of law enforcement, which
accorded the sovereign's subjects greater protection than mere foreigners, pass
away. American constitutional practice used to draw a sharp distinction between
citizens and noncitizens.

The American militias have plenty of antigovernment antecedents in American history, yet, like a photograph's negative, their backlash against the global market outlines the devaluation of law. What is lost is belief in the national community and the process of political representation. The militias' way of separating "them" from "us" is not primarily religious; rather it is a cocktail of populism and local nationalism, sometimes tinged with religion. In their gruesome contortion, the federal government and its law was not "us" but "them," the enemy whose officials were not fellows but foes to be killed, people seen in bizarre cahoots with sinister forces of internationalism.

In these circumstances, the status of international law is buffeted by cross currents. From one direction, it is more relevant. Traditional international law always sat uneasily with U.S. traditions, for it too was based on Westphalian notions of state sovereignty and nonintervention in the affairs of sovereigns. States, not people, were the concerns of traditional international law. The Founding Fathers could be tenacious about America's own sovereignty: witness the War of 1812. But states had to be legitimate to be sovereign. It was the arbitrariness of sovereignty that the Founding Fathers had sought to escape.

Now, though, international law is moving in a very "American" direction: people are coming to matter, and what happens inside national borders is more and more regarded as a legitimate concern of the international community. To the extent that sovereignty, borders, and all the trappings of the Westphalian state are becoming less important in international law, that law should be more relevant.

Yet from the other direction, the planet is still far from having any real alternative to states and state action, particularly when it comes to enforcement. It took a coalition of willing *states*, however covered by the legitimacy of international law, to impose peace on Saddam Hussein, decency on the Bosnian Serbs, or minimal orderliness on Zaire's succession. There is still a mismatch between the forces that are driving international politics and the forces of international law. When it comes to enforcing treaties regulating private activity, such as global warming, national power remains crucial.

The Market State Implies Dramatic Changes in "Private" Responsibilities
This is the obverse of the previous implication. Traditionally, private actors were objects, not subjects of international politics. States, or groups of states acting through international institutions, might try to regulate private behavior, but nonstate actors had little corresponding authority or opportunity for setting norms. To that extent they were free riders on the international order. Of course, private efforts to influence state policies are a familiar feature of democratic politics, and those efforts ran to the international policies of states. We see them now in the U.S. debate over according most-favored-nation (MFN) status to China. Occasionally, private companies have acted more creatively, for instance in Dupont's role in rallying chemical companies to support, not oppose, the Montreal Protocol's ban on damaging fluorocarbons, or the private law-making in maritime affairs. But those instances have been rare.

The transition to the market state implies a vast increase in the responsibility of private actors, from companies and individuals to so-called nongovernmental organizations (notice that the label is itself a remnant of the old order!). They are becoming, in ways hardly realized, let alone charted, not the objects of the international order but its subjects, its architects. They are becoming the setters of international norms, not free riders on rules set by states.

ASSESSING INTERNATIONAL ORGANIZED CRIME

The difficulty of defining terms in new circumstances runs through all the essays in this book. Of the three words in its subject—international organized crime—the one that is ostensibly least ambiguous, *crime*, is itself elusive. What is against the law in one place is not everywhere so. Given the prim rules of their Communist past, when Russians talk of their mafia, they lump together what Americans would call crime with what we would label aggressive but acceptable economic behavior—usurious interest rates and harsh repayment terms, for instance.

International and *organized* are more slippery still. In today's world, almost every event has some tail that runs beyond the nation in which it occurred. And virtually all crimes involving more than one person require some "organization." It is useful, especially at first, to impose a relatively high threshold for both terms. Thus, if a Mexican immigrant mugs me in Santa Monica, I have been the victim of crime but not an "international" crime. (I as statistic, though, may become part of a larger debate about people flows, but that is worth holding separate, at least analytically.)

The two dimensions interact. Suppose my muggers are two, both Mexican immigrants, their weapon is one smuggled across the border, and their getaway plan involves returning back across the border. The crime would then have more claim to being labeled both international and organized. One would still want, though, to imagine a continuum. At one end would be spontaneous crimes committed by individuals. The other end, harder to describe, would involve repeated crimes ("business lines") involving networks of people holding many different passports, operating across borders. The watchwords would be *repetition, network,* and *cross-border.* The network and the use of borders would need to be necessary, not merely convenient (my Mexican muggers probably could as safely have disappeared into one of Los Angeles's barrios). For my purposes, the initial focus should be toward that end of the continuum.

In this era of the market state, "national security" is much harder to define than it was during the cold war. For starters, it probably needs to refer to the security of people in a state or nation, not that *of* the state or nation. That makes the definition both more expansive and less. It is more expansive in that it drives the definition of security toward the everyday. It may be less in that, to the extent that the institutions and icons of the nation-state are being threatened, those institutions and icons are already becoming devalued (though citizens may still cling to them).

In principle, in the distinction between purposive threats and threats without threateners, international organized crime would traditionally have qualified as the latter to the extent that its perpetrators did not intend to do America *as a state* harm. They set out only to enrich themselves. Their targets were on the whole private citizens and institutions, not state institutions. In that, they would have been sharply distinguished from terrorists; if terrorists engaged in crime to support their terrorism, the two actions would have been distinguishable, at least in principle.

International organized crime also has other attributes of threats without threateners. It is chronic, not acute. The point at which drug trafficking ceased being, for Colombia, a lucrative annoyance and become a threat to established order and institutions of governance was a matter of definition. The "war on drugs" has no end, but neither, unlike traditional war, does it have a defined beginning. It required cooperation across states almost by definition. If government levers were relevant, those levers were, for the United States at least, not primarily in the hands of the federal government. All those levers depended very much on the cooperation of private citizens. And to the extent crime depended on willing "victims" or collaborators—in the profits reaped from drug use, gambling, prostitution, or money laundering—governments had either weak levers or none at all.

As a threat without threateners, international organized crime might still threaten national security in four ways—by destabilizing friendly governments, by risking wider violence, by materially affecting the economic well-being of citizens, or by sharply offending cherished values. I take the security of the United States as my example, for convenience's sake. It is a mixed example, for on the one hand, the United States is a weaker state than those of Western Europe or northeastern Asia, and so it feels the implications of the market state sooner than they do. On the other hand, it remains the strongest government on the globe, at least in the traditional attributes of interstate power. The depression, hot war, and cold war gave Americans more government, and more federal government, than had been the custom. The United States, a strong nation but a weak state, came to resemble the European state form with which America's founders had broken. At the same time, immigration was making the American nation more and more heterogeneous.

Consider each possible threat in turn:

Destabilizing Friendly States
On first glance, the states most threatened by international crime are either, like Colombia, not very important or, like Russia, not exactly friends. Yet the end of the cold war surely has overturned definitions of friends, and Mexico is both important and a friend (as the Canadian saying has it, "whether it wants to be or not"). The difficulty with assessing this threat is knowing what "destabilizing," that most frequent of government monikers for what it opposes, actually means. It seems to mean one of three things—that established government institutions lose control, risking wider violence; that governments lose the capacity to cooperate with the United States on measures deemed important; or, a variant of the second, that forms of governance America dislikes emerge. The first of these merges with the second threat.

Of the second consequence of destabilization, the sharpest examples have arisen from drug trafficking. There, the issue is cause and effect, the trade-offs governments have been forced to make. Peru was standoffish about pursuing the war on drugs with the United States during much of the 1980s. Fear of being too closely associated with Washington was part of the reason, but that merged with a larger dilemma: the campaigns against trafficking and against terrorism were in ugly opposition, for to destroy peasant incomes by eradicating coca was to hand the Sendero Luminoso easy opportunities for recruiting. Hence, when compelled to choose, the Peruvian government pursued the war against the guerrillas and let that against drugs languish.

Or for Mexico, the more it involved its army in fighting drugs, the more it risked corrupting that army, one of the country's few relatively clean and cohesive institutions. In these cases, crime had not really destabilized governments. What it had done was force upon them hard choices, which they sometimes made in ways of which the United States disapproved. Even with Colombia, where drug criminals negotiated with the government, the outcome seems not quite rightly described as destabilization. Rather money had created forces—political forces in the sense that they became interested in outcomes of governmental authority— powerful enough to again confront a government with unhappy choices.

For the third consequence of destabilization, the emergence of ugly forms of governance, including the lack of governance, the question is whether international crime's current spurt is mostly the artifact of transition. Take Russia as an example. There is no doubt that there is more crime in Russia and that it is more organized than in the rest of the world. Since chaotic gang wars during 1990–1994, the number of gangs in Russia has been falling but the remaining ones have become larger and more effective. The result has been fewer but stronger gangs. There is less indiscriminate killing but more targeted assassination, for instance of uncooperative businessmen or too-interested journalists. An estimated 80 percent of all businesses pay an average of a tenth to a fifth of their profits in protection money. And, according to a 1993 commercial survey, four-fifths of all U.S. firms operating in Russia had at least once violated the Foreign Corrupt Practices Act by paying a bribe.

The Russian mafia reportedly invests as much as a third of its own income to buy political protection. Hence, for all talk of tackling crime, not one of the major killings has been solved, nor has any senior crime figure been brought to trial in Russia. Russian gang leaders have only been prosecuted abroad, in Austria, Italy, and the United States.[9] Meanwhile, the Russian mafias have forged a number of links to counterparts abroad—for instance, with the Sicilian mafia to allow it to operate in northern Europe, or by exchanging cocaine for heroin with the Colombian cartels. These are, however, alliances of convenience, which are both temporary and cynical.

The economic transition has created lucrative opportunities for organized crime. When old structures have collapsed but not been replaced, and when rules are weak and enforcement weaker, black markets arise. Members of the old regime may use special knowledge or access to derive economic rent. "Protection rackets" flower. Drug money provides capital for new illicit ventures, along with incentive for criminal alliances across nations. Thus far, there is little evidence that organized crime has trafficked in nuclear materials—it has other, richer product lines—but the possibility cannot be ruled out. There was, for instance, a search in 1994 for plutonium a German businessman claimed was circulating on the black market.[10]

If its transition proceeds, will Russia then become more like Italy or the United States, where organized crime prospers but does not threaten basic institutions of government? Or will Russia's spiral down resemble Colombia or worse, where new, uglier elites displace traditional leaders and the nature of governance is up for grabs? No one can know, but there are good grounds for optimism. Having had a state that was too strong, Russia was bound for a time to have one that was too weak. Not having had capitalism, it was almost bound to have a period of "cowboy capitalism," as inappropriate rules and institutions were replaced by none at all. Over time, with luck, better economic institutions and the rule of law will grow, not eradicating opportunities for organized crime but containing them.

As other of the world's dinosaur regimes come unglued, crime is likely to be one of the results. For instance, North Korea already has its own black market. Suppose a collapse in the North came or impended. North Korea's leaders and senior commanders would know their futures were in trouble and would have an incentive to look to organized crime for succor or money. They might bring to the bargaining unconventional weapons, including nuclear devices. Havana was a playground of the U.S. mafia before the Cuban Revolution and could again become so. Depending on how the Castro regime collapses, there could be an ugly period of unrestrained rules and appetites, in this case not far from U.S. shores and this time with mafiosi from many nations engaged.

Risking Wider Violence
Here, it is useful to distinguish between violence that is more or less endemic to the criminal activity and violence that is a spillover. Unhappily, endemic violence seems inversely related to organization. That is, fighting is most intense when the criminal "market" is disorganized, as contenders battle for turf, distribution rights, or market share. That was true some years ago for the Cali and Medellín drug cartels; over time, perhaps sobered by the cost of violence, they became less contenders than collaborators. More anecdotally, drug-related gang violence on the streets of the United States also seems most intense when turf is in question, when new contenders threaten old market holders.

Neither the good news nor the bad from this observation is very good. The good news is that violence may dampen as crime becomes more organized, but the price may be more of the crime, more efficiently managed. And the bad news is that globalization almost ensures a fresh supply of immigrants and other contenders for old markets. So it has been with Chinese, Southeast Asian, Russian, and other new arrivals to the United States.

Most of the spillover violence from international organized crime so far has reflected criminals' efforts to protect themselves from law enforcement. In some places that has meant alliances, tacit and explicit, with other groups that share the government as an enemy—terrorists, for instance. In others it has meant threatened violence or hostage-taking to release comrades or secure safe passage. There seems little reason why criminals should sell their violent services to governments or terrorist groups: What is there to sell when the buyer is already proficient in violence? The other possibility of concern is not that criminals will engage in violence but that they will facilitate it, by selling nuclear or other weapons of mass destruction to renegade states or terrorist groups. In 1996, there were no seizures of nuclear material in the United States, but there were two cases involving conspiracies to import radioactive material into this country.[11]

Harming Economic Well-Being
From a pure economic perspective some crimes, like extortion, impose plain economic losses on their victims. Others, however, can increase a person's well-being by providing goods and services—gambling or prostitution, for instance—that the open market doesn't. Even protection rackets might contribute to well-being if the buyer of protection is subject to many predators and the cost of protection is not too high. The calculation then turns, in economic terms, on whether the secondary costs to society, enforcement costs or social ills, outweigh the private gains to the consumers. If most of the secondary costs are those of enforcing the law, society has the option of legalizing the activity. In the United States, one after another state has made just that calculation for gambling and has legalized it, though there are now the beginnings of a debate over the distributional effects of legalized gambling.

Economically speaking, trafficking in illegal drugs might also be regarded as providing a valued good which the market doesn't since the "victims" are in a strict sense willing ones, at least initially. However, the social costs of drug use seem appallingly high. The question at issue, one endlessly and fruitlessly debated between North and Latin Americans, is whether those social ills arise from the crime of supply or the crime of demand. If there were no demand, there surely would be no supply, but the reverse is not the case. If there were no supply from abroad, there would still, it appears, be some demand for mind-altering substances, and that demand would be satisfied by domestically grown substitutes or by chemicals ("designer drugs"), though the alternatives might conceivably be more expensive, more easily controlled, or less harmful in their social side effects.

Offending Important Values
Whether the international order is driven by interstate relations or global economics, not just money matters to citizens. Values matter as well. Organized crime offends those values, though in different measure in different places, and it imposes trade-offs on governments and peoples that both seek to avoid. Legalizing some illicit drugs could, on the analogy with gambling, reduce the power of organized crime and diminish violence. It probably would do so at the price of more drug use, though how much is a debated subject. In the end, though, legalization has not gotten on the agenda less for practical reasons than fundamental

ones: it simply seems wrong to most Americans. It offends their values, as it does citizens in other countries.

WHAT IMPLICATIONS OF THE MARKET STATE?

International organized crime will challenge U.S. institutions and conceptions of governance. It will be more than a nuisance, but less than a real threat to national security. That is the tentative conclusion of the foregoing effort at defining terms and categories. The same conclusion might not hold for other countries, for Colombia, for instance, not to mention the Comoro Islands.

It surely will challenge national institutions and conceptions of governance. If the United States has not quite recognized that the American state is being devalued by the market state, international crime is one of a number of examples that drive home how ill-suited U.S. government institutions are to the transformed international order. U.S. institutions—the Pentagon and National Security Council and so on—all were progeny of the cold war. They reflect the primacy of the balance of power defined in political and military terms. The CIA, for instance, is barred from law enforcement. It was hardly an accident that the Clinton administration felt impelled to create a National Economic Council in an effort to rebalance the government's attention. Nor was it much of a surprise that the initiative had little effect.

The foregoing has uneasily straddled the divide between the old and the new international orders, a traditional conception of national interest and elements of the emerging market state. International politics will be similarly straddled in the years ahead. But speculating further, what might be the implications for international organized crime of the transition to the market state? I conclude with two.

The first is that international concern over organized crime is likely to grow but international capacity to deal with it will diminish. Crime will offend the pocketbooks and values of more and more of the planet's citizens, but, for a time at least, national and international institutions for dealing with it will be devalued. For instance, there seems to be growing awareness that bribery in pursuit of international contracts is ultimately bad even for the nations whose officials are bribed, and so it is possible to imagine something like the U.S. Foreign Corrupt Practices Act becoming a norm for international commerce. The rub is that interest in the norm is likely to run ahead of capacity to enforce it, as both national and international institutions, rooted in the nation-state order, wither.

Over a longer time period, as Asia becomes more dominant in the international economy, new values will be injected into the process, and institutions will be shaped accordingly. Today's detached, rather amoral multinational corporation, built on American conceptions of the separation of public and private (not to mention of God and Mammon) may, under the pressure of the market state, give way to something more assertive and tinged with values.

The second is a deeper question about what "destabilization" means. Not to understate the venality of crime, but much of what today's Russia is undergoing is a familiar process of old elites being threatened, then displaced by newer ones.

The process has ugly overtones, but, then, so did the nineteenth century's displacement of pastoral aristocrats by money-grubbing industrialists. After all, in this century the Kennedys have gone from rum-running to American royalty in two generations.[12] Yesterday's elite in Latin America was nationalist and faintly Marxist, skeptical of the United States. Today's is technocratic, educated in the United States, and more internationalist, likely to care more for meeting Bill Gates than Bill Clinton.

So the question returns to whether countries important to the United States are foreordained by organized crime to a downward spiral. Or are they, rather, in the midst of transitions that will reach steady-state when institutions and practices solidify—albeit steady-states that may include high levels of crime and politics that have been refashioned in part by new elites? On this score, as with the reshaping of values and institutions by the market state, only time will tell.

NOTES

1. This discussion draws on my "The Changing Security Agenda," RAND, P–7918, (1995).
2. New York: W.W. Norton, 1992.
3. The classic text on this point is Raymond A. Bauer, Ithiel de Sola Pool, and Lewis Anthony Dexter, *American Business and Public Policy: The Politics of Foreign Trade* (New York: Atherton Press, 1963).
4. My RAND colleagues and I argue for constructing such a partnership, real this time, with America's European allies. See David A. Gompert and F. Stephen Larrabee, eds., *America and Europe: A New Partnership for a New Era* (Cambridge: Cambridge University Press, 1997).
5. Robert D. Kaplan's evocative article contributed to the attention to—and perhaps also the misunderstanding of—failed states. See "The Coming Anarchy," *Atlantic Monthly*, Feb. 1994.
6. The consensus on this point is broad enough to make one nervous. It is, for instance, the theme of Robert Reich's work. For a terse popular formulation, see Peter F. Drucker, "The Age of Social Transformation," *Atlantic Monthly*, Nov. 1994.
7. This term is owed to Philip Bobbitt and much of the discussion has been enriched by conversations with him. We were surveying the same intellectual terrain from somewhat different directions. See his forthcoming book, *The Shield of Achilles*.
8. IMF, *World Economic Outlook*, 1997, p. 29.
9. See International Institute for Strategic Studies, *Strategic Comments* 3, no. 3, Apr. 1997.
10. See *Washington Post*, 23 July 1994, A11R.
11. From Statement of Louis J. Freeh, FBI director, before the Senate Appropriations Committee, Subcommittee on Foreign Operations, Hearings on International Crime, 12 Mar. 1996, cited at www.fas.org/irp/congress/1996_hr/s9603.
12. I once found myself at a conference coffee break in Liechtenstein, standing next to that country's crown prince. In my best American, I stammered a question about his family. His answer began in the tenth century. I had read that his family once owned extensive lands north and west of its present holdings, and I inquired about that. He said that sometime in the thirteenth or fourteenth century his forebearers had been invited to dine with the Hapsburgs. After dinner, they had been given the choice of dying or relinquishing their land. The episode made me think that if one stole it a half millennium ago, one is European aristocracy, if one stole it a century ago, one is American old money; twenty years ago makes one nouveau riche, while a year ago makes one a convicted felon!

OFFSHORE MONEY

3

Jack A. Blum

INTRODUCTION

International organized crime and large-scale narcotics trafficking depend on the money laundering and banking services provided by the world of offshore banking and finance. The offshore financial world is made up of countries and political subdivisions that use their sovereign status to protect the wealth of foreign customers from the civil and criminal law of their own countries. These "haven" jurisdictions provide a home for banks, international business corporations, securities brokers, and insurance companies, which are used by the owners of all kinds of offshore assets. All of their transactions are, for the most part, shrouded under a blanket of secrecy.

Offshore financial activity has grown steadily and quietly for the last forty years. Today the banking and investment activity that takes place in offshore jurisdictions is an important part of overall global finance. Based on the booking of deposits and loans,[1] the Cayman Islands are the world's fifth-largest banking center. The islands are home to 520 banks and more corporations than people. The Netherlands Antilles are the fourth-largest source of foreign investment in the United States. The British Virgin Islands are home to nearly 180,000 corporations.

From their beginnings offshore havens have serviced the money-laundering needs of organized crime, but their real growth came because of the flight of noncriminal money from the political power of the nation-state. The movement of money offshore was facilitated by improvements in communications technology, computer hardware and software, and transportation. The fact is that assets in the offshore havens are a mixture of legal money, fleeing tax and regulation, and the proceeds of criminal activity. This mixture confuses the issue—

customers who want to hide legitimate money from the tax collectors argue the case for the offshore system; the crooks take advantage of the cover that the presence of legitimate money provides.

Offshore financial operations undercut two of the most important historical prerogatives of the nation-state—economic regulation and taxation. Because so many assets have moved offshore, even the largest nation-states are finding it difficult to control their own economies. The shift of assets offshore has forced countries to rely on payroll taxes, sales taxes, and value added taxes. The offshore system has made the collection of estate taxes, corporate income taxes, and personal income taxes on income derived from investment very difficult. Insurance companies, mutual funds, banks, and trading companies all use the offshore environment to avoid regulation.

Offshore finance is an especially important issue for the Americas. A dozen jurisdictions in the Caribbean and Central and South America either operate offshore financial centers or contribute essential elements to the offshore mixture. The other countries of the hemisphere provide the centers' best customers. For example, the total amount of money held offshore by Argentine nationals exceeds by far the Argentine national debt. United States capital markets invite investment money from the offshore centers. The money that comes to the United States through offshore facilities helps keep New York the financial center of the world.

This chapter will review briefly the colorful history of the offshore financial trade and trace the government decisions and market forces that brought it into existence. It will describe how criminals, tax evaders, international businesses, corrupt politicians, and even some governments use the offshore financial world. It will consider the implications of the remarkable recent growth of offshore centers for law enforcement, financial regulation, and government revenue. Although the principal focus of the discussion will be the impact on the Americas, the problem is worldwide, the implications global.

Money laundering is the term used to describe the process by which criminals hide money that comes from illegal activity. In the early days of organized crime it referred to hiding illegal money from police and tax authorities. Today the term includes the process of getting illegal currency into the banking system without having the deposit reported to the government.

Over a period of years the U.S. government took steps to make depositing unaccounted-for cash in banks as difficult as possible. Congress passed laws that required financial institutions to report cash deposits of $10,000 or more. At first the reporting requirements were not enforced. In the early 1980s the Bank of Boston was prosecuted for failure to file the required Cash Transaction Reports (CTRs), and a tremor went through the American banking establishment. When the Bank of Boston entered a guilty plea, other American banks fell in line and began to insist on the proper reporting of cash transactions. The criminals responded by using nonbanking businesses—jewelry stores and car dealerships. In response, the laws were changed to require reports from any business that deals in large amounts of cash. Finally, in the late 1980s, new laws required banks in the United States to report suspicious transactions and to refuse business from customers they did not know.

To get around the rules, criminals sought holes in the U.S. banking system. For a time they tried *smurfing*—a term used to describe making many deposits of amounts just under $10,000 to get around the reporting requirements. The courts quickly closed that loophole. As the U.S. system closed, criminals shipped the currency out of the country for deposit abroad.

Getting currency into the bank, around the reporting system, at home or abroad is called *placement*. Once the money is in the form of a bank entry, the launderer hides its criminal origin through a series of complex transactions. Police call this *layering*. The launderer then makes the proceeds available to the criminals in an apparently legitimate form. The term for this is *integration*.

Like major corporations, large criminal organizations need access to the world's banking system to manage their affairs. Retail crime produces cash. Drug addicts do not use checks or credit cards and drug dealers do not accept them. The cash drug dealers get is heavy, dirty, and dangerous to keep on hand. Criminal organizations have a hard time shipping it to pay foreign suppliers and contractors and to bribe public officials. Currency does not pay interest; thus each day criminal proceeds are kept in the form of cash they lose interest. To function efficiently, criminal businesses must turn their currency into bank entries.

A large-scale marijuana smuggler, Leigh Rich, described his cash problem to me while sitting in the visiting room of a federal prison. "When a big load came in, they paid us in cash. The cash was very hard to hide. We started using large picnic coolers as containers. We stored the cash-filled coolers in a house we rented. Pretty soon the coolers were going over window level and we worried about what the neighbors would think was going on. We could not hire guards. After all, they could turn the guns on us and take the money. Obviously we could not call the police and ask for protection." In the end Rich and his colleagues shipped the money by charter plane to the Cayman Islands where, at the time,[2] the banks took U.S. currency, no questions asked. "After a while," Rich continued, "the amounts of cash became so large the banks were embarrassed and told us to go somewhere else. We moved the cash to Panama and began using BCCI [The Bank of Credit and Commerce International]."

Panama was, and is, an especially useful jurisdiction for money laundering because it uses the U.S. dollar as its currency. Bringing large amounts of U.S. cash to a bank in Panama is routine business. A money launderer testified that he had shipped cash to Panama on pallets aboard regularly scheduled Eastern Airlines flights. The cash was shrink-wrapped in PVC. The money was offloaded into waiting armored cars the minute the plane touched down in Panama City. The launderer's testimony was confirmed by the testimony of an Eastern Airlines pilot who described how his plane was routinely directed to an isolated area of the airport so the cash could be unloaded before the plane was allowed to go to the gate to unload passengers.

When the federal authorities arrested and convicted Rich, the government recovered approximately $10,000,000 that it said represented his illegal profits.

Most likely the $10,000,000 was a fraction of what Rich had earned in the drug business. Yet the U.S. government has never found any more money or even evidence that more money existed. Rich has laundered it effectively. In all probability Rich hid his money by using the working tools of the offshore financial world. The most important of these is the international business corporation, or IBC. IBCs are corporations chartered in jurisdictions that give tax-free status to firms that do no business at home. These jurisdictions allow the beneficial ownership of the corporation to be concealed.[3] The way the ownership of the corporations is hidden depends on the country. Some countries, such as Panama, use bearer share companies. When bearer shares are involved, whoever holds the physical certificate owns the company. Straw men do the incorporation and are the initial shareholders. They then give the stock to the true owners.

Local lawyers act as corporate officers and directors. Most of them make it a point of not knowing who their clients are. Their role is limited to opening various bank accounts in the name of the corporation, following telephoned and faxed instructions, and forwarding financial statements. Recently Panama passed legislation that requires lawyers who act as officers and directors to know who the real owner of the company is. In response a large Panamanian law firm became an agency of the government of Belize so that it could form Belize corporations for its customers on the spot. Belize has no rules requiring identification of beneficial ownership.

Other jurisdictions allow "nominee" shareholders, officers, and directors. In these jurisdictions, mostly common law, such as the Cayman Islands and the British Virgin Islands, trust agreements that are a private matter bind the nominees. The trust agreements are usually hidden under lawyer-client privilege. The trust agreements bind the nominees to follow the instructions of the grantor or the beneficiaries. Again, the main function of the trustee is to open bank accounts, follow client instructions, and forward statements. The offshore corporation then becomes the vehicle for opening bank and brokerage accounts. If the corporation is introduced to the bank by a local lawyer or accountant, the bank will open an account without further question. Offshore banks and brokerage firms offer asset management accounts. A customer can invest in any asset through these accounts and leave it in the custody of the bank trust department. If a customer is nervous, the offshore bank can ask a major New York bank to open a custodial account for the corporation. In a domestic "custodial" account, investments are held in a "street name" and are fully segregated from the assets and liabilities of the bank itself. If the bank fails, trust assets are not owned by the bank and are not tied up in the bankruptcy proceedings.

A professional offshore money specialist and money launderer in the Cayman Islands told me that he could invest my money in any market in the world through the most reputable institutions, no questions asked. He also assured me that I would remain completely anonymous. He proposed setting up an offshore corporation—an IBC—for me, which his bank would manage. The corporation would then have an asset management account at his bank's trust department. The trust department would then invest the money on my instruction anywhere in the world. He asked me for a fee of $5,000 to set up the company and an additional $2,000 to manage it each year.[4] His fees were way above the going market. I can set up a Cayman corporation for just over $1,000 and a British Virgin Islands corporation for a bit less.

This launderer was part of a small army of professionals who are available to "structure" offshore protection for clients. He and his thousands of colleagues will, for a fee, plan the proper mixture of corporations, jurisdictions, and institutions to maximize protection. The roster of accommodating professionals includes lawyers, accountants, and trust officers.

If you cannot use it, then hidden money is worthless. Criminals and tax evaders want to use the money without leaving a paper trail and without arousing suspicion. The latest developments in technology have made that increasingly easy. Offshore banks will now issue debit cards, which, according to one ad in the *International Herald Tribune*, will "keep you in touch with your offshore funds." The card can be used in any cash machine around the world and as a credit card for purchases. The records stay in the bank secrecy jurisdiction, out of reach of the government where the transaction took place.

The latest—and potentially most difficult—problem in the control of money laundering is the control of cybercash. *Cybercash* is the term used to describe smart cards that can be "filled" with amounts of money. Using a code, the holder can authorize the deduction of "cash" from the card. Cybercash and smart cards may make the idea of controlling cash transactions obsolete.

A favored technique for repatriation of large sums of money is to disguise the incoming money as proceeds of a foreign bank loan. The person wanting the money back in his home jurisdiction sets up a deposit at an offshore bank. The bank then "lends" the depositor his own money. Sometimes the loan is not repaid and the bank just keeps the deposit. Sometimes the loan is repaid with interest. The interest payment gives the "borrower" the ability to take tax deductions and move even more money offshore.

As governments discover money-laundering techniques and crack down, criminals invent new ones. Recently, for example, U.S. money launderers have been buying currency from drug dealers at a 20 percent discount. They pay for the currency with funds they generate outside the country. The first step in the process is the purchase of a desirable product at the wholesale level in the United States for cash. They then ship the goods to the country whose currency they want. They then sell the goods at or below cost and use the proceeds to pay the criminals.

Sophisticated practitioners of the art of hiding assets mix and match countries of incorporation, institutions, and trustees. For example a British Virgin Islands corporation might have an account at a Panamanian bank. The Panamanian bank receives the cash. The bank balance is then transferred by wire to the account of a Netherlands Antilles corporation in a Cayman Islands bank. The possible permutations and combinations are endless and are an investigator's nightmare.

The combination of high-powered computers and sophisticated electronic communications have made it possible to set up a complex system of conceal-ment by e-mail, fax, and phone from anywhere in the world. If a government is hot on the trail of a criminal's assets, skilled launderers can move it from one financial maze to another in seconds. Cost is the only constraint on the level of protection. Each corporation, trust agreement, and bank account added to the maze carries a management fee. Each transaction carries a fee. The professionals who do the planning, especially planning for criminals, are expensive.

Today's offshore financial world is a "Bermuda Triangle" for money launder-ing, financial fraud, and tax investigations. Information on ownership, money transfers, trust arrangements, and banking connections is, with rare exceptions, unavailable because of secrecy laws. If it is available, then so many jurisdictions are involved and so many hurdles must be cleared that the police give up. Inves-tigators move on to greener pastures out of sheer frustration. For example, even the jurisdictions that have signed mutual legal assistance treaties with the United States can provide information only when they know what they are looking for. Thus if the Drug Enforcement Administration (DEA) asks the Caymans for information on a particular drug dealer, the request will be useless without the name of the IBC the drug dealer is using to hide his assets.

To make matters worse, many otherwise reputable institutions will create completely false paper trails to document illicit transactions. For a fee—usually 1 percent—the bank staff will create fictitious invoices, back-to-back letters of credit, and dummy intermediaries to conceal the origin and destination of goods and money. In a recent case I worked on, a large bank gave an American busi-nessman a false invoice for machinery for his employer's factory. He paid the invoice to the bank's controlled shell corporation. The bank then deposited the money in his trust account.

Obviously, what works for criminals will work for anyone who wants to hide money. Some people are hiding from creditors, some from spouses and ex-spouses, although most are hiding from tax collectors and regulators. In civil matters, even the few tools available to the criminal investigator are lacking. For example, there are a number of offshore jurisdictions that have signed mutual legal assistance agreements with the United States and that are participating in the effort to control drug money. Uniformly, these jurisdictions refuse all coop-eration in civil tax matters.

Many multinational corporations use subsidiaries in tax-free jurisdictions to conceal the true amount of profit they earn in high-tax jurisdictions. To lower the profit in the country where something is manufactured, a corporation will sell the product to its own tax haven subsidiary at a minimal profit, or even at a loss. The subsidiary then sells the product to the marketing subsidiary in the high-tax jurisdiction at a high price, allowing the company to claim that its prof-its were earned in the tax haven jurisdiction. In other cases, corporations operate various service subsidiaries from tax haven jurisdictions. Thus, shipping compa-nies and finance subsidiaries are often sited in low-tax jurisdictions and their charges are inflated to move the money beyond the reach of the home country tax collector. This problem is usually referred to as the *transfer pricing* problem and has been the subject of acrimonious debate and complex legislative proposals for decades.

A variant of transfer pricing is the *parking,* or offshore *booking,* of commodities positions, deposits, and loans to avoid taxation and local controls and limits on trading. Because of the electronic nature of financial transactions, decisions on the situs of a transaction have no real connection to the place. A financial transaction can be placed anywhere the parties want by simply hitting a few computer keys.

Corporate insiders and investment bankers have used offshore corporations to conceal their ownership of stock. By doing that they avoid the rules that require them to report when they buy or sell the stock. By using IBCs they also avoid rules that require them to wait for a period after a company goes public before taking their stock to the market.

As it has since the 1950s, the offshore financial world offers a home to insurance and mutual fund management companies that most jurisdictions would regulate heavily. Some of the offshore insurance business is legitimate and some is not. To give an extreme example of the illicit, an insurance company in the British Virgin Islands wrote fire insurance for Korean grocers in Los Angeles in the late 1980s. The British Virgin Islands does not regulate insurance. When the Korean grocery stores burned in the 1993 Los Angeles riots, the grocers tried to collect. They discovered that the "insurance company" was an answering machine. It had no assets, no claims office, and was a pure fraud. The grocers had no recourse because they had no one they could identify to sue. The money they paid in premiums disappeared into a maze of offshore accounts.

A current boom business is the sale of offshore mutual funds. The funds are not subject to reporting and disclosure requirements. Many funds are taking extraordinary risks and are dealing in questionable investments. Their accounting practices are largely unsupervised. This boom is reminiscent of the offshore fund boom of the 1960s that took hundreds of millions from the hands of unsuspecting investors. The perils of the present boom are illustrated by the recent apparent fraud in two offshore mutual funds managed by Morgan Grenfell, the British merchant banking subsidiary of Deutsche Bank. The funds invested in unlisted offshore corporations. The fund managers arbitrarily assigned the company shares high values. Deutsche Bank wound up covering more than $100 million in losses.

Today's complex tapestry of offshore finance was woven a strand at a time by a mix of people and institutions. Taken a piece at a time, much of the offshore activity is legal and, arguably, legitimate and justifiable. When the system is considered as a whole, it raises very difficult policy issues. If international organized crime is to be controlled, then these policy issues will have to be tackled, even if it makes other powerful interests unhappy.

The history of the illegal use of offshore financial institutions that follows is abbreviated and incomplete. Historians can discuss only criminal activity that has been reported and has become public. Criminal money laundering and tax evasion are consensual and rarely surface are in public. The tax haven countries and the financial institutions in them depend on secrecy. The names of most tax evaders who have used them are unknown. The stories of successful criminals and con men who have used them to launder their illegal profits are also unknown.

ILLEGAL USE OF OFFSHORE FINANCIAL INSTITUTIONS

Myer Lansky was a pioneer in the field of criminal money laundering.[5] Lansky started as a bootlegger in the 1920s. He was a friend and colleague of Lucky Luciano and Jimmy "Blue Eyes" Alo, two well-known gangsters. When Prohibition ended, he went into illegal gambling, first in New York and later in Hallandale, Florida. In 1939 he went to Cuba to take over the operation of the casinos at Oriental Park, Havana's major racetrack. During World War II Lansky cemented his relationships with high-level gangsters by helping engineer cooperation between the U.S. government and Luciano. Luciano was then serving a jail term. The Office of Naval Intelligence needed his help on the New York City docks. Luciano arranged to have his gangsters protect shipments of war matériel against sabotage. He also had his men provide intelligence on Axis agents working the waterfront. When the war ended, because of his cooperation, Luciano was paroled from prison and deported to Sicily. From his new base of operation, some historians believe, he established himself in the heroin business. Lansky stayed in contact with him and traveled to see him. Many believe he handled Luciano's finances. During the late forties Lansky expanded his illegal casino operations in Florida and began to invest in Las Vegas. In Las Vegas he built the Flamingo Hotel in partnership with Benny "Bugsy" Seigel. The Flamingo project and Lansky's other casino investments were successful and he developed a reputation as a money man worthy of respect. It was during this period Lansky began to move money to Switzerland to the Exchange and Credit Bank, which he controlled, to keep it out of reach of the Internal Revenue Service (IRS). Lansky recognized that legal gambling casinos offered the chance to skim money. Other businesses have physical inventories and cash register receipts. Gambling casinos do not leave auditors much to work with. It is easy for a casino owner to declare as much or as little income as he feels like. If an owner is skimming, he counts the cash each night when the tables close. When the total reaches the *handle*—the amount needed to cover expenses and some modest profit—the balance disappears. Lansky became an expert on skimming and moving skim money out of the reach of the IRS.

Gambling casinos can also be used to make criminal money look legitimate. A casino can claim that it made substantial profits because some high rollers played and lost, and no auditor can challenge the claim. Lansky used the casinos for that as well. When Fulgencio Batista returned to power in Cuba in a 1952 coup, he gave Lansky a major opportunity. The Cuban casinos had developed the reputation of being run dishonestly. American high rollers were complaining that they were being cheated at the tables. Batista invited Lansky to return to Cuba to clean them up. For Lansky the timing was perfect. He was under pressure in the United

States because of the Kefauver crime hearings. Local law enforcement had targeted his main places of business in Florida and New York. Despite its tropical temperatures, Havana was the perfect place to avoid the heat. Lansky quickly became the controlling force in the Cuban casino business. Working with New Orleans and Tampa mob figures, Lansky helped build, refurbish, and operate a number of gambling casinos and hotels. Batista relied on his judgment in deciding who should be allowed to enter the Cuban casino business.

Lansky's return to Cuba coincided with the drug smugglers' decision to route their heroin destined for the East Coast of the United States through Cuba. The circumstances suggest that Lansky used Cuba and the Cuban casinos to cover the movement of large amounts of organized crime money related to the heroin trade.[6] Cuba became a center for laundering mob cash. The Cuban casinos had bank accounts in Miami. Each evening they took checks and cash to Florida for deposit. From those accounts the money was transferred back out of the United States. It is highly likely that the Cuban casino deposits included and covered much of the organized crime profit from the East Coast.

Lansky's Cuban adventure ended with the Cuban Revolution. When Batista fled Cuba on New Year's Eve, December 31, 1959, Lansky was at the peak of his power and influence. He tried to hang on as Fidel Castro consolidated his power, but the new government banned the lottery and all other forms of gambling. It nationalized Lansky's showcase Riviera Hotel along with all the other foreign property in October 1960.

Forced out of Cuba, Lansky and his Cuban business colleagues moved back to Florida to regroup. They became interested in the Bahamas as a possible alternative to Cuba and started to do business there. John Pullman, an acquaintance of Lansky from the time of Prohibition days, operated as one of his Bahamian point men. Pullman established The Bank of World Commerce in the Bahamas in 1961. The Bank of World Commerce laundered money through accounts it maintained in Florida at the Bank of Perrine. The Bank of Perrine accepted mob cash and credited the cash to the Bank of World Commerce accounts. No records of the true ownership of the accounts or the identity of the depositors were kept in the United States.

The Bank of Perrine had a similar arrangement with another Bahamian bank, Castle Bank. Castle was owned by a Chicago lawyer, Burton Kanter, and a Miami lawyer and former CIA agent, Paul Helliwell. Castle became the target of an IRS investigation as the result of a narcotics investigation. Allen Palmer, a drug trafficker, had received checks from the Chicago account of Castle Bank. The IRS began a careful look at the bank. During the course of its investigation of the bank, an IRS agent managed to get his hands on a briefcase that contained a copy of the entire account list of the bank. The list identified around three hundred depositors and thirty-nine brokerage accounts. The names included the rich and powerful as well as mobsters and thugs. Among the most prominent hidden account names were members of the Pritzker family, owners of the Hyatt Hotel chain. Although IRS superiors had approved the way its agents got the contents of the briefcase, the failure to get a search warrant became a major problem with the cases that the IRS then attempted to make. Ultimately, the Castle investigation fell prey to political pressure.[7] Donald Alexander, Nixon's commissioner of Internal Revenue, neutered the agency's criminal division and tried to shut down the Castle investigation. Although cases were made as the result of the "briefcase" information, they were few in number. Finally, in 1980 the *Wall Street Journal* reported that the last of the Castle tax investigations were shut down at the request of the CIA. The CIA said that if the investigations continued, then they might disclose CIA sources and methods.

Swiss bank secrecy and the fabled Swiss numbered accounts trace their origin to the rise of Nazi Germany. The Swiss offered their banks as a haven for the funds of Jews who were being persecuted. The numbered account was a way of insuring that the Nazis could not trace the money deposited. Soon, Europeans of all nationalities were using Switzerland to protect their assets against the impact of the world war. Several corporations went so far as to structure themselves through incorporation in Switzerland so that they could continue to function no matter which side won. The key was a Swiss holding company that did not make public the names of its shareholders.[8]

What worked against the Nazis worked against American criminal investigators who tried to trace mob money Lansky had hidden in Switzerland. Throughout the 1950s and 1960s the Swiss aggressively protected their bank secrecy against all foreign law enforcement requests. This encouraged organized crime figures to buy control of several Swiss private banks and use them to manage money and hide assets. One of the banks that fell under mob control was the Exchange and Investment Bank of Geneva, which was purchased by two of Lansky's associates.[9]

In the late 1950s Bernie Cornfeld established Investor Overseas Services (IOS). His concept was a simple one—help the middle class in countries with nonconvertible currencies move their money offshore. Cornfeld knew that for years the very rich in the Third World had used their businesses and their connections with the foreign operations of American and British banks to get their money out of their own countries. The very rich did not want their assets to be subject to high taxes, confiscation, and the possibility of government instability. Cornfeld wanted to give the average citizen the same chance.[10] Working with a legal mastermind, Edward Cowett (Harvard Law '54), the IOS companies and funds were structured to take full advantage of lax securities laws, tax breaks for offshore corporations, and a mix of jurisdictions to stymie potential litigants and investigators. Cornfeld's salesmen fanned out over Latin America, Europe, and Asia and brought back suitcases filled with money. In Latin America the money was collected by Sylvain Ferdmann, a bank employee who traveled regularly to all of the twenty Latin American countries where IOS did business.[11] The money was invested in IOS's stable of mutual funds. The most audacious fund was the "Fund of Funds," a mutual fund that invested in other mutual funds. IOS mutual funds were established in unregulated "offshore tax havens," principally Panama and the Bahamas, and were managed from Switzerland.

At the heart of Cornfeld's scheme was a system that would allow his investors to disguise their illegal investments in IOS funds from their own governments. The currency IOS salesmen smuggled from Latin America was deposited at the IOS-controlled International Credit Bank of Geneva. The deposited money was then "loaned" back to the depositor and the "loan" proceeds were immediately invested in the Cornfeld mutual funds. The Latin American investor would show the loan on his books as money borrowed to promote foreign business. Further, the investor could then pay "interest" on the loans quite legally.

IOS had a wild ride in the early 1960s as it accumulated more than $1.5 billion from investors. But the stunning success was not meant to last. In 1966 the Brazilian police raided IOS's offices in Brazil. They arrested thirteen IOS salesmen and seized the files of more than 10,000 Brazilian clients. Realizing the dangerous situation he was in, Cornfeld hired a former American intelligence officer to get his men out of Brazil before they could be tried. Although the plot to rescue the staff succeeded, IOS was charged with smuggling more than $100 million out of Brazil during an eight-year period. The Brazilians banned further activities and began to investigate the IOS clients for tax evasion and currency control violations.

The Brazilian assault scared potential investors and cut into the IOS cash flow. It also made other governments take notice. In 1967 the Swiss tired of Cornfeld's efforts to make his Panamanian mutual fund business look Swiss by maintaining headquarters in Switzerland. The Swiss government forced Cornfeld to move across the border to France. Cornfeld was convinced—probably correctly—that the Swiss government was responding to pressure from Swiss banks which did not appreciate the competition for offshore dollars from a relative upstart. Cornfeld and his associates understood that they could do anything they wanted to with the money they took in. They knew that an Argentine who violated the laws of Argentina by shipping his money out of the country would not want to admit his own criminal activity by filing a lawsuit over how the money was managed. They also knew that if the IOS operation spread the responsibility for the funds among several jurisdictions—none with any financial regulation—lawyers for the Argentine citizen would face the dilemma of which entity to sue, where to file the suit, and if he won, where to find money to collect. As one author put it:

> a fund incorporated in Panama but mismanaged from a villa overlooking Lake Lugano in Switzerland by a Greek principal and sold through a Liechtenstein distributor to Brazilian investors was unlikely to receive much attention in a Panamanian court of law. Because the new breed of international funds was incorporated outside of the major markets in which they were sold, they were not initially subject to national regulation. That was the essence of "offshoreness."[12]

What Cornfeld pioneered quickly spawned many imitators. By the late 1960s there were more than 150 offshore funds in operation with stated assets of more than $3.5 billion.

In 1968 a military revolt changed the government of Panama. General Omar Torreos, commander of the Panamanian National Guard, took over. The United

States wanted to assist Torreos, who was seen as a reformer and something of a populist. As part of the assistance plan the U.S. Agency for International Development sponsored an economic study for the government of Panama. The study, which was done by a team of economists from the University of Wisconsin, suggested that Panama had all the necessary requisites to become an important international banking center. The country had excellent communications facilities, was a transportation hub, and used the U.S. dollar as its currency. The report noted that the country already had laws authorizing bearer share corporations. What it needed was banking secrecy and a provision opening the Panamanian market to branches of international banks. Responding to the recommendations, Panama revised its banking laws and the offshore banking sector took off. In short order more than fifty international banks opened offices in Panama City.

When the Bahamas became independent in 1973, the prospect of being subject to rules generated by a locally elected black government unnerved the Bahamian offshore banking community.[13] Many of the banks either moved outright or opened operations in the Cayman Islands, which remained as a British crown colony.[14] The bankers who moved away from the Bahamas were, to some degree, reflecting the concerns of their customers. For a bank secrecy/tax haven country to be effective it must have political stability, a foreign service capable of protecting the secrecy, and access to a court system that has an element of fairness. British crown colonies meet all of these requirements. As a result, they have, over the years, been the most successful offshore banking centers.

In the late 1960s the offshore mutual fund industry was rocked by one scandal after another:

- A con man named Allen Lefferdink set up Mutual Funds of America Limited. He used investors' money to invest in his own management company and then to buy an unregulated offshore insurance company and two unregulated offshore banks. Lefferdink ran his empire from the yacht *Sea Wolf* which cruised the Caribbean. When he disappeared, he left behind a series of empty bank accounts and corporate shells. Investigators estimated his take at $15 million.
- Walter Voss ran fraudulent mutual funds that invested in unlisted shell companies. His base was Panama. He is estimated to have defrauded investors of some $10 million.
- Jerome Hoffman incorporated the International Investors group in Liberia. Hoffman's company then set up two funds in Bermuda, Real Estate Fund of America and the Fund of the Seven Seas. Hoffman himself had offices in London. When Hoffman's operations collapsed, he was shown to have helped himself to $12 million. He was eventually arrested in Rome and spent time in jail in the United States.

Lefferdink, Voss, and Hoffman were merely warm-up acts for the master offshore con man, Robert Vesco. Vesco was an ambitious New Jersey businessman who had his attention drawn to the offshore business by Clovis McAlpin. McAlpin, who operated fraudulent offshore funds himself, encouraged Vesco to open his own offshore fund. He wanted to buy a Swiss bank in partnership with Vesco so they could follow the IOS pattern and disguise hot money as "loans" to investors. At first they tried to buy the Exchange and Investment Bank of Geneva. When they realized the Exchange and Investment Bank was mob-controlled, they settled for a smaller bank, the Standard Commerz Bank of Lucerne. The initial Vesco mutual fund venture failed and the bank deal turned out to be unsuccessful as well. But Vesco's appetite was whetted.

The police raids in Brazil, the pressure from the Swiss, and the bear market of the late 1960s combined to create a crisis at Cornfeld's Investors Overseas Services. The operation was forced to give up its most lucrative business—cash smuggling from Latin America. It lost the endless flow of new investment dollars, and without those dollars the management company, which carried outrageous overhead including the cost of Cornfeld's chateau, exotic cars, and young women, could not continue to function. Cornfeld's disaster became Vesco's opportunity. After a year of negotiations in which Vesco offered Cornfeld less and less for his IOS stock, Vesco wound up buying it for next to nothing. In the space of another year he managed to convert the IOS mutual funds to closed-end funds that could not be redeemed. The money left—some $260–$300 million—was then "invested" in a series of shell companies scattered around the world. From there the money disappeared into a maze of accounts and corporations controlled by Vesco. Vesco, using the stolen IOS money, became the world's most flamboyant fugitive. He was partial to large private jets, palatial homes, and large yachts. By then under indictment in New York for his role in the illegal funding of the 1972 Nixon presidential campaign, he made substantial payments to Bahamian government officials for protection from extradition. For a time he operated from Nassau and carried a Bahamian diplomatic passport.

Gorman Bannister, the son of a well-connected Bahamian bag man, told me that for a time Vesco operated a unique bank in Nassau. "If you were a government official," Bannister said, "the bank opened an account for you. You could make withdrawals, but you never had to make a deposit."

Vesco purchased a home in Costa Rica that had once been the residence of the United States ambassador. He became a confidant and financier of the president, Pepe Figueres, and agreed to finance a number of his harebrained economic schemes after he left office. However, his real hold on the country came from his purchase of tens of millions of dollars of Costa Rican-dollar-denominated bearer bonds. When I visited Costa Rica in 1974 to investigate Vesco's activities, I was told that he had the power to create an instant financial crisis in Costa Rica by demanding that all the bonds in his possession be redeemed at once.

Vesco also developed business connections with the then-rising head of Panamanian intelligence, Manuel Noriega.[15] These connections later became the basis for work he did for the Cuban government in running the United States blockade of Cuba.

Vesco's most significant investment was in the narcotics business. He used some of the money he took from IOS to finance the large-scale production and distribution of cocaine. Cocaine is a capital-intensive business. It takes more than six months for cocaine to move from the farms through the processing labs and into the distribution network. Along the way farmers, chemists, chemical suppliers, government officials, transporters, and distributors all have to be paid. Until Vesco arrived on the scene cocaine was a mom-and-pop business. Small-time farmers sold their leaf to small-time refiners who in turn sold it to small-time smugglers. The smugglers moved a few kilograms at a time. Vesco changed all that by using his money to finance rapid growth and vertical integration. He worked with Carlos Lehder and the emerging Medellín cartel to turn the cocaine business into a vertically integrated multinational enterprise that shipped hundred of kilos at a time.

Vesco and Lehder bought the island of Norman's Cay in the Bahamas. They made Norman's Cay a transshipment center for cocaine. Its air conditioned hanger provided a central storage and warehousing facility. Large planes from Colombia offloaded cocaine at Norman's Cay. The cocaine was then transferred to small planes and fast boats for the run past U.S. Customs. As the result of excellent investigative reporting by Ira Silverman and Brian Ross, the Norman's Cay operation wound up on NBC News in the United States and became a target of American law enforcement authorities.

The pressure from the United States on the Bahamas and Costa Rica finally forced Vesco to seek refuge in Cuba. The asylum in Cuba was arranged by Pepe Figueres, who called Fidel Castro and personally asked him to take care of his friend.[16] Vesco used his Cuban travel papers to flit between bases of operation in Panama and the Bahamas. In Panama he worked with Manuel Noriega to help the Cubans run the American embargo. The Cubans shipped their export products to the Colon free-trade zone where they were packed, labeled "product of Panama," and shipped to the United States. For a period of time most of the frozen lobster in Miami came from Cuban fishermen. Contraband goods destined for Cuba were shipped to the free-trade zone with paperwork that showed they would be shipped on to other destinations. Once in the zone the goods were diverted to Cuba.

In his blockade-running activities Vesco worked closely with the Cuban military officers, the Ochoa brothers, and General Delaguardia who were executed in 1990 for smuggling drugs. The Cubans suspected that he was involved in the drug case, but did not charge him. He was placed under tight surveillance and later was under a form of house arrest. In 1995 the Cubans formally arrested Vesco for unauthorized business dealings. They claimed that he had attempted to market a Cuban pharmaceutical without government permission.

In the early 1970s as part of the growth of the Eurodollar market, United California Bank, then the largest multistate bank holding company in the United States, decided to buy a bank in Basel, Switzerland. The bank they bought was a small bank that had been used by organized crime to launder money. After they bought the bank, the management of United California discovered that under Swiss secrecy law it could not send its own staff in to audit the books of its new subsidiary.

Suddenly empowered by the credit standing and the name of United California Bank, two traders at the Basel subsidiary went on a cocoa-buying binge in the world's commodity markets. They were trading for themselves at the same time. When the market peaked, the traders sold their personal positions and left the United California Bank in Basel owning most of the world's cocoa crop. The traders abandoned their desks and disappeared. The Swiss arrested the president of the bank, Paul Erdman, and forced United California to spend $70 million unwinding the cocoa positions and supporting the bank.

About the same time another California bank was looking for a way into the petrodollar market. Bank of America had never done Middle East business and did not have the contacts to compete with the major American banks that had historically operated overseas. To get around this shortcoming they joined forces with an engaging Pakistani banker who had set up operations in Abu Dhabi. The banker, Aga Hassan Abedi, sold them on the idea of being a joint venturer in a "Third World bank." As Abedi saw it, the bank would service the needs of the developing world. It would be a dollar bank, but would operate outside the regulatory sweep of the United States. The joint venture was called the Bank of Credit and Commerce International (BCCI). It was incorporated in Luxembourg and in the Cayman Islands. Its main office was in London and its "shareholders," other than Bank of America, were in the Middle East. In the best offshore tradition the bank was regulated nowhere. Abedi used London the way Cornfeld used Switzerland. He made the bank appear to be regulated by the Bank of England because he kept his office there.

In fact the bank was a fraud from the beginning. The bank had no real capital. To create capital accounts it used the bank in the Caymans to "lend" money to "shareholders" who then invested in the bank in Luxembourg. Similarly, the bank in Luxembourg lent money to other shareholders who bought stock in the bank in the Caymans. The problem was that most of the shareholders were unaware that they had borrowed money or that they had invested in the bank. Cynical bank insiders called them RAFs, or "rent-a-faces." Abedi could get away with his chicanery because the bank was unsupervised and each bank entity used a different auditor. As a result the auditors were unable to compare notes and find out that each bank had capitalized the other. BCCI made its money by servicing the truly criminal side of the world business community. The bank offered letter of credit services to smugglers, gun runners, and drug dealers. Instead of the usual .5 to 1 percent fee, this bank was able to charge its criminal clientele 12 percent. The bank laundered drug money, hid funds for terrorists and intelligence services, and assisted corrupt government officials who wanted to keep their money out of sight and away from their own country. Not surprisingly, one of the biggest branch operations was in Nigeria. The demand for illicit offshore services was so great that by 1980 it was one of the world's fastest growing banks. Despite the rapid growth, and perhaps because of nervousness with the management of the bank, the Bank of America gave up its interest and moved on. On paper, BCCI bank assets just kept growing.

In 1980 the bank applied for a license to do full retail business in England and was turned down. The problem was that the bank would not release complete information about share ownership, which rightly made the Bank of England nervous. Later however, the British changed their banking laws and opened the London market. In the deregulatory frenzy BCCI was given a full retail banking license.

From time to time the issue of the responsibility for the regulation of BCCI would arise, but each country involved disclaimed responsibility for the bank's worldwide operations. Luxembourg said that it did not have the capacity to regulate the bank on a worldwide basis. The Cayman Islands had no regulation to speak of, and the British disclaimed responsibility for the bank's worldwide supervision. Ultimately, BCCI was to be regulated by a "college" of regulators made up of bank authorities from a number of countries. In November 1988 a U.S. customs sting operation code named C-Chase led to the arrest of several bank officials in Tampa. The customs agents taped the bank officials as they offered to launder drug money through the bank. The bank argued to U.S. government authorities that the bankers involved were on a frolic of their own and that money laundering was against bank policy. Later investigation showed that this was not the case and that board minutes stating the money-laundering policy had been fabricated to fool skeptical regulators.

At the same time the C-Chase operation was underway, I was investigating the bank for the Senate Foreign Relations Committee's Subcommittee on Narcotics Terrorism and International Operations. The bank's name had come up in connection with money laundering in Panama. Witnesses, including Leigh Rich, told the subcommittee that they had been referred to BCCI by Noriega. One witness, José Blandon, thought that Noriega owned a share of the bank. This testimony led me to other bank employees, who began to lay out the massive fraud inside the bank, the worldwide scope of its criminal activities, and its widespread distribution of money to buy political influence. I passed the information to the members of the C-Chase team of prosecutors, who chose to focus on the events in Tampa and nothing more. One of the IRS agents repeatedly tried to bring the bank to the attention of the Federal Reserve Board, but he had no response. Despite the obvious questions raised by C-Chase and the information in the Senate investigation, the bank continued to do business. Later investigation showed that between 1980 and 1991, when the bank was closed, there were more than two hundred criminal referrals relating to the bank in the United States alone.

In March 1989 I made arrangements with agents involved in C-Chase to tape a series of conversations I had with a former high-ranking bank employee. In those conversations, the employee described the bank's criminal behavior. The prosecutors decided to do nothing with the tapes, which were not even transcribed for another year. In the face of the unwillingness of the federal authorities to move against the bank as a whole, I took the information about the bank to the New York County District Attorney, Robert Morgenthau, who began a comprehensive investigation. The work of his office forced the bank regulators to close down the bank worldwide in June 1991.

BCCI added some new twists to the uses and abuses of the offshore system. It bribed central bank officials in the developing world to direct central bank deposits to it. It told politicians in Third-World countries that BCCI could help them avoid the strictures of the World Bank and the International Monetary Fund (IMF) by protecting their money from international creditors. In fact, BCCI needed the central bank deposits to avoid its own liquidity crisis. For example, Nigeria needed a loan to get around a currency crisis. The Nigerian leadership did not want to follow IMF conditions on loans. The Nigerian military government considered the IMF's requirements too onerous and politically dangerous. BCCI stepped into the breach and gave Nigeria a $2 billion loan without conditions. A BCCI-related company, Attock Oil, took the repayment in the form of Nigerian crude oil at a below-market price.

Peru's president, Alan García, deposited Peruvian foreign exchange reserves at BCCI as part of his plan to renounce all of Peru's foreign debt. He too did not want the IMF or commercial creditors to seize Peru's foreign bank holdings when he announced that Peru was refusing to pay foreign creditors. García's use of BCCI's offshore facilities was perhaps the most extreme example of offshore "asset protection."

When BCCI was closed by the coordinated action of the central banks in 1991, law enforcement agencies seized tons of documents in London, New York, Miami, and the Cayman Islands. When the documents were examined, investigators discovered that key memoranda were written in Urdu—a language none of the relevant regulators could speak or read. Moreover, the investigators focused on those documents that dealt with fraud inside the bank, not those relating to tax evasion and criminal activity by the bank's customers.

Although BCCI was the most flamboyant example of offshore services for criminals and criminal organizations ever to surface, it coexisted and did business with other legitimate banks for eighteen years and, during that time, successfully avoided serious questions about its activities.

The savings-and-loan scandal and the insider trading scandals of the 1980s both had offshore connections. Virtually every insider trading case made by the government led to an offshore account set up to hide the questionable trades. The Securities and Exchange Commission and the U.S. federal prosecutors were able to locate the accounts and identify the owners because they had help from cooperating witnesses who traded information for shorter jail terms. Without the help of cooperating insiders, the money would have remained hidden. Again and again, stolen savings and loan money disappeared offshore. The most brazen example was provided by David Paul, flamboyant chairman of Miami's Centrust Savings. Centrust left the government holding the bag for $2 billion when it failed in 1992. Paul had used bank funds to purchase old master art that he put in his living room, to pay for a yacht which he used for political fund-raising, and to decorate lavishly the Centrust Towers bank headquarters with gold bathroom fixtures and custom-designed china and crystal. When Paul was convicted, the government tried to recover his $400 million pension trust, which he had the bank set up for him in the Channel Islands. The attempt failed, and Paul will have his pension when he returns to society.

A succession of scandals since BCCI has underscored the failure of regulators to deal with the offshore phenomenon in a systematic way. In 1994 Nicholas Leeson, a trader in the Singapore office of Barings Bank, lost the bank's entire net worth in trades he made on the Singapore derivatives market. Leeson has been convicted of bank fraud in Singapore, but the issue of whether he was really acting without the knowledge of his superiors is still unresolved. The underlying question is how a bank that operates outside its home jurisdiction in countries with limited regulation can be regulated properly.

The Venezuelan banking system collapsed in 1994 following the failure of Banco Latino, a bank that had shifted a significant portion of its assets offshore. As the Venezuelan Central Bank began to investigate, it discovered that virtually every bank in the country had an offshore operation which it used to get around the country's system of currency controls. The Venezuelan banking system and the offshore subsidiaries were used by Colombian drug traffickers to get around Colombian money laundering controls.

In 1995 Daiwa Bank's New York office reported to its American regulators that it had lost more than $1 billion in trading on U.S. Treasury obligations. The bank attempted to portray the problem as one of a rogue trader who traded without authority over a period of eight years. It soon became clear that the officials of Daiwa had known of the problem for many months before they let the regulators know. The bank officials had discussed hiding the losses by transferring the transactions to their lightly regulated Cayman Island subsidiary. The discovery that a transfer to an offshore jurisdiction had been proposed as a way of covering the losses shocked the Federal Reserve. The Fed realized, apparently for the first time, that the Bank of Japan and the Japanese Ministry of Finance had not been supervising the activities of Japanese banks in the "offshore" jurisdictions. The Fed, in cooperation with the Japanese authorities, then began a massive emergency effort to examine the books of the Japanese banks' offshore activities to insure that there were no other hidden problems.

In the spring of 1996 the largest Japanese Bank, Sumitomo Bank, announced that it had sustained losses of more than $1.5 billion in illicit trading of copper futures. The losses stemmed from the collapse of a decade-long effort on the part of Sumitomo traders and an official of Codelco, the Chilean copper company, to rig the world market price for copper. The Codelco official was paid for his services in offshore accounts and the scheme was never seen by regulators because most of the trading activity took place in the offshore world.

The list of dictators who looted their countries and hid the money in offshore accounts is long and disheartening. The Marcos family is thought to have hidden at least $500 million from the government of the Philippines. Some Marcos money was located in Switzerland but the cost and legal complexity of tracking the rest has defeated the best efforts of the Philippines agency charged with the task. The Duvalier family left Haiti with an estimated $50 million. The money moved through Canadian banks and from there to France and England. Carelessness on the part of the Duvaliers almost allowed the Haitian government to recover the money. Investigators got a court order freezing certain London accounts hours after they had been cleaned out. General Noriega deposited his illicit funds in a numbered account at BCCI and maintained BCCI credit cards for his wife and daughter. Three Latin American ex-presidents are all thought to have hidden millions they made illegally during their terms of office. Venezuela has arrested and imprisoned its former president, Carlos Andrés Peréz, and Venezuelan investigators have been unsuccessfully tracking his finances for the last several years. Alan García has been the subject of ongoing investigations in Peru relating to the attempt made to build a mass-transit system in Lima. The system was never finished but the money to build it disappeared. The ex-president of Brazil, Fernando Collor de Mello, was impeached and is thought to have successfully hidden illegally obtained wealth offshore.

Offshore banking as a cover for government corruption exploded in the case of Raúl Salinas, the brother of the former president of Mexico. Investigation showed that Mr. Salinas had $120 million hidden in offshore accounts, which he could not explain. The foreign accounts had been arranged by the Citibank private-banking department through its Mexico City office. This discovery raised the immediate question of whether Citibank had known the possible illegal origin of the funds and had been party to helping Salinas launder the money. In response to press inquiries, Citibank said publicly that its private-banking department dealt discreetly with very wealthy customers and that it could not assume the burden of checking the legality of their activities. Privately, a number of bank security officials have told the government that their banks exempt private-banking customers from the normal vetting process the banks use with new customers. At the time of writing, American law enforcement officials were trying to determine whether the work done by Citibank to help Raúl Salinas hide his assets was in exchange for favors given by the Salinas family to the bank's operations in Mexico.

Thus far, I have focused on the criminal and the marginal. However, the most important driving force behind the offshore financial business has been the development of the *Eurodollar* market. Eurodollars are what bankers call dollars deposited outside of the United States. In the immediate post-World War II period, virtually all dollar lending was done in the United States by American banks. After all, in the postwar world, it was the American banks that had the dollars. Foreign borrowers agreed to repay American banks, with interest, in dollars. The borrowers agreed to take all risk of currency fluctuation.

Some dollars did remain offshore. The Soviet Union needed dollars to participate in world trade. However, the Soviets could not risk keeping their dollars in American banks. They had two serious problems. First, the Czarist government of Russia had issued bonds that had been renounced by the Soviet Union. The Soviets feared that holders of the Czarist bonds might use the U.S. courts to go after Soviet deposits in American banks in the United States. Second, and more important, the United States had a history of seizing and freezing foreign assets held in the United States as a political tool. As the cold war grew increasingly tense, the Russians feared that the United States might seize its bank accounts at any time. In response, the Russians began holding and lending dollars out of the Moscow Narodny Bank branch in Paris. The loans bore dollar-related interest rates and were to be repaid in dollars. When the Russians started their dollar banking, other international banks generally were reluctant to hold deposits and make loans in currencies other than the currency of their own country. The reason was simple prudence. In a liquidity crisis, a bank turns to its central bank for loans to help it through. But central banks are limited to issuing their own currency. The Bank of England cannot create dollars. That privilege is the exclusive province of the U.S. Federal Reserve Bank. In turn the Federal Reserve has no mandate to help foreign banks operating outside of the United States and not chartered in the United States that get into liquidity trouble in their dollar accounts.

The Soviets ignored the risk. Their experiment was a great success and the practice of allowing dollar accounts soon spread to other European banks. The spread was accelerated by the 1956 decision of the U.S. government to seize the U.S.-based dollar assets of all of the participants in the Suez crisis, including all of the assets of countries in the Arab world. Although the freeze did not last long, the Arab governments took the point. They moved their money out of American banks and into what was now called the *Eurodollar* market. The growth of the Eurodollar market coincided with the use of the U.S. dollar as the currency of choice in world trade and as the world's reserve currency. The bankers and their customers soon began to understand the full potential of the market. For much of the postwar period the United States attempted to control interest rates on deposits and loans through Regulation Q. This regulation kept the interest on both deposits and loans quite low. As soon as depositors and lenders discovered a way to operate outside the framework of regulation, they jumped at the chance. Soon money poured out of the United States to find the higher interest rates offered in the Eurodollar market. At first the government responded with an interest equalization tax, but all that did was put American institutions at a competitive disadvantage. The tax was short-lived. The offshore market prospered. There were the further issues of reserves and control of the money supply. Within national markets the central bank regulates the supply of funds and the amount of lending a bank can engage in. It does this by establishing reserve requirements. For example, a bank may be allowed to lend only 80 cents for each dollar on deposit. When banks dealt in Eurodollars through "offshore" subsidiaries, they had no regulatory limit. Each deposit became a loan, which in turn became another deposit. When there are no reserve requirements, the cost of money is lower and the potential for profit is higher. This spurred the booking of loans and deposits in offshore havens.

Yet another push came from the Vietnam War. Financing the war created a huge negative balance of payments. In 1965 President Johnson established voluntary capital controls to prevent the movement of funds outside of the country. The voluntary approach failed and in 1968 the controls became mandatory. The immediate response of the American business community was to stop repatriating foreign profits. Instead of bringing the money home, the companies put it in the newly opened branches of American banks in the Bahamas. Under the control regulations the offshore money was free of restrictions. Almost overnight Nassau became one of the world's most important banking and Eurodollar centers.

When oil prices skyrocketed in the early 1970s, the Eurodollar market took off again. The Arab oil-producing countries already had their dollars outside the reach of the U.S. government in foreign banks in London. Only now the amounts became astronomical. London was awash with billions of "petrodollars." Foreign banks used the flood of dollars to begin to compete for U.S. corporate borrowing business. Soon every bank in the United States felt that it had to be in London and in the "offshore" market to get its share of the business.

By the mid-seventies the banking world was relishing the discovery of operations in an unregulated market. Banks could buy money on the overnight London interbank market and then sell the money to borrowers worldwide. Because the dollar was freely convertible and traded in a very broad and deep market, borrowers could use the loan proceeds in any country in the world. Because the market worked freely across borders, the bankers could "book" loans and deposits anywhere they wanted. By booking loans in the offshore world, the bankers could avoid withholding taxes on interest payments and taxes on deposits.

In 1975 the Senate Foreign Relations Committee's Subcommittee on Multinational Corporations began to explore the issues raised by the explosion of the Eurodollar market. As a member of the staff working on the investigation, I traveled to the major banking centers both on- and offshore and met with dozens of prominent bankers. The questions were straightforward. What were the risks of a market in which banks borrowed short in the overnight market and lent long around the world? What about the explosion of loans to developing countries, which, at that time was called "petrodollar recycling?" Who would pick up the pieces in the event of a default or in the event of a liquidity crisis? Should there be any regulation? If there was regulation, who would take responsibility for the supervision of the foreign operations? The home country? The host country? What were the implications of allowing banks in the Eurodollar market to operate without reserve requirements? Did it mean that the Fed could no longer control the money supply?

The bankers answered that the market would solve all the problems. They argued that there could never be a real liquidity crisis because deposits that fled a particular bank would always reappear on the interbank market. They argued that the long-term loans to the developing world did not crate a problem. A few of them admitted that in the end there was always the Federal Reserve Board to protect the market. Lee Prussia, then cashier of the Bank of America, explained it to me this way: "We are not worried about sovereign lending. Countries do not go away and one way or another their loans get repaid. At worst the loan is rescheduled and it takes us a while to get our money. In the meantime we can meet our liquidity needs by borrowing from the Fed." A few of the bankers I talked to went further and explained that they thought their banks were too big and too important to be allowed to fail.

At the same time it was obvious that there were risks. The banking system could fall victim to bad credit judgments, trading and currency risks, and liquidity problems. The problems of the Herrstat Bank failure in Germany and the failure of Franklin National Bank showed that markets were now connected in unexpected ways and that the cost of a mistake for the Federal Reserve system could be quite high. The Herrstat failure led to large losses for a Seattle bank that had money invested in the "safe" overnight London interbank market. The Franklin problem was the result of improperly controlled currency trading and the activities of a "rogue" trader. The Fed pumped billions of dollars into the bank to keep it afloat until it could be sold.

When the subcommittee began to press for detailed information on the nature and amount of Eurodollar and petrodollar deposits and the corresponding loan commitments, the presidents of six of the largest American banks in the international market and two governors of the Federal Reserve met with the committee in executive session to argue that the investigation was too sensitive to be allowed to continue. The Fed's representatives argued that "the problem is that the information is so sensitive that if the risks are discussed in public the discussion might trigger the very crisis of confidence the committee says it seeks to understand and prevent." The Fed's presentation carried the day and the subcommittee decided not to go further in public.

The preliminary subcommittee investigation represented the high-water mark of public government efforts to question the shape of the offshore market. From then on U.S. government policy was made in private by the Federal Reserve. The Fed viewed its role as protecting the market and meeting the competitive needs of its banking constituency. It chose not to question the evolution of the offshore banking market into a private system for handling the gyrations of stateless money. It tacitly accepted the proposition that an international banking system that undermined the ability of individual states to regulate economic activity was good.

The 1974 Herrstat failure led central bankers to the conclusion that international financial markets were interconnected and that regulators would have to understand and deal with the connections. The Basel group of G-10 central bank governors responded by creating the Committee on Banking Regulation and Supervisory Activities. This committee drew up the "Basel Concordats" of 1978 and 1983 on international regulation. These agreements divided the responsibility for regulating international banking operations among the home and host governments, and set standards for consolidated worldwide financial reporting. In 1987 the Basel committee hammered out an accord on capital adequacy designed to protect the banks against credit risks from borrowers and other banks. It was not until 1993 that the committee addressed the risks that come from foreign-exchange trading, open futures positions, and liquidity squeezes.

The weaknesses of the Basel agreements were highlighted by the failure of supervision in the BCCI, Barings, Daiwa, and Sumitomo cases. The Basel committee has been in the position of playing catch-up. Its pace is glacial and progress tortured because each central bank governor defends his own national position. The ability of the marketplace to stay ahead of the regulators by creating new risk instruments beyond the understanding of supervisors is startling. The speed with which new risks can lead to destructive losses is equally startling.

When skeptics like me raise questions about the risks inherent in allowing banks to operate in offshore secrecy havens, international regulators argue that there is no problem. They say that because they required the banks to keep copies of their offshore books in their home countries, the banks are subject to complete examination. What the regulators do not admit is that the examiners who look at offshore bank books in a bank's home office cannot see the loan documentation and correspondence relating to the underlying relationship. Those papers tell an examiner far more that the numbers on ledgers and balance sheets.

By the early 1980s booking bank deposits and loans in tax havens became commonplace. And as transportation and communications improved, the ease with which a loan could be booked "offshore" increased dramatically. "Jurisdictions" became segregated sections of a computer hard drive. "Moving" money from one to another was a simple matter of a few keystrokes. Many offshore bank "branches" were brass plates on the wall of a lawyer's office.

BCCI provided the most extreme example of the possibilities. It opened a Bahamas branch even though it had no license and no office there. The "branch" was a fiction created on the bank's Miami computer. If a drug dealer wanted to deposit cash without a record being sent to the federal government, the BCCI officials would book the deposit to the Bahamas branch. They would then record a "shipment" of currency from the nonexistent Bahamas branch to Miami and deposit the cash at another Miami bank as an interbank transfer.

At the other extreme is the case of Citibank. Citibank booked many of its foreign-exchange positions in the Bahamas in the 1970s to avoid the trading limits put on its branches by individual governments. A Citibank trader reported the "parking" and the related "cooking of the books" to the SEC, and both the SEC and the House Commerce Committee investigated. The investigation found that Citibank had established a "Nassau Desk" in the New York office that handled the record keeping for all the "parked" business. In an effort to make the foreign operation look real, Citibank tried to keep parallel books in Nassau. The problem was that the operations were complex and the Bahamian bookkeepers were incompetent. The books never seemed to match. Despite all of this, Citibank was never charged with wrongdoing in the United States, and the debate was mooted by the evolution of completely electronic worldwide trading.[17]

The operating philosophy in the banking world is absolute faith in pure market economics. Decisions on booking turn on minimizing taxation and regulation and nothing more. Today many international bankers believe that because of the global marketplace no government regulation of the offshore market is possible. Moreover, many of them believe that any attempt by the state to control private wealth is immoral. In a panel discussion with a group a Bahamian bankers I asked this question: "Would anyone who is not a Bahamian citizen or running a business in the Bahamas do banking business in the Bahamas if the underlying transaction were legal and untaxed in his home country?" My question was greeted with rage. After the panel discussion I received a serious letter from a distinguished member of the audience. He argued that inasmuch as all taxes and all regulation of private wealth were immoral, the government of the

Bahamas was helping decent people around the world fight the immorality of their own governments.

It is reasonable to argue that without the development of the Eurodollar market and the offshore finance business, the explosion in international trade and economic growth of the last fifteen years would never have occurred. The unregulated international markets created credit and supplied money in amounts that far exceeded the niggardly horizons of the world's central bankers. Further, the presence of unregulated offshore markets has forced individual governments to give up their attempts to control the flow of capital and restrict international trade. Around the world, restrictive government policies have changed and markets have opened. Moreover, the offshore financial markets have taken the heat off politicians who would never have been able to change the system on their own. In country after country political figures have been able to say, "I had no choice. We had to change the system and open markets or we would have been overrun by international forces."

The offshore market has hastened the development of technology and methods that have made international business easy and seamless. Letters of credit, wire transfers, and other international banking transactions have become routine. On a recent trip around the world I was able to avoid changing currency by using a debit card in cash machines in seven countries. I withdrew funds from my account in real time in the local currency. No rational person would want to give up these conveniences and improvements merely to fight money laundering by criminals.

The negative side of the balance sheet has some painful entries. The offshore banking world has proved difficult to regulate. The Basel Concordat that divided regulatory responsibility created a "college of regulators" to deal with BCCI. As it turned out, the college had no dean and the bank was never subjected to effective regulation. When the Bank of England was confronted with evidence that the bank's operations were supported by massive fraud and that its books had been cooked, the response was to try to move the bank from London to Abu Dhabi and to get the ruler of Abu Dhabi to pick up the losses.

While trade and income have risen worldwide, income distribution is getting progressively worse. The very rich are adept at using the offshore system to keep their wealth intact and out of the world tax system. Corporations have used the offshore system to move income to low-tax jurisdictions. As a result, governments are finding that as a practical matter their ability to tax is limited to payroll and consumption taxes. It is no coincidence that the growth of the offshore world corresponds with the growing revenue problems all governments now face. Every major industrial country is running a budget deficit. In many cases the deficit exists despite a growing economy and draconian efforts to cut back public services. In many countries the inability of the government to collect taxes has made the construction of essential infrastructure impossible and has deprived the government of the tools it needs to solve economic problems. The case of Mexico is instructive.

In September of 1995 members of the Mexican Congress told me that Mexico collects about 10 percent of the income tax it believes is due from Mexican citizens. Mexican tax authorities receive fewer than one million returns. Mexican bankers said that all the wealthy Mexican families had set up offshore IBCs to hold their assets. Every important Mexican bank has a Cayman Islands subsidiary to manage the holdings of wealthy clients. The offshore accounts are also supporting the Mexican system of corruption. At the end of each six-year term the outgoing administration has taken advantage of the system to enrich itself and its supporters. The money leaves the country. As a result, at the end of each six-year term, there is a financial crisis, which the new administration is forced to deal with. For the last three crises the solution has been an American bailout of some sort. The bailouts are justified in terms of saving the economy of the United States' most important neighbor and trading partner. Because the Mexican government cannot raise revenue and cannot afford to take steps that will solve its massive employment and infrastructure problems, the economy has become increasingly dependent on the narcotics business. At the beginning of the present administration Mexican government officials promised their American counterparts that they would pass money-laundering legislation. The legislation passed in May 1996—two years later. It has yet to be implemented. The problem is that the banking system is insolvent because of the financial crisis. The government has no funds and is therefore incapable of dealing with massive insolvency in the banking system. As long as the drug money continues to flow, the cash flow through the banks allows the government and the bankers to ignore the underlying problems. At the heart of all these problems is the operation of the offshore market.

- If Mexican officials could not hide the bribes they take offshore;
- If the identity of the real owners of companies that acted as middlemen in dealings with the Mexican government were known; and
- If the wealthy of Mexico could not move their money offshore to hide from the tax collector;

would it not be reasonable to assume Mexico would be in a better position to solve the drug problem and deal with its other crises?

SOME POSSIBLE SOLUTIONS

Until now the focus of the offshore discussion has been on money laundering, and most of that has been about the placement of U.S. dollars in foreign banking systems. As I see it, the real issue is the willingness of some nations to rent their flags or the flags of their associated territories to anyone who wants to conceal the true nature of a business transaction and anyone who wants to operate in a regulation-free environment. The problem is that the institutions they charter and the activity they choose not to regulate or tax have an enormous impact on the rest of the world. The central question is: why should any major country recognize the international business corporations of offshore havens?

If any system of tax and regulation is to work, the price of entry to major markets must include a willingness to open the door to civil and criminal investigation. Thus if a British Virgin Islands (BVI) corporation wants to do business in the United States, there should be full transparency for that corporation in the BVI legal system. As matters now stand, the only role of the BVI government is to block any effort to make its corporations and their owners responsible for their actions outside the BVI.

A financial system designed to operate outside the reach of political and social control may be the dream of free-market enthusiasts but it invites gross abuse and creates intolerable social problems. The gross abuse is evident—the offshore markets have given criminal enterprises the space to become as large as the largest legitimate enterprises. The criminal enterprises have used the offshore markets to corrupt and subvert the societies they deal in. Those little islands that make a living offering safe harbor to criminals are analogous to pirate ships that prey on legitimate commerce.

The offshore system has given rich individuals and international business the ability to opt out of national tax systems. That ability enables them to profit from societies without contributing to them. The revenue loss is serious enough to undermine essential services and undercut the power of the state. It also raises fundamental questions about the nature of the social contract in the modern world. Is playing by the rules of society required only of the lower classes? If that is so, can democracy function?

The international legal system is decades behind the development of the international financial system. Both private and public international law are still mired in the concepts of sovereignty developed in the eighteenth and nineteenth centuries. The law of nations assumes that the sovereign controls what goes on within the borders of the nation-state. Because of the development of the offshore world, the nation-state has lost control of money and the money has lost the protection of the state and its legal systems. If there is no workable international civil law system to settle disputes in the offshore world, how long can it last?

A financial system that operates outside of regulatory control places the entire world economy at risk. The only possible guarantors of the offshore system are the very nation-states that have been left behind. At the moment it is the central banks of the major nations that are insuring the liquidity of the institutions operating in the offshore realm. They appear to be ready and willing to support the markets, the banks, and brokerage firms to help the system weather crises. But the offshore markets have become very complicated. Some derivative contracts are so complex that the risks involved are nearly impossible to predict.

The possibilities for fraud and abuse in this complex system are so significant that there can be no assurance that all the central banks could save the system if a real crash ever got started. There is no international criminal system to track down the fraud or to deter it. There is no international bankruptcy system to deal with the wreckage when a major failure occurs.

Short of abolishing offshore financial operations altogether, there are a number of changes that can be made to improve the system and to ameliorate some of the more serious problems it creates. The most obvious way to control the use of the offshore financial system by organized crime is to end the IBC—the international business corporation. These corporations and the anonymity they provide are at the heart of almost every money laundering scheme.

There should be international agreement that no jurisdiction should be allowed to charter corporations that do business in the country of origin and have no identifiable responsible officers or directors. There should also be international agreement that any bank or brokerage firm caught falsifying commercial documents to support client fraud or tax evasion should be subject to severe penalties. The false paper factories of the Bahamas, the Channel Islands, and the other havens should be shut down.

The "old boy network" system of regulation favored by the Bank of England and other central banks should be replaced. The modern transnational banking operations are far too complicated to rely on one person vouching for another's behavior. Banks must be audited by expert supervisors who understand international operations and who can evaluate modern high-risk instruments.

The major industrial nations should not allow their banks and brokerage firms to open branches or subsidiaries in jurisdictions that do not allow home country auditors to do on-the-premises examinations. An on-site examination is an essential element in preventing criminal activity and fraud. Free-trade zones should be put out of business.

Free-trade zones such as the Colon free-trade zone in Panama have become centers for illegal commercial and financial activity. One of the most important branches of BCCI was in the Colon free-trade-zone, which was then and continues to be a center for the smuggling of goods and weapons all over the hemisphere. Bank secrecy protection should not cover criminal activity or tax evasion. Jurisdictions that do not accept this proposition should be cut out of the world banking system.

NOTES

1. Statistics on the volume of deposits and loans booked through British possessions are almost impossible to obtain. Neither the World Bank nor the Federal Reserve have accurate numbers. My assessment is based on interviews with bankers and experts at both institutions who have been trying to develop accurate statistics.
2. The Cayman Islands have since adopted strict controls on cash deposits. As a result, the flow of criminal currency by the plane load to the island has stopped.
3. IBCs are quite inexpensive to incorporate. An off-the-shelf corporation in the British Virgin Islands is about $1,000, in the Caymans $1,200, and in Bermuda about $5,000.
4. Interview with John Mathewson, chairman of Guardian Bank and Trust Co., Georgetown, Grand Cayman. Mathewson is under indictment in the Northern District of New Jersey for money laundering.
5. In his book *Little Man Meyer: Lansky and the Gangster Life* (Boston: Little Brown and Co., 1991), author Robert Lacey argues that Lansky's role in money laundering is greatly exaggerated. He argues Lansky did not become involved in laundering until the early 1960s and then in connection with John Pullman, a bootlegger-turned-banker who opened the Bank of World Commerce in Nassau.
6. Lansky's partner in his Cuban gambling enterprises was Santos Trafficante who just happened to flee New York after the murder of Albert Anastasia. Anastasia had been negotiating for a piece of a rival casino at the new Havana Hilton Hotel at the time he was shot. Just three weeks later the high "commission" of organized crime met in upstate New York at the so-called "Appalachian" summit. I believe that the key organized crime figures wanted to head off a gang war that would expose something

much more important than who controlled gambling in Havana: the way they moved their money out of the country and concealed it from the IRS.

7. For the definitive account of the Castle Bank investigation, see Adam A. Block, *Masters of Paradise: Organized Crime and the Internal Revenue Service in the Bahamas* (New Brunswick, NJ: Transaction Publishers, 1991).

8. See Anthony Sampson, *The Sovereign State of ITT* (New York: Stein and Day, 1973).

9. Robert Morgenthau, the United States attorney for the Southern District of New York, identified the bank as being beneficially owned by Ben Seigelbaum, a reputed mob money man, and Ed Levinson, a Las Vegas gambler who fronted for Lansky.

10. See Charles Row, *Do You Sincerely Want to be Rich* (London: Andre Deutsche, 1971), a book about Cornfeld and the establishment of IOS.

11. Earlier in his career, Ferdmann had done the same thing for John Pullman at the Bank of World Commerce.

12. Robert A. Hutchison, *Vesco* (New York: Praeger, 1974).

13. A similar transfer of offshore interests is underway in anticipation of Hong Kong's reversion to China. Dozens of Hong Kong corporations have moved to the Cayman Islands and Bermuda. Jardine Matheson, the most famous Hong Kong firm, is now on the Bermuda stock exchange.

14. The Caymans had been governed as a dependence of Jamaica. When Jamaica became independent, the Caymans elected to remain a crown colony.

15. I learned of these connections in 1974 in a meeting with Padre Nuñez, Pepe Figueres's priest. He told me that he had overheard Vesco discussing the business dealings during the baptism of Pepe's grandchild. Vesco was the godfather. The father is the current president of Costa Rica.

16. Conversation with Manuel Piniero, Havana, Cuba, June 1990.

17. For a detailed account of the Citibank "parking" problem and the ensuing investigation, see Robert A. Hutchison, *Off the Books: Citibank and the World's Biggest Money Game* (New York: William Morrow, 1986).

SMUGGLING WARS: LAW ENFORCEMENT AND LAW EVASION IN A CHANGING WORLD

4

Peter Andreas

INTRODUCTION

The regulation and monitoring of cross-border flows is central to the modern state's claims of territorial sovereignty. However, the focus and concern vary significantly across time. In the post-cold-war era of global economic integration, many states are less concerned about deterring cross-border military threats or imposing tariffs on cross-border commerce and are, instead, more concerned about policing prohibited cross-border economic activities.[1] Enhanced state efforts to police these prohibited activities—such as the smuggling of drugs, people, and dirty money—contrast sharply with the general trend toward opening borders and reducing the role of the state in the economy.

The United States is perhaps the leading example of this bifurcated trend. The post-cold-war U.S. security agenda, it seems, is increasingly dominated by concerns over crime fighting rather than war fighting; law evasion rather than military invasion. The rising prominence of law enforcement concerns is reflected in the transformation of the federal policing apparatus. During a period when most federal agencies are merely surviving, law enforcement is thriving. Budgets are growing,[2] agency missions are expanding, new and tougher laws are being implemented, policing is becoming more federalized and internationalized,[3] national security and law enforcement institutions are increasingly integrated, and more sophisticated and powerful surveillance technologies are being developed. In short, "reinventing government" in this case is more about redeploying, rather than reducing, government.

Among the leading concerns are criminal organizations engaged in a wide variety of prohibited cross-border activities. A conference report from the Center for Strategic and International Studies even calls organized crime the "New Evil Empire," concluding that: "The dimensions of global organized crime present a greater international security challenge than anything Western democracies had to cope with during the cold war."[4] Echoing this view, Senator John Kerry warns, "Organized crime is the new Communism, the new monolithic threat."[5]

But what exactly is the nature of this threat? To a large extent, transnational criminal enterprise involves some form of smuggling, defined by my dictionary simply as the practice of bringing in or taking out illicitly or by stealth.[6] Of course, criminal groups engage in many other illegal activities (extortion, fraud, theft, and so on), but the cross-border dimension of their business largely involves smuggling in one form or another. The following analysis highlights the paradoxical, double-edged, and even interdependent relationship between the business of smuggling and the business of trying to thwart it.[7]

SMUGGLING: THE UNDERSIDE OF GLOBAL TRADE

Smuggling is an extraordinarily diverse form of trade that is as old as trade itself. Today it includes, for example, trafficking in hazardous waste and chlorofluoro-carbons (CFCs), arms and nuclear material, antiquities, precious stones and metals, psychoactive substances (such as heroin and cocaine), money, pornography and other entertainment products, and animals and animal products.[8] And, of course, there is the booming business of human smuggling, itself a diverse enterprise involving the trafficking in immigrants, prostitutes, babies,[9] and even body parts (thanks to modern technologies that make it possible to store and ship high-demand organs, such as kidneys, livers, and bone cartilage).[10]

The United States is by far the world's number one smuggling target, with illegal drugs and immigrants leading the list of imports. The United States is also probably the single largest exporter of smuggled goods—if one considers, for example, all the American-produced cigarettes, pornographic material, money, weapons, stolen cars, and hazardous waste that are smuggled out of the country every year. Of course, most of the attention is on what is coming into the country rather than on what is going out. For example, complaints by Mexico that large quantities of illegal weapons from the United States end up south of the border in violation of Mexican gun control laws generate relatively little concern in Washington (particularly in comparison to the concern expressed over the smuggling of drugs and people into the United States). Even as the United States puts out an annual report card on the law enforcement efforts of drug-exporting countries, the magnitude of illegal exports from the United States suggests that Washington would have to grade itself rather poorly if the evaluation were to focus on smuggling in general.

It is important, however, to keep in mind that while the total volume and profitability of smuggling into and out of the United States and elsewhere may be much higher today than ever before, as a percentage of overall trade it is possibly no more (and very possibly much less) significant today than in the past. The method and speed of smuggling, the size, structure, and location of the smuggling organizations, the content of state laws along with the intensity and form of their enforcement, the commodities being smuggled and their origin and destination point, and the nature and level of consumer demand have all changed over time. It is striking how little has actually been written about the history and practice of smuggling.[11] Indeed, while the story of the emergence and spread of a global trading system has been endlessly told and retold, the "underside" of trade is generally ignored.

Laws and consumer demand are the most basic determinants of what smugglers smuggle. For example, in a world of high tariffs, much of smuggling is composed of the clandestine trade in legal commodities to avoid import or export duties. This has long been a serious concern for the U.S. government, given that customs duties were virtually its only source of revenue for much of the nation's history.[12] Even on the eve of World War I, approximately half of all federal revenue was still generated through customs duties.[13] Smuggling was, of course, already a well-established and widespread practice prior to the founding of the country. Prominent American merchants made fortunes in illicit trade before the Revolutionary War. Indeed, smuggling was an integral part of commerce in the colonial period.[14]

In a world of low tariffs, on the other hand, the main concern inevitably shifts from evading tariffs on legal commodities to evading prohibitions on commodities deemed dangerous. Still, even in a world of low tariffs, variations in domestic taxes on some high-demand products, such as cigarettes and alcohol, provide enormous incentives for smuggling. Thus, even as illegal drugs flow into the United States, mass quantities of a legal drug (American cigarettes) flow out (for example, smuggled to Canada, where domestic cigarette taxes are much higher). Similarly, German law enforcement officials worry about not only the smuggling of illegal drugs from Poland but also the clandestine influx of cigarettes—a highly profitable and sometimes violent business partly run by Berlin-based Vietnamese crime groups.

Another important but too often overlooked type of smuggling that persists in a low-tariff environment is the smuggling of legal commodities that are obtained illegally, such as stolen cars, computer chips, and other high-technology products. The cross-border trade in stolen cars is a multibillion-dollar business, and cars are one of the leading smuggled commodities that move from richer to poorer countries. Well-known crossing points include the U.S.-Mexico border and the Eastern borders of the European Union.[15]

As the trend toward market liberalization and an increasingly open global trading system continues, prohibitions rather than tariffs and quotas increasingly drive the business of smuggling. For at the same time as there has been a general liberalization of trade, there has also been an increase in the selective criminalization of trade through prohibitions. Some prohibitions, such as those against heroin and cocaine, are virtually universal. Others are more nation-specific, such as the variations in prohibitions against the trade in pornographic material. One nation's tolerated pleasure may be another nation's abominal vice. For instance, while American entertainment products are promoted and consumed across much of the globe through legal trade, in some places these products are available only by smuggling. The smuggling of American videotapes into Iran, for example, is a lucrative business, just as it was in the Soviet-Bloc countries before the fall of the Iron Curtain. Even the illegal use of satellite dishes in mainland China may be considered an electronic form of smuggling American entertainment products.

The lack of broad agreement on many prohibitions certainly undermines their effectiveness, but even when a certain degree of consensus exists, there remains enormous variation in how and (how much) it is enforced. Note, for example, the variations in national drug laws and their enforcement despite the existence of a global drug "prohibition regime."[16] Thus, while the Dutch approach to regulating drugs is less punitive than the U.S. approach, the U.S. approach is certainly less punitive than the draconian Indonesian approach. These variations often create significant tensions between states, as well as distinct opportunities and constraints for smugglers.

There is also great diversity in what trade is prohibited (and by whom) over time. Contrast, for example, the American regulatory approach toward alcohol today and the prohibitionist approach of the 1920s; today's prohibitionist approach toward cocaine and opium products and the free-market approach of a century ago; China's effort to prohibit American and British opium exports in the nineteenth century and America's efforts to prohibit Chinese alien smuggling in the late twentieth century; today's global prohibition against the slave labor trade and the legal trade in slaves in previous centuries; the prohibitions against money laundering and the trafficking in endangered species that did not exist even a few decades ago. Depending on the political winds and dominant social norms of the day, what is illegitimate trade in one era may be legitimate trade in another.

Just as some countries and regions have a special niche in legal trade, so too do different countries and regions have a niche in illegal trade. The industrialized countries dominate legal trade; illegal trade is an area of significant comparative advantage for many developing countries. This awkward and sobering reality is not, of course, formally recognized by the leading international institutions (such as the International Monetary Fund (IMF), the World Bank, and the World Trade Organization) that monitor global trade patterns and urge developing countries to specialize based on the principles of comparative advantage.

Thus, asparagus is officially listed as Peru's most important agricultural export, but coca products are unofficially the country's number one export. (Indeed, illegal drugs are the most important export for a number of countries across the Western Hemisphere, Africa, South Asia, and Southeast Asia.) While drugs are the single most important smuggled commodity worldwide,[17] for many countries the importance of smuggling extends well beyond the drug trade. Madagascar, for example, is on the extreme periphery of the global economy in terms of legal trade, but is a major player in the $10-billion clandestine trade in endangered species, such as rare turtles and snakes, with the United States as a major importer.[18] While South Africa's dominance in the diamond trade is well known, far less known is its dominance in the rhino-horn- and ivory-smuggling trade.[19] Russia, China, and Brazil are leading exporters of smuggled gold. Developing countries also have a comparative advantage in the export of low-wage workers, many of whom are prohibited in the countries they enter. El Salvador, for example, has exported a large percentage of its labor force to the United States, and this labor force, in turn, generates crucial foreign exchange for the Salvadoran economy through remittances.

Many countries specialize in transshipment. Panama, for example, is a free-trade zone not only for legitimate trade but for a great deal of illegitimate trade as well, including the clandestine movement of money, weapons, and people. Chinese smuggled to the United States are routinely routed through Panama to purchase false travel documents.[20] Paraguay has long been a major smuggling transshipment hub, including serving as a distribution center for the smuggling of American cigarettes and other products into South America.[21] Mexico is a major producer of marijuana and heroin, but it is also the most important transshipment point for Colombian cocaine to the U.S. market.[22]

The economic importance of smuggling suggests that there is not just a formal, above-ground dimension of regional and global interdependence, but an informal, underground dimension as well. For some countries, it is the smuggling-based part of the economy that is most responsive to (and integrated into) U.S. and global markets. Moreover, smuggling provides an alternate avenue of upward mobility for entrepreneurial but marginalized social groups that have little access to legitimate business opportunities. And in some cases, upward mobility through illegal trade may provide a mechanism for some groups eventually to break into more legitimate trade (which can also provide a convenient cover for illegitimate trade).

Advances in technology and global transportation networks have dramatically reduced the time and cost of smuggling. Historically, waterways have provided the primary channel for smuggling. The development of road and rail networks considerably expanded the smuggler's options, as did the arrival of the automobile. Today, the traditional land and sea methods and routes of previous eras remain essential, but growing access to airspace and now cyberspace (for example, in the case of intellectual property and pornography via the Internet) has further expanded the possibilities and opportunities for smuggling. Literally anything that crosses a national border can be used for smuggling, ranging from the most common and conventional (such as car trunks and luggage) to the most desperate and dangerous (human ingestion) to the most ingenious (stuffing cocaine into jalapeno peppers) to the most unstoppable (the airwaves).

But while the methods of smuggling are as diverse as what is being smuggled, most smuggling parallels the methods and routes of legal commerce. Governments consequently face an increasingly awkward but unavoidable predicament: policy measures that facilitate the flow of legal trade—improved transportation systems, deregulation of shipping, privatization of ports, and so on—also unintentionally facilitate illegal trade. Furthermore, as the speed and volume of trade continues to increase due to economic liberalization, so too does the difficulty of "weeding out" the illegal from the legal.

This problem is particularly apparent, for example, along the U.S.-Mexico border, where the formal processes of economic integration (increased trade, business and tourist travel, financial flows), are paralleled by a more informal and clandestine process of economic integration based on smuggling. And it is very much a two-way street: illegal immigrants and drugs flow north, and weapons, dirty money, and stolen cars flow south. Illegal flows in both directions are intertwined with legal flows, frustrating border inspectors who must keep the ever-increasing volume of cars and trucks moving quickly in order to avoid long traffic jams. While U.S. officials estimate that much of the cocaine that enters the country from Mexico is smuggled through official ports of entry in commercial cargo conveyances, only a small percentage of the vehicles that cross the border can realistically be inspected.[23] In 1996, 254 million people, 75 million cars, and 3.5 million trucks and rail cars entered the U.S. from Mexico.[24] Even though the U.S. Customs Service is deploying more resources and personnel to the southwest border through "Operation Hard Line," the sheer volume of legitimate crossings guarantees that the border will remain porous.

Smuggling organizations come in all forms and sizes. While smugglers are often lumped together as "organized crime," this is highly misleading due to the extreme variation in the levels of organization and degree of criminality. Smuggling is an illegal transnational enterprise, but how organized and how criminal often depends on what is being smuggled and the intensity and form of state control efforts. (Indeed, increased law enforcement can turn disorganized smuggling into organized smuggling.) Today's smugglers range from independent entrepreneurs, to loose networks of transnational gangs, to highly developed and sophisticated criminal organizations.[25] The image of an octopuslike global network of crime syndicates that runs the criminal underworld through its expansive tentacles is a fiction invented by sensationalistic journalists and politicians. If this picture matched reality, the challenge to law enforcement would actually be far less serious: one need only cut off the octopus head, and the tentacles would die with it.

What makes it so difficult to put smugglers out of business is that not only are there so many heads in so many places but also every time one head is cut off, a replacement head grows back, and every time one smuggling place is closed down by law enforcement, another place emerges. For example, U.S. law enforcement pressure on cocaine smuggling through south Florida in the early 1980s simply caused traffickers to shift to Mexican smuggling routes. More effective air interdiction efforts also caused traffickers to rely more on commercial cargo shipping.[26] Successful law enforcement initiatives can deter and even eliminate individual smugglers and smuggling organizations, but this rarely leads to a significant and extended reduction in smuggling. In the 1980s, for example, impressive law enforcement initiatives against Italian organized crime families in the United States resulted primarily in a redistribution rather than a reduction in criminal enterprise, with other crime groups—Colombians, Chinese, and Russians, for example—more than happy to fill the void.[27]

Smugglers are in many respects similar to their counterparts in legitimate businesses. Smugglers do, after all, engage in some rather conventional business practices, including subcontracting, joint ventures and strategic alliances, use of offshore bank accounts, diversification through investment in various sectors of the economy, and of course, the use of money and influence to gain government favor. Just as major transnational corporations employ lawyers, transportation and communications specialists, security guards, accountants, and distribution and sales managers, so too do some of the larger smuggling organizations.[28] Not surprisingly, many smugglers simply view their activities as a business that happens to be illegal. They would no doubt agree with Adam Smith's contention: "A smuggler is a person who, although no doubt blameable for violating the laws of the country, is frequently incapable of violating those of natural justice, and would have been, in every respect, an excellent citizen had not the laws of his country made that a crime which Nature never meant to be so."[29]

But if smuggling is a business like any other, it is also a business unlike any other. Its illegal nature gives the business some peculiar characteristics: for example, business disputes between smugglers may be resolved by killing rather than suing each other, high profits are as much a product of laws and law enforcement as they are of market demand, and the relationship to the state can be rather unpredictable and costly.

The state-smuggler relationship is a paradoxical one, defined by irony and contradiction: the smuggler is pursued by the state, but at the same time is kept in business by the state. The smuggler is dependent on the state in multiple ways. The most obvious and essential point is that state-created and enforced laws provide the very opening for (and high profitability of) smuggling in the first place. In this sense, states literally create business for criminal organizations. Just as alcohol prohibition helped fuel the growth of Italian organized crime in America, drug prohibition has been a major impetus for the emergence of many of the more recent crime groups. This is not meant to suggest that alcohol and drug prohibition has been the sole reason that these crime groups have emerged, but prohibition laws have obviously been the most powerful conditioning factors.

Recent trends in immigrant smuggling into the United States illustrate how law enforcement creates and shapes the business of smuggling. Past patterns of illegal immigration from Mexico, for example, can be characterized almost as a form of self-smuggling (i.e., the traditional role of the smuggler was limited and localized). However, the recent tightening of border controls has significantly increased the immigrant's dependence on the connections and skills of professional people-smugglers. The cost of being smuggled across the border has consequently risen with the risks. These higher smuggling fees (in some cases more than doubling), in turn, are fueling the growth of increasingly sophisticated and well-organized binational people-smuggling organizations in the Southwest borderlands. As Miguel Vallina, the assistant chief of the border patrol in San Diego notes, "The more difficult the crossing, the better the business for the smugglers."[30] Moreover, as law enforcement intensifies, many small-time smugglers are being pushed out of the business, replaced by larger criminal organizations that have the skills and connections necessary to evade law enforcement.

Similarly, immigrant smuggling operations in Central America have been transformed by law enforcement pressure in recent years. As the International Organization for Migration reports, "as authorities in the region stepped up the border control and enforcement efforts, migrant traffickers have had to grow in sophistication in order to survive. Links to transnational crime syndicates have consequently been established."[31] While American officials push for more and tougher enforcement against alien smuggling in the region, they also warn, "As enforcement efforts become more effective ... we can expect the smugglers to become more sophisticated and hard-core criminal groups to become involved in this extremely lucrative trade."[32] Thus, not only do smugglers depend on state laws for their existence, but the enforcement of such laws often creates better-organized and more skillful smuggling groups.

Laws and their enforcement also mean that smugglers necessarily interact symbiotically with elements of the state apparatus. While some smugglers attempt to intimidate or violently neutralize the state, the general rule is that they must buy off key state officials because they cannot entirely bypass or bully them. Smugglers may be seen as purchasers of a much-needed service monopolized by the state: the nonenforcement of the law. Corruption, in the form of bribes and payoffs, functions as a kind of informal tax on smuggling and is viewed by the smuggler as a necessary (even if costly) business expense. As law enforcement pressure increases, so too does the corruption tax. Moreover, smugglers may rely on corrupt state officials not only to insure that their operations are not targeted by enforcement but also to provide protection against (and/or to eliminate) rival smugglers and at times even to provide protection against other state authorities (meaning different police agencies can end up shooting at each other).[33]

Corrupt officials provide other essential services as well, such as fraudulent documents (passports, visas, naturalization cards, and so forth) that facilitate smuggling, most notably immigrant smuggling. For example, document-selling is a booming business throughout Central America, the primary passageway for the estimated 100,000 Chinese who are smuggled to the United States every year.[34] Corruption scandals involving immigrant-smuggling has lead to the replacement of immigration directors in Panama, Guatemala, and Belize.[35] While not reaching such high levels of corruption, U.S. immigration officials are far from immune.[36] In 1994, the *New York Times* reported, "No agency of the government is more vulnerable to corruption than the INS, where front-line workers, paid little more than the minimum wage, give out green cards and other coveted documents that are worth thousands on the black market. Year after year, dozens of employees are arrested for taking bribes or related crimes."[37]

Although difficult to quantify, current trends along the southwest border may reinforce rather than remedy the corruption problem. As border controls tighten, the incentive to offer bribes and/or buy entry documents from those doing the controlling also increases. Moreover, as smuggling groups have become more sophisticated, organized, and profitable (due to the higher demand and cost of their services and the heightened risks involved in providing these services), the capacity and means to corrupt has also grown. Thus, bribing corrupt officials is, in a sense, the equivalent of paying an informal tax or entry fee—and the incentive to both pay and collect the fee increases as traditional methods of clandestine entry become more difficult and risky. Indeed, partly in response to this potential for increased corruption, the U.S. Attorney's Office for the Southern District of California established a Border Corruption Task Force in 1995 and has prosecuted an unprecedented number of cases.[38]

These dynamics suggest both the power and limits of the state: even as the state fails to deter smuggling, there is no smuggling without the state. Laws and the selective nature of their enforcement are what makes smuggling possible. When pressured by the state, most smugglers simply wish to evade rather than attack or even overtly challenge the state. Of course, this is not meant to dismiss or belittle the serious threat (sometimes violent) that smugglers can pose to state institutions and/or the rule of law. (In some notorious cases, smuggling and the state apparatus virtually merge so that the illegal activity becomes a public enterprise. The Garcia Meza regime in Bolivia and the Noriega regime in Panama are particularly well known examples.)

Just as smugglers depend on the state, so too does the state depend on smugglers, although in a very different sense. This dependence takes multiple forms. In some cases, the economic dependence on smuggling can be significant. In a number of Latin American drug-exporting countries, such as Peru and Bolivia, the foreign exchange generated from smuggling enters the cash-strapped financial system through the central bank (which in turn boosts foreign-exchange reserves and helps service the foreign debt), while the jobs generated from such smuggling cushion the unemployment crisis and other social dislocations created by economic restructuring.[39] Regardless of how sincere and intense the government's battle against drug smuggling may be, the immediate economic repercussions of suddenly winning the battle would be severe.[40] What Jorge Domínguez observed in the 1970s remains true in the 1990s: "Many developing countries are not likely to achieve their priorities . . . without a measure of smuggling."[41]

A different kind of economic dependence is generated through corruption. Interestingly, while the response to corruption in regulating the legal economy in many developing countries has been to reduce state intervention (i.e., reduce rent-seeking), the response to corruption in regulating the illegal smuggling economy is to increase state intervention (which can increase rent-seeking). Consequently, the very rent-seeking behavior that market-based reforms were designed to curb in the legal economy is thriving in the illegal smuggling economy. Moreover, as rent-seeking in the legal economy is reduced, some political systems may become more dependent on revenues generated from the illegal smuggling economy.

The bribes and payoffs from smugglers not only supplement the meager incomes of corrupted law enforcement officials but also, in some cases, help sustain entire police agencies. Mexican law enforcement is one of the most notorious case of this phenomenon, particularly along the major smuggling corridors into the United States. While drug smuggling is the main culprit, other forms of smuggling can also provide significant payoffs. For example, Tijuana police reportedly take as much as $40,000 in bribes per month to allow the operation of safe houses where immigrants being smuggled through Mexico into the United States are temporarily housed.[42]

The Mexican government's response to drug-related corruption (partly due to U.S. pressure) has been to expand the role of the military in drug enforcement, but the likely result is not less corruption but rather a redistribution of the rewards of corruption from the police to the military. Suggestively, two Mexican army generals were arrested in early 1997 on drug-related corruption charges, including the head of Mexico's antinarcotics office.

Beyond corruption, however, it is important to emphasize that there are also legal channels through which resources from smuggling are directly transferred to the state, most notably asset forfeiture laws. In the U.S. case, for example, asset forfeiture has turned drug control (and anti-organized-crime initiatives in general) into a revenue-generating activity for both federal and local law enforcement. In one well-publicized case, U.S. law enforcement will retain $7.9 million of the $9 million confiscated from the U.S. bank accounts of Mario Ruiz Massieu, who had been Mexico's deputy attorney general and top drug enforcement official in 1993 and 1994.[43]

State officials also depend on smugglers to carry out their antismuggling mission. Law enforcement cannot do its job without at least minimal assistance from smugglers. The reason is that smugglers are the primary source of information on smuggling; to obtain this information, officials must constantly bargain and negotiate with smugglers. A number of drug smugglers, for example, received lenient sentences for providing information that lead to the sentencing of Noriega by a Florida jury. At a lower and less-publicized level, this type of bargaining is the standard operating procedure. The line between legality and illegality can become rather blurred. Law enforcement officials may overlook the activities of one smuggler in exchange for information that leads to the busting of other smugglers.

Most importantly, however, it is the very persistence of smuggling (and the perception of it as a growing threat) that is most critical for sustaining and expanding law enforcement. In other words, even though law enforcement fails to deter the business of smuggling (and in some ways helps sustain the business), smuggling also keeps law enforcement in business. This is particularly critical in an era of austerity, shrinking budgets, and antigovernment ideology. In many countries, the growth of law enforcement is the most striking exception to the general rollback of the state.

Indeed, in some cases, security and intelligence agencies designed to deter military attacks have embraced antismuggling tasks. In the U.S. case, the Pentagon has transformed itself from a reluctant ally of drug enforcement to a frontline participant. Strict rules against the use of the military for law enforcement functions have gradually been loosened since the early 1980s.[44] Intelligence agencies, such as the CIA, are also becoming more enthusiastic about law enforcement as they attempt to reinvent themselves after the cold war. Moreover, the drug war and other antismuggling efforts provide a new home not only for cold warriors but for cold-war technology leftovers. For example, some experimental technologies off-limits to law enforcement before the end of the cold war are now being adapted for border control.[45] Using old security institutions and technologies for new security missions may be an awkward and expensive fit, but bureaucratic incentives and political pressures continue to push in this direction.

CONCLUSION

As long as borders and trade restrictions (whether in the form of prohibitions or tariffs and quotas) have existed, there has been smuggling. And absent the emergence of a truly borderless free-market global economy (an option that is neither desirable nor politically viable), there always will be smuggling. And just as the business of smuggling will persist, so too will the business of policing smuggling. Thus the endless game of hide-and-seek on and across borders continues. But while the rules of the game are set by states, playing the game has become evermore difficult for those agencies charged with the task of law enforcement. While on the one hand, law enforcers are becoming bigger, better, and smarter players, on the other hand, the smugglers are increasingly advantaged by the same state-promoted economic and technological changes that benefit legal commerce—deregulation of trade and finance, privatization, free-trade agreements, improvements in communications and transportation infrastructure, and so on.

There has, of course, been some important law enforcement progress in recent years. For example, progress has been made against the smuggling of stolen cars,[46] and some animal species would no doubt become extinct without trade prohibitions. Progress has also been made (and much more can be made) in the area of controlling money laundering, if one considers that controls were virtually nonexistent a decade ago. (At the same time, however, money laundering has been facilitated by the continuing deregulation of financial markets.) Prohibitions have proven more effective in cases where supply is unusually scarce and transport is highly cumbersome (and in some cases, extremely dangerous to the carrier, such as the smuggling of nuclear material). Legal market alternatives also reduce the demand for smuggling (for example, the smuggling of toxic waste for improper disposal is prohibited, but there are legal and increasingly efficient disposal alternatives to dumping). Law enforcement can also be relatively more effective not only when consumer demand is low but also when the nature of the demand is not one of dependence. (For example, an animal collector purchasing a rare parrot smuggled from Mexico is a different kind of problem from an addict purchasing cocaine smuggled from Mexico.)

In those smuggling cases where supply is plentiful and demand is strong (in terms of both level and dependence), there is an obvious need for a fundamental reevaluation not only of the law enforcement game plan but also of the game itself. Illegal drugs and immigrant labor are the main cases that fall into this category. Together, they also happen to represent a sizeable percentage of global smuggling activity. Many criminal justice officials readily admit that unless the demand side of these problems (consumers of drugs and employers of immigrant labor) are fully confronted with more than token measures, antismuggling efforts can at best have only a marginal impact.

This is particularly true in the case of the United States, the world's number one consumer of illegal immigrant labor and drugs. It is interesting to note that among advanced industrialized countries, the United States has the toughest penalties for immigrant smuggling and related activities, yet is amongst the lowest in terms of penalties against employers.[47] Remarkably, only about 2 percent of the FY 1996 INS budget was devoted to employer sanctions enforcement. The lack of policy attention to the workplace contrasts sharply with the unprecedented attention being devoted to the smuggling of immigrants across the southwest border. The imbalance in policy priorities is also enormous in the case of drugs. Only about a third of the federal antidrug budget is devoted to demand-side measures (treatment, prevention, and education). A 1994 RAND study concluded that $34 million invested in treatment reduces cocaine use as much as $366 million invested in interdiction or $783 in source-country programs. Nevertheless, a supply-side drug enforcement campaign continues to overwhelm attempts to promote a public health approach to drug problems.[48] Despite the economic logic for policy reevaluation, political and bureaucratic logic continues to push for escalation, as ever more resources and energy are devoted to playing the antismuggling game. Playing the game, it seems, has become an end in and of itself.

NOTES

Research was made possible by a fellowship from the Foreign Policy Studies Program at the Brookings Institution, and a Social Science Research Council–MacArthur Foundation Fellowship on Peace and Security in a Changing World. I would also like to thank the Center for U.S.-Mexican Studies (University of California at San Diego) and the Weatherhead Center for International Affairs (Harvard University).

1. Some of these activities would fall into the category of *gray area phenomena,* defined as "Threats to the stability of nation-states by nonstate actors and nongovernmental processes and organizations." See Jim Holden-Rhodes and Peter A. Lupsha, "Gray Area Phenomena: New Threats and Policy Dilemmas," *Criminal Justice International,* 9, no. 1, Jan.–Feb. 1993, 11.
2. Funding for federal law enforcement has nearly doubled in the last five years alone, and continues to rise. The Justice Department's budget increased from $3.9 billion in fiscal year 1986 to $13.7 billion in 1995—making it the fastest (and one of the only) growing cabinet departments. The increase in funding is particularly noticeable in the case of drug control and, more recently, in immigration control. The budget of the Immigration and Naturalization Service (INS) more than doubled between 1993 and 1997. The boom in drug control spending began earlier: since 1981, the United States has invested about $65 billion in federal drug law enforcement.
3. The most comprehensive account of the internationalization of U.S. law enforcement is Ethan Nadelmann, *Cops Across Borders* (University Park: Pennsylvania State University Press, 1993).
4. Linnea P. Raine and Frank J. Cilluffo, eds., *Global Organized Crime: The New Evil Empire* (Washington D.C.: Center for Strategic and International Studies, 1994).
5. Quoted in R. T. Naylor, "From Cold War to Crime War: The Search for a New 'National Security' Threat," *Transnational Organized Crime,* 1, no. 4, winter 1995, 37.

6.   *The American Heritage Dictionary*, 2nd. ed. (Boston: Houghton Mifflin, Second College Edition, 1982).

7.   This is an example of what sociologist Gary Marx calls the interdependence between rule breakers and rule enforcers. See Gary Marx, "Ironies of Social Control: Authorities as Contributors to Deviance Through Escalation, Nonenforcement and Covert Facilitation," *Social Problems*, 28, no. 3, Feb. 1981, 221–46.

8.   See John Nichol, *The Animal Smugglers* (New York: Facts on File Publications, 1987).

9.   See, for example, Nancy Baker, *Baby Selling: The Scandal of Black-Market Adoption* (New York: The Vanguard Press, 1978).

10. Dick Ward, "The Black Market in Body Parts," *Criminal Justice International*, 7, no. 5, Sept.–Oct. 1991.

11. The word *smuggler* apparently emerged during the English civil wars of 1642–1649. A royal proclamation was announced in 1661, "for the prevention and punishment of all frauds on the Customs committed by . . . a sort of lewd people called 'smuckellors,' never heard of before the late disordered times, who make it their trade . . . to steal and defraud His Majesty of His Customs." Geoffrey Morley, *The Smuggling War: The Government's Fight Against Smuggling in the 18th and 19th Centuries* (Alan Sutton Publishing, 1994), 4.

12. William Von Raab, Introduction to Carl E. Prince and Mollie Keller, *The U.S. Customs Service: A Bicentennial History* (Washington D.C.: Department of Treasury, U.S. Customs Service), vi.

13. Laurence F. Schmeckebier, *The Customs Service: Its History, Activities and Organization* (Baltimore: The Johns Hopkins University Press, 1924), 2.

14. In the case of Boston smuggling, see John W. Tyler, *Smugglers and Patriots: Boston Merchants and the Advent of the American Revolution* (Boston: Northeastern University Press, 1986).

15. Author interviews with law enforcement officials on the German-Polish border and on the U.S.–Mexico border, 1996.

16. Ethan Nadelmann, "Global Prohibition Regimes: The Evolution of Norms in International Society," *International Organization*, 44, 1990, 479–526.

17. The Organization for Economic Cooperation and Development estimates that as much as $122 billion is spent annually in the United States and Europe on heroin, cocaine, and cannabis. Cited in Paul Stares, *Global Habit: The Drug Problem in a Borderless World* (Washington D.C.: Brookings Institution, 1996), 1.

18. Donovan Webster, "The Animal Smugglers," *New York Times Magazine*, 16 Feb. 1997.

19. De Wet Potgieter, *Contraband: South Africa and the International Trade in Ivory and Rhino Horn* (Cape Town: Queillerie Publishers, 1995).

20. *Washington Post*, 23 Oct. 1995.

21. Jorge Dominguez, "Smuggling," *Foreign Policy*, Fall, 1975.

22. See Peter Andreas, "U.S.-Mexico: Open Markets, Closed Border," *Foreign Policy* (Summer 1996).

23. Ibid.

24. Report to Congress, Office of National Drug Control Policy, Washington D.C., September 1997.

25. See Lee, this volume. Also see the country case studies, this volume.

26. "Operation Hard Line: First Anniversary," Department of the Treasury, U.S. Customs Service, Washington D.C., February 23, 1996.

27. For an overview of some of these cross-border crime groups, see Phil Williams, "Transnational Criminal Organizations and International Security," *Survival*, 36, no. 1, spring 1994, 96–113.

28. Ibid.

29. Quoted in Jorge Domínguez, "Smuggling," *Foreign Policy* (fall 1975): 164.

30. *Los Angeles Times*, 5 Feb. 1995.

31. International Organization for Migration, "Trafficking in Migrants: Some Global

and Regional Perspectives" (paper submitted for the Regional Conference on Migration, Puebla, Mexico, 13–14 March 1996), 5.

32. Presidential Initiative to Deter Alien Smuggling: Report of the Interagency Working Group, Washington D.C., Dec. 1995.

33. In the case of Mexico, see Andres Oppenheimer, *Bordering on Chaos* (Boston: Little Brown and Co., 1996), 301.

34. *Washington Post*, 23 Oct. 1995.

35. Presidential Initiative to Deter Alien Smuggling: Report of the Interagency Working Group, Washington D.C., Dec. 1995.

36. *Los Angeles Times*, 5 Feb. 1995.

37. *New York Times*, 11 Sept. 1994.

38. Author interview, Office of the U.S. Attorney for the Southern District of California, 28 Feb. 1997.

39. This is not to deny that drug smuggling also has some negative economic consequences. See Thoumi, this volume.

40. In the case of Peru and Bolivia, see Peter Andreas, "Free Market Reform and Drug Market Prohibition: U.S. Policies at Cross-Purposes in Latin America," *Third World Quarterly*, 16, no. 1 (1995).

41. Jorge Domínguez, "Smuggling," *Foreign Policy* (Fall 1975): 162.

42. *Los Angeles Times*, 5 Feb. 1995.

43. *New York Times*, 16 Mar. 1997.

44. Although not authorized to make arrests, U.S. military personnel engage in a wide variety of support activities, such as surveillance and intelligence, road and fence maintenance, and training.

45. See Sandra Dibble, "Star Wars Arrives at the Border: High Tech Developed by the Military, CIA May Aid Enforcement," *San Diego-Union Tribune*, 18 Mar. 1995.

46. Author interviews with U.S. and German law enforcement officials, 1996.

47. *Trafficking in Migrants*, no. 12 (Sept. 1996).

48. For a discussion of a public health approach to drug problems, see Eva Bertram, Morris Blachman, Kenneth Sharpe, and Peter Andreas, *Drug War Politics: The Price of Denial* (Berkeley and Los Angeles: University of California Press, 1996).

TRANSNATIONAL CRIMINAL ENTERPRISE: THE EUROPEAN PERSPECTIVE

5

Elizabeth Joyce

Attempts among European Union (EU) member states to formulate a common approach to such matters as transnational crime cannot disguise the wide range of problems and policy responses across the continent. Although the EU might enhance the prospect of cohesive European policy on trade, security, and other interregional concerns, the existence of a European perspective on just about anything is, for the most part, an illusion. Yet for the purpose of comparison with the Western Hemisphere it is possible to identify a particularly European outlook on transnational crime which, although perhaps clearly perceptible only in contrast to U.S. attitudes, is no less powerful for that.

Analysis of a European approach to transnational organized crime can provide a comparative antidote to examination of the Western Hemispheric approach. Europe and the Western Hemisphere share many of the same problems and responses. In the field of drugs, nearly all the countries of both regions are signatories to the UN conventions that are part of the foundation of the international drug control regime. Yet U.S. dominance of Western Hemispheric law enforcement cooperation inevitably defines the context in which transnational crime is discussed in both North and South America. One consequence of this has been that critical analyses of U.S. foreign policy on transnational law enforcement have sometimes conflated questions about the propriety of U.S. unilateralism in this sphere and the appropriateness of international law enforcement cooperation in general. In the case of Europe, multilateralism in law enforcement cooperation is not a reaction to the dominance of a single actor, but rather a consequence of the demands of integration.

Transnational crime is interpreted here as any illicit activity or activity conducted by illicit means that involves the penetration of national borders. In examinations of transnational crime, particular consideration is usually given to the large-scale delinquencies perpetrated by organized crime. Yet cross-border crime can also be considered as a continuum ranging from the tourist's smuggled bottle of duty-free whisky in excess of allowances to the shipment of a multimillion-dollar cache of arms or drugs arranged by a highly organized criminal enterprise with substantial resources at its disposal. This has traditionally been the European view of transnational crime, although it is a view that is increasingly prone to reinterpretation. If transnational crime is perceived as a continuum, it is more likely to be perceived as a law enforcement concern and less likely to be addressed as a problem of national security.

Europeans have traditionally been more reluctant than U.S. citizens to consider crime, whether domestic or transnational, as a threat to national security. For Europe, the "war" against drugs has always been a metaphor. This is not the case in the Americas, where the war is both a figure of speech and a literal description of policy; with the growing involvement in drug control of the United States Department of Defense and several Latin American armed forces, drug trafficking—the main transnational crime that concerns the United States—has become clearly established in the United States as a security issue. Military rhetoric infused discussion of transnational crime in the 1980s. Lending greater credence to the notion that transnational crime was an urgent security threat was the link that some U.S. policymakers saw that it had to the more traditional cold-war security threat posed by leftist insurgents in Latin America. Representative Charles Rangel, Chairman of the Committee on Narcotics Abuse and Control, noted: "We must destroy not only the drug traffickers' operations, but those people who have joined with them to overthrow our democratic friends in the area."[1] One danger of perceiving transnational crime as a security threat is the inherent, ultimately unrealistic, belief that a country (or region) can be made secure at its borders, and that the ultimate objective, as in a literal war, entails the neutralization of that threat.

MUTABLE BORDERS

In contrast to the United States position, Europeans have not in the past readily treated transnational criminal enterprise as a security matter. This European reluctance to conflate crime and security has deep roots as well as being conditioned by the circumstances that define contemporary security concerns. It has affected the way European policy is formulated and implemented, how governments conceive of cooperation and collaboration with other states, and the priority they accord to transnational law enforcement and international regimes.

Europe has more frontiers dividing far smaller slices of land than in most of the Western Hemisphere. Europeans travel frequently between countries by train, car, and on foot, and treat the crossing of borders more nonchalantly than U.S. citizens. Residents of Chamonix in France routinely choose between their local supermarkets in Switzerland, Italy, and France to take advantage of favorable exchange rates. The Channel Tunnel has reduced the distance between Britain and France to a twenty-minute train ride. Europe has a long history of transnational crime in the form of frequent yet low-level smuggling, arms dealing, and illegal migration across its myriad frontiers. The stakes are not necessarily always high. Europeans have traditionally been blasé about a certain level or type of transnational crime, treating it as mundane and inevitable. Americans in the Southwest are aware as never before of the permeability of the United States border with Mexico but, for most Americans, U.S. borders are a distant phenomenon. In Latin America, borders are frequently remote and inaccessible.

Yet U.S., Latin American, and European policymakers all wrestle with the same problem: how to encourage transnational licit commerce while strengthening border controls against illegal migration, smuggling, and other forms of cross-border crime. Some policymakers advocate more regulation: "Every country must develop tough new policies aimed at restoring its borders so that they are again meaningful protection against criminals, drugs, weapons, and illegal immigration."[2] Europeans have no such faith in the power of borders. They cannot acknowledge the concept of "restoring" borders as a means of protection, because borders on their continent have seldom protected them from anything. In Europe, borders, and even nationality, are mutable, open to interpretation and negotiation. Paradoxically, the New World's borders are older and much firmer than those in the Old World.[3] Europe's mutable borders have complex associations with national and ethnic identity and, in a very practical way, security threats.

Moreover, in contrast to the United States, language and culture rather than borders have acted as natural barriers to transnational crime in Europe. Once a criminal activity is at the point of developing into organized transnational crime, language and culture have often acted as a barrier to its spread in Europe, while actually acting as a conduit in the United States. The Italian Mafia did not foster links with communities in Italy's European neighbors, but with the discrete criminal organizations run by Americans of Italian origin in the United States.[4] The IRA did not solicit funds for illegal arms deals in the rest of Europe, but in the United States. In both cases, established ethnic communities that retained social and familial links in other countries while being based in a heterogeneous U.S. society fostered the growth of transnational crime. There is some evidence of such criminal transnational networks active in Europe, including the presence of "units" of Sicilian migrants in Germany involved in the German heroin market and the alleged activities of Hong Kong Triad groups in Britain, the Netherlands, and Spain.[5] Nevertheless, the lack of common cultural ground between European states has often proved to be a disincentive to large-scale transnational crime inside the region.

MOTIVATIONS FOR EUROPEAN COOPERATION ON LAW ENFORCEMENT

Notwithstanding European skepticism about the efficacy of borders as a means of protection, there has been a growing movement towards multilateral cooperation in Western Europe in recent years, and it is worth examining why this has occurred. In the last twenty years, there have been five factors that have encouraged the development of a European law enforcement response to transnational organized crime. The first is the existence of terrorism, traditionally the principal European transnational security threat. Even where terrorist forces act internally in a given country, they often commission transnational crime—arms smuggling, drugs smuggling, and the crossing of borders in operations—in the course of their activities. The need to combat terrorism was the original motivation for establishing international law enforcement cooperation in Europe. The second factor is the increasing attention that European countries have paid to drug trafficking in the last decade. The third is the political and economic transformation that has occurred in Eastern Europe and the former Soviet Union. Concern about drugs and Eastern Europe, in particular, has helped produce a growing consensus, even among European states unwilling to agree to a federal "European" approach to transnational law enforcement, that multilateral cooperation is an essential part of European security. The fourth factor is the existence of massive amounts of EU fraud, the consequence of integration itself, and much of it undertaken, according to the European Commission, by organized groups of transnational criminals.[6] The fifth factor is concern about illegal immigration and its alleged links with organized crime.

Terrorism, the Initial Motivation

Until recently, terrorism rather than the illicit movement of goods across borders was the prime concern of European transnational law enforcement. Europeans have never felt secure. The threats that have traditionally inspired European fears are qualitatively different from those that inspire Americans. Terrorism has provided a far greater threat to Europeans than to Americans since the end of the Second World War. Moreover, transnational crime has traditionally been far lower down the list of perceived threats in Europe than in the United States. Germany, Italy, France, Spain, Britain, and Ireland have all endured decades of insecurity generated by the threat of terrorism. The bombing of the federal building in Oklahoma City in 1995 was surprising to Europeans in the degree to which even this incident, with 168 deaths, failed to shake Americans' faith in their own security from the threat of terrorist attack on "soft targets'—government buildings and public transport systems—a common feature of life at one time or another in most major European cities. In recent years, Spanish, British, and Irish citizens have perceived ETA, the IRA, and the Ulster paramilitary groups to be more immediate and dangerous threats to their safety than any drug trafficker or transnational criminal. In Europe, transnational crime has traditionally been regarded as a security threat largely in the degree to which it is interdependent with political terrorism.

In Europe, as in many parts of Latin America, political terrorism (that is, politically motivated violent crime) has facilitated transnational crime and vice versa. Transnational crime—as well as the domestic variety—has provided money, arms, and equipment for terrorist activities. Yet, conversely, political violence has created a reservoir of arms, a network of international contacts, and a culture of impunity conducive to the commission of large-scale nonpolitical transnational crime. This has been the legacy to a greater or lesser extent in Ireland, the former Yugoslavia, and Central America. The need to tackle terrorism was the prime motivation behind European cooperation on transnational crime from 1975, when European security forces began to undertake cooperation and exchange strategic intelligence within the Trevi Group.[7]

Drugs and European Heterogeneity

Although the EU and its member states are signatories of the 1988 Vienna Convention, there is less popular consensus on drugs in Europe than in the United States. Most governments in Europe find it difficult to rally support for a hard-line approach to drug control without a great deal of opposition, although this reflects a wide variety of opinion in Europe on drugs rather than a strong trend towards liberalization. Such heterogeneity tends to find expression at the sub-state level rather than in national policy.[8] The Netherlands has been rare in implementing national policy guidelines on drugs that differed significantly from those of its neighbors. Nevertheless, movements for the decriminalization of cannabis have won nonpartisan support in many countries.

Attitudes towards drugs in France encompass the full range of opinion in Europe. France has ruled out any liberalization of its drug laws and has been the most vocal of EU member states in opposition to the more permissive drug laws of its neighbor, the Netherlands. President Jacques Chirac has insisted that France needs to retain border checks on its northeastern frontiers to protect itself from Dutch drug trafficking, effectively blocking full implementation of the EU's Schengen "open borders" agreement, an agreement first reached in the 1980s to eliminate border controls between most of the EU member states to accelerate the effects of the single market.[9] Yet attitudes within the French government illustrate the willingness of public figures to dissent publicly from the status quo even while their government commits itself to maintaining it. French Environment Minister Dominique Voynet has said explicitly that she has smoked cannabis and that she favors its legalization. In the campaign preceding France's June 1997 elections, French Prime Minister Lionel Jospin admitted to smoking marijuana and hinted that he favored decriminalization. That he made these statements at such a sensitive time suggested that he had calculated that a liberal position on drugs might win him votes, or at least not lose him support.

In Europe, leaders in the debate on drugs have also emerged from unexpected quarters. In Britain, drug czar Keith Hellawell, while serving as West Yorkshire Chief Constable, called for a national debate on drug decriminalization. These public figures can often count on quite considerable popular support for a debate on the basic principles of drug policy, and those who openly support decriminalization are approved by a vocal minority. After the 1997 British elections, a vigorous decriminalization campaign emerged to oppose the new Labour government's hard line on drug control. Some 300 campaigners openly smoked cannabis in front of police in Hyde Park to protest drug laws. Europeans also often appear willing to encompass liberal approaches to illicit drug treatment. In September 1997, 70 percent of Swiss voters in a national referendum, initiated by an antidrug organization, approved a government scheme to give regular doses of heroin to addicts. Research had shown that among Swiss addicts participating in an existing scheme crime levels have fallen by 60 percent, and some estimates claimed that the cost of supporting the users with heroin was lower than the cost of treatment and jail for users on the streets.[10]

The Dutch Case
In the context of these varying responses to illicit drugs, the Netherlands does not appear to regard its drug policy as particularly radical. The Dutch government has said that its drug policy is little more than an attempt to formalize and regulate a type of decriminalization that is already de facto in force in Britain, France, Germany, and even the United States; that is, that users in possession of small quantities of soft drugs are rarely prosecuted.[11] Implicit in this view is the sense that the Dutch government considers its neighbors to be hypocritical in their condemnation of its approach to drugs.[12]

That Dutch policy disturbs rather than outrages its neighbors is largely thanks to the fact that the Netherlands has never actually legalized drugs. Public prosecutors have discretionary powers to prosecute for possession. Pressed regularly since 1976 on legalization, the government has always argued that such a move would violate the UN illicit drug conventions to which the Netherlands is a signatory. In short, the UN conventions have acted as the limits to Dutch liberalization on drugs. Europe's response to drugs is heterogeneous but within limits.

And, more important, at the state level the EU poses even greater limits to heterogeneity. When the Netherlands changed its liberal policy on drugs in 1995, it did so only to placate its European neighbors. The prospect of the full implementation of the Schengen Agreement brought the debate to a head, rather than any internal Dutch motivation. A joint statement accompanying Schengen obliges the Netherlands to ensure that its neighbors are not inconvenienced by Dutch drug policy. The Dutch interpreted this to mean a thorough surveillance of the points of sale, particularly those in border regions. Despite the deployment of large numbers of Dutch police at borders and ports, and the arrest in 1994 of more than 800 people at the frontiers for drug offences, the French government was not satisfied and blocked implementation.

Thus, in 1995, the Dutch government produced a review that recommended major changes and restrictions to its drug policy, despite the fact it regarded the Dutch approach as a success. The amount of cannabis individuals could buy in coffee shops without fear of prosecution would be reduced from thirty grams to five. In addition, the availability of cannabis would be reduced through limits on the number of retail outlets, and serious drug users would be required to undertake compulsory rehabilitation.[13] The government stated explicitly that the only reason it was considering major amendments to a policy that it considered effective and satisfactory was because of its neighbors' concerns about "drug tourism" whereby users from France, Belgium, Britain, and Germany were crossing Dutch borders to take advantage of its permissive policies and importing cannabis bought there to their own countries. It also published the report simultaneously in five languages, a clear indication that the policy statement was intended as much for the other EU member states as for the Netherlands itself.

France acting simply as an interested neighbor could hardly have forced a change in Dutch drug policy. France's leverage with the Netherlands was Dutch commitment to the EU. A threat to sabotage the EU Schengen agreement proved an effective instrument. Dismantling EU internal borders has thus resulted in more than law enforcement cooperation; the Dutch case suggests strongly that there will be some homogenization of national policies on cross-border crime. In this instance, however, the French remained unsatisfied with Dutch policy and continued to block Schengen implementation, while the Dutch were left with a policy that was from their point of view not as satisfactory as their previous arrangements. Multilateralism can mean that no one gets what they want.

EU Fraud

Transnational organized crime is capable of subverting and manipulating public policy for profit, and the EU itself is a rich resource for organized crime. Organized criminal groups have targeted EU agricultural subsidies, commercial policies, structural policies, and even direct EU expenditure, according to the EU's own investigative unit, the Unité de Coordination de la Lutte AntiFraude (UCLAF). UCLAF was created in 1988 to collaborate with the member states in investigating the transnational fraud that costs EU taxpayers millions of dollars a year. The unit has a particular concern about organized crime's involvement in EU fraud. Much of this fraud involves the loss to governments of excise duties and VAT (Value Added Tax); some involves the systematic extraction from the EU of funds and subsidies on fraudulent terms. Sometimes such frauds involve criminals in only one member state; more usually, the network is transnational. Cigarette smuggling is the chief activity of transnational crime syndicates engaged in large-scale EU fraud. The UCLAF reported the detection of some 800 million ECUs avoided in customs duty, VAT, and excise in 1996.[14] Such is the EU's concern about cigarettes that in 1994 it set up a Cigarettes Task Force whose only remit is to investigate cigarette-related fraud. More recently, similar task forces have been set up for olive oil and alcohol.

The methods and resources for such fraud are similar to those used in the trafficking of illicit substances. The networks use large EU ports for transit and rely on the large volume of transactions to mask their activities; they give a false description of goods or specify false destinations outside the EU. UCLAF believes that most of the organizations involved are formally established as companies outside the community but have a chain of partner and front companies inside the union that use a network of customs and tax warehouses.[15] In one operation, French, Belgian, and Spanish law enforcement officials found that criminal groups had been loading cigarettes from Benelux ports onto ships ostensibly bound for West Africa. The cigarettes had then been unloaded in international waters off the coast of Spain into specially adapted high-speed boats destined for the Spanish black market. An estimated 220,000 cartons (more than 2.2 billion cigarettes) reached the Spanish market in this way in 1996, costing the EU around 175 million ECUs in lost revenue. Similar shipments of alcohol avoid excise duty in this way, and the financial impact is considerable: a single truck-load of alcohol supposedly bound for Eastern Europe but actually destined for another member state represents around 500,000 ECUs in excise duty.[16] Exports of beef, olive oil, wine, and other products have all been treated in the same manner.

In addition, outwardly respectable individuals perpetrate more recondite forms of EU fraud that do not require the use of high-speed boats and secret warehouses. As UCLAF admits, there are irregularities and fraud in all sectors of the EU budget. Half of the cases involve agricultural funds, which represent half the community budget. In 1995, UCLAF and the member states detected 1,853 cases involving agricultural fraud, amounting to 316 million ECUs.[17] Other cases have recently included the artificial inflation of costs on vocational training courses (Spain and Britain) and the creation of dummy vocational training courses (Italy) to defraud the EU's European Social Fund; fictitious research into hydroelectricity (Ireland) and a renewable energy project (Germany); and the embezzlement of EU funds from a humanitarian operation in the former Yugoslavia (France). These instances of fraud are neither novel nor typically European, but they have an interesting status in the context of the EU. Although some may have involved citizens in only one member state and are not therefore considered to be transnational crimes in the traditional sense, they are transnational in the sense that the money acquired is defrauded of all fifteen member states. In the case of fraudulently claimed agricultural subsidies worth millions of dollars, organized criminals operating in only one country nevertheless acquire their profits from taxpayers in all fifteen member states. Policing integration itself is one of the challenges that the Europeans have had to face.

Eastern Europe

Rapid social, political, and economic change, as well as the impoverishment of large parts of the population in Eastern Europe, has made countries there more viable as transshipment platforms and markets for drugs and other illegal goods. The Balkan route, a significant route but by no means the only one, has always been important for European smugglers who have transported heroin from Afghanistan via Turkey to Europe as well as cigarettes, arms, and other products to and from Europe through Bulgaria, Romania, and Macedonia, with the Adriatic coastline of Italy often the first port of call. In recent years the Balkan route has become particularly difficult to police. Combatants in the former Yugoslavia used profits from smuggled drugs, oil, arms, and cigarettes to finance war, and there is now evidence that trafficking profits—one estimate put the figure at around $36 million per year—flow into the state coffers of Serbia and Montenegro.[18] Eastern European countries have also rapidly become prominent as drug "producer" countries. Some experts believe that Poland has become the main manufacturer of illicit amphetamines in Europe.[19] Underemployed pharmaceutical companies in the Czech Republic and Slovakia are also reportedly producing the synthetic illicit drugs that are popular in the European youth market.[20]

Transnational criminal enterprises based in Western Europe also have the opportunity to widen their markets to the east. There is evidence that drug traffickers have undertaken agreements with Italian organized crime syndicates to franchise Eastern Europe's drug market, and that Colombian traffickers have formed business alliances with criminal groups in Russia.[21] Stronger trade links with eastern neighbors provide greater cover for illicit commerce. Products hereto in short supply in Eastern Europe and the former Soviet Union are in demand on the black market. The theft of motor vehicles in the EU for resale in the Baltic republics, the Ukraine, Russia, and central Asia has become a major problem. Bulgarian and Russian criminal groups are believed to be particularly active in this area.[22] In this respect, the European car theft problem resembles similar problems in the Western Hemisphere, where vehicles stolen in more affluent countries are resold elsewhere.[23] Germany is concerned about the traffic in nuclear-weapons grade material acquired from the former Soviet Union and potentially available for sale to terrorist groups, organized criminals, or even states attempting to create some kind of strategic nuclear capability. The German Bundeskriminalamt has identified several hundred individuals it suspects of involvement in this type of smuggling, most of whom are German, Czech, Polish, and Russian.[24]

Countries in Eastern Europe offer safe havens for transnational criminals, a source of weapons and intelligence, and easy money laundering facilities for criminal earnings, with the economies of the region still cash-based and open to any convertible currency. Viktor Ilyukhin, chair of Russia's parliamentary Security Committee, has reported that organized crime controls 55 percent of capital in the country, and 80 percent of all voting stock, while another estimate has organized crime controlling 15–25 percent of the nation's banks.[25] Europe also benefits in unprecedented ways from crime in the east. Criminals based in the former Soviet Union annually spend more money on property in Britain than Britain gives in aid and credits to the former Soviet states.[26]

Many of the Eastern European countries lack the institutional mechanisms to address drug trafficking and other forms of transnational crime effectively. Where those countries are about to accede to the EU—Poland, Hungary, and the Czech Republic, in the first instance—the EU member states are strongly motivated as a group to strengthen cooperation and provide assistance. The aim is twofold: to assist in the development of national drug policies in Eastern Europe and to promote cooperation with the EU and its member states. Poland, for example, has experienced a dramatic rise in drug consumption and trafficking in recent years, as well as being a key producer of amphetamines. Yet until 1997, the Polish police did not even have a drugs unit, and in 1995 the Polish police detected only 97 cases of drug smuggling.[27]

The EU provides assistance to Eastern Europe on drugs through its Phare cooperation program, and EU member states offer bilateral cooperation. The EU spends more on external drugs aid in this region than any other, through its Phare Drug Program.[28] One of the focal points for international law enforcement cooperation, however, is run by the United States, which is also extremely active in Eastern Europe: the FBI-run International Law Enforcement Academy (ILEA) in Budapest has rapidly become a key training facility for officials from all over the region.

Illegal Immigration and Transnational Organized Crime

Perceptions of transnational crime are inevitably bound up with a country's interactions with its neighbors. In the Western Hemisphere, the United States border to the south separates the United States from a region that is far poorer and less economically successful, where the illicit movement of people and goods across a border often offers the best opportunity for personal improvement. The same conditions have not, until now, applied in Western Europe. Europeans could perhaps afford to be relatively blasé about transnational crime within Western Europe because in the later years of this century, European countries have been roughly equal in economic terms. (Spain and Portugal were exceptions to this rule, but were isolated from the rest of Europe by political as well as economic circumstance.) During the cold war, there was little need to worry about excluding economically less fortunate neighbors to the east because they were very effectively being kept in by their own governments.

The prevention of illegal immigration is a traditional role for border law enforcement. However, the collapse of emigration controls in Eastern Europe has propelled immigration toward the top of the EU security agenda, on a par with transnational organized crime. One of the main priorities when the EU member states discuss transnational organized crime is the coercive "trafficking in human beings" allegedly perpetrated by transnational organized crime. In April 1997, the EU Ministers of Justice endorsed an action plan drawn up by the EU's High Level Group on Organized Crime, which stressed the importance of "trafficking in drugs and human beings, corruption, money laundering and terrorism." EU Commissioner Anita Gradin, speaking on April 14, 1997 on the sexual exploitation of children, argued that the prevention of child sexual abuse was dependent on European coordination and, therefore, the ratification of the Europol Convention.

THE INSTITUTIONAL INCENTIVE FOR EU COOPERATION ON TRANSNATIONAL CRIME

Although there are strong external motivations for multilateral cooperation in Europe—including the presence of terrorism, drug trafficking, and the consequences of profound transformation in Eastern Europe—European integration itself has been a driving force that has helped produce multilateral law enforcement cooperation in the region as it is currently configured, even though cooperation on law enforcement between EU member states remains intergovernmental rather than federal. Since the early 1990s, a specifically European set of security and law enforcement priorities has emerged from institutional development. European responses to transnational organized crime are embedded in the broader EU integration process and the political debate it generates. At the European level, the EU member states' current response to transnational crime is characterized by a preoccupation with institutions and with the problem of how to coordinate and reconcile policy and law among the fifteen existing member states as well as new members in Eastern Europe. The 1992 Treaty on European Union envisaged greater cooperation on law enforcement. There is much about what emerges from Europe that is specifically European. Yet the concrete steps that EU member states and their neighbors are taking towards multilateral cooperation on transnational organized crime, being still the stuff of political rhetoric in other regions of the world, are making the region a pathfinder in such matters.

European cooperation on transnational organized crime is an integral part of the wider regional EU project. As the heated disputes over monetary union and the introduction of a single European currency demonstrate, integration is not a smooth process. Nevertheless, closer union has occurred rapidly during the last decade, expedited by the Single European Act of 1986, which formally envisaged the EU as a single market, "an area without internal frontiers in which the free movement of goods, persons, services and capital is ensured" (Article 8a). Essentially, this meant the removal of the EU's internal borders to create one vast internal market.

The removal of the EU's internal borders is a forcefully symbolic act as well as a practical necessity. But no one involved in the process of European integration ever underestimates the power of symbols. In the last decade, the progress of Schengen has been a fairly reliable barometer of fears and enthusiasms about European integration. This is partly why the process has been so painfully slow and fragmented. A timetable is agreed and, usually at the eleventh hour, objections are raised, and the process either jolts further forward a few steps or halts yet again for months (sometimes years) as new compensatory measures to guard against transnational crime and illegal migration are added. Greater economic integration makes closer law enforcement cooperation on transnational crime a practical imperative, and discussion of cooperation on law enforcement raises some of the most emotive issues of national sovereignty. For this reason, the process of reaching a *modus vivendi* between member states has been slow and complicated, and remains far from complete.

Nevertheless, over the past decade, the compensatory measures in the sphere of law enforcement cooperation for a process originally designed to relax the movement of goods, services, and people have created a complex network of operational rules and regulations, including detailed measures on hot pursuit, cross-border surveillance, asylum, the status of refugees, illegal immigration, and the common computerized system for the exchange of personal data.[29]

Disagreements over sovereignty hampered the establishment of Europol, a European police agency formally established on October 1, 1998 to coordinate customs and police cooperation on terrorism, drug trafficking, and other serious transnational crime. In 1991, German Chancellor Helmut Kohl suggested the creation of a European police force, which Germany originally envisaged as a European FBI, whose initial brief would be the gathering of police intelligence on drug trafficking. Britain, in particular, vigorously opposed the initiative. In the early 1990s, the British government saw the initiative less as a practical means to fight crime and rather as instrumental in Germany's ambition to create a federal Europe. London argued against any operational powers to investigate crime being ceded to Europol, demonstrating that, as always, some of the greatest obstacles to the EC's ability to act in its own right lay in the member states and their perceptions of the community's identity and role.[30] Britain eventually came to accept the principle of Europol (being, with Germany, one of the two EU countries that make more use of the agency's resources than any others),[31] while insisting that cooperation on law enforcement remain a purely intergovernmental matter.

For now, Europol is an intelligence-sharing agency whose remit has been extended from intelligence on drug trafficking to include the traffic in women and children for prostitution, as well as smuggling of stolen cars and nuclear material. It has no executive or investigative powers, and it cannot monitor terrorism or keep personal computerized records on criminals. Although Europol's immediate future is uncertain, it will probably become a pillar of international law enforcement cooperation, and its establishment will clearly have an impact on Interpol: European countries provide more than half the funding for Interpol, and Germany would like to see at least some of this money diverted to Europol.[32] It is, however, far from being a European version of the FBI; to characterize it as such is to misunderstand the EU and the legal and political constraints that divide and bind its fifteen member states.

Many law enforcement officials and diplomats remain skeptical about Europol. They point to the legal and operational difficulties involved in exchanging intelligence quickly and effectively among fifteen countries where a multiplicity of languages and institutional differences are involved. They tend to argue that an improved Interpol-type arrangement is the best that can be hoped for, and that to take Europol much further into operations would be neither feasible nor desirable. There has been less discussion lately of "harmonization" of the different legal arrangements, and more of "approximation." A second type of suspicion toward police cooperation focuses on the potential "democratic deficit" and the potential threat to civil liberties involved in any widening of police powers at the supranational level.[33] This is a reasonable concern, although Europol is set up under a convention which, according to EU rules, cannot be changed without unanimous approval from member states and ratification by each national parliament. Several countries, Germany most vocally, would like to see Europol move out of the intergovernmental sphere, where it is subject to the scrutiny of elected national representatives, and into the supranational field.

LAW ENFORCEMENT COOPERATION AND THE PROBLEM OF SOVEREIGNTY

The European case demonstrates to the rest of the world the practical and political difficulties of criminal law enforcement cooperation. Transnational organized criminal groups in Europe are persistently widening their spheres—both in geographical and operational terms—and grasping opportunities created by integration and other changes. A response that goes beyond the exchange of data between discrete law enforcement agencies is not easy to organize. Effective cooperation may require surrender of some of the core prerogatives of statehood in the spheres of criminal justice, law enforcement, and security. The distribution of intelligence to foreign countries and the extradition of one's own citizens, both common elements of international law enforcement cooperation, can be seen as examples of such surrender.

Fear of loss of sovereignty informs many European responses to all aspects of EU integration, but criminal justice is a special case by virtue of its internal security status. Yet once it is acknowledged that current forms of international cooperation are inadequate to address transnational organized crime, the dilemma becomes one of deciding how much sovereignty, in terms of criminal justice, a country or group of countries is prepared to cede to counteract transnational organized crime. A country might decide that the potential loss of sovereignty that criminal penetration of its borders poses is greater and more threatening to national welfare than loss of sovereign discretion required for an effective response.

In the Western Hemisphere, the problem of sovereignty and law enforcement is discussed in the context of U.S. relations with smaller and weaker states. U.S. unilateralism in law enforcement cooperation often produces resistance to aspects of law enforcement cooperation regarded as legitimate between European states. Other countries in the hemisphere resist U.S. attempts to expand cooperation on law enforcement and complain that the United States is insensitive to the dilemmas of smaller, weaker states and that they are being forced to act in accordance with U.S. interests even when they are incompatible with their own. Small Caribbean islands protest that they have been bullied into accepting ship-rider agreements that allow U.S. law enforcement officials to board their ships to search for illegal shipments but make no provision for reciprocity. Colombia claimed in 1996 and 1997 that the United States had unfairly judged it to have made inadequate progress on drug control, leading to its "decertification." The Mexican government protested in early 1997 that DEA agents should not carry firearms while working in Mexico. Other states in the Western Hemisphere complain, with varying degrees of validity, of a lack of reciprocity in cooperation: that their coast guards are not allowed to board U.S. ships to search for drugs, that Americans are not being extradited to stand trial in their countries, and that their armed policemen cannot roam the streets of Baltimore looking for Americans to arrest. Being almost inevitably embedded in the politics of U.S. foreign policy in the region, the legitimate problems of operational cooperation on law enforcement in the Western Hemisphere are often less clearly identified, understood, and addressed than in the European case.

The European process of developing intergovernmental and supranational law enforcement institutions that seek to address transnational organized crime is often clumsy, long-winded, and overly bureaucratic, but this process is an inescapable part of creating an international policy space for criminal law enforcement, hereto largely a domestic policy area. EU cooperation on crime involves, at the very least, fifteen member states working together. Problems are inevitable, but the goal is cooperation on equal terms. In light of European cooperation on transnational crime, Western Hemispheric cooperation often does not look like cooperation at all, but rather the attempt of one country to persuade, encourage, or coerce other countries to act in its interests, a coincidence of interests being an optional extra rather than a basic requirement. The United States sometimes dresses up its foreign relations on transnational crime in the borrowed robes of multilateralism, but this is seldom more than an attempt to put a more internationally acceptable gloss on the unilateral promotion of U.S. interests. Latin American commitment to multilateral cooperation is also lacking, often seeming to be little more than a rhetorical response to U.S. pressure. At the 1998 Summit of the Americas in Santiago, participants agreed that the Organization of American States (OAS) might act as a potential focal point for multilateral efforts on drugs, administering a multilateral judgment of member states' drug control efforts with the potential to replace the United States' certification process. It is worth bearing in mind that the OAS's Inter-American Drug Abuse Control Commission, the vehicle for this effort, has often almost withered away for lack of attention and funding, turning at times to the EU for funding because it could not raise sufficient interest among its own member states.

An optimistic assessment of cooperation on transnational crime in the Western Hemisphere may see it coming to resemble European cooperation as a serious and productive collaboration between states. Assuming the further development of liberal trade regimes in the Western Hemisphere, the United States might find itself in a more collaborative relationship with its neighbors in several policy areas, including but not confined to law enforcement. Open borders, more liberal trade arrangements, and greater communications between states provide more opportunity for illicit commerce. Transnational crime in the Western Hemisphere, as in Europe, will expand. U.S.-Mexican trafficking and illicit migration have already escalated in line with the growth in cross-border trade. The question is how perceptions of this growth in transnational crime shape U.S. and Latin American policies. The recognition that a balance must be struck between liberty and security from crime, whether in Europe or the Western Hemisphere, is also a recognition that transnational criminal enterprise is something from which neither region can entirely be protected.

NOTES

The author would like to thank the Fulbright Program in Belgium for the EU-US Senior Scholarship that provided the opportunity to research this chapter.

1. United States. Congress. House of Representatives Select Committee on Narcotics Abuse and Control. *Cocaine Production in the Andes* (Washington D.C.: GPO, 1989), 16.
2. U.S. Deputy Assistant Secretary of State for law enforcement and crime Jonathan Winer, quoted in: Peter Andreas, "U.S.-Mexico: Open Markets, Closed Border," *Foreign Policy* 103 (Summer 1996), 53.
3. Disputed borders in the Western Hemisphere have seldom led to outright conflict in recent times, Ecuador's short-lived 1995 war with Peru being a notable exception. By contrast, Germany's borders have been redrawn several times this century, most recently when West and East were reunited. Austria's independence was recognized only in 1955, prior to which it had been swallowed by the German Third Reich and later divided into four zones occupied by the USSR, the United States, Britain, and France. Further east, the boundaries and national identities of those who live within them are even more complex. In Italy, a substantial minority of northern Italians would, for their own economic and political benefit, like to see their region secede from the rest of the country. Geographically distinct from mainland Europe, the British Isles have some of the world's most idiosyncratic national border arrangements. England and Scotland, despite the 1707 Act of Union, have substantially different legal systems. The current frontier between two EU member states, Britain and Ireland, was made only in 1922 with partition, and Ireland did not become a sovereign state until 1937.
4. According to Savona, Sicilian Mafiosi entered the United States during the early 1960s, establishing a nucleus there which subsequently acted as an intermediary in heroin-trafficking from the Middle East. In the mid-1980s, it was estimated that 70 percent of heroin entering the United States came through Sicilian connections. See Ernesto U. Savona, "The Organized Crime/Drug Connection: National and International Perspectives," in H. Traver and M. S. Gaylord, eds., *Drugs, Law and the State*, (Hong Kong: Hong Kong University Press, 1992), 120.
5. Phil Williams and Ernesto U. Savona, *The United Nations and Transnational Organized Crime* (London: Frank Cass, 1996), 14, 17,
6. UCLAF, *Annual Report 1996*, Brussels: European Commission (1997).
7. Although initially concerned with terrorism, the remits of the Trevi Working Groups eventually covered public order matters and, from the mid-1980s, transnational organized crime, including drug trafficking, bank robbery, and arms trafficking. See Monica den Boer, "Justice and Home Affairs: Cooperation without Integration," in: H. Wallace and W. Wallace, eds., *Policy-Making in the European Union*, 3rd edition, (Oxford: Oxford University Press, 1996), 394–5.
8. Most well known at this level in the sphere of drug control is the "Frankfurt approach," a transnational movement of city authorities (including Frankfurt, Hamburg, Amsterdam, and Zurich) that supports policies that attempt to control rather than limit the use of drugs, according to the principles of harm reduction. The "Stockholm approach" was prepared as a response to the Frankfurt resolution when the heads of 21 European capitals signed a resolution entitled "European Cities against Drugs' which took a more traditional line against drugs and eschewed the reclassification of any drugs under the UN conventions.
9. In an attempt to accelerate the process, Belgium, France, Germany, Luxembourg, and the Netherlands signed the Schengen Agreement in 1985, which was to involve the abolition of virtually all controls at mutual borders. Other countries have since joined the core five; most of the Scandinavian countries will probably join soon.

Only Denmark, Britain, and Ireland, of the 15 EU member states, have deliberately chosen to remain outside the agreement.

10. *Manchester Guardian*, 29 Sept. 1997.
11. Ministry of Health, Welfare and Sports (VWS), *Drugs Policy in the Netherlands* (The Hague: VWS, 1995).
12. Other European countries have ruled that possession of "soft" drugs need not be an indictable offence. The German Federal Constitutional Court in Karlsruhe ruled in March 1994 that an individual should no longer be prosecuted on the grounds of having committed an indictable offence if found in Germany in possession of cannabis deemed to be for personal use. Dutch policy takes this approach one step further by reasoning, according to the principles of harm reduction, that if drug use cannot be eliminated, it is prudent to regulate its use. The Dutch approach, implemented since 1976, attempts to separate the markets for "hard" drugs (heroin, cocaine, and amphetamines) and "soft" drugs (cannabis products). The intention is to prevent users from progressing from soft drug use to hard drug use when exposed to a criminal underground that markets both products. Coffee shops are allowed to sell small amounts of cannabis without fear of prosecution. Until recently, users could possess up to 0.5 grams of hard drugs, or 30 grams of cannabis unless the offender was also suspected of trafficking or another drug-related crime. Hard drug users are more routinely prosecuted and are the prime reason for the rapid recent expansion of Dutch prison capacity.
13. In some respects, the review did propose greater liberalization by taking a radical view of domestic cannabis cultivation. It advocated raising tolerance for domestic growers of cannabis. The idea was that tolerance of a cottage industry of small growers of Dutch cannabis—known as *nederwiet*—would reduce the involvement of organized crime in cannabis supply. See VWS, *Drug Policy*.
14. UCLAF, *Annual Report 1996* (Brussels: European Commission, 1997), Section 3, 3.
15. Ibid., 3.
16. Ibid., 4.
17. Ibid., 6.
18. *Washington Post*, 21 Nov. 1996, A34.
19. Interview, senior British law enforcement official, Sept. 17 1996.
20. *Phare Fight against Drugs*, no. 3, November 1997, 7.
21. IRELA, *Cooperation in the Fight against Drugs: European and Latin American Initiatives*, October 1995, Madrid: IRELA, 30.
22. Phil Williams and Ernesto U. Savona, *The United Nations and Transnational Organized Crime* (London: Cass, 1996), 28.
23. Williams and Savona cite the FBI's claim that four out of five vehicles worth more than $15,000 awaiting dockside clearance in an unnamed Caribbean country were stolen. Ibid. 28.
24. Williams and Savona, *The United Nations*, 23.
25. Mark Galeotti, "Cross-Border Crime and the Former Soviet Union," *Boundary and Territory Briefings* 1, 5 (1995), 14.
26. Galeotti, "Cross-Border Crime," 14.
27. Reuter, "Polish Police Pledge Crackdown on Drugs," 11 Feb. 1997.
28. The EU's Phare programs are directed toward 13 countries of Eastern Europe and cover all aspects of EU cooperation with the region. A parallel framework, Tacis, exists for the former Soviet states.
29. den Boer, "Justice and Home Affairs," 397.
30. Britain's objections managed to slow down the establishment of Europol by several years but could not prevent it entirely. By 1996, German Foreign Minister Friedrich Bohl was asserting that "the goal of the Federal Government is . . . to build Europol up into an effective European police force." *Allgemeine Zeitung*, 26 Oct. 1996 (translation provided by the Press and Information Office of the Federal Government).

31. *The Independent*, May 6, 1996, 8.
32. The basis for the International Criminal Police Organization (Interpol), an international police organization, was created in 1914 at an international conference organized by Prince Albert of Monaco, and attended by 300 participants from 15 countries, although the decision was not implemented until 1923. Now Interpol has some 174 member countries. Interpol is useful in the exchange of data and intelligence between police forces, and has real value in creating opportunities for members of different law enforcement agencies to get to know one another and their modes of operation, thus facilitating cooperation. Like Europol, Interpol is not an operational organization. Critics describe it as being little more than an international bulletin-board to which police forces can attach their "Wanted" posters. Europeans have tended to make more use of the institution than countries from other regions: in 1994, the European region accounted for 80 percent of all messages that passed through the organization. The United States is virtually alone in providing no data to Interpol, despite occupying some of the key positions in the organization.
33. John Benyon, "Policing the European Union: The Changing Basis of Cooperation on Law Enforcement," *International Affairs* 70, 3 (1994), 516–17. See also, Martin Elvins, *Drugs and the State in a Global Network*, Paper presented at the South African Institute of International Affairs, June 5, 1997.

THE IMPACT OF THE ILLEGAL DRUG INDUSTRY ON COLOMBIA

6

Francisco E. Thoumi

INTRODUCTION

During the last twenty-five years Colombia has become a leading producer and trafficker of illegal drugs. Its drug entrepreneurs turned coca, opium poppy, and marijuana into important crops, manufactured cocaine and heroin, and established themselves as the main smugglers of those drugs into the United States and as important suppliers of Europe.[1] It is undeniable that this illegal industry has had a great impact on Colombia; however, while certain effects are easy to identify and measure, many others are not, making it difficult to answer some questions, the provisional answers to which are a necessary prelude to effective public policy. Among these questions are the following: What is the actual weight of the industry in the country's economy? What are its effects on fiscal and macroeconomic policies and management? Would the destruction of the industry cause an economic crisis? What have been the industry's effects on the democratic process, local governments, peace negotiations, armed forces, political parties, and corruption? These are all complex and difficult questions. In this chapter I attempt to respond to those questions, but I acknowledge the difficulty of obtaining definite answers. First, I summarize the evidence on the industry's economic impact, then I focus on the social and political effects. I end the chapter with a short summary and some conclusions.

THE ECONOMIC IMPACT

What economic effects of the illegal drug industry might one hypothesize? The abundance of foreign exchange the industry generates can cause overvaluation of the currency and loss of competitiveness for other exports and the domestic production that competes with imports. The industry can cause regional booms and busts in coca, poppy, and marijuana growing regions and in the cities where drug traffickers are concentrated. It can have a significant impact on employment; it promotes money laundering; it can distort consumption, investment, and import patterns as traffickers and their associates choose to invest and consume assets that are useful to launder their revenues; and it raises expectations of quick wealth and encourages high-risk speculative investments.

The Industry's Structure and Its Income Distribution

Because of the price and profit structure of the industry, its economic impact depends crucially on the stage of the business in which a country participates.[2] First, due to sharp price increases as drug processing advances and as drugs move from the mainly producing countries to mainly consuming ones, income is much greater in the smuggling and marketing stages than in the agriculture and manufacturing ones. Second, most of the industry's employment takes place in the agricultural stage of the business. Third, income is distributed very widely in the agricultural stage; it becomes increasingly concentrated as the manufacturing stages advance, is highly concentrated in the smuggling phase, and from then on it becomes deconcentrated to the point that retailers' income distribution is again very dispersed.[3]

The illegal drug industry in Colombia is diversified, and Colombians are involved in it in complex ways. Marijuana production and exports began around 1970 and were responsible for a boom in the northwest of the country in the mid- and late 1970s.[4] Marijuana lost importance after a government eradication program in 1979. Since then, cocaine refining has become the main drug industry. During the first stage of the cocaine boom, coca paste was imported from Peru and Bolivia. By the early 1980s coca plantings had developed, mainly in the Caguán and Guaviare regions (Jaramillo, Mora, and Cubides 1989; Molano 1987). Most illegal crops grow in natural reserves or public lands (*baldíos*), in isolated, hard-to-reach regions where there is little or no state presence, almost no infrastructure, and in which power is frequently exercised by either guerrilla or paramilitary organizations. During the last five years illegal plantings have grown quite rapidly. Today Colombia is the second-largest coca-producing country after Peru, having surpassed Bolivia (Uribe 1997). In the 1990s Colombia developed the poppy industry, which has now become an important producer of opium and heroin (Barragán and Vargas 1995). Marijuana is still produced, mainly for the domestic market, and current acreage has declined relative to the 1970s.

The illegal drug industry has many actors: peasants who grow illegal crops and produce coca paste, cocaine base, opium, and heroin; local buyers who gather those products and refine them further when necessary; manufacturers who refine cocaine and heroin; the cartels that coordinate some of the refining activities and smuggle the drugs and market them out of the country; guerrilla organizations that protect crops, peasants, and labs, and charge "export" and "value added" taxes in the growing and processing regions; white-collar professionals such as chemists, pilots, lawyers, financial advisers, and accountants; bodyguards and other security forces, including paramilitary organizations; politicians; financial-sector professionals who are money-laundering accomplices, and so on. As witnessed by the current social and political crises, the involvement of Colombian society in the illegal drug trade has been pervasive.

It is very difficult to draw an accurate picture of the organization of the illegal drug industry in Colombia. First, drug organizations are continuously changing as they try to foil law enforcement efforts and search for new raw material and intermediate goods sources, export routes, and markets. Second, the secrecy required by illegality is a strong disincentive to develop a highly structured organization in which workers at the bottom know their bosses and their actions. Third, high profit incentives and low barriers to entry induce independent operators to spring up at various steps of the business.

According to U.S. intelligence services (Zabludoff 1994), in the early 1990s Colombia's drug exports were controlled by ten to fourteen large organizations that coordinated all parts of the business, from buying coca paste to selling wholesale in the United States, Europe, and in some cases, even selling to middle-level traffickers in the United States. However, there were many mom-and-pop operations that produced and smuggled small quantities of drugs. They also argued that the Cali cartel controlled up to 80 percent of the cocaine marketed in that country. Castillo (1996) argues that many organizations were independent but they had contact with the large cartels and frequently cooperated and coordinated their actions with them. For example, Castillo argues that in the late 1980s Pablo Escobar required smaller organizations to contribute financially to his political fight against extradition, and that the Cali cartel required contributions from the North Valle exporting organizations to fund the 1994 presidential campaign of Ernesto Samper. Castillo also argues that Escobar issued the equivalent of "export licenses" to smaller groups and required payments of an "export tariff." The growing heroin traffic appears to be controlled by the smaller groups.

The Industry's Size

Estimates of Colombian illegal drugs' value added and of the actual narco-dollars that enter the country's economy are highly uncertain and difficult to assess. Most of the industry's value added is generated by the roughly tenfold increase in cocaine price between Colombian and U.S. wholesale prices, an even larger difference between Colombian and European wholesale prices, and by the larger price increase within the mainly consuming countries. The industry's value added can be looked at as a remuneration for risk and is not related to factor costs in Colombia. It is not known how high are the smuggling costs confronted by Colombian traffickers, although it is reported that they can range from 15 to 50 percent of the selling price in the United States. Still, when cocaine is exported, the Colombian exporter has to bring into the country only a proportion of his revenues to pay to cover his Colombian costs. The rest can be laundered and invested anywhere else. As good capitalists, drug traffickers respond very well to market incentives and tend to bring their capital to Colombia when they think it is profitable to do so. The lack of correlation between the unexplained flows in the Colombian balance of payments and the estimates of Colombian traffickers' earnings confirms this point (Thoumi 1995a).

Data about the size and structure of the industry are inaccurate, difficult to obtain, and frequently derived from secondary and indirect sources that at best provide a fuzzy approximation to reality.[5] To illustrate this point, consider the amount of cocaine produced and exported by Colombian drug organizations. To begin, it is necessary to figure out the size of the coca crop in Colombia, Peru, and Bolivia. Then conversion factors from coca leave to coca paste, cocaine base, and cocaine must be determined. These vary with weather conditions, the density of the plantings, the amount and types of fertilizers and herbicides used, the skills of chemists and the type and quality of the chemicals used, the type of coca plants and their age, and the time between the moment leaves are harvested and the actual refining process. Furthermore, since improved varieties have been developed and yields have increased, it is also necessary to estimate the effects of technological change on output.

Other data requirements to estimate the industry's value added are: (1) the actual inputs used in the chemical and agro-industrial processes and their prices[6]; (2) price data on coca paste, cocaine base, and cocaine; (3) the share of the Bolivian and Peruvian paste and base that is controlled and internationally marketed by Colombians; (4) the non-Colombian value added in the smuggling process, that is, the amounts paid to foreign pilots and smugglers, bribes, and other transportation costs; (5) the Colombian smugglers' share of each foreign market (United States, Europe, Japan, and other countries) where wholesale prices are different; (6) losses in the production process and by seizures. Every estimate adds uncertainty to the final figure.[7]

The impact of the industry on Colombia depends on the industry's value added within the country, excluding the value added in the smuggling process, and on the amount of revenue brought from abroad. Further estimation problems arise if one takes into consideration the involvement of Colombian expatriates in drug marketing outside the country. Their profits are not Colombian value added, but they can be invested in Colombia, and at least a share of them is (Thoumi 1995a).

It is also possible to estimate the industry's size from the consumption side. To do so it is necessary to figure out world consumption and to use that estimate to derive backward the Colombian market share. This approach also has great weaknesses. Little is known about consumption in several markets, and prevalence data based on surveys do not provide detailed consumption information.[8] It is well known that consumption-based estimates are substantially lower than production estimates, raising further doubts about the latter's accuracy (De Rementería 1995; Steiner 1996; Reuter 1996).

During the last twenty years there have been several attempts to estimate the size of some parts of the illegal drug industry (Junguito and Caballero 1979; Ruiz

Hernández 1979; Gómez 1985, 1988, 1990; Kalmanovitz 1990; Sarmiento 1990; Urrutia 1990; Kalmanovitz and Bernal 1994; Barragán and Vargas 1995; Rocha 1997; Uribe 1997; among others. These studies are summarized in Thoumi 1995a; Steiner 1996; and Rocha 1997). The estimates have a wide range, depending on the set of assumptions made. Cocaine value added estimates range from as little as $0.7 billion to as much as $5 billion; most estimates are in the $1.5 to $3.5 billion range. These figures compare with 1991 estimates of total GDP of about $51 billion and total official merchandise exports of $7.3 billion.

All estimates have important biases. First, reliable data about actual transportation cocaine costs through the Caribbean and Central America to the United States is not available.[9] Second, some Colombians are involved in trafficking within the United States, Europe, and other markets, as witnessed by the large number of Colombians jailed around the world on narcotics charges, but there are no studies that estimate their income and what they send back to Colombia. Third, estimates available do not include marijuana revenues or those generated by the recent development of opium and heroin exports.

On balance, it is likely that these biases underestimate the size of the industry's value added relevant to Colombia, that is, that which ends up in Colombians' hands in and out of the country and that is likely to be brought back to Colombia at some point in time. To figure out the bias, it is necessary to weigh the income generated by opium and heroin and marketing outside Colombia, which is likely to be "large," against the possibly underestimated costs of Colombian traffickers in the smuggling stage. On balance, it is likely that the current studies underestimate the relevant Colombian drug income.

Money-Laundering Constraints[10]

The economic effects of the illegal industry also depend on how difficult is it to launder income and capital. In Colombia there are significant constraints. Money laundering itself is a relatively new policy issue and has only recently been considered a crime in many countries. For a long time Colombia has had "illicit enrichment" legislation that was unenforceable. This was used as the basis of the money-laundering legislation developed during the last decade (Garzón 1997).[11]

Income, asset, and foreign-exchange laundering is a complex phenomenon. Laundering is commonly defined as a process through which illicitly obtained income and capital become disguised to appear legitimate (Cárdenas 1995, 1; Falco et al. 1997, 33). This definition implies a coincidence between legitimacy and legality; but in Colombia, where there is a great gap between de jure and de facto behaviors, it is important to separate them (Thoumi 1995a). Indeed, there are many illegal but legitimate actions, that is, approved by the mores and values of the society or of some of its subgroups. Besides, in Colombia, asset and income laundering are closely related to the weak legitimacy of the Colombian state and property rights (Thoumi 1995c).

For the purposes of this chapter, it is convenient to define *asset and income laundering* as the process through which illegally obtained assets and income are disguised and become identified as legal, separating the concepts of legality and legitimacy. This transformation from illegality to legality requires hiding the origin of the assets and income and minimizing the risk of origin identification after the process. The transformation risks depend heavily on whether laundered income and capital are legitimate: when they are illegal but legitimate, laundering risks and costs are substantially lower.

Asset and income laundering implies the existence of processes for dirtying assets and income (Thoumi 1995a, 1996). In countries where many laws and regulations related to economic activity are evaded, *legality* and *illegality* are words connoting costs and benefits, rather than moral judgments (De Soto 1986). Any profit-maximizing firm will try to obtain the benefits of legal and informal operations while avoiding the costs of both. This is why in Colombia there is a long tradition of individuals and businesses continually dirtying and cleaning assets, that is, evading taxes and regulations, hiding legal capital and making it thereby illegal, and vice versa. From any entrepreneur's viewpoint, the decision to have a proportion of her operations above board and the rest below board is similar to any portfolio management decision in which she has to choose between assets that provide different risks and returns.

To break many economic laws and regulations is legitimate in Colombia, and the government has had to adapt to it. During the last twenty-five years there have been more than ten tax reforms, most of which have included amnesties that recognize the existence of and encourage capital-dirtying systems since they lower the expected costs of future laundering.

In any country every individual has the capacity to dirty and launder an amount of income and capital. Specifically, there is an amount of illegal income that a person can spend and capital that she can accumulate without confiscation or penal sanctions. The risks of those actions increase with income and asset size, but also depend on the individual's behavior, on his or her ability to develop a social support network, on the type of assets invested and consumed, and on the degree of law compliance in the society. The key to successful laundering is to not engage the attention of the authorities or to launder through socially legitimate means.

Conspicuous personal behavior lowers laundering capacity while a modest, low profile increases it as it raises the probability that the laundering operation will not be identified. Social support networks lower the risk for any criminal organization. The capacity to launder is higher when one counts on a loyal and large group of relatives, childhood friends, classmates, and so on, who collaborate in the process. The need for these networks is directly related to the size of the income or assets to be laundered. Assets that are difficult to price and those widely used by other businesses to hide capital are good laundering channels. In Colombia, real estate is in this category. Lastly, in societies where breaking economic laws is widely accepted and legitimate, laundering is easier than where the opposite is the case.

It should be noted that what is sometimes called *asset laundering* does not increase the amount of laundered capital in the society. For example, if a real estate transaction is recorded for a lower sum than the actual one, then the purchaser who paid illegal cash obtains a legal asset while the seller has to hide the excess price. This amount of hidden capital is just transferred from one individual to another who may have a higher capacity to hide such assets because he engages in other activities that can be used to shelter them.

In the idiom of law enforcement, laundering is an *asset-focused phenomenon*. For example, if a crack dealer from a U.S. ghetto goes on a cash-spending spree at a fancy shopping center, then the Department of State does not consider this action to be money laundering because the cash was spent for nondurable consumer goods. For ghetto kids to launder money, they have to end up with an asset to show for it.

The prevalence of dirtying and laundering activities makes it very difficult for a society to legislate against money laundering. Attempts to do so can create a conflict between the law and social mores. For example, any law that defines laundering to cover all illicit income and capital will face strong social opposition. To avoid this problem, current legislation in many countries, including drug-producing ones, criminalizes laundering only when the income or assets are related to illicit drug trafficking[12]; it does not affect income and capital stemming from the violation of many laws and regulations, like nondrug smuggling, tax evasion, and fraud. The legislation implicitly differentiates between dirty but cleanable and dirty but noncleanable assets. Colombian laundering legislation, while it has unusual breadth, covers only income and assets obtained from the illegal drug industry, kidnappings, extortion, and public-sector corruption.

As argued, individuals have a limited capacity to dirty and launder capital without risk of confiscation. Countries also have limits on the amounts that can be laundered within their borders. These depend on the size and structural characteristics of the economy. Laundering illegal drug money in Colombia requires two different and related steps: first, dollar-denominated assets have to be brought into the country and converted into peso-denominated assets; second, those should be disposed of (consumed or invested), minimizing the confiscation risks.

There are few ways to bring illegal assets into the country , and each has limits. Besides, bringing assets into the country per se does not launder them. The most common ways to bring illegal assets into Colombia are contraband of goods; *technical contraband* (import underinvoicing, export overinvoicing, and other trade-related tricks); foreign-exchange cash imports sold to the central bank as labor remittances and other transfers or sold in the black (now parallel) market; purchases of assets in Colombia paid for abroad; and establishing fictitious transnational corporations that invest in Colombia. There are also less-known financial transactions that achieve the same result, like purchasing some Colombian foreign debt bond issues that are sold in foreign currencies but may be redeemed in pesos.

All of these channels are limited. Contraband is limited by local demand; by the need to bring in easily hidden and sold goods whose origin does not have to be justified by the purchaser[13]; by export controls in foreign countries; and by the need to have a collaborating exporter.[14]

Technical contraband is limited by demand for imported goods and price information available to customs officials. It frequently requires the complicity of customs officials and the trade partner (exporter or importer).

Central bank foreign-exchange purchases as labor and other remittances depend on the bank's willingness to accept those funds without asking too many questions about their origin. During the last two decades the bank has changed its policy several times. When the bank eases its purchase requirements, it is said that it "opens its sinister window," and vice versa when it increases them.

Recent estimates of contraband and illegal flows hidden in the current account of the balance of payments show modest amounts (Rocha 1997). On average, the estimates show that these two systems have been used to bring in about $1 billion a year, a figure that highlights the difficulty of bringing in illegal capital.

The Colombian parallel foreign-exchange market is also small and highly volatile. Changes in monthly inflows of a few million dollars have significant effects on the exchange rate. For long periods of time the parallel exchange rate remained below the official one, a unique case in the world that reflects the laundering difficulties.

Asset purchases paid for abroad are also limited and require finding a Colombian resident who wants to invest abroad or who is leaving the country. Capital is highly profitable in Colombia and capital flight has not been significant. It tends to depend more on security factors than on profitability.

Investment opportunities limit the formation of fake transnational corporations to bring in capital. Furthermore, if these are used to purchase existing enterprises, they require the seller's complicity.

Colombia has intermittently issued foreign debt bonds redeemable in pesos, a practice that began more than twenty years ago. These are bearer issued bonds, and their interest and possible capital gains are exempted from Colombian taxes.[15] Recent bond issues approved by Law 55 of 1992, Decree 700 of 1994, and Decree 4308 of 1995 fall into this category. These issues have not been large; the last one in 1995 was for only $80 million. Whoever buys these bonds abroad can use them to convert foreign exchange into pesos, making the state a possible accomplice in a money-laundering operation (Thoumi 1996).

As mentioned above, some means used to bring in dirty foreign exchange do not launder it. For instance, contraband sales in the country do not launder those assets since they remain illegal. The operation increases the assets' safety, they might actually become legitimate, and the need to hide them might decrease since the government will find it very difficult to expropriate them. However, they remain illegal. A similar situation arises when the foreign-exchange bonds mentioned above are cashed in pesos.

The structure of the Colombian economy also imposes important restrictions on the use of the illegal capital once it is in the country. Indeed, the small size of the "laundromat" makes it difficult and costly to launder large amounts of capital. Rocha (1997) shows that Colombia's macroeconomy is easily affected by illegal capital flows precisely because it is difficult to launder large amounts. The limitations of three possible money-laundering investments—the purchase of existing firms and urban and rural real estate—are discussed below.

The Colombian private sector developed in the mist of a lack of trust among market participants. Transaction costs and uncertainty are high, property rights are weak, and the state is not seen as a fair judge, or referee, to enforce contracts and solve conflicts. The structure of the private sector reflects these characteristics.

The public sector's failure to provide effective contract enforcement mechanisms is a strong incentive to integrate vertically and to form economic conglomerates that include financial, manufacturing, advertising, marketing, and retailing firms. Each conglomerate has internal contract enforcement systems that facilitate transactions among their members. It is possible for some of these groups to become monopolists in some markets, but contrary to what took place in the United States in the nineteenth century, most of their rents are not monopolistic: they result from the entrepreneurs' ability to transact within the conglomerates at lower costs than their competitors.

The development of economic conglomerates is a private-sector reaction to the market environment in which it operates. Conglomerates have been a major obstacle to the development of a meaningful stock market since the traded companies are controlled by them, but they have also protected large parts of the formal sector from being penetrated by drug capital. Stock purchases are not attractive to drug entrepreneurs, foreign mutual funds, or domestic investors since those firms are closed companies managed according to the strategy of the conglomerate that controls them. Given the thin stock market, large stock investments require prior agreement with the conglomerate owners. Laundering large amounts using most stocks traded on the stock exchange requires the complicity of the financial conglomerates, who are bound to be very uneasy about acquiring mafiosi as, in effect, junior partners in the enterprise.

According to Colombia's conventional wisdom, urban real estate is an important laundering instrument for drug capital. Barranquilla experienced a real estate boom during the early 1970s when marijuana developed in the Sierra Nevada de Santa Marta; Cali and Medellín had similar experiences during the 1980s cocaine boom. Most real estate transactions in Colombia are recorded at lower than real values, and buyers transfer hidden capital to sellers. However, if an investor wants to launder his capital using real estate, then he must keep possession of the properties or transfer them to front men (*testaferros*) or companies. For instance, if illegal drug funds are used to finance a building project that is then sold and recorded at lower-than-real values, the buyers launder capital through the purchase. In this case the drug industry that finances the project launders somebody else's dirty capital! There is no doubt that urban real estate has been used to launder some drug money, but it has only a limited capacity to serve as a laundering vehicle. Using it on any scale leads to price inflation, overbuilding, and unproductive investments.[16]

Drug money has also flown into rural land. Illegal entrepreneurs or their *testaferros* have bought large tracts, mainly in areas of recent settlement where property rights and state presence are weak.[17] These purchases have frequently taken place in areas of strong guerrilla activity. Drug entrepreneurs have contributed to the creation of self-defense paramilitary groups that fight the guerrillas and thereby raise land values. Rough estimates (Reyes 1997) indicate that illegal drug money has been used to purchase some 4 to 5 million hectares of grazing land. These include a large proportion of the best grazing land available in the country. Further investments are likely to be smaller than in the past as available lands are of lower quality. Recent legislation that facilitates land expropriation is another disincentive to further land purchases by drug entrepreneurs.

The Industry's Effects

Macroeconomic Effects

The macroeconomic effects of the illegal drug industry are complex. The industry has plainly increased the supply of foreign exchange, thus producing effects reminiscent of other export booms; but those effects have been ameliorated by Colombia's macroeconomic management. In contrast with other Latin American countries of similar or larger size (until the 1990s triumph of neoliberalism), Colombia has distinguished itself by avoiding populist governments with their concomitants of runaway fiscal deficits and periodic hyperinflation (Urrutia 1991). Indeed, Colombian macroeconomic management has been remarkably stable. The country had been able to cope with export booms and busts relatively well and was the only one in the region that avoided the Latin American debt crisis of the 1980s.

The increased supply of foreign exchange generated by the illegal drug industry also has different effects in Colombia than in the rest of the region because its effects are less direct. As noted above, most profits are made in the smuggling stage; the amount needed to pay for illegal exports is only a small proportion of total export revenues. Since most income is earned in the currency of the country to which the drugs are delivered, drug capital inflows are largely a function of the same factors influencing other capital inflows, namely interest rate differentials between Colombia and the international markets, mainly the American one, and devaluation expectations in Colombia (Urrutia and Pontón 1993).

Colombian macroeconomic policies changed significantly in 1990, when the country engaged itself in an economic liberalization process similar to that followed by other Latin American countries. The main economic policy changes were[18]:

1. The elimination of exchange controls that had originally been put in place as far back as in 1931 and tightened in 1967. These changes allowed Colombians to have financial accounts and to borrow abroad, and legalized the parallel foreign-exchange market.
2. A decline in import tariffs and the elimination of import quotas and most import licenses.
3. A labor market liberalization making it easier to lay off and fire workers.
4. The establishment of a program to privatize publicly owned companies,

including banks that had been purchased by the government during a financial crisis in the early 1980s.

5. The promotion of direct foreign investment.
6. The promotion of private retirement funds as an alternative to public social security.

Complementary measures included attempts to modernize the judicial system, development of simpler ways to enforce contracts, support of alternative development programs in coca growing areas, reform of the bidding systems for state suppliers, and other measures to eliminate privileges and corruption. All these changes were designed to create a modern capitalist society and had the support of the World Bank, the Inter-American Development Bank, the International Monetary Fund, and several U.S. government agencies. Similar to other developing countries that follow like policies, economic liberalization was accompanied by very large external capital inflows.

In late 1994 the U.S. Drug Enforcement Administration (DEA), wary of the growing influence of the illegal drug industry on Colombia, argued that country's new economic policies provided the illegal industry with inroads into the economy that would make it more difficult to monitor and control (U.S. DEA 1994). First, U.S. drug enforcement officials insisted that elimination of exchange controls made it easier to bring large sums of drug money into the country disguised as foreign investment capital. Second, the privatization of publicly owned banks allowed drug lords to purchase these banks and develop an ostensibly legitimate infrastructure through which to hide and launder capital. Third, officials warned that Colombia lacked restrictive money-laundering laws, which made it easy for drug money to enter the country and penetrate the national economy. Fourth, U.S. officials insisted that the recent construction boom experienced in the country "has been financed primarily by large investments using drug proceeds" (U.S. DEA 1994).

The Colombian government's response to the DEA was quite forceful (Banco de la República 1994). It argued that the DEA's paper "was without any empirical and theoretical basis,"[19] was biased against the government, contradicted many "statements from other U.S. agencies and the Federal government" and "expresses implicitly its preference for a heavily nationalized economy with very little space for the private sector." Important points raised by the government included: (a) the large capital inflows received by Colombia had occurred in all Latin American countries that had followed similar policies; (b) earlier controls had not prevented drug moneys from coming to the country; (c) liberalization did not eliminate the requirement to register capital brought to the country; (d) the construction boom was being financed by a significant increase in credits from savings and loan associations; (e) the financial-system liberalization required "financial institutions to get to know their customers and carry out direct surveillance of transactions"; (f) the privatization of financial institutions had been under the surveillance of the banking superintendency, and no drug moneys had been detected in bank purchases.

This debate illustrates the difficulties associated with trying to identify strong macroeconomic causal relations.[20] On one hand, it is likely that economic liberalization programs facilitate money laundering. On the other hand, it is also true that illegal drug capital flows follow the same pattern as other capital movements, and that the government has instituted systems to control illegal flows. However, within the Colombian environment of widespread acceptance of illegal economic activities, corruption, contraband, and a large underground economy, one has to question whether any of the central bank policies are likely to be effective.

The DEA's paper also illustrates the effects of placing illegal drug policies in a paramount position to which all other policies have to be sacrificed. Indeed, one of the main problems raised by antidrug policies anywhere is the sacrifice they demand of other policy interests including human rights.[21] The DEA's implicit request that Colombian macroeconomic policies should be shaped by its antidrug effort is a good example of the high costs society is asked to pay to achieve repressive drug policy success.

Regional and Sectoral Effects

The impact of the illegal drug industry at the local level has been large at times in cities like Barranquilla, where many marijuana exporters were located, and Medellín, where a large proportion of the cocaine entrepreneurs once lived. These cities experienced *Dutch disease* symptoms when marijuana and cocaine were booming.[22] Similar effects are evident in coca-producing regions, where income boom-and-bust cycles follow coca prices (Thoumi 1995a).

During the 1980s the Medellín export syndicate invested heavily in rural land in the Middle Magdalena Valley. This was a recently settled region where property rights are still questionable, and an area that had a strong guerrilla presence. The drug investors promoted the establishment of "self-defense" paramilitary groups that fought the guerrillas and coincidentally attacked peaceful proponents of a more egalitarian society. During the 1990s rural land investments by the drug industry continued.

Although precise figures are impossible to obtain, Reyes (1997) demonstrates that drug industry rural land purchases have been large. He estimates that drug moneys have purchased around 4 to 5 million hectares of the best and easiest-to-administer grazing lands of the country. (About 10 percent of the country's grazing lands). Reyes's findings indicate that most purchases have been of large ranches and that drug money has not penetrated *minifundia,* or modern agricultural areas. Small purchases have taken place only in areas near cities or in tourist places, where land value increases are expected. These have been minor, however.

Other export syndicates have adopted a lower profile, investing primarily in manufacture, urban real estate, and services. While there is some revealing evidence of these investments, there is almost none concerning the moneys earned by those who have sold chemical precursors, on helped drug traffickers launder their capital and buy "security" from the police and the armed forces. Nor is anything of consequence known about the investment activities of the chemists who help refine cocaine and heroin, the smugglers who help launder drug capital, the small-time drug dealers who have returned from the United States, and so on. In other words, a significant proportion of drug-related income never surfaces and thus may be laundered easily, particularly in a country were money laundering and dirtying is an old art.

For most of the last twenty-five years, the employment effects of the illegal drug industry have been significant in a few isolated regions of Colombia, but not at the national level. However, coca and poppy plantings grew substantially during the 1990s, and coca and poppy growers organized themselves with guerrilla support, so that by 1996 they became a force with which the government had to reckon. In late 1996 peasant protests against aerial coca fumigation, instigated by guerrilla organizations, mobilized some 120,000 peasants and turned coca spraying into a social issue of national magnitude (*Semana* 1996b).

Structural Effects
Independent of the actual amount of foreign exchange brought into the country by drug entrepreneurs and of its macroeconomic effects, there is no doubt that the impact of the industry on Colombia's economy has been quite large. According to national accounts data, private-sector capital formation during the 1980s averaged $2.8 billion a year. A substantial proportion of that amount must be connected to drug exports. After all, any criminal organization exporting fifty or more tons of cocaine a year would have profits that compete with those of the largest financial conglomerates of the country.[23] The bottom line is that any estimate of the size and profits of the illegal drug industry, no matter how conservative, highlights the capacity of the illegal drug industry to change the economic power structure of the country (Thoumi 1995a).

While it can be argued that the drug industry has penetrated many economic activities, it cannot be argued that the performance of the Colombian economy has improved because of drug income. Indeed, the Colombian GDP's rate of growth during the postcocaine era (late 1970s on) has been about 3.2 percent, while it averaged 5.5 percent during the preceding thirty years. This decline cannot be explained by the Latin American foreign debt crisis of the 1980s, which Colombia avoided, or by worse terms of trade or other external conditions during the 1980s than the three earlier decades.

Most Colombian economists who have studied this issue concur that, on balance, the illegal drug industry has had a negative effect on the performance of the Colombian economy. In particular, the drug industry has acted as a catalyst accelerating a process of "delegitimation of the regime." Delegitimation in turn has contributed to the country's stagnation due to increased violence, transaction costs, expenditures in security, increased uncertainty, and a decline in trust, in part fortifying a climate of violence and impunity that has induced "clean" capital flight and larger security costs. This has promoted expectations of very fast wealth accumulation that produced highly speculative investments and increases in bankruptcies, embezzlements, and so forth (Thoumi 1995a, 1995c; Rubio 1996b). Recent studies confirm that the increased level of criminality has had a significant negative effect on the country's income growth rate. Rubio

(1996a, 32b) finds that "the cost of crime in terms of lost growth exceeded 2 percent per year, without including its longer term effects on factor productivity and capital formation."

Most economists also agree that Colombia can do quite well without the illegal drug economy. Colombia has a diversified economy, and before the growth of the illegal drug industry, it generated a significant amount of manufacturing and other exports. Colombia's macroeconomic management has been very prudent and stable, and as I mentioned earlier, the country was the only one in Latin America that avoided the 1980s external debt crisis. If drugs were to disappear today, then the most likely worst-case scenario would be a mild recession for a couple of years, a blip on the screen (Sarmiento 1990; Thoumi 1995a). After this brief period of purging, more rapid growth would ensue.

SOCIAL AND POLITICAL EFFECTS

Some social and political "effects" of the illegal drug industry, like the increased show of wealth and the use of illegal drug moneys to fund political campaigns, are obvious. There is no question that the illegal drug industry has permeated Colombian society: it brought increased violence and criminality,[24] corruption of the political system, a growing social tolerance for criminal and deviant behaviors, and a get-rich-quick mentality. These social and political effects are widespread and more important than any possible economic effect, because they impact the basics of social organization.

In early 1984 members of the Medellín cartel tried to obtain directly at least regional political power. Pablo Escobar ran for Congress and got himself elected; Carlos Lehder established a political movement with strong nationalistic overtones, but it did not progress. Pablo Escobar also developed a strong support base, mainly in some Medellín suburbs and his nearby hometown, Envigado, where he financed public works, housing, and a welfare system. The Medellín cartel invested heavily in rural land, mainly in the Middle Magdalena Valley and areas of the Antioquia and Córdoba regions, where they promoted the formation of self-protection paramilitary groups that fought the guerrillas. These groups have been funded by traditional landowners and by the drug industry and responded to the need to protect property and life in those regions where guerrillas used kidnapping and extortion to finance themselves.

The Medellín cartel did not hesitate to use violence against journalists, other private-sector personalities who opposed them, and public officials. Their early victims were lower-level judges and law enforcement authorities. However, in late April 1984 they escalated by killing Rodrigo Lara Bonilla, the justice minister. The list of victims since then has been long and varied, including politicians, cabinet ministers, judges, journalists, policemen, military personnel, presidential candidates, and others who opposed the drug trade.[25] The 1989 presidential campaign was particularly infamous: three presidential candidates were assassinated. The victims of the violence generated by the Medellín cartel transcended the establishment, because terrorism was also used as a weapon.

During the late 1980s and early 1990s large bombs were frequently employed randomly to create chaos.

The Cali cartel has followed a low-profile political strategy. It developed a strong support network in Cali that included public employees, politicians, and a large cadre of taxi drivers and other common folk. They did not use violence openly against the political establishment and did not appeal to terrorism. Indeed, some of their violence was applied to gain public support, like their "social cleansing" of petty thieves, prostitutes, homosexuals, and other "throwaways" (*desechables*) in Cali.

By 1990 the regime was in a deep "delegitimation" crisis of which the evident power of the drug mafias in comparison to the formal state apparatus was only one element, albeit a possibly catalytic one. The underlining elements of the crisis were as follows[26]:

1. An elitist and undemocratic political system that appealed to widespread clientelism to co-opt the opposition but that was unable to cope with the fast changes of the Colombian society and to democratize it (Leal 1989; Leal and Dávila 1990).
2. A very inefficient state, including a congested and dysfunctional judicial system that nobody trusted. The state had lost its monopoly on violence and its capacity to enforce contracts and protect property rights.
3. Extremely fast growth of criminal and noncriminal underground economies, particularly marijuana and coca growing, and cocaine manufacturing and exporting.
4. Extremely high violence levels comparable to those of countries at war.
5. Guerrilla organizations that had operated for more than forty-five years and that controlled large rural areas.
6. Paramilitary groups that grew as self-protection landowner organizations against the extorting guerrillas and their kidnappings. They control parts of the country and have links with the armed forces.
7. A very high level of nonpolitical and nonmilitary associated violence that has prompted many analysts to claim that Colombians have few internalized behavioral constraints and that they show a total disregard for the effect of their actions on other people (Kalmanovitz 1989; Herrán 1987).

The deep social crisis and the need for significant reforms were first recognized by the Betancur administration (1982–1986), which promoted a dialogue and negotiations with guerrilla movements. The Barco administration (1986–1990) continued seeking reforms that led to a Constitutional Assembly to reform the constitution. The Gaviria administration (1990–1994) approved the new constitution and implemented drastic institutional changes.[27]

Political reforms were of paramount importance to tackling the crisis. The new constitution is very long and complex. To achieve its main goals of "modernizing" the country and promoting democracy, it establishes systems to encourage political participation and the development of grassroots organizations and to increase the government's accountability. One important change that has played a key role in the current crisis has been the creation of a strong "prosecutor general" office independent of the executive branch.

One of the most publicized features of the new constitution is the prohibition against extradition of Colombian nationals. This has been interpreted by at least some elements of the American government as evidence that the illegal drug industry has corrupted the Constitutional Assembly. Recent work by Lee and Thoumi (1998) shows that the influence of the drug industry on the assembly was mainly indirect. Extradition had become a sore issue among "extraditable" drug traffickers (those conspicuous enough to be requested by the American government) who unleashed a "war" against the state, marked by a rash of random explosions. This violence turned public opinion against extradition. The elections for the Constitutional Assembly were peculiar. It was the first time that the left participated as an independent party after the Gaviria administration's peace negotiations with some of the guerrillas, and the left obtained the largest percentage of the vote on record. This representation was against extradition on ideological grounds. The illegal drug industry did support some elected candidates to the assembly, but given the composition of the assembly and the mood of the country at the time, the illegal industry did not have to "buy" assembly members to have extradition declared unconstitutional.

The drug industry did influence the *congresito* (little congress) that followed the Constitutional Assembly and had to ratify the decrees taken by the president during the interim period between the two constitutions. Some of these decrees dealt with the *sometimiento* policy of Gaviria that allowed drug traffickers to turn themselves in, plead guilty to one relatively minor crime, and receive a short sentence (Lee and Thoumi 1998).

Independent of what happened at the Constitutional Assembly, Colombia's polity was and is very vulnerable to illegal drug moneys. The country's geographic segmentation, the isolation of many regions where there is virtually no state presence, combined with political parties that have not had a strong ideology or centralized organizations has produced an environment conducive to the development of the illegal drug industry.

The "National Front" arrangement to end violence in the 1950s amounted to a real power cartel of the two traditional parties that distributed the government as a bounty. The "National Front" divided all government jobs "equitably" (50 percent to each party) and alternated the presidency between liberals and conservatives. It depoliticized the two traditional parties (Leal 1989; Leal and Dávila 1990), which have always been associations of local political leaders (*caudillos*), and converted them into electoral machines whose main purpose was to distribute the public bounty, which included government jobs, the *situado fiscal* (budget funds assigned to each congressman to distribute at will), and the "commissions" on government investment projects and purchases.

In many of the coca- and poppy-growing areas, guerrilla organizations substituted for the state and provided the needed support and protection to plantings and labs (Uribe 1997). In this environment, illegal agriculture, manufacturing, and exporting could be done with the help of local social support networks, which are relatively cheap (Thoumi 1995a) and do not require corruption at high political levels.

As shown above, the "laundromat" is quite small in Colombia relative to the income and capital generated by the illegal drug industry. Small farmers, manufacturers, and exporters can use their own families and friends to launder sums that are large relative to Colombians' incomes but that are small in the large scheme of the illegal drug trade.[28] However, laundering large sums requires support and protection at high social and political levels. In Colombia it is impossible to launder large sums (say $10 million) inconspicuously. The concentration of the industry in a few large cartels in the export stage has forced those cartels to seek political support at the highest level in order to protect their investments and also to fend off extradition.

Colombian society has been ambivalent toward the illegal drug industry. In an environment in which virtually everybody breaks economic laws, one marked by radical individualism, an appalling lack of human solidarity, and an ethics of inequality that encourages people to gain wealth at any cost, it is very difficult, if not impossible, to single out one illegal economic activity as evil or to be punished while others are socially tolerated.

The Colombian government has been able to obtain widespread support for antidrug activities and to implement strong antidrug policies *only* when illegal drug entrepreneurs have used terrorist tactics against key social figures and have been seen as a social threat to all other consequential social groups. The lack of societal support would make it difficult for the government to implement harsh antidrug measures even when political leaders at the top had the "political will" to do so. In many Colombian circles the simplistic statement "when there is demand there is supply" is frequently used to justify the country's involvement in the drug industry, particularly when the United States pressures the government.[29]

From the early 1970s, when the illegal industry began to grow in Colombia, until the end of the Gaviria administration, Colombian governments argued that drug trafficking was a global problem that Colombia could not solve, and that the country's fight was against narco-terrorism. However, after Pablo Escobar was killed and the Medellín cartel was dismantled, at the end of the Gaviria administration, the United States began to pressure Colombia to fight a "war on drugs," not just a war against "narco-terrorism." These pressures would have been felt by the Samper administration regardless of how his campaign was financed.

The fight against narco-terrorism itself increased the government's vulnerability to the drug industry because the demise of the Medellín cartel was achieved, at least partly, with the collaboration of the Cali cartel. According to the DEA and other sources, the two main cartels had fought for control of some U.S. markets, mainly New York City, and had other conflicts in Colombia. The two main cartels formed alliances with different segments of Colombian society with disastrous political effects. The Medellín cartel promoted the development of paramilitary groups to protect their rural investments and developed some links with army personnel. The Cali cartel developed better intelligence capabilities against the Medellín cartel than the police itself and established alliances with the police and politicians.[30] The police also helped the cartel's social-cleansing campaign against "throwaways" in Cali, and army personnel helped clean the Middle Magdalena Valley of guerrillas. The Cali cartel supplied the police vital information that led to the demise of Pablo Escobar and his organization. The Medellín syndicate, led by Pablo Escobar, offered a bounty for the head of each policeman, which resulted in many of them being killed. The conflicts between the cartels and their links with different parts of the government resulted in divisions and widespread distrust among government offices fighting the war on drugs.

The war against narco-terrorism had other effects: it eliminated the most violent bullies from the illegal business and promoted an increase in sophistication among the remaining traffickers. The Cali organization took advantage of Colombia's clientelistic system to build a political support base. This was accomplished by funding politicians and their campaigns. As noted above, the election campaign of the Samper administration was heavily financed by the illegal drug industry, which caused an unprecedented political crisis,[31] the highlight of which was a presidential trial in Congress forced by the prosecutor general.[32] The trial had to deal with two main issues: first, whether Samper knew that illegal drug moneys had entered his campaign, as Fernando Botero, the campaign director claimed, and secondly, whether campaign expenditure limits had been broken and the campaign accounting falsified to collect state matching funds. It was not possible to prove that Samper knew about drug funds entering his campaign. Samper alleged that he had been too busy with the political aspects of the campaign to bother with its finances. Botero claimed that he had discussed campaign finances with Samper, but could not present definitive proof.[33] A related point that strengthened the president's position was simply that at the time of the campaign, Colombia did not have enforceable antimoney laundering legislation.

With respect to the second issue, violation of campaign expenditure limits, one of the provisions of the 1991 constitution established that the government would provide matching campaign funds as long as the total campaign expenditures did not exceed certain limits. This was potentially a stronger accusation and one that Samper could not dodge because compliance was legally his responsibility, independent of whether he was aware of any violations. The accusation was simply that Samper's campaign had exceeded the limits and had altered its accounting to claim government funds. This implied that the campaign had defrauded the state of more than two million dollars, a clearly defined and easy-to-prosecute crime. However, Samper got off on a technicality. Because of the continuous inflation experienced in Colombia, expenditure limits have to be established by the Electoral Court six months ahead of each campaign and published in the *Diario Official*. The Electoral Court did not meet these requirements and in 1995 the Consejo de Estado (Council of State) declared the expenditure limits unapplicable. Interestingly, both presidential candidates had expressed knowledge of the limits, and both campaigns had sought ways around them. In Colombia's legalistic system, with its literalist interpretative tradition, whether either the spirit of the law or justice is respected is irrelevant![34]

Samper's trial is another example of the high societal price of fighting the "drug war" at any cost, that is, making it into a *jihad*, overriding every other national goal and moral or prudential constraints. Independent of whether Samper knew about or authorized or condoned the entrance of drug moneys to his campaign coffers, the legal case against him was very weak.[35] First, illicit enrichment legislation had not been "typified," that is, the crime itself had not been defined and the legislation was unenforceable. Second, most drug funds came from legal companies that fronted for the cartel and contributed checks from legal accounts in approved banks. Third, the illicit enrichment legislation required Samper's personal net worth to have increased, which did not happen since all moneys were spent in the campaign. The trial was an attempt to turn a political issue into a criminal one. In a country where perhaps the main problem is the weakness of the legal and judicial systems, attempts to bend the law to achieve a political goal set dangerous precedents.

Besides the legal weaknesses of the case against Samper, the political establishment whose stronghold was the Colombian Congress that tried the president had too much to lose with a presidential conviction. The evolution of the clientelistic political system weakened the two traditional parties while inhibiting the development of political alternatives. Samper was indicted and tried by a Congress controlled by the two party machines. A significant number of congressmen and other politicians had received support from the drug industry and were also at risk. The weak and corrupt political system did not provide a viable political alternative to Samper, and the opposition was unable to muster a majority in Congress to convict him.

Samper survived, but at a high cost. The country was divided, and government expenditures and policies were used to anchor the weak administration. Indeed, labor unions, financial conglomerates, guerrillas, paramilitary groups, some private sector associations, some political groups and nongovernment organizations, and so on, sensed the weakness of the government and tried to extract from it as many favors as possible in exchange for their support or nonaggression.

The Samper administration arrived in power with the goals of lowering inflation, increasing social sector expenditures, and deepening democracy. These goals fell victim to an administration whose main goal was to simply survive. Thus the "social pact" established to control price increases caused mainly by inertial inflation was not respected because any group that felt needed by the government was able to force favorable price, wage, or government expenditure increases. Possible peace negotiations in Colombia were another important victim of the crisis. The weak government lacked credibility and the power to launch a strong peace process, in which one would like to have the participation of the armed forces, guerrillas, paramilitaries, and parts of the drug industry related to those organizations.

Colombia-United States relations deteriorated to historically low levels. In

1996 the United States government "decertified" Colombia for the first time and exerted other very strong pressure on its Colombian counterpart. The latter responded with strong antidrug efforts. Nevertheless, the official U.S. version discounted Colombia's efforts on the grounds that they were the result of its own pressure and not of the Colombian government's conviction. The direct effects of "decertification" have been minor, since the United States did not apply any discretionary economic sanction. Decertification prohibits export-import bank credits (which are not relevant for Colombia) and requires the U.S. executive directors at the World Bank and the Inter-American Development Bank to oppose any project for Colombia outside those dealing directly with the antidrug effort. However, the United States does not have veto power in any of these institutions and has not lobbied other countries to block any loans. The United States has taken some discretionary measures, but these have been mostly symbolic, like canceling Samper's and other politicians' tourist visas.

The indirect decertification effects—such as a discouragement of direct foreign investment, higher interest rates on private sector loans to Colombia, and a shift of some Colombian industries abroad in anticipation of possible trade sanctions—can become important.[36] On March 31 1997, the U.S. government decertified Colombia again, a controversial decision in view of a full certification of Mexico, a country whose government has also been infiltrated by the illegal drug industry.[37]

AS A WAY OF CONCLUSION

A balanced view of the effects of the illegal drug industry on Colombia shows that insofar as the economy is concerned, the effects have been important but not yet overwhelming and that not only can Colombia's economy survive but it can improve without illegal drugs. On the other hand, because Colombian political and social systems were more vulnerable, the illegal industry's effects on them have been dramatic.

The current political crisis has reached a depth unknown in twentieth-century Colombia. The country's economy, known for its resiliency, is finally showing signs of significant deterioration, and Colombians feel they are in a mist of a social crisis. Pessimism about current and future social, political, and economic conditions among Colombians has risen to unprecedented levels.[38] *Semana's* 1996 survey attributes the large increases in pessimism to a widespread feeling of collective social failure.

There is no question that the illegal drug industry has had dramatic effects on Colombian society and that the current political crisis was triggered by the industry's financing of Samper's presidential campaign. However, the causal relations between drugs and crisis are not easy to ascertain.

One main issue is whether the Colombian political and social conditions led to the development of the illegal drug industry in the country, or whether this event was just the result of malevolent chance. If the latter is true, then the causality is clear and goes from illegal drugs to violence, corruption, and so forth.

If, as argued elsewhere (Thoumi 1995a), Colombia developed its competitive advantage in illegal drugs because it had the best conditions for the industry to grow there, due in significant measure to the weakness of the regime, then the causality goes the other way: the social, political, and economic environment in Colombia was the cause of the industry's location in that country. In that case, the illegal drug industry has acted mainly as a catalyst and accelerator in a process that had already begun. Within this framework, one should look at what has been happening in Colombia as an evolutionary process in which the drug industry is playing a role, but in which the causal relation between illegal drugs and social problems and crises is not well defined, since those variables interact and feed each other with no happy end in sight.

NOTES

1. Recent reports suggest that Mexicans have been wrestling control of the U.S. market from Colombians.
2. Typical prices in the coca-cocaine industry circa 1996 were $300 to $500 for the leaves required to produce a kilogram of cocaine; $500 to $700 for the paste processed with those leaves; about $1,000 for the cocaine base; $1,500 to $2,000 f.o.b. of a wholesale kilogram of cocaine; $14,000 to $20,000 c.i.f. per kilogram of cocaine at the port of entry in the United States, and higher prices in Europe. The street value of a kilogram of cocaine sold by the gram diluted to 60 or 70 percent purity reaches $120,000 and more.
3. The large variations in employment, income, and income concentrations are one of the main reasons why the effects of the illegal industry in Colombia are very different from those in Bolivia and Peru (Thoumi, 1995b).
4. The main study of this development is Ruiz-Hernández (1979).
5. The difficulties inherent to the data are well known (Thoumi 1995a; Clawson and Lee 1996; Reuter 1996).
6. All inputs used to produce cocaine can be substituted. When one input market is controlled, producers use others or develop new ways to obtain the same result.
7. Similar estimation problems arise in poppy-opium-morphine-heroin, marijuana, and synthetic drugs.
8. Typical questions asked in those surveys are: Have you ever consumed a particular drug? Have you consumed it within the last year? Within the last month? These questions do not provide good data about frequency, patterns, and amounts consumed each time.
9. DEA estimates that recently Mexicans have charged a 40 to 50 percent commission in specie to smuggle cocaine to the United States. DEA also estimates costs of about 10 to 15 percent when smuggling is done directly by Colombian traffickers. The proportion of drugs exported using various routes is not known and varies through time.
10. This section is based on Thoumi (1996).
11. The development of this legislation has also advanced in other countries. See Lamas (1995) for the Peruvian case.
12. This is the case of the Peruvian legislation, although money-laundering sentences increase if the money laundering is related to armed subversion (Lamas 1995).
13. For example, a legal importer frequently uses legal imports to shield similar goods imported illegally.
14. One of the most notable complicity examples is given by the U.S. tobacco industry that exports ridiculously large amounts of cigarettes to Panama, Aruba, Curaçao, Margarita, and other Caribbean islands knowing that many of those products are

smuggled into Colombia. Aruba's cigarette imports are four times its GDP! (Steiner 1996).

15. It seems that these bonds were designed to be sold to Colombians who had taken capital out of the country, legitimating exchange control evasion.
16. There are many reports about the several hundred apartments that the Cali cartel had in that city. Most of them were vacant. One has to wonder how many more they would have purchased if they had not been captured. Chances are not many, because they were simply an economic waste.
17. Reyes (1997) gives a detailed picture of this process.
18. See Thoumi (1997) for a detailed discussion of these events.
19. Indeed, the DEA does not have strong economics capabilities and its paper lacked the rigor of World Bank, IMF, or Colombian government reports.
20. Urrutia and Pontón (1993) and O'Byrne and Reina (1993) are good examples of well-grounded yet polar views about the importance of illegal-drug capital flows.
21. The literature about this issue is substantial and growing. See, for example, Balakar and Grinspoon (1984), McWilliams (1996), Husak (1992) and Peele (1989).
22. The term *Dutch disease* refers to the effects of a primary product boom on the producing area. The main point is that the boom raises labor and other local costs, making the region less competitive in the production of other goods and services. When this happens, the region imports more goods and services and its economy tends to become specialized in the booming product and services that cannot be imported.
23. A back-of-the-envelope estimate places export profits at about $10,000 per kilogram or $500 million per fifty tons. *Semana* (1996a) estimates that in 1995 the four largest formal-economy financial groups had profits of $530, $140, $480, and $190 million respectively.
24. The World Bank (1997) based on Pan American Health Organization data, indicates that during the late 1980s and early 1990s Colombia had approximately 90 violent deaths per 100,000 inhabitants, a figure that had increased from about 20 ten years earlier. The corresponding figure is about 10 in the United States, the most violent developed country. Other Latin American countries known for their violence, like Brazil and Mexico, show up at about 18 in the late 1980s-early 1990s. Data on kidnappings are weaker than those for violent deaths because many kidnappings are not reported to the authorities. Still, journalistic reports suggest that during 1995 and 1996 Colombia experienced 40 to 50 percent of all the kidnappings in the world!
25. Thoumi (1995a) provides a partial victim's list.
26. These points are developed in Thoumi (1997).
27. Santos Calderón's (1989) collection of newspaper articles provides an excellent chronology and analysis of the events that led to the Constitutional Assembly.
28. For instance, a drug-trafficking family is likely to be able to launder say $200,000 a year without raising suspicion.
29. For example, in a recent column, Alfonso Cano (1997) condemns the United States's "double morals" after that country's "decertification" of Colombia: "With its characteristic arrogance, the United States government self-proclaims a universal veto power over cocaine and heroin producing countries, whose only sin has been the unfortunate fact that some of its citizens decided to turn its lands into immense plantings of coca and poppy, to use its industrial complexes to process, elaborate, and distribute the drugs derived from those plants, all in order to supply the growing number of psychoactive drug consumers in the world, who paradoxically, are mainly young Americans." This statement is particularly revealing because the author is the brother of Guillermo Cano, the editor of *El Espectador*, who was assassinated by the Medellín cartel ten years ago, and because it appeared in *El Espectador*, a newspaper with an antidrug tradition that has been a victim of several terrorist attacks.
30. Interview with DEA Washington personnel in December 1992. The DEA version has been ratified by recent works (Castillo 1996).

31. By the end of 1996, Fernando Botero, the former director of Samper's campaign and former minister of defense, Santiago Medina, the former campaign treasurer, and former senators Gustavo Espinosa and Alberto Santofimio were serving sentences. Former campaign manager Juan Manuel Avella, former Attorney General Orlando Vásquez-Velásquez, former Comptroller Manuel Francisco Becerra, former senators Eduardo Mestre, Armando Holguín Sarria, and José Guerra de la Espriella, former representatives Tiberio Villarrreal, Alvaro Benedetti, Ana García de Petchalt and Rodrigo Garavito, former head of the presidencial guard Coronel Germán Osorio and General Farouk Yanine were detained and being tried. However, Ernesto Samper remained in power.

32. Vargas, Lesmes, and Téllez (1996) present a very detailed journalistic account and analysis of the events of 1994, 1995, and 1996 that led to and included Samper's trial.

33. It is true that it cannot be proven that Samper knew. However, chances are very slim that he did not know. Samper and Botero spent many hours together every day during the campaign and campaign finances were a key campaign issue, specially after the first round, when the campaign found itself very short of funds.

34. Samper's campaign falsified its accounting to comply with the limits. Andrés Pastrana, the other presidential contender, nationally divided the campaign into "his" campaign in Bogotá and seven regional campaigns he claimed were not part of "his" campaign. Even doing so, "his" campaign exceeded the limits, but he got off the hook when he received a favorable ruling that established that the actual campaign limit was equal to the limits set by the Electoral Court plus the government matching funds received. This interpretation presents a logical problem since the amount of matching funds is not determined by the amount spent itself but by the amount of votes received, implying that the limits are determined after the election returns are known. In any case, this issue became mute when the expenditure limits were dismissed. Such is life in the tropics!

35. López-Caballero (1997) analyses the case against Samper, highlighting its weaknesses and legal contradictions.

36. For example, Colombian flower producers have tried to move some of their operations to countries like Ecuador and Costa Rica.

37. The U.S. Department of State's version is that Colombian president Ernesto Samper actively sought campaign funds from the drug industry while Mexican President Ernesto Zedillo actively opposed the industry. Apparently it is not important being Earnest, but it is important being Samper or Zedillo.

38. *Semana* (1996c) shows that in December 1994, at the beginning of the political crisis, 38 percent of Colombians believed that conditions in the country were improving while 31 percent believed they were worsening. Subsequent surveys showed continuous increases in the proportion of those who believed conditions were worsening and continuous declines among those who believed conditions were improving. By the end of October 1996 only 9 percent believed in improving conditions while a whopping 86 percent believed conditions were worsening.

WORKS CITED

Balakar, James B., and Lester Grinspoon. 1984. *Drugs in a Free Society*. Cambridge: Cambridge University Press.

Banco de la República. 1994. Comments to the Document Colombian Economic Reform: the Impact of Drug Money Laundering within the Colombian Economy, Published by the Intelligence Division of the United States Drug Enforcement Agency [sic] (DEA). Bogotá.

Barragán, Jacqueline, and Ricardo Vargas. 1995. Amapola en Colombia: economía illegal, violencias e impacto regional. In *Drogas poder y región en Colombia*, vol. 2, ed. R. Vargas. Bogotá: CINEP

Cano Isaza, Alfonso. 1997. De la doble moral y la extradición. *El Espectador*, 9 Mar., 2–A.

Cárdenas, Jorge Hernán. 1995. The Anti-Money Laundering Effort: Some Elements for Analysis. Washington, D.C.: World Bank. Mimeo.

Castillo, Fabio. 1996. *Los nuevos jinetes de la cocaína*. Bogotá: Oveja Negra.

Clawson, Patrick L., and Rensselaer W. Lee III. 1996. *The Andean Cocaine Industry*. New York: St. Martin's Press.

De Rementería, Ibán. 1995. *La elección de las drogas: Exámen de las políticas de control*. Lima: Fundación Friedrich Ebert.

De Soto, Hernando. 1986. *El otro sendero: la revolución informal*. Lima: Editorial El Barranco.

Falco, Mathea, et al. 1997. *Rethinking International Drug Control: New Directions for U.S. Policy*. Task Force Reports, Council on Foreign Relations, New York.

Garzón, Edgar. 1997. Estudios sobre aspectos legales y praxis del narcotráfico y lavado de dinero en Colombia. *Drogas ilícitas en Colombia: su impacto económico, político y social*, ed. F. Thoumi. Dirección Nacional de Estupefacientes and UNDP, Bogotá: Editorial Planeta.

Gómez, Hernando J. 1985. Colombian Illegal Economy: Size, Evolution and Economic Impact. Brookings Institution, mimeo.

———. 1988. La economía illegal en Colombia: tamaño, evolución e impacto económico. *Coyuntura Económica* 18, no. 3 (Sept): 93–113.

———. 1990. El tamaño del narcotráfico y su impacto económico. *Economía Colombiana*, nos. 226–227 (Feb.–Mar.): 8–17.

Herrán, María Teresa. 1987. *La Sociedad de la mentira*. 2d. ed. Bogotá: Fondo Editorial CEREC—Editorial la Oveja Negra.

Husak, Douglas N. 1992. *Drugs and Rights*. Cambridge: Cambridge University Press.

Jaramillo, Jaime E., Leonidas Mora, and Fernando Cubides, eds. 1989. *Colonización, coca y guerrilla*. 3d. ed. Bogotá: Alianza Editorial Colombiana.

Junguito, Roberto, and Carlos Caballero. 1979. La otra economía. *Coyuntura Económica*. VIII, no. 4 (Dec.): 103–39.

Kalmanovitz, Salomón. 1989. *La Encrucijada de la sinrazón y otros ensayos*. Bogotá: Tercer Mundo Editores.

———. 1990. La economía del narcotráfico en Colombia. *Economía Colombiana*, nos. 226–27 (Feb.–Mar.): 18–28.

Kalmanovitz, Salomón and Rafael H. Bernal. 1994. Análisis macroeconómico del narcotráfico en la economía colombiana. *Drogas, poder y región en Colombia*, vol. 1, ed. Ricardo Vargas. Bogotá: CINEP.

Lamas, Luis. 1995. Estudio sobre aspectos legales y praxis penal del control del lavado de dinero en el Perú. Lima: UNDP.

Leal, Francisco. 1989. El sistema político del clientelismo. *Análisis Político*, 8 (Sept.–Dec.): 8–32.

Leal, Francisco (ed.). 1996. *Tras las huellas de la crisis política*. Bogotá: Tercer Mundo Editores–FESCOL–IEPRI (UN).

Leal, Francisco and Andrés Dávila. 1990. *Clientelismo: el sistema político y su expresión regional*. Bogotá: Tercer Mundo Editores.

Lee, Rensselaer W. III and Francisco E. Thoumi. 1998. El nexo entre las organizaciones criminales y la poítica en Colombia. *Ensayo y Error*, 4, April.

López, Andrés, in collaboration with Olga Lucía González. 1997. Costos para el gobierno colombiano del combate a la producción, la comercialización y el consumo de drogas y a la violencia generada por el narcotráfico. In *Drogas ilícitas en Colombia: su impacto económico, político y social*, ed. F. Thoumi. Dirección Nacional de Estupefacientes and UNDP, Bogotá: Editorial Planeta.

López-Caballero, Juan Manuel. 1997. *La Conspiración: el libro blanco del juicio al presidente Samper.* Bogotá: Editorial Planeta.

McWilliams, Peter. 1996. *Ain't Nobody's Business If You Do: The Absurdity of Consensual Crimes in Our Free Country.* Los Angeles: Prelude Press.

Molano, Alfredo. 1987. *Selva adentro: una historia oral de la colonización del guaviare.* Bogotá: El Ancora Editores.

O'Byrne, Andrés, and Mauricio Reina. 1993. Flujos de capital y diferencial de intereses en Colombia: ¿Cuál es la Causalidad? In *Macroeconomía de los flujos de capital en Colombia y América Latina,* ed. Mauricio Cárdenas and Luis J. Garay. Bogotá: Tercer Mundo Editores–FEDESARROLLO–FESCOL.

Peele, Stanton. 1989. *Diseasing of America: Addiction Treatment Out of Control.* Lexington, MA and Toronto: Lexinton Books.

Reyes, Alejandro. 1997. La compra de tierras por narcotraficantes en Colombia. In *Drogas ilícitas en Colombia: su impacto económico, político y social,* ed. F. Thoumi. Dirección Nacional de Estupefacientes and UNDP, Bogotá: Editorial Planeta.

Rocha, Ricardo. 1997. Aspectos económicos de las drogas ilegales en Colombia. In *Drogas ilícitas en Colombia: su impacto económico, político y social,* ed. F. Thoumi. Dirección Nacional de Estupefacientes and UNDP, Bogotá: Editorial Planeta.

Rubio, Mauricio. 1996a. Crimen y crecimiento en Colombia. In *Hacia un enfoque integrado del desarrollo: ética, violencia y seguridad ciudadana, encuentro de reflexión.* Washington, D.C.: Inter-American Development Bank.

———— 1996b. Reglas del juego y costos de transacción en Colombia. Centro de Estudios sobre Desarrollo Económico (CEDE), Universidad de Los Andes, Documento CEDE 96–08, Bogotá.

Ruiz Hernández, Hernando. 1979. Implicaciones sociales y económicas de la producción de la marihuana." In *Marihuana: Legalización o Represión,* ed. Asociación Nacional de Instituciones Financieras. Bogotá: Biblioteca ANIF de Economía.

Reuter, Peter. 1996. The Mismeasurement of Illegal Drug Markets: the Implications of Its Irrelevance. *Exploring the Underground Economy,* ed. S. Pozo. Kalamazoo, MI: W. E. Upjohn Institute.

Santos Calderón, Enrique. 1989. *Fuego cruzado: guerrilla, narcotráfico y paramilitares en la Colombia de los ochentas.* Bogotá: Fondo Editorial CEREC.

Sarmiento, Eduardo. 1990. Economía del narcotráfico. In *Narcotráfico en Colombia: dimensiones políticas, económicas, jurídicas e internacionales,* ed. Carlos G. Arrieta et al. Bogotá: Tercer Mundo Editores-Ediciones Uniandes.

Semana. 1996a. "Los cuatro grandes." 731: 56–64, 30 April–7 May 7.

————. 1996b. Aquí estamos y aquí nos quedamos. 745: 32–35, Aug. 13–20.

————. 1996c. "Pesimismo." 757: 24–34, Nov. 5–12.

Steiner, Roberto. 1996. Los ingresos de Colombia producto de la exportación de drogas ilícitas. *Coyuntura Económica* (Dec).

Thoumi, Francisco E. 1987. Some Implications of the Growth of the Underground Economy in Colombia. *Journal of Interamerican Studies and World Affairs* 29, 2 (Summer).

————. 1995a. *Political Economy and Illegal Drugs in Colombia.* Boulder, CO: Lynne Rienner.

————. 1995b. Los efectos económicos de las drogas ilegales y las agendas de política en Bolivia, Colombia y Perú. *Colombia Internacional* 29: 7–17 (Jan.–Mar.).

————. 1995c. Derechos de propiedad en Colombia: debilidad, ilegitimidad y algunas implicaciones económicas. Bogotá: CEI-Uniandes, *Documentos Ocasionales,* 38, Apr.-June.

————. 1996. Legitimidad, lavado de activos y divisas, drogas ilegales y corrupción en Colombia. *Ensayo y Error* 1:1 (Nov).

————. 1997. U.S., Colombia Struggle Over Drugs, Dirty Money. *Forum for Applied Research and Public Policy* 12:1 (Spring).

United States Drug Enforcement Administration (DEA). 1994. Colombian Economic

Reform: The Impact on Drug Money Laundering within the Colombian Economy. Drug Intelligence Report, Washington, D.C. Sept.

Uribe, Sergio. 1997. Los cultivos ilícitos en Colombia. *Drogas ilícitas en Colombia: su impacto económico, político y social.* ed. F. Thoumi. Dirección Nacional de Estupefacientes and UNDP, Bogotá: Editorial Planeta.

Urrutia, Miguel. 1990. Análisis costo-beneficio del tráfico de drogas para la economía colombiana. *Coyuntura Económica* 20, 3:115–26 (Oct.).

———. 1991. On the Absence of Economic Populism in Colombia. In *The Macroeconomics of Populism in Latin America,* ed. Rudiger Dornbush and Sebastián Edwards. Chicago: University of Chicago Press.

Urrutia, Miguel, and Adriana Pontón. 1993. Entrada de capitales, diferenciales de interés y narcotráfico. In *Macroeconomía de los flujos de capital en Colombia y América Latina,* ed. Mauricio Cárdenas and Luis J. Garay. Bogotá: Tercer Mundo Editores–FEDESARROLLO–FESCOL.

Vargas, Mauricio, Jorge Lesmes, and Edgar Téllez. 1996. *El Presidente que se iba a caer.* Bogotá: Editorial Planeta.

World Bank. 1997. Crime and Violence as Development Issues in Latin America and the Caribbean. Presented at the seminar The Challenge of Urban Criminal Violence, The State of Rio de Janeiro and Inter-American Development Bank, Rio de Janeiro, 2–4 Mar.

Zabludoff, Sid. 1994. Colombian Narcotics Organizations as Business Enterprises. In *Economics of the Narcotics Industry,* ed. U.S. Department of State and Central Intelligence Agency. Conference Report, Washington, D.C. 21–22 Nov.

THE DECENTRALIZATION IMPERATIVE AND CARIBBEAN CRIMINAL ENTERPRISES

7

Anthony P. Maingot

INTRODUCTION

On September 12, 1998, Deochan Ramdhanie, considered one of the major "drug lords" of the island of Trinidad and who was serving a life sentence, simply walked out of jail and disappeared. It was soon revealed that the total bribes that secured the cooperation of corrupt police were over U.S.$1 million and that Ramdhanie was already in Venezuela where, according to local police sources, he had good connections and "direct links with the Colombian cartels."[1] The escape seemed to exasperate the society, which, according to the major daily, had seen too many commissions of enquiry into the drug trade, police corruption, and the government's apparent incapacity to control either. "Hereinafter," editorialized the *Trinidad Guardian*, "how this matter is handled can speak volumes about the society's ability to win this war on drugs."[2] Nearly two weeks after the escape, the government had made no official statement about the matter, which led the same paper to conclude editorially that: "This is, in a word, a scandal!"[3] On October 7 it was announced that Ramdhanie had been captured in Venezuela by a "joint operation" of the Venezuelan police and the U.S. Drug Enforcement Administration (DEA).[4]

It is this sense of local frustration with native capabilities in the face of obvious transnational criminal links, combined with the evidence of increasing American involvement, which has led some observers to question whether these islands are, indeed, viable. Some believe that, given the enormity of the challenges from organized crime, they are not, and that the United States should consider officially taking on police duties.[5] The problem with such approaches, however, is that they focus too narrowly on the small islands and fail to understand how the "viability" issue should also be broached vis-à-vis larger countries that manifest all the elements of threat from organized crime. The fact that no reasonable person would suggest a direct policing role for these lareger countries indicates that the operative variable in the question of viability is size. As plausible as such an assumption is, the issue of size and viability is best left as an empirical question rather than as a given.

Let us, for the sake of argument, take an example with strong parallels to the Ramdhanie case in Trinidad: the Cuntrera family and the Venezuelan-Italian connection.

The case of Pasquale Cuntrera and his family, who were all Italian citizens, had long been a scandal in Venezuela, where they operated as influential businessmen. Accused in Italy of mafia connections, including drug running, Cuntrera was suddenly "removed" from Venezuela by Italian Carabinieri Commandos. He was then sentenced by an Italian court to 21 years incarceration. None of this was ever fully explained in Venezuela. In May of 1998, Cuntrera, supposedly sick and provided with a wheelchair, simply wheeled himself out of an Italian appeals hearing and disappeared.[6] Cuntrera was eventually arrested by a joint Italian-Spanish-Interpol operation in Malaga, Spain, just as he was to board a chartered flight back to Venezuela, where, according to an in-depth report of Rome's *Corriere della Sera* (May 26, 1998, 1, 13), "he had many friends." It is instructive to realize that these "friends" must have obviously survived a major Venezuelan-Italian antinarcotics operation in mid-1997 in which some fifty individuals belonging to over a dozen Italian mafia families had been arrested.[7] The journalistic version was that the Venezuelan-Italian connection had replaced the Colombians as the main merchants and transporters of both cocaine and heroin through the Caribbean to Spain, where the goods were received by Spanish gangs under local Italian mafia control. According to local officials, these Venezuelan operations were laundering their monies through the offshore centers not just of the Caribbean but of Switzerland, Spain, Italy, and Kuwait. That the mid-1997 sweep had not dismantled the Cuntrera family was made evident with the arrest in May of 1998 of another Cuntrera said to be "a major official of the Cuntrera clan."[8]

U.S. sources are very specific about what makes both Venezuela and Brazil very attractive to major international cartels and, as a logical extension, puts the islands of the Caribbean at great risk. The first element is geography: they both border at least one of the major producing countries, Bolivia, Peru, and Colombia. Secondly, there is widespread corruption in the police and judiciary. Third, major opportunities exist for laundering the proceeds: lax banking laws, extensive networks of nonbanking financial institutions (that is, currency exchange houses), and virtually unregulated networks of casinos, bingo halls, and multiple other games of chance. Finally, their increasingly open economies provide ever-increasing opportunities for fraudulent invoicing of both imports and exports, participation in privatization programs, and entry into the extensive, and historically unregulated, expansion of real estate holdings.[9]

One can conclude, therefore, that there is nothing occurring in the islands that was not occurring, writ large, on the mainland. Having said this, it still begs the question as to whether size is the key variable in the viability question. A brief review of other aspects of organized crime in the insular Caribbean will explain why size is indeed a key factor and why the polity and civility of these small states are indeed threatened.

In February 1998 the Colombian magazine *Semana* described the widespread links of the Russian mafias with the Cali cartel. *Semana*, quoting Russian sources, spoke of over 4,000 Russian groups. In fact the story had already been broken by Douglas Farah of the *Washington Post*.[10] The Russians could offer the Colombians several things: sophisticated weapons, contacts in New York, Miami, Puerto Rico, and several Caribbean offshore banking centers (Antigua, Aruba, St. Vincent), as well as a cocaine-for-heroin exchange arrangement in Europe.

In July 1998, the *Miami Herald* probed the Miami dimension of the Russian mafias–Cali cartel network.[11] Miami is central to the scheme. "There is no need for Russian criminals to come [to Colombia]," says the Russian ambassador in Bogotá, "they make all their contacts with Colombian gangs in Miami."[12] This is not a new role for Miami, which in many ways plays a Caribbean-wide role not unlike that of Venezuela. "What elevates Miami to the top of Russian organized crime in the U.S. is the access to banks in the Caribbean and drugs in Latin America," says the head of the FBI's organized crime branch in Miami. A dozen Russian gangs are believed to be operating in Miami.[13] It should come as no surprise, therefore, that increasing numbers of Caribbean islands are offering the same as Miami and more: not just bank secrecy but also something called "economic citizenship." For $25,000–$50,000, places like Grenada, Belize, St. Kitts, and Antigua offer the Russians new passports to travel with. Dominica even allows them to adopt new names on the new passports. Indeed, Larry Rohter of the *New York Times* quotes a U.S. official who described St. Kitts as the English-speaking Caribbean state that came "closest to devolution into a narcostate."[14] Others describe the Dominican Republic as the "center of the drug trade."[15] A perceptive anthropologist with a good knowledge of Surinamese politics describes the dominant party, the National Democratic Party (NDP), as divided between the genuine ideological nationalists and "the organized crime, narco-mob."[16]

The fact is that no matter where you look in the hemisphere, the threat of drugs is present. In the Caribbean this same threat raises the question of viability. In the Caribbean, drugs and the international cartels who handle them are now seen as a threat to the very foundations of civil society,[17] a threat to sovereignty,[18] and a threat to turn the concept of a "war" into less than an analogy and more of a literal description of Caribbean reality.[19] What is more, experts in intelligence fear that the war is being lost.[20] It is well known that the crackdown in South Florida and the Bahamas in the 1980s led to a shift in drug routes from the Caribbean to Mexico and Guatemala and the rest of Central America. In the Caribbean, except for Puerto Rico, which has continued to be targeted both for transshipment and as a market in its own right, drug runners shifted their routes. As a consequence, the Caribbean's share of the trade was said to have dropped to about 30 percent of the total.

By the mid-1990s, however, a new upsurge in movements through the Caribbean became evident. As indicated in Table 7.1, it is now calculated that the Caribbean handles close to 40 percent of the cocaine moving to the U.S. and Europe. Additionally, the shipments appear to be getting larger. In June 1996, officials on the French island of St. Barthélemey (25 square miles) discovered a cache of 863 kilograms, while officials in Suriname captured a shipment of 1,226 kilograms in a remote jungle village.

How can this resurgence in Caribbean routes be explained? One hypothesis is that the increasing power of the Mexican cartels has made it too expensive for the Colombians to use Mexico exclusively and has forced them to divert their routes to the Caribbean islands.[21] It is calculated that the Mexican "surcharge" to the Colombians was 50 percent while the Dominican-Puerto Rican gangs charged them only 20 percent.[22] Another is that the U.S. had moved many of its resources to the Mexican border, leaving the Caribbean relatively unpatrolled. A third is that organized crime in Brazil and Venezuela has sought outlets in the Caribbean using criminal connections established in the 1970s and 1980s, which were still in place, but now considerably enlarged and diversified. It is this diversification which provides the capacity to shift routes. A fourth, and most plausible, explanation is that of conjuncture: all three situations occurred virtually simultaneously, providing the move to the Caribbean with even greater impetus.

**Table 7.1   Cocaine in Transit at any Time
in Mexico, Central America, and Caribbean (1996)**
(estimated metric tons)

Total Transiting at any Time:		1,054 t
A. Transiting the Caribbean:	394 t	(37.38% of total)
(a) Through Western Caribbean (toward Belize, Mexico, and from there also Cayman Islands, Jamaica, Cuba, Haiti):	60 t	
(b) Through the Central and Eastern Caribbean:	154 t	
(c) Through the Caribbean to Europe:	180 t	
B. Transiting through Mexico, Central America, and Pacific:	660 t	(62.61% of total)
(a) Through the Pacific towards Central America and Mexico:	250 t	
(b) Through Central America to Mexico	50 t	
(c) In Mexico from Central America, Pacific, Western Caribbean, and own production:	360 t	

Source: U.S. Joint Interagency Task Force East, in UNDCP, *Focus on Drugs*, IV (January, 1997): 1, 2.

Whether the Caribbean shore is three-tenths or four-tenths of the trade, it has invariably represented big profits in the Caribbean. If one keeps in mind the small size of most of the islands, one realizes that even the relatively small amounts of drugs (usually packages weighing less than 200 kilograms) being transshipped from Colombia via Venezuela through the Eastern Caribbean, for instance, have had dramatic consequences for each island, consequences this study documents. Comparative street prices for a kilogram of cocaine (Table 7.2) make a fundamental point: no matter what the route, it pays to get the drug from Colombia to Florida and from there to points North.

There are various to Florida through the Islands. In fact, the Caribbean is akin to a series of bridges between producers and the higher-paying markets. It makes perfect economic sense to try to control and organize each of these bridges and so profit from the whole trade, from production to transshipment and sale in the United States. The benefit is compounded if there is also control over the laundering of those U.S.-provided gains.

All this is to introduce our central research questions: (1) What is the degree of centralized organization in the drug trade in the Caribbean? (2) What are the forces favoring centralization or decentralization?

WHICH STRATEGY IS BEST? THE PRESUMPTION OF CENTRALIZED CONTROL

The director of the newly created United Nations Drug Control Program (UNDCP) in the Caribbean relates a private conversation he had with a commissioner of police from the region. That commissioner was challenging the very rationale for establishing regionwide counternarcotics programs such as those being advanced by the UNDCP. In the commissioner's opinion, the drug problems of 29 different countries were like fingerprints: no two were identical, and, for that same reason, no two strategies to combat them could be identical either.[23] The director of the UNDCP disagreed. He noted that "1996 has created a new awareness that the drug war can be won ... if only we take up the challenge in a concerted manner." Which point of view provides the best starting point for a strategy?

In early 1997, Colombian authorities discovered a highly sophisticated, satellite-based communications center operated by one of the cartels. From Bogotá they were communicating and providing direction to operators in Mexico, Los

Table 7.2 Street Prices per kilogram Cocaine—Fourth Quarter, 1994	
Lesser Antilles	US$ 5–7,000
San Juan	US$ 10.5–13,000
Miami	US$ 16.0–22,000
North Florida	US$ 24.0–26,000

Source: DEA, Miami Field Division, January 1995

Angeles, New York, Miami, Madrid, Luxemburg, Berlin, and many other points on the globe. It had as cover a legitimate company specializing in international communications.[24] It is this type of information that contributes to the presumption of a centralized command and control.

By the early 1980s there existed a regionwide assumption that the Caribbean was being "Colombianized"; that is, that not only was the region's trade coming under the control of Colombian cartels, but that the nature and frequency of criminal violence on individual islands were taking on Colombian proportions and, indeed, being run by Colombians. Additionally, there was a sense that the criminals were winning, that the existing antinarcotics strategies were not working. In the words of the chairman of a Senate subcommittee, in the face of the cartels, with organization "like a military campaign," the U.S. effort was invariably one day late and a dollar short.[25] Even the director of the UNDCP, the most important regionwide center in the antinarcotics strategy, admits, "the political will to act against drug lords is undoubtedly growing strong while the antinarcotic flesh—the implementation of these policies—remains weak and fragmented."[26] In the face of this menace, the region and the international community responded. In 1995, new offices for the regional study and combat of the drug trade were opened in the Caribbean. In November, the DEA and the FBI opened new regional offices in Puerto Rico where, according to one official, "major drug trafficking organizations [are] completely controlled by the Colombian mafia."[27] Besides being a major market itself as well as a key transshipment center for drugs, Puerto Rico is a significant money-laundering center. In Jamaica, construction began on a new Caribbean Regional Drug Trafficking Center, which would serve the eighteen English-speaking countries of the area. Ground was also broken for a police-military post at Pedro Cays, 40 miles south of Jamaica, a favorite drop-off point for drugs moving up the islands and destined for the U.S. mainland. Legislation punishing money laundering was being prepared by the island's Ministry of National Security. There were grand juries sitting in the U.S. Virgin Islands looking at drug-related police corruption and even murder; there were commissions of enquiry sitting in the Bahamas looking at the widespread corruption that has characterized government in those islands over the past two decades, and in island after island, the New Scotland Yard, the DEA, and the FBI were operating alongside local authorities. In fact, one is tempted to say that the drug trade has engendered a benign form of "recolonization" of the Caribbean as agencies of the U.S., the Netherlands, the U.K., and France intensify their surveillance and investigation of the problem. The very size of the trade passing through the Caribbean on its way to the U.S. and Europe (see Table 7.1) explains this generalized concern.

On the self-evident assumption that the remedy must fit the illness, the critical question is: What is the nature of this Caribbean disease now generally referred to as "Colombianization?" What are its specific institutional and behavioral characteristics? Are the trends in the deepening and broadening of the drug trade, for instance, a consequence of the centralization and coordination of criminal activities from and by Colombian drug cartels? Certainly the regionwide propensity to speak of "Caribbean organized crime," "cartels," or "mafias," reflects the widely held belief that there is some form of centralized organization, if not outright control. Usually it is perceived to be Colombian control, although there are those who claim that other "mafias" are gaining not just ascendency but regionwide dominance. The Dominican Republic, says a student of the problem, is now considered by the DEA to be "the command, control and communications center for Caribbean drug trafficking activities. Dominican organizations oversee and monitor most of the logistical requirements to move cocaine...."[28] In the 1980s such an organizational role was assigned to the Jamaican posses.

An effective multilateral anticrime policy must be informed by accurate appreciation of the "centralization" hypothesis. If, for instance, one discovered that what exists is an island-to-island opportunistic and mostly ad hoc coordination or cooperation in a hemisphere-wide business, this would certainly put the burden of counternarcotics operations on each sovereign national actor. It would call for national governmental assaults on criminals in individual islands rather than the traditional dependence on U.S. actions against some presumed centralized organization. In terms of U.S. national policy, this might mean giving higher priority to assisting local law enforcement agencies. However, where local governments are hopelessly corrupted, it could mean taking a more unilateral interventionist approach.

Before answering the question of whether the trade in the Caribbean is centralized or decentralized, some definitional clarification is necessary.

WHAT IS "ORGANIZED CRIME"?

Up to 1986, most U.S. government studies assumed that organized crime was synonymous with the mafia.[29] In that year, a presidential commission, while calling the drug trade the single most important criminal problem in the country, admitted that instead of a single "mafia," what existed were many different crime organizations which "operate independently and occasionally in collaboration with other groups." This was hardly a novel hypothesis. As Diego Gambetta notes, the Italian scholar Leopoldo Franchetti theorized over a century ago that what existed was an industry in which many organized criminal groups with similar operating styles took part. In other words, the *mafioso* exists, but not *the mafia*.[30] Both Franchetti and Gambetta make it clear, however, that a fundamental part of that *mafioso* operating style is tight organization and a hierarchical command structure specifically geared towards expanding its sphere of power and profits.

Table 7.3 is an attempt to synthesize some important studies on organized crime. What they share is a view of organized crime as a rigidly organized, hierarchical, and ongoing effort to control a total criminal enterprise or trade. It is neither ad hoc nor *territorially limited*. Is the Caribbean drug trade "organized crime" in this sense? For instance, assuming that the Cali cartel fits such a description for Colombia, does it also exert a regionwide control which is tight, hierarchical, and enduring? Are the three reputed "mafias" in Trinidad (organized, as these groups tend to be worldwide, on ethnic lines[31]), or the Jamaican "posses," or the Dominican "mafias" subordinate to the Cali cartel, or are they autonomous players that act sequentially, segmentally, and locally in a chain of individual conspiracies running from producer to consumer? Because of the secrecy involved, direct empirical evidence is difficult to come by. My attempt to illuminate the structure of the Caribbean drug business will depend on a series of assumptions.

One of our operating assumptions is that there is a natural and logical tendency among all those involved in the "business," Colombian producers and Caribbean transshippers alike, to maximize the gains of their participation, to increase their profits by controlling more and more links in the chain—that is, centralizing the operation. Call it the centralization imperative. It is logical to assume that since the centralization imperative operates in all groups, there will be conflict, and the group best organized in terms outlined in the conceptual scheme (Table 7.3) will emerge victorious. The empirical question becomes: What factors exist in the Caribbean that militate against any one group achieving regionwide control?

Table 7.3 Defining "Organized Crime": Conceptual Approximation

1. Despite a preference for laissez-faire ideologies, it is *nonideological* in an opportunistic way.

2. Its *capacity to adapt* in order to meet a variety of demands for its services provides it with *strong continuity* over time.

3. The adaptability and continuity are facilitated and enhanced by (i) milieus of *generalized corruption* which are not of its creation, indeed, they precede the emergence of the organization; (ii) the acquiescence or indifference over long periods of major military actors creating "blowback situations"; (iii) the total or significant control of a given territory (urban or rural) in which it can operate freely and profitably.

4. It is most efficient when based on ethnic ties utilizing ethnic loyalties among its overseas diasporas and networks.

5. It has an organization which is hierarchical and whose top command has the *capacity* to coordinate and implement (enforce) at least the following:
   (1) the use of force or the credible threat thereof
   (2) recruitment: access and membership
   (3) control of the bulk of the profits (value added) from any series of transactions through total or near monopoly control
   (4) strategical planning to achieve a range of goals, especially the "control" or at least neutralization through corruption or/and violence of crucial political/civilian/military actors
   (5) enforcement of secrecy and loyalty

Sources: F. Hagan, "The Organized Crime Continuum: A further specification of a new conceptual model," *Criminal Justice Review*, 8 (1983): 52–57; M. Maltz, "On Defining Organized Crime," *Crime and Delinquency*, 22 (1976): 338–46; Dennis J. Kenny and James O. Fiuckenauer, *Organized Crime in America* (Belmont, CA: Wadsworth, 1995), 1–28; Diego Gambetta, *The Sicilian Mafia* (Harvard University Press 1993).

Even as we recognize the imperative to centralize, we can also understand that when there is an opportunity to maximize gains by acting independently, people do so. We call this the imperative to localize. One factor militating in favor of the imperative to localize (and, thus, against centralization) is the difficulty and thus high cost of transporting the merchandise. Part of the difficulty and high cost is the need to keep shifting routes. There are costs and risks in bringing new members into the conspiracy. There is some incentive, therefore, to shift the risk to local entrepreneurs as long as there is an understanding as to the distribution of the final take. Here is where the elements of capability for violence and capacity to exact loyalty come in, since one has to assume that given the size of the criminal enterprise, there is always the temptation to carve out an individual share of the enormous sums involved.

The going price of transporting the drugs from Colombia to Miami in 1994 ran from $2,800 to $10,000 per kilogram. The price per kilogram dropped as the size of the cargo increased, but even so it was incentive enough to encourage individual entrepreneurs using commercial vessels and aircraft to make the Caribbean run. There are, of course, "private" planes operating, but these tend to be stolen and sold to the traffickers at high prices, increasing the cost of the "run." Between January and September 1994, seven twin-engine airplanes were stolen in the Bahamas and five were later sighted at El Dorado airport in Bogotá, Colombia. Traffickers pay $400,000 each for these aircraft, and this is just the beginning of a series of costs.[32] There are also the indeterminate but presumably large sums to "grease" and "protect" the trade through bribes and general corruption. The UNDCP calculates that of every $10,000 in transportation costs (Colombia to United States), $2,000 goes to local pay offs. For 1995, that calculates out to over $400 million in bribes to local Caribbean officials and agents.[33] Michael Woods estimates that the figure was between $400 and $600 million in 1996.[34] The more complex and circuitous the routes, the more influential the local contacts, the less centralized control, the higher the costs to the exporter.

How should one then weight the relative strength of each imperative? One way would be to do a detailed study of each of the 34 islands and mainland countries in the Caribbean Basin, each with its own fingerprint, to quote the police commissioner. The Bureau of International Narcotics and Law Enforcement Affairs of the U.S. Department of State does just that every year. As valuable as these studies are, they need to be handled with careful skepticism because they have a political purpose: to help the president decide on which nation to "certify" and "decertify."

Another approach is to select those cases which appear to be most active at the present time, and derive from those cases broader generalizations. There are two dangers incident to such extrapolations. One is the fallacy of tautological explanation; the other, the fallacy of post facto explanation. Our critical understanding of crime and corruption is always after the fact, that is, after the damage has been done. Given the capacity of organized crime to adapt and shift strategies (see Table 7.3), our discovery of today's center is already a day late.

Here we try a different approach. We assume that there is one central enterprise—getting the merchandise from producers to markets. We then trace one naval operation in that enterprise, explaining the situation at each leg of the ship's voyage, and searching for the possible presence in each of those stops of the characteristics of our conceptual model. One value of this approach is that rather than selecting our case a priori, we let the criminals select it for us. The case (Table 7.4) is drawn from DEA files and allows us to probe the probable levels of organization or localization as they existed in the mid-1990s.

This is obviously a very broad outline, but it is about as much information as researchers without clearance can access. Aside from the facts that some drugs were loaded off Jamaica and were discovered in Tampa, there is not much specific information. The challenge lies in adducing as many conclusions from such data as will help shed light on the central research problem: Did the voyage of the drug ship involve one business undertaking controlled by one organization, or was it a series of conspiracies, each maximizing its possible gain from the ultimate payoff—the sale of the drugs? The specific question makes it clear how difficult this area of research is. Did the ship arrive in Trinidad with the secret compartments in place and offload a cargo, or were the compartments added in Trinidad where it was taking on cargo? What do the changes of ownership imply; a subterfuge for a single owner or new owners at different legs or stages of the voyage?

Table 7.4 Tracing a Drug Shipment

1. **February–July, 1994:**
   M/V *Carib Coast* is docked for unspecified repairs in **Trinidad.** While there, the vessel changes ownership and is renamed M/V *Avior.*

2. **July 28, 1994:**
   Avior sails to **Jamaica**

3. **August 4, 1994:**
   Avior sails to **Honduras.** Sets sail and claims to be adrift with mechanical problems somewhere in the Caribbean.

4. **August 6, 1994:**
   Returns to Jamaica, where no mechanical problems are reported.

5. **Sometime in August:**
   Avior rendevouses off Pedro Banks, Jamaica with two Colombian "go-fast" boats known to have left from Canal del Dique, **San Andres Islands,** Colombia. Ship returns to Jamaica and takes on a load of gypsum.

6. **September 2, 1994:**
   Avior unloads gypsum cargo in Santo Domingo, **Dominican Republic.** There the ownership of the vessel is again changed and it is renamed M/V *Inge Frank.*

7. **September 9, 1994:**
   Sails into **Tampa Bay, Florida** and schedules dry dock repairs similar to repairs done in Trinidad.

8. **September 16, 1994:**
   U.S. Coast Guard boards the *Inge Frank* and locates secret steel and cement compartments containing 1,948 kilograms of contraband cocaine.

The drug cargo seized was 1,948 kilograms, which at a 1994 estimated cost of delivery of $4,500 per kilogram, amounted to a payout of $8,766,000. Not an inconsequential sum certainly. But given the complexity of the route and the change in ownership, was it a sum which would have satisfied an agent only involved in the transportation? One can hypothesize two ways: (1) the localization imperative hypothesis: the ship added some value at several stages by delivering drugs or other illegal cargo in several ports to locally based criminal groups which, controlling the local market, added the real value to the drug; or (2) the centralization imperative hypothesis: one group controlled the whole operation, expecting to make its real profit from the street sales of the drug in the U.S. which, at the going Miami price, would have been $42,856,000 (1,948 kilograms at $22,000 per kilogram).

We can get closer to an answer to the central query by analyzing sequentially the situation in each of the six countries involved in the trip.

Trinidad and Tobago

According to the Department of State's 1995 *International Narcotics Control Strategy Report* (hereinafter referred to as the 1995 Report), "Trinidad and Tobago is not a major producer, consumer or trafficker of illegal drugs, precursor chemicals or a significant money laundering center."[35] Based on this, one would hesitate to conclude that M/V *Carib Coast* arrived in Trinidad for anything other than legitimate repairs and might assume that the transfer of ownership and name was a legitimate business transaction. Unfortunately, the 1995 Report on the situation in the island was only partly true. It appeared to be correct only with regard to the absence of cocaine production and of precursor chemicals. In all other areas the drug trade was thriving. In fact, only one year later, the 1996 Report stated that the island, located only seven miles off the Venezuelan coast, "is a significant transit country for cocaine. Heroin has also been intercepted.... It is a producer and exporter of marijuana. Narcotics-related violence, money laundering and drug abuse are growing problems." Our analysis tends to confirm the 1996 assessment. Cocaine seizures alone increased 100 percent between 1995 and 1996 (from 342 kilograms to 746 kilograms),[36] still only a fraction of the 2,000 kilograms believed by the DEA to transit through the island each month.

In the fourth quarter of 1994, local authorities claim to have destroyed 1,540,000 marijuana plants. Yet marijuana was readily available anywhere on the island. Most cocaine seizures were made off "mules" transporting the drug strapped to their bodies. Substantial amounts must be getting through, since the price per kilogram in Trinidad is U.S.$5,000, half of the price in Barbados or St. Lucia. The island serves as a major transshipment center for the Eastern Caribbean, and what is not transshipped is increasingly being consumed locally. Trinidad is also rapidly becoming a significant center for money laundering. Sources in the banking community, who wish to remain anonymous, have for some time alleged that there was significant money laundering taking place on the island. Only recently did former minister of national security, Russell Huggins, admit that it was a "very serious problem," especially since the local money launderers have extensive international links.[37]

Reflecting all this are the escalating violence and corruption that afflict the society. On Thursday, June 22, 1995, the former minister of national security and attorney general, Selwyn Richardson, was assassinated in what can only be called a profession "hit." The response in the region reveals something of the way the situation in Trinidad and Tobago is perceived by those in the Caribbean who follow events closely:

> So they have murdered the Trinidad politician and lawyer who had so deservingly won the enviable reputation of "Mr. Clean" in a society riddled with *bobol*—corruption—and where mafia-style killings and shocking violent crimes are reminiscent of the crime scene in Jamaica.
> (Veteran Caribbean journalist Rickey Singh, *Weekend Nation*, June 23, 1995, 9)

> I know he is someone who has stood up vigorously and vehemently against the drug trade and it looks as though someone like him has to be silenced . . .
> (Sir James Mitchell, Prime Minister of St. Vincent, *Weekend Nation*, June 23, 1995, 16)

> I'm afraid that the carnage and the assassination will continue. Heaven knows who is going to be next.
> (Ex-Minister of Legal Affairs of Trinidad and Tobago, Hector McLean, *The Barbados Advocate*, June 23, 1995, 13)

While these are the all-too-evident manifestations of the drug trade, potentially the greatest damage is what is occurring, through drug-related corruption, to the very structures which should be stemming the problem: the security and criminal justice systems. Despite multiple well-documented requests by the United Kingdom and the United States for extradition of alleged major drug kingpins, not a single person had been extradited nor had one single significant drug dealer been convicted in a Trinidad court. Witness intimidation and even murder were some of the reasons why.

The situation with the security force is arguably even more threatening. Their suspected involvement in the drug trade had been the subject of an enquiry which generated a report, the Scott Drug Report, submitted to Parliament in 1989. While the report was silent as to the names of drug dealers, it left no doubt as to the seriousness of the local situation with respect to drug traffic and drug addiction. Fifty-one police officers were suspended, and Police Commissioner Randolph ("Rambo") Burroughs resigned after being indicted as a drug dealer. He was acquitted after a long trial. As subsequent events would prove, including the murder of a policeman in a failed illicit drug operation, the situation was worse than that revealed by the government. By the early 1990s, the evidence of drug-related criminality, and the participation of members of the security forces in it, had become so serious, and public concern so strongly expressed, that the newly elected government of Patrick Manning went abroad for help. The United Kingdom responded to a request from the newly elected government by sending a high-level investigative team from New Scotland Yard. The general conclusion of this foreign team was that corruption was evidently widespread within the police force, but that a more thorough investigation was not possible for three reasons: (1) After seven four-week tours, the British detectives were still not sure who they could trust in the Police Service; (2) They had no "clout" and were given none by the Trinidad and Tobago government and thus could not compel testimony; and (3) worst of all, their work was being actively sabotaged by corrupt higher-ups. "There had been promotions, transfers, and acting appointments," said the foreign investigators, "which have had the effect of giving a clear message to the honest element in the police service that the old and corrupt guard was still very much in control."[38]

Corroboration for the New Scotland Yard assessment came on June 20, 1994, when the minister of national security of Trinidad and Tobago reported to Parliament that major parts of the documentation and evidence collected by New Scotland Yard had disappeared. His explanation was typical of the political bureaucratese which some officials of democratically elected governments in the region are using to explain their incompetence or incapacity in the face of organized crime's growing role:

[T]he loss of the New Scotland Yard documents] is a kind of problem that I would find it extremely difficult to lay blame at the footsteps of any Government, because the Government does not have control over the police files, the court files, and that sort of thing. [39]

Trinidadians can be excused for being cynical, knowing that none of the over one hundred officers identified as corrupt by the New Scotland Yard Report had been sanctioned even as the attorney general discussed new bills to deal with the nature of bail and to install one-way mirrors in identification parades. A former minister of national security, George Padmore, condemned the disingenuousness of the government's excuses at a time when the drug problem had taken on "octopus-like proportions" and the Police Service appeared to have "careened out of control."[40]

The assassination of ex-attorney general Selwyn Richardson is evidence that Padmore had not been off the mark. It also revealed, however, that there had been no decisive actions by the Trinidad government to regain control over law and order, justice, and simple civility on the island. In July 1995, the leader of the opposition, Basdeo Panday, threatened several times to use Parliament to reveal the names of government ministers involved in the drug trade. At the time of this writing, none have been revealed. Meanwhile, drugs continue to be transshipped through the island in large quantities.[41] On January 18, 1998, a ship carrying over a ton of cocaine to Trinidad was stopped before it arrived at its destination.[42]

Local cultivation and export of marijuana was also increasing; on January 8, 1998, a celebrated national track star was arrested (along with two Jamaicans) as they were about to ship out a load valued at U.S.$10 million.[43]

While the government—and the society generally—appears immobilized, the strain on that historically divided multiethnic society intensifies as each ethnic group (Indian, Black, and Syrian-Lebanese) accuses the other of being the "god-fathers" of the trade. These accusations raise important questions about the tendency toward localization. While the general "softness" (propensity for corruption) of the society facilitates the penetration of any cartel seeking to control and centralize the business, the ethnic division exerts pressure toward decentralization and diversification of the trade. It appears that Indo-Trinidadian gangs control the shipping from Venezuela only 8 miles away across the Gulf of Paria. The distribution in the urban ghettoes appears to be in the hands of Afro-Trinidadians. Large shipments and transshipments up the islands appear to be in the hands of rogue members of the security forces and of members of the well-to-do classes with access to large yachts and small trading ships. Since none of these groups appears to have control of organizations outside the island, they are presumed to pass the business on to other organizations once the drugs arrive at those destinations.

The ship, now named M/V *Avior*, sailed to Jamaica, where the nature of the drug trade differs quite radically from that of Trinidad/Tobago.

Jamaica

The Jamaica in which the newly named drug ship M/V *Avoir* arrived was, in the words of its then-commissioner of police, Col. Trevor MacMillan, in a "pre-Colombianization" stage.[44] It is not clear whether the commissioner meant that metaphorically or literally. Did he mean to say that the Colombians were actually doing the organizing, transporting, and enforcing of the drug trade? There are episodic incidents consistent with the latter hypothesis. In March 1997, a 45-foot motor vessel of Colombian registry was located off the Boston area of Portland, Jamaica. A number of "white aliens" were seen disembarking and being whisked out of the area by local contacts. Soon thereafter, "professionally" executed arson destroyed a well-known eatery in the area. No further information is available on this incident. But speculation in the national press was that a professional "hit" was carried out.[45]

Certainly there is enough evidence that the trade is growing and becoming more complex. According to the island's major paper, U.S.$1.3 billion in crack cocaine was confiscated and 2,400 drug-related arrests made in the first 6 months of 1995. [46] The same paper later reported that seizures of cocaine had gone from 274 pounds in 1994 to 1,200 pounds in 1995, but then declined to 236 pounds in 1996. Arrests went from 1,597 in 1994 to 3,354 in 1995, and then down to 3,263 in 1996.[47] There is little reason to question the 1995 Report's description of Jamaica as a "major producer of marijuana ('ganja') and a *flourishing* trans-shipment site for South American cocaine. . . ."[48] Far less persuasive is its conclusion that there is no evidence of money laundering. In fact, Jamaica had been witnessing increases in the trade, in local use, in money laundering, and in the number of drug-related arrests. Jamaica appears to be deep into the traffic in and through the Caribbean. Increasing, according to then-deputy and by mid-1997 commissioner of police, Francis Forbes, is the use of small aircraft for airdrops along the coast. The craft are reputed to be registered in the Bahamas and owned by Bahamians who are often residents in the United States. Even the involvement of Jamaicans in the drug trade in the United States is not new, though the growth of that involvement has been precipitous.

The unique nexus between politics, ganja, arms smuggling, and organized crime in Jamaica goes back to the mid-1960s. There are no equivalent cases elsewhere in the region. The trafficking in ganja and the links with the political parties began very early, building up steam in the 1960s.[49] Already by 1977 a major study noted that "the size of the ganja industry, and the vested interests which relate to it, help to explain part of the political and criminal violence which occurred in Jamaica during the 1960s."[50]

While the word "posse" ("yardie" in the U.K.) was not widely used in the 1960s, the districts of origin and names of the gangs which later became notorious have a familiar ring: the Max, Blue Mafia, Dunkirk, Phoenix, and Vikings. In the 1960s they were called "criminals" and "hooligans," and were known to be the "soldiers" of various leaders in both dominant political parties—the Peoples National Party (PNP) and the Jamaican Labour Party (JLP). It is precisely this native origin, their links with political parties, their deep roots in the local culture and, fundamentally, their tight links with the Jamaican diaspora in the U.S. and the U.K. which explain their independence of action in the growing drug trade, and their capacity to shift from ganja to cocaine. According to a Jamaican researcher, "the first known and proven" case of Jamaica's involvement in the international cocaine trade occurred in February 1975. Although this involved a prominent businessman, the posses—originally recruited in the slums of Kingston—soon took control of the business.[51]

The capability to penetrate and operate in the American market has been one of the telling characteristics of the Jamaicans. In the decade of the 1970s, the United States became well acquainted with the violent Jamaican posses. Two in particular, the Shower Posse (originally with close ties to the JLP), and the Spangler Posse (originally close to the PNP), were operating with some 5,000 members in each posse throughout the United States. By the end of the 1980s, the GAO calculated that there were some 40 posses in the United States with perhaps 22,000 members.[52] An integral part of their trading scheme was smuggling guns. In October 1984, Jamaican authorities discovered two barrel-loads of guns shipped from Miami. This turned out to be part of an arsenal of 210 weapons purchased in Miami and Fort Lauderdale by the Shower Posse.[53] This would be minor compared to what would follow. The discovery on January 6, 1989, of a container in the port of Kingston loaded with U.S.$8 million in arms illustrated that the problem had wider ramifications. Of West German manufacture, the weapons were shipped from Portugal on a Panamanian registered ship and were destined to be shipped from Jamaica to an unspecified group in Colombia. It took a joint effort of Jamaican, British, U.S., and Colombian intelligence to break the Jamaican link of what was called "an international network of drug traffickers and terrorists."[54] The Panamanian ship was owned by Bluewater Ship Management Inc. of Panama. Both the company and its British (naturalized Panamanian) president had previously been linked to illegal arms shipments, cocaine distribution, and the laundering of drug-related monies. This certainly seemed to be a chain of separate conspiracies by different groups cooperating for their own individual gain.

These posses are said to be organized hierarchically into leader(s), lieutenants, and street-level soldiers. The crucial point of their organization is that there is no centralization of the various posses; loyalty is to the leader of each posse and to the district in Jamaica of their origin and their most loyal following. This tight, territorially based bonding helps to explain why the turf wars which naturally exist between trading groups take on additional violence among these posses. While it is quite logical that, as the posses switch from ganja and hashish oil to cocaine and crack cocaine, their contacts with the Colombians increase, their established structures and organization militate against subordination to the Colombians. The new cocaine contacts with the Colombians take various forms, but some of the better-known routes appear to be by "fast boat" from the San Andres y Providencia archipelago of Colombia, and by air on any of the two airlines with Jamaican connections: SAM, which flies from Medellín, and COPA, which flies from Panama. It is said that increasing numbers of Colombians are going to Jamaica on 30-to-60-day visas to organize multikilogram shipments by container and other commercial craft into the United States.[55] Notwithstanding this contact, the U.S. Justice Department maintains that the Jamaicans control their own organizations, manage very tightly the transshipment through Jamaica into the United States, and, once there, are in full control of the marketing and the laundering of profits.[56] As the *New York Times* reported, Jamaicans buy a kilogram of cocaine from the Colombians at wholesale prices ($5,000) and retail it for $120,000 in street sales.[57] Today the Jamaicans control over 25 percent of the crack cocaine trade in over 80 U.S. cities, as well as a few Canadian and British ones. In the Southeastern United States from Miami, Florida, to Myrtle Beach, North Carolina Jamaican control is said to reach between 60 and 80 percent of the trade. A recent report from Jamaica, citing FBI sources, listed the following weekly earnings of the four major posses operating in the U.S.[58]:

Shower:	$4.0 million
Spangler:	$3.5 million
Jungle:	$2.7 million
Dunkirk:	$2.0 million

There is no evidence that the Jamaican link of the chain is organizationally part of any unitary, Caribbean-wide criminal enterprise. The posses' involvements in the trade have shifted as the commodities traded have shifted, with no known fundamental changes in their structure, loyalties, and long-term prospects.

In the late 1980s, after many years during which the Jamaican electorate had chosen many a new government without any serious debate or discussion of the Jamaican drug problem, a dramatically changed perception of the threat became evident. The drug dealers, wrote the foremost pollster at the time, Carl Stone, were "crippling Jamaica . . . the very future and livelihood of this country and its people are at risk." Such was his sense of threat that he urged that steps be taken "in a hurry" to stop this trade, including making "any constitutional changes necessary."[59] What explains such a dramatic switch, and what does it say about the nature of the threat to the security of Caribbean countries? The answer is that it was a response to some very real challenges to the Jamaican state's control over its public health and economic activities.

Perhaps most urgent was the realization that what was generally called the Jamaican "drug culture" was no longer limited to ganja. As Stone himself discovered in his first major foray into drug use on the island, there had emerged a "syndrome" of multiple drug use at all levels of the society. The traditional wad of ganja was now a "spliff"—ganja sprinkled with cocaine.[60]

Then there was the threat to the economy. Between 1987 and 1989, several major shippers stopped shipping goods out of Jamaica: Evergreen Lines had already paid $137 million, and Sea-Land Services, $85 million in fines to U.S. customs; the Kirk Line had one of their ships confiscated in Miami (released after the payment of a fine); Air Jamaica was suffering from constant fines imposed because of drug finds, and the Free Zone manufacturers were said to be in a "tailspin" because of the use of the port by drug lords.[61] In the midst of all this, Jamaica was experiencing a flood of imported weapons.

How to explain the phenomenal growth of this trade and the relative silence about it on the island? Part of the explanation, of course, lies in the delicate issue of the gangs' political ties, present or past. This goes with a general penchant for sweeping drug-related crimes under the carpet for fear that they might affect both tourism and foreign investment. It has taken the writings of courageous journalists to fill the void. In October 1994, Jamaican *Gleaner* columnist Dawn Ritch began revealing the links between crime, drugs, and politicians. Despite the well-documented columns, in November 1994, the deputy commissioner of police skirted the issue, claiming not to have seen Ritch's columns. He gave the following "philosophical" (to use his own words) responses to the query: "Why do Jamaicans regard crime as the number one national problem?"—"When social conditions exist which do not comfortably accommodate all social classes on an equal level, it is not uncommon for crime to increase. . . ."[62]

The redoubtable Ms. Ritch was not about to be silenced. In the face of considerable pressure to "keep quiet," she published facts taken from police records. She pointed to the constituencies that Jamaicans call "garrison constituencies" because the gangs exercise such control that the police have to be "garrisoned" in fortified stations. In August 1994 this author toured one of the constituencies mentioned by Ritch (under the "protection" of the popular local parish priest). The Mercedes Benzes of the drug "dons" were everywhere in evidence, signs that the drug trade was flourishing. With the police presence limited to single highly protected "garrisons" in each neighborhood, the fear of the residents was palpable.

It is understandable that Jamaicans would want to protect their reputation and that of the all-important tourist industry. Less understandable has been the long silence from Washington about the local role of the posses. One week before the visit to Washington in 1989 of recently reelected, and newly conservative, Michael Manley, the DEA office in Jamaica denied that there was any link between the posses operating in the United States and any of the Jamaican political parties. "The monies made by the posses in the United States," said Manley, "stayed in the United States."[63] When the major posses host the most significant constituency parties, sharing gifts with everyone, and when the battles in the United States spill over to the island, one can hardly stand on such diplomatic niceties. Jamaica recorded 656 murders in 1993 and 650 in 1994. These were non-election years, with increasingly sophisticated weaponry joining the fray.

There is plenty of evidence that the drug-related problems of so much concern in the 1980s continue to grow. There is also evidence of decline in the integrity of the security forces. In 1994 the Narcotics Division of Jamaica's Police Services seized and destroyed J$1.3-billion-worth of crack cocaine, ganja, and cocaine powder. Then, in October 1995, Jamaican narcotics detectives intercepted an aircraft bringing J$111 million in cocaine. But, in January 1996, it was reported that a significant part of the seized cargo had disappeared from the Narcotics Department's vault. Such is the distrust and lack of investigatory capabilities that three U.S. polygraph experts were brought in to help with the investigation. Officials were talking darkly about a possible "syndicate" operating in the police force.[64]

According to Minister of National Security K. D. Knight, Jamaica is making every effort to contain this trade since it represents a threat to the island's national security:

> ... if the smugglers are successful to any significant degree, there will be no ship willing to transport Jamaican bauxite.[65]

It is not just the container cargo and small aircraft which are involved. In early June 1995, virtually the complete staff of UPS carrier service in Kingston were caught red-handed loading cases of marijuana onto a UPS courier plane. The plane was seized by Jamaican authorities. One week later, a DHL courier service plane was stopped; ganja-laden honey bottles were on board.[66] When not only the sea shipping lanes but also the airlines and the courier services are polluted, an export-driven economy faces disaster.

Contrary to the 1995 Report's assertion that no money was being laundered in Jamaica, sources at the central bank (the Bank of Jamaica) report that "billions" of dollars are being laundered. The *Jamaican Weekly Gleaner* quotes a source in the Bank of Jamaica: "significant deposits of foreign currency were crucial to the stability of the economy, so [the government] decided early not to ask commercial banks to question the source of the incoming funds."[67] It is an extraordinary indication of the importance of this dirty money that a committee established in 1993 to try to have Jamaicans serving jail sentences in the United States returned to Jamaican jails so that they could be close to their families, gave as a reason for ameliorating punishment that these criminals "contribut[ed] to the development of the country by providing . . . much-needed foreign exchange."[68]

Jamaica appears finally to be mobilizing to take on what Jamaicans themselves are calling the "war on drugs." Evidence of this is the secondment of Colonel Trevor MacMillan from the army to the police and the constant attention and honors being bestowed on him even after his retirement. As he collected yet another award, this time in New York, MacMillan related how he is changing a police force which he found with low morale and little equipment but, worse, in which "criminality, corruption and power abuse were prominent features."[69] It is evident, however, that it has taken the society a long time to mobilize against the drug trade. It was long assumed that, to the extent that there was a mafia, it was the Colombian one and that this was a concern for the United States. Now there is ample awareness that Jamaica has its own mafias, making profitable links with the Colombians or anyone else who will enrich their coffers, and which pose real threats to the economy and political system. Despite the discovery of occasional boats and small planes coming from abroad, in Jamaica the localization imperative has real strength.

Honduras

Judging from newspaper reports, citing sources in the DEA, by the late 1980s, Honduras had become a significant transshipment center for cocaine that the Medellín cartel was shipping north.[70] This development was facilitated by the dramatic relaxation of ethical standards generally and in the Honduran armed forces specifically, that accompanied the U.S. use of the country as a base for insurgency against the Sandinistas of Nicaragua.[71] In other words, Honduras was another of the many "blowback" states in the region. The military were in an excellent position to take advantage of the proceeds of this trade. The civilian powers were thoroughly corrupt and not interested in probing too deeply into military corruption. No one else, at times not even the U.S. Embassy, it appears, was interested in probing either, since national security and geopolitical concerns had priority. Additionally, the military controlled the police and, as such, had a monopoly of force and surveillance. As if all this did not give them latitude enough, the military also administered the country's airports (only three out of the 215 airstrips had surveillance) and ran the nation's merchant marine.

No evidence surfaced of a direct and ongoing link between the military itself and the Medellín cartel. Instead, officers appear to have relied in the 1980s on a Honduran national, Jos Ramon Mata Ballesteros, who was also connected with Col. Antonio Noriega in Panama. As reported by U.S. Senator John Kerry:

> According to antinarcotics officials, he was the contact between the Colombian cocaine suppliers and the Mexican smugglers. He heads the so-called Padrino

trafficking organization, which supplies cocaine to the United States . . . operates in Peru, Mexico, Colombia, and Honduras. [72]

When U.S. pressure was finally applied on the military, they promptly arrested Mata and secretly moved him to the United States. With that, a major link between the Colombians and the Hondurans was broken, and a big gap was left in the whole operation.[73] It is difficult to say just what quantity of drugs are presently moving through Honduras, especially since there are U.S. radar systems operating in the southern part of the country, now truly looking for drug flights rather than, as before, possible Sandinista movement.

Whatever drugs do move out of Honduras through the Caribbean route, rather than up through Mexico, probably leave from the Bay Islands which lie off the northern coast of Honduras. A number of conditions make this an ideal transshipment point. Aside from the obvious geographical one of being able to escape the surveillance of U.S. radar and being within range of the Colombian islands of San Andres y Providencia, there are ethnic and economic reasons. Settled in the early nineteenth century by English-speaking Belizeans and Jamaicans and other West Indians, the Bay Islanders share a common ethnicity with the inhabitants of other archipelagos in the Western Caribbean as well as similarities in economic life. Besides fishing, the Bay Islanders have traditionally served as crew on regional and oceanic vessels and engaged in small-scale smuggling. For the past decade and a half, the islands have been experiencing a boom in the tourist industry, and the once-peaceful islands are now littered with pleasure craft of all sizes and nationalities but with little surveillance and control by the Honduran armed forces. The islands are ideal stop and drop-off points for the flow coming through the next set of islands at which the drug ship M/V *Avoir* stopped.

In Honduras there appears to be a differentiated situation: on the mainland, the tendency was towards localization; on the offshore Bay Islands, the Colombians probably had the upper hand. In the final analysis, however, the major movement up to Mexico, Guatemala, and the United States went through the local cartel dominated by Mata Ballesteros. Colombian operations appear to be exercised through subordinates on the islands of San Andres y Providencia.

San Andres y Providencia

The archipelago of San Andres y Providencia belongs to Colombia and is located some 110 kilometers southwest of Jamaica. It is inhabited by English-speaking people of West Indian descent, who, like the people of the Bay Islands, have long existed as fishermen, as crew on ocean and interisland vessels, and as smugglers. Because San Andres has always been a free port serving mainland Colombians, the smuggling business was always more important than it was in the Bay Islands. Yet San Andres never brought in the kind of money and wealth that the Sanandresianos began to notice starting some fifteen years ago. The erstwhile bucolic existence of these islands has been replaced by high-rise hotels, fancy discos, shops with expensive clothing and merchandise, and yacht havens chock-full of vessels of every description and price.

The islanders know exactly to what this wealth is attributable and colorfully dubbed it the "lobster route." This is an operation which began with the Medellín cartel and is said to be controlled today by the Cali cartel. Drugs and fuel are flown in from the mainland, either delivered at the airport in San Andres or dropped offshore, and picked up by speedboats the islanders call *voladores.* These cargoes are delivered to larger vessels which ply the Caribbean. The word is that the Mosquito coast of Nicaragua was once their principal destination; today it is the Bay Islands, Jamaica, and the Dominican Republic. According to a well-placed source, a Colombian police report called San Andres the "epicenter" of the nation's drug exports. In addition to drugs, the archipelago trades in arms, precursor chemicals, and counterfeit dollars, and it provides the services necessary for money laundering.[74] Another major service, according to a report of the Colombian navy, is that: "They can take an old ship, restore it to service, pack it with a ton of cocaine, and have if off the Jamaican coast, all in 30 hours." All these activities, noted the source, take place with brazen openness. Soon after that report was made public, *Cambio 16* reported that "the major" drug dealer on San Andres had been arrested. The individual was said to be at the service of the Cali cartel and to have business associations with Italians and Jamaicans established on the island.[75] On this critical launching point, there can be no doubt that the Colombian cartels, first the Medellín and now the Cali cartel, are in full control. One can also assume that the purpose of our drug ship in going there was to collect a cargo. The ship's next destination is now part of the major route into Puerto Rico and the United States.

Dominican Republic

The drug ship M/V *Avior* delivered its load of Jamaican gypsum and in the seven days it was in port in Santo Domingo, the ownership and the name of the ship changed. We know that when it left harbor as M/V *Inge Frank,* it was carrying a ton of cocaine. It should come as no surprise that the drug trade and the accompanying corruption of officials are today a major problem on that island. At a "Technical Anti-Drugs Summit" held in Puerto Rico in May 1995, the head of Puerto Rico's DEA office spoke of the "Colombianization" of the region.[76] He was not the first to so characterize it, but the characterization seems especially apt for the situations in Puerto Rico and the Dominican Republic. The most tragic evidence that this is indeed so is the increase in professionally executed murders of those in the trade, of those combating the rot, and of those involved and soiled but fallen from grace. There is also a real effort to influence the nation's politics. In late March 1996, Puerto Rican authorities seized $511,592 in $20 bills hidden in food cans. The destination was the Dominican Republic and there, according to the Dominican then-drug czar, Contraalmirante Julio Cesar Ventura Bayonet, it was an attempt by Dominican "narcos" to influence the upcoming elections.[77]

Today, the first point of contact for the Puerto Rican operators is the Dominican Republic. The rest of the Caribbean plays an essentially supporting role to this U.S./New York/Miami/Puerto Rico/Dominican Republic axis. The DEA claims that Colombians are directly organizing groups and routes in the Dominican Republic.[78] It is nevertheless indisputable that the Dominicans have a formidable set of their own organizations. Michael Woods claims that the role of Dominican criminals has "dramatically evolved" as a result of their association with the Colombians. Previously, Dominicans were limited to acting as pickup crews and couriers assisting Puerto Rican criminals in drug-smuggling ventures. "Now," say Woods, "Dominican traffickers are smugglers, transporters, and wholesalers."[79] Through their infrastructure support from Colombian traffickers, they have been able to dominate a significant portion of the market in U.S. East Coast cities. Like the Jamaicans, the Dominicans have created truly binational societies between the U.S. and the Dominican Republic. The U.S.-based Dominicans are called "Dominicanyorks" and are resented in the Dominican Republic, in major part because they have been stereotyped as being drug dealers.[80] They are, of course, not all drug dealers, but there is no doubt that there are powerful Dominican drug rings operating in New York with very tight contacts with the trade back home. Additionally, with no Dominican legislation against money laundering, the Dominican drug lords have literally flooded the island with dollars and in that way have penetrated the island's banking, business, judiciary, police, and even Congress. According to much of the growing literature on the subject, this penetration and corrupting of the Dominican system has taken place virtually unhindered and certainly with near-total impunity.[81]

The establishment of a new Dominican National Directorate for Drug Control is part of the expansion of such local efforts throughout the Caribbean. This is one case, however, where the evidence does not warrant optimism about controlling the crime wave. One obstacle is the apparent absence of a mafia controlled by one or even a few *capos*. The state fights a Hydra of decentralized and localized gangs without hierarchy or enduring central control, opportunistically engaging in whatever conspiracies are necessary to carry on the lucrative business. The drug ship could as well have been offloading a cargo for one group on the island and taking on the product of another for delivery to Tampa, where it was finally interdicted.

CONCLUSION

Despite its relative insignificance in the total scheme of U.S. geopolitical and geoeconomic concerns, the Caribbean retains a certain *droit de regard*. Its location, the shared mutual interests, and its potential for causing a good deal of trouble to the United States all make it so. The Caribbean not only provides bridges between the producer and the consumer of drugs; in addition, its modern banking system provides virtually impenetrable shelter for the profits and investments of that criminal industry.[82] It is a sobering thought that no matter what route we might have chosen through the Caribbean, we would have found elements of locally organized crime.

The facts revealed in this study show that of the five ports used by the drug ship before reaching the United States, two (Jamaica and the Dominican Republic) show very strong tendencies toward localization, two (Trinidad and Honduras) show mixed localization-centralization tendencies, and one (San Andres) is clearly under the central control of the Cali cartel. At least with respect to this slice of the overall drug trade in the Caribbean, there are no grounds to assume the existence of one organized—that is, centralized—criminal conspiracy (as defined in Table 7.3) that we can call "the Caribbean mafia." There does not appear to be an organized hierarchy showing continuity over time and long-range planning. What appears to exist are Colombian-organized criminal syndicates or cartels that utilize the many local organizations, taking advantage of geopolitical opportunities (such as shifts in U.S. interests and emphases) and of the general milieu of corruption in which they operate. We are confronting many local gangs, mostly, like the Jamaican posses and the Dominicans, without a centralized, hierarchical structure even in the islands themselves.

The critical question, of course, is whether the sliver of reality we have analyzed here is representative of the larger Caribbean reality. Some key testimony presented to the U.S. Senate's Committee on Foreign Relations a decade ago tends to support our conclusion[83]:

As regards the Bahamas:

> . . . the basic problem was a lack of central leadership. . . . you pay off one guy and somebody wouldn't agree with him, and you had no way of keeping track of how many people you had to pay off to accomplish a goal.

As regards Mexico:

> Senator Kerry: "Was there a dispute between the Mexican drug traffickers and the Colombian?"
> Mr. Rodriguez: "Yes." [over money control]
> Senator Kerry: "Do the Colombians operate in Mexico now?"
> Mr. Rodriguez: "No. The Mexicans operate in Mexico, and the Colombians cooperate with the Mexicans where they are allowed to. But the border belongs to the Mexicans."

This might explain the hypothesis discussed above, that the shift to the Caribbean stems from the localization of the Mexican criminal enterprises.

As regards Haiti and the heavy involvement of the military in the trade:

> Senator Kerry: "Do you know whether or not the drug trade in Miami involving the Haitians is controlled from Haiti?"
> Mr. Quintana: "It is my understanding that it is."

There is some evidence that the dismantling of the major drug cartels in Colombia has contributed to this proliferation of drug operators. Mireya Navarro of the *New York Times* quotes U.S. federal officials to the effect that decimation of the Medellín and Cali cartels "has fragmented the drug trade, giving way to dozens of smaller trafficking groups that, while not as big or efficient as the cartels, require more manpower and better intelligence gathering to combat."[84] In this sense, the situation in the Caribbean has at least superficial similarities to the evolving situation in Colombia and certainly to the description of organized crime in Russia. Stephen Handelman describes a "hydra-headed" phenomenon of between 3,000 and 4,000 gangs which control up to 40 percent of all Russian economic activities. Despite the plurality of groups, they all feed off the changing social and economic circumstances of the country. "The hazy boundary between criminal and legal business activity," says Handelman, "has allowed mafia groups to penetrate most areas of the Russian economy, giving them disproportionate influence."[85] As was noted in the case of Italy, what appears to exist is not a mafia but rather *mafiosi* and an atmosphere conducive to a *mafiosi* style.

Given this reality, the best strategy would appear to be to deal with each of these mafias in their home base even as the efforts against the Colombian cartels continue. There are, of course, several problems with a strategy that emphasizes localization, and policymakers should take these into account.

First, in the Caribbean—and elsewhere—the issue of sovereignty complicates any cross-border initiative. Beyond thin-skinned sovereignty, the intractable mix of constitutional systems with their own justice, security, and intelligence programs work to frustrate collective action. It is doubtful any "pan-Caribbean" activity can be successfully carried out. Not even among the English-speaking countries of CARICOM are the prospects for real transborder cooperation anything but dim. When the prime ministers of Jamaica and Trinidad called for a coordinated effort against the growing trade in drugs, their proposals did not go any further than the speeches they gave at an inaugural dinner.[86] Since that date, each Caribbean government has approached issues of antidrug coordination differently.

While Trinidad and Tobago hastily signed a "hot pursuit" agreement with the United States in 1997 (popularly known as the Shiprider Agreement), Barbados and Jamaica held off signing. They insisted, and eventually got, a pledge that random pursuit of suspected traffickers into their territorial waters would first require their express permission. Unfortunately, given the underdeveloped state of the defense structures, insisting on such a requirement seems to be foolhardy. One can sympathize with a U.S. Department of State spokesman when he told a recent conference that in order to protect their sovereignty from abuse by a big government, "Caribbean countries wind up permitting their sovereignty to be invaded by big criminals."[87] Perhaps the clearest case of this is Suriname, where state authorities have resisted the extradition to the Netherlands of former military dictator Desi Bouterse on drug-smuggling charges.

A second weakness of the localization strategy is a hangover from the cold war: our lack of cooperation with the Cuban authorities. The many cays off the southeastern coast of Cuba continue to be favorite airdrop points, easily accessible to speedboats operating out of the Bahamas and the Florida Keys.[88]

Finally, and crucially, the consequences of "globalization" have swept up the Caribbean in dramatic changes. For the small nations of this region, this means closer commercial and other ties with the United States, including offshore services of all types such as tourism, banking, electronic betting, and medical schools. Puerto Rico has 75 daily flights to the mainland and no exit immigration controls. The seaport of San Juan is the third busiest in the United States. Competing with San Juan to be the "hub" of inter-Caribbean trade and transportation is Miami, a virtually open city and locus of many illicit activities ranging from gun-running and alien smuggling to money laundering.[89] It is a sobering thought that the drug ship in this study was only one of 111,000 vessels that entered U.S. seaports that year; less than 5 percent of this traffic is ever inspected. A significant element in the mass migratory movement is the problem of the new binational criminal gangs, as we saw in the case of Jamaica-U.S. posses and the so-called *Dominicanyorks*. This is a new phenomenon as far as the Caribbean is concerned, and the full implication for the islands of this growing phenomenon—the migration and then deportation of criminal aliens—has yet to be analyzed. It stands to reason that if they are considered threats to U.S. national security, they surely must be even larger threats to their country of origin.

Globalization is, at least for now, an irreversible trend. Along with the many advantages it undoubtedly brings to these struggling economies, it is indisputable that it favors the multiplication of many local criminal enterprises feeding off that monstrous and gruesome multinational enterprise called the drug trade. All this brings us back to our original question: Will this criminality undermine democratic governance in the region, or, put in another way, are these states viable?

On a trip to Colombia in 1996, Fabio de Pasquale, Italy's formidable Mafia-combatting magistrate, distinguished the situations of the two countries: organized crime, he said, could not even remotely be considered a threat to Italian national security. Just the opposite might well be the case in Colombia.[90]

Magistrate de Pasquale was defining "national security" in a particular way. As long as organized crime used illegitimate means to gain "legitimate" ends, such as wealth, social status and honor, and the political influence of any organized group, "the state" itself—even "democracy"—was secured. Italy functioned for half a century with the Christian Democrats, heavily influenced by the Mafia.

The fact is that we already have, and have had, such criminal-influenced states in the Caribbean. And, they continue to operate "democratically." On the other hand, we have cases where it can be argued that illegitimate means are used for illegitimate and illegal ends. In Aruba, for example, it is evident that there are— as there is elsewhere in the region—substantial transshipment, warehousing, and money-laundering activities taking place.[91] But in Aruba, corruption has also penetrated the mass media, the employment market, and, not surprisingly, politics. Government coalitions are made and dissolved by the local traffickers and money launderers. Yet Aruba enjoys elections, free enterprise, and a booming tourist industry, and signs virtually all counter-drug agreements.[92]

In the case of Aruba, as elsewhere in the Caribbean, the issue of "viability" cannot be discussed separately from the idea of democracy as sovereign consent, that is, the will of the people. Both concepts need the kind of analytical review that has not yet been given. The point to be made is that there is locally "organized" crime in virtually every state in the Caribbean Basin. The most plausible hypothesis is that unless more effective countermeasures than what those of the late 1990s are put in effect, the progression towards more Aruba-type "viable" but only semidemocratic states is what the future holds.

NOTES

1. *Trinidad Guardian*, 20 Sept. 1998, 1.
2. *Trinidad Guardian*, 24 Sept. 1998.
3. *Trinidad Guardian*, 28 Sept. 1998.
4. *Trinidad Guardian*, 7 Oct. 1998, 1.
5. See Elliot Abrams, "The Shiprider Solution: Policing the Caribbean," *The National Interest* (Spring 1996), 86–97.
6. *New York Times*, 23 June 1998, 4.
7. *El Universal*, 20–30 June 1997.
8. *El Universal*, 4 Oct. 1998, 1.
9. See U.S. Department of State, Bureau of International Narcotics and Law Enforcement Affairs, *International Narcotics Control Strategy Report. Executive Summary*. Washington, D.C.: Department of State Publications, Mar. 1998, 67, 68, 102, 103, 114, 178, 179, 250.
10. *Washington Post*, 27 Sept. 1997, 1, 16.
11. See Tim Johnson and Juan Tamayo, *Miami Herald*, July 3–5, 1998.
12. *Miami Herald*, 3 July 1998, 26.
13. *Miami Herald*, 5 July 1998, 18.
14. *New York Times*, 30 June 1997, 4.
15. Joseph Rogers, "Unwanted Fame," *Hemisphere*, 7, no. 3 (1997): 38.
16. Gary Brana-Shute, "Sisters in the Woods: Ethnicity and Power in Guyana, Suriname and Trinidad and Tobago," Unpublished manuscript, November 1998, 20.
17. West Indian Commission, *Time For Action: The Report of The West Indian Commission* (Black Rock, Barbados, 1992).
18. Ivelaw Griffith, *Drugs and Security in the Caribbean: Sovereignty under Seige* (University Park, PA: The Pennsylvania University Press, 1997).
19. Elizabeth Joyce, "Conclusion," in Elizabeth Joyce and Carlos Malamud (eds.), *Latin America And The Multinational Drug Trade* (London: Institute of Latin American Studies, 1998), 193.
20. This is the chilling conclusion of an agent with long experience in the region. See Michael J. Woods, "Countering Transnational Crime in the Caribbean," Unpublished Master's Thesis, Joint Military Intelligence College, Aug. 1997.
21. "Drug Trafficking on the Increase in the Caribbean," *Focus on Drugs*, 4 (Jan. 1997): 1.
22. Michael Woods, "Countering Transnational Crime," 12.
23. Sandro Calvani, Foreword, UNDCP, *No One Is an Island*. UNDCP Activities Report, 1997 (Bridgetown, Barbados, February 1997), 1.
24. *Semana* (Bogota), 19 May 1997, 38–39.
25. Ibid., 47.
26. Calvani, *No One Is An Island*, 2.
27. *Miami Herald*, 16 Nov. 1995, 2.
28. Joseph Rogers, "Unwanted Fame," *Hemisphere*, 7, no. 3 (1997): 38.
29. See G. Blakey, *Organized Crime in the United States: A Review of the Public*

Record (Bellevue, WA.: Northwest Policy Studies Center, 1987); August Bequai, *Organized Crime, The Fifth Estate*, (Lexington: Lexington Books, 1979); Timothy S. Bynum, *Organized Crime in America: Concepts and Controversies* (Money, N.Y.: Criminal Justice Press, 1987).
30. Cited in Diego Gambetta, *The Sicilian Mafia* (Cambridge: Harvard University Press, 1993), 101.
31. See F. Ianni, *Black Mafia: Ethnic Succession in Organized Crime* (New York: Simon Schuster, 1972).
32. Interviews with the DEA, Miami Field Division, 5, 6 Dec. 1995.
33. Calvani, *No One Is an Island*, 3, no. 1.
34. Woods, "Countering Transnational Crime in the Caribbean," 41.
35. U.S. Department of State, Bureau of International Narcotics and Law Enforcement Affairs, *International Narcotics Control Strategy Report* (Washington, D.C.: Government Printing Office, 1995), 310.
36. Calvani, *No Country Is an Island*, 3, no. 1.
37. *Trinidad Guardian*, 26 May 1995, 3.
38. G. Seaby, *Final Report for the Government of Trinidad and Tobago on Investigations Carried out by Officers from New Scotland Yard* (London, 20 July 1993, Paragraph 8.4.1).
39. *Sunday Guardian* (Trinidad), 25 June 1994, 141.
40. George Padmore in *Sunday Guardian*, 26 June 1994, 6.
41. *Trinidad Guardian*, 11 Nov. 1997, 1.
42. *New York Times*, 19 Jan. 1998, 6.
43. *Trinidad Guardian*, 4 Nov. 1997, 1.
44. Commissioner of Police Col. Trevor MacMillan at a private meeting of the Jamaica Think Tank, Montego Bay, Jamaica, 29 Oct. 1994. The author was present.
45. *Jamaican Weekly Gleaner*, 27 Mar.–2 Apr. 1997, 8.
46. *Jamaican Weekly Gleaner*, 16 June–22 June 1995, 1.
47. *Jamaican Weekly Gleaner*, 15–21 Dec. 1995, 11. Reports for 1995 and 1996.
48. *The 1995 Report*, 180.
49. See Vera Rubin and Lambros Comitas, *Ganja in Jamaica* (The Hague: Mouton Press, 1975).
50. Terry Lace, *Violence and Politics in Jamaica, 1960–1970* (London: Frank Cass, 1977), 160.
51. Barry Chevannes, *Background to Drug Use in Jamaica* (Kingston: ISER Working Paper no. 34, 1988).
52. U.S. General Accounting Office, *Nontraditional Organized Crime* (Washington, D.C.: Government Printing Office, 1989).
53. *Daily Gleaner*, 4 Oct. 1984, 1.
54. This section draws heavily on A. P. Maingot, *The United States and the Caribbean* (London: The Macmillan Co., 1994), 142–62; and Laurie Gunst, *Born Fi' Dead* (New York: Henry Holt, 1995).
55. Interviews, Miami DEA Field Division, 5 Dec. 1995.
56. U.S. Department of Justice, *Attacking Organized Crime: A National Strategy* (Washington, D.C.: Government Printing Office, 1991).
57. *New York Times*, 19 July 1987, 10.
58. *Jamaican Weekly Gleaner*, 1–7 Dec. 1995, 2.
59. Maingot, *The United States and the Caribbean*, 142–62.
60. See Carl Stone, *National Survey on the Use of Drugs in Jamaica* (Kingston, 1990), 35–40.
61. Maingot, *The United States and the Caribbean*, 142–62.
62. *Jamaican Weekly Gleaner*, 12–18 Nov. 1994, 15.
63. *Jamaican Weekly Gleaner*, 27 Mar. 1989, 11.
64. *Jamaican Weekly Gleaner*, 27 Mar. 1989, 11.

65. *Jamaican Weekly Gleaner*, 23–29 June 1995, 6.
66. *Jamaican Weekly Gleaner*, 23–29 June 1995, 2.
67. See Editorial, *Jamaican Weekly Gleaner*, 17 Sept. 1993, 19.
68. *Financial Gleaner*, 24 June 1994, 1.
69. *Jamaican Weekly Gleaner*, 16–22 June 1995, 21.
70. See J. LeMoyne, "Military Officers in Honduras are Linked to the Drug Trade," *New York Times*, 12 Feb. 1988; D. McManus and R. Ostrow, "Alto militar hondureno es sospechoso de narcotrafico," *El Nuevo Herald*, 13 Feb. 1988; A. O'Connor, "U.S. Agents Say Honduras Is Major Cocaine Transport Point," Reuters Service, 23 Feb. 1988.
71. See Mark B. Rosenberg, "Narcos and Politicos: The Politics of Drug Trafficking in Honduras," *Journal of Inter-American Studies and World Affairs*, 30, nos. 2, 3 (summer/fall 1988), 143–65.
72. *Drugs, Law Enforcement and Foreign Policy*, part 3, 154.
73. See the testimony on Matos Ballesteros in Ibid., part 3, 150–165.
74. *Semana*, (Bogota), 668, 21–28 Feb. 1995, 27.
75. *Cambio 16*, (Bogota), 95, 3–10 April 1995, 35–46.
76. *El Nuevo Dia*, 18 May 1995, 26.
77. Calvani, *No One Is an Island*, 5, n. 5.
78. Interviews, Miami DEA Field Division, 6 Dec. 1995.
79. Woods, "Countering Transnational Crime in the Caribbean," 56.
80. See Luis E. Guarnizo, "Los Dominicanyorks: The Making of a Binational Society," in Anthony P. Maingot (ed.), Trends in U.S.-Caribbean Relations. *The Annals of the American Academy of Political and Social Science*, 533 (May 1994), 70–86.
81. The literature on corruption in the Dominican Republic is growing rapidly. The following works by M.A. Velazquez Mainardi are important: *El narcotrafico y el lavado de dolares en Republica Dominicana* (Santo Domingo: Editora Corripio, 1992); *Corrupcion e Impunidad* (Santo Domingo: Editora Tele-3, 1993).
82. See Anthony P. Maingot, "Offshore Secrecy Centers and the Necessary Role of States: Bucking the Trend," *Journal of Inter-American Studies and World Affairs*, 37, no. 4 (Winter, 1995), 1–24; "Offshore Banking in the Caribbean: The Panamanian Case," in Joyce and Malamud, eds., *Latin America and the Multinational Drug Trade*, 149–71.
83. *Drugs, Law Enforcement and Foreign Policy*, Hearings of the Subcommittee on Terrorism, Narcotics and International Communications, Committee on Foreign Relations. One Hundredth Congress, First Session. Three Parts. (Washington, D.C.: Government Printing Office, 1988).
84. *New York Times*, 31 May 1998, 14.
85. Stephen Handelman, "The Russian 'Mafia'," *Foreign Affairs*, 73, no. 2 (Mar./Apr. 1994): 83.
86. *Jamaican Weekly Gleaner*, 24 Apr. 1989, 25.
87. Jonathan M. Winer, "Problems and Strategies to Attack Narcotics, Crime and Corruption in the Caribbean," Paper, Georgetown University Conference on the Caribbean, 17 June 1997.
88. Interviews, DEA Miami Division, 6 Dec. 1995.
89. See Anthony P. Maingot, "Laundering the Gains of the Drug Trade: Miami and Caribbean Tax Havens," *Journal of Inter-American Studies and World Affairs*, 30, nos. 2, 3 (Summer/Fall 1988), 167–87.
90. *El Tiempo*, July 7, 1996, B–2.
91. U.S. Department of State, Bureau for International Narcotics and Law Enforcement Affairs, *International Narcotics Control Strategy Report*, Washington, D.C.: March 1997, 163–68.
92. *International Narcotics Control Strategy Report*.

TRANSNATIONAL CRIMINAL ORGANIZATIONS IN BOLIVIA   8

Eduardo A. Gamarra

INTRODUCTION

On December 20 in the town of Chimore, located in the coca growing region of the Chapare, President Hugo Banzer Suárez symbolically pulled the last coca plant of the 7,000 hectares Bolivia was obligated to eradicate in 1997 under the terms of bilateral agreements with the United States. Banzer also unveiled a promise to eradicate all coca grown in the Chapare by the year 2002. This is not the first time that a Bolivian head of state has promised to eradicate coca and to face head-on narcotics trafficking. In 1962, Bolivia pledged before the United Nations to wipe out all coca within two decades. And in the mid-1970s, during Banzer's own tenure as de facto president (1971–1978) Bolivia also pledged to wipe out the production of coca. Paradoxically, the coca-cocaine industry emerged as a significant dimension of Bolivian politics and economy during those very same years. Rather than disappearing, the coca-cocaine cycle has become a very significant component of Bolivia's polity, society, and economy.

In 1996, 48,100 hectares were under cultivation in Bolivia, which could yield up to 75,100 metric tons of coca leaf. The production of cocaine also increased, reaching a high of 66 metric tons in 1993, and according to the U.S. State Department's Bureau of International Narcotics and Law Enforcement Matters, 215 metric tons are potentially available from Bolivia. Although estimates are notoriously unreliable, U.S. government agencies calculate that the value of exports of cocaine base and hydrochloride (HCL) peaked in the late 1980s at about $450 million. According to the same sources, total income generated and retained in Bolivia was about $300 million. The most credible figure of the industry as a percentage of gross domestic product is between 4 and 5 percent.

Another important dimension of the Bolivian coca-cocaine cycle is the size and significance of the population employed in this industry. While there is a great deal of disagreement about the specific size (the best estimate is somewhere between 200,000 to 250,000), it is evident that this population has achieved great political importance. In 1997, for example, coca growers elected two of their principal leaders to the Bolivian Chamber of Deputies. The capacity to mobilize resistance to eradication and interdiction efforts was notorious before their leaders achieved such high office.

Pessimism about the plan is rooted not only in the rather well-known dimensions of Bolivia's coca-cocaine industry—such as organized coca growers movements—but also in the recent realization that the transnational criminal organizations (TCOs) may have surpassed the capacity of law enforcement efforts in this Andean country of 7.5 million inhabitants. For many years, the presence and significance of these organizations were dismissed in most studies of Bolivia. This chapter attempts to fill a bit of the gap by providing a historical overview of organized transnational crime in Bolivia. Given the production potential of cocaine base and HCL in Bolivia, transnational criminal organizations have been an important player, yet only former agents of the Drug Administration Administration (DEA) and journalists have delved into any type of systematic analysis of these structures and their significance in Bolivia.

For at least two decades, four traits have characterized Bolivian transnational criminal organizations: family-based enterprises; close linkages with police institutions and with the armed forces; stable, although not necessarily single, connections to international criminal networks; and diverse relationships with government officials and political parties irrespective of regime type or ideology.

Bolivian TCOs developed behind the protective cover of the attention given to Colombia's infamous drug cartels. This chapter provides an analysis of the Santa Ana cartel, a major drug-trafficking organization that spans three decades of involvement in transnational crime. This TCO reveals that Bolivia was much more active in the production and export of cocaine hydrochloride than has been commonly asserted. As early as 1978, Bolivian organizations were able to deliver refined cocaine to distribution networks on both the East and West coasts of the United States. Moreover, they were also quite eclectic in the establishment of international strategic alliances. Bolivian linkages with Mexican, Colombian, and other organizations were in place long before the recent curbing of the Medellín and Cali cartels.

Bolivia's TCOs have restructured, retooled, and accommodated to changing circumstances dictated by the changing nature of the marketplace, more effective law enforcement efforts, or transformations in the domestic political scene. While they flourished under military authoritarian governments, the transition to democracy and the democratization process did little to slow them. In fact, democratization and the introduction of market-oriented reforms provided an environment that enhanced the capacity of TCOs to expand and consolidate.

A BRIEF BACKGROUND

Organized drug trafficking from Bolivia has been present for a number of decades and has always been a source of corruption and generation of wealth.[1] Anecdotal accounts claim that the first traffickers were immigrants, primarily of Lebanese descent, who made small fortunes from the export of cocaine. A popular view is that Lebanese immigrants made fortunes illegally and then moved into respectable business ventures that quickly earned them acceptance from the native oligarchy.

The 1950s witnessed a significant shift in Bolivia as international smuggling organizations discovered cocaine. According to one account:

> By about 1955 as communication and air transportation to Bolivia improved, organized Cuban narcotics traffickers had, in concert with elements in La Paz and Cochabamba, brought on line a significant coca paste conversion capability and an embryo illicit cocaine manufacturing capability. By the late 1950s, Bolivia and more specifically La Paz and Cochabamba had become the major source for coca paste for the clandestine manufacture of cocaine in Cuba. This traffic with Cuba gradually ended between 1959 and 1960 when the Cuban narcotic traffickers in Havana and Santiago fled to the United States, Mexico and Colombia following the Castro takeover.[2]

International organizations developed linkages with Bolivian traffickers and more significantly with members of the Bolivian police and other security agencies.[3] Between 1956 and 1964, under the government of Movimiento Nacionalista Revolucionario (MNR), a significant linkage developed between government officials and international trafficking organizations.[4]

From this point onward, every government has faced accusations of linkages with drug-trafficking organizations. The most significant connections developed under the military governments that ruled Bolivia between 1964 and 1982, for two fundamental reasons. First, in the late 1960s and early 1970s international demand for cocaine and other drugs increased. In this context, military governments turned a blind eye to emerging trafficking organizations. Then, in the early 1970s, as trafficking networks shifted, a few prominent families from the Santa Cruz and Beni departments established contacts with the emerging Colombia cartels.

The transition to democracy in 1982 did little to undo the linkages of trafficking organizations to government officials. Since 1982, four consecutive governments have faced accusations of official complicity with drug organizations. Moreover, all major political parties have been accused of funding their political campaigns with money from major criminal organizations. In the 1990s, transnational criminal organizations have achieved an important presence in Bolivia.

The origins of Bolivian transnational criminal organizations are rooted in the military dictatorship of General Hugo Banzer Suárez (1971–1978). Many accounts have noted the influence on the military government of prominent Santa Cruz families allegedly tied to narcotics.[5] Several undisputed events link Banzer government officials and close relatives of the general to narcotics trafficking. Two former government officials, Marcelo Ibañez, minister of agriculture, and Walter "Pachi" Atala, undersecretary of labor, became very significant players in the narcotics connections leading to the infamous 1980 García Meza coup, to be discussed below. In 1974, Banzer's son-in-law, Luis "Chito" Valle, was asked to leave Canada after a Bolivian government official toting a diplomatic passport was arrested at the airport with a suitcase filled with cocaine presumably addressed to Valle.

Owing mainly to the cold war and Banzer's anti-Communist dictatorship, Washington showed little interest in Bolivia's emerging trafficking organizations or in the allegations of official involvement. In 1973, the newly formed DEA opened an office in the U.S. embassy in La Paz, staffed by two agents. Fighting drugs in the 1970s, however, took a back seat to fighting Communists. Infatuated with Banzer's implementation of a national security doctrine to purge leftists, for most of the 1970s U.S. officials looked the other way when charges surfaced that prominent members of the government were linked to the cocaine industry. Between 1972 and 1974 U.S. assistance totaled nearly $150 million, an exceptionally high figure considering that Bolivia had only 5 million inhabitants. A GAO audit endorsed the nature of U.S. assistance on national security grounds:

> Developments within Bolivia, due to its central location in South America, have a great impact on the Latin American community. Political stability has been the overall U.S. objective in Bolivia and since the August 1971 revolution this stability has increased.

The United States also provided grant-in-aid military equipment to Bolivia of about $3 million annually to finance the maintenance of internal security. In the mid-1970s the United States was satisfied with the Banzer government's counternarcotics efforts. The aforementioned GAO report concluded that the government had:

> strengthen[ed] its [counternarcotics] organization structure and increased measures to control the trafficking of narcotics. It has issued a new drug law providing stiff penalties for drug offenders. These efforts, while significant, are inadequate to control the manufacture of cocaine from coca. Improved Bolivian financial support and coordinated efforts between the Bolivian government and its agencies are needed.

The Banzer government established the first National Directorate for the Control of Dangerous Substances (DNCSP). Housed in the Ministry of Interior, the DNCSP centralized all counternarcotics efforts, ranging from controlling the cultivation of coca leaf to drug-abuse prevention programs. Between 1972 and 1974, Bolivia received $200,000 in U.S. assistance as part of a USAID public safety program aimed at teaching police organizations methods to control drug trafficking.

In 1975, based on the premise that coca farmers would substitute coca for legal crops if these were properly identified and funded, the State Department funded a pilot program to identify viable crops. In 1977, the Bolivian government established an agency called Proyecto de Desarrollo (PRODES) Chapare-Yungas that, in conjunction with the University of Florida at Gainesville, established a number of experimental nurseries for the production of plant material seedlings to be distributed to farmers.

During a visit by Secretary of State Henry Kissinger in September 1976, the Banzer government agreed to expand investigations into alternate crops in exchange for economic assistance and Bolivia's ratification of the Single Convention on Narcotic Drugs of 1961, a key event from the perspective of future efforts to eradicate coca. In signing the convention, the Bolivian government committed itself to the eradication of all coca crops, except for those used by the pharmaceutical industry, by the year 1990.

The late 1970s, however, did not witness a reduction in the production of coca. Instead, between 1976 and 1981 farmers in the Chapare and elsewhere abandoned traditional food crops to grow coca, as the production of coca increased from 15,600 hectares to 55,000. Stated bluntly, crop substitution programs appeared to spawn greater coca plantations.

The focus on crop substitution dominated Banzer's counternarcotics efforts in the 1970s. Interdiction efforts clearly took a back seat. In 1976, for example, the DEA had only two officials in La Paz to assist the Bolivian government in its narcotics control enforcement measures. Between 1976 and 1980, the State Department's Bureau of International Narcotics Matters provided $9.5 million in assistance to Bolivia. These efforts were clearly minimal if contrasted with the efforts underway in 1990.

Toward the end of the 1970s, the Carter administration's concern over human rights violations by the military government were not overshadowed by revelations about the involvement of officers in the drug trade. The narco-military connection did not become a major U.S. policy issue until the brief democratic interlude in 1979 and 1980. In the early months of 1980, paramilitary squads linked to the armed forces kidnapped and murdered Luis Espinal, a Catholic priest who, as director of the weekly *Aquí,* had threatened to reveal names of officers involved in the cocaine industry and other forms of corruption. The Espinal murder was the tip of the iceberg. In early 1980, Bolivian organized crime had already reached very important dimensions.

THE PIONEERS: *LA CORPORACIÓN*

For more than a dozen years, one organization established an almost complete monopoly over the Bolivian coca-cocaine industry. From its humble beginnings as a coca paste supplier to the Colombian traffickers, the Santa Ana cartel, also known as the Cartel de los Techos and "La Corporación," became a multifaceted transnational criminal organization headquartered in the Beni department. At its most profitable stage, it was capable of delivering cocaine by the ton into southern California through Mexico and shipping millions of dollars out of the United States in profits. The Corporacións origins hark back to the military dictatorships of the 1970s and the role of Roberto Suárez Gómez, who came to be known as the "King of Cocaine."

While little is known about the origins of Suárez's organization, this has not prevented a series of books and articles speculating widely and contributing to the numerous myths that surround this man's drug organization. Available evidence tells a very simple story. For most of his life, based in Santa Ana del Yacuma, in the Beni department, Suárez was primarily dedicated to raising cattle in his large ranch. At some point in the mid-1970s, Suárez claims that he was approached by Colombian traffickers who requested the use of his ranch's runway to load coca paste onto small planes destined for refinement labs in Colombia. In exchange, Suárez received $10,000 per flight.

Suárez developed a number of important contacts in Colombia, especially in Medellín, and rapidly acquired a reputation as a reliable supplier of coca paste. At the same time, however, Suárez sped toward the consolidation of his own operation, with direct links to the United States and a number of strategic alliances throughout Brazil, Colombia, the Caribbean, and Mexico. He had put together a fleet of about twenty-eight planes to pick up the paste and fly it into the Beni, on the border with Brazil, where the Colombian traffickers would pick up the supplies. Suárez was also able to deliver cocaine to Miami, Florida, without consulting with his Colombian partners.[6] According to Michael Levine, in the late 1970s Suárez was in fact uniting all major Bolivian drug producers into a single monopoly organization. As shall be seen and as has been the case in Colombia, the goal of any drug-trafficking organization has been to establish a monopoly over the production and commercialization of the product. Thus, the potential for the development of violent conflict resolution mechanisms has always been latent in Bolivia.

As Suárez's reputation grew internationally, so did his clout domestically. By the late 1970s, Suárez had developed a powerful organization with key alliances with members of the armed forces, politically powerful families, especially in Santa Cruz, and prominent political figures in La Paz.[7] In Santa Cruz, Edwin Gasser and his son José Roberto were critical to the Suárez organization. The Gasser family's involvement in narcotics was documented as early as 1971 when, at least according to some sources, it financed the August 21, 1971, coup that brought General Hugo Banzer Suárez to power.[8] In the 1970s, Santa Cruz became noteworthy for the proliferation of drug-trafficking organizations, many of which allegedly had linkages to the Banzer government. Another significant member of the Suárez Clan was Alfredo "Cutuchi" Gutierrez, who was arrested in Miami in a DEA undercover operation orchestrated by Michael Levine.[9]

The Suárez organization developed its own coca cultivation network, its own maceration pits, and refining laboratories in the Bolivian Chapare, the largest coca-producing region, and throughout the Beni. In short, Suárez no longer depended on the Colombians to conduct his business. As was the case with other trafficking organizations in Bolivia at the time, international strategic linkages were developed early and were quite diverse. Contrary to common interpretations, Colombia was only one of many routes employed by Suárez and other Bolivian organizations.

Establishing a Monopoly

In the late 1970s, as Suárez's organization expanded and achieved international prominence, Bolivia was in the throes of a turbulent transition from military-based authoritarian rule to democracy. Returning civilian politicians were watched with great suspicion and concern by most sectors of the armed forces, the Bolivian right, and most conservative forces in the country. The newly elected civilians faced a particulary problematic set of relations with the military. This was especially the case in 1979 when the National Congress, acting as a grand jury, heard charges of human rights violations and corruption against General Banzer Suárez and dozens of his collaborators.[10]

General Banzer's accusers were primarily members of the Bolivian Socialist Party; as a result, sectors of the military played the anti-Communist card well, seeking not only to end the congressional inquiry but also to murder the disrespectful leftist politicians. To achieve this end, a wing of the army established alliances with Roberto Suárez and other traffickers as well as with prominent civilian members of the Bolivian right. The result was one of the most nefarious alliances ever conceived in Bolivia and the July 17, 1980, coup that brought General Luis García Meza to power.

General Luis García Meza overthrew the feeble civilian government of Lidia Gueiler Tejada and installed himself in the governmental palace with the stated goal of remaining there for a twenty-year period. Not long after García Meza sat in the presidential chair, U.S. intelligence sources claimed that the coup had been financed by Roberto Suárez. As a result, it came to be known as the "cocaine coup."[11]

At the time of the July 17, 1980, coup, Suárez's fortune was estimated by some to have reached $300 million, although these estimates were probably exaggerated. Rumors also abounded not only that Suárez was wealthy but also that he had his own armed force, complete with Harrier jets. As with many traffickers in the remote areas of the Bolivian Beni, Suárez used his fortune to dot the landscape with good deeds, ranging from soccer fields to health posts and schools. This "Robin Hood" image served him well, as few in these isolated villages were willing to turn in their benefactor to authorities.

In the 1970s, Suárez was a respected cattle rancher; in a sense, his drug business was no different from that family-run affair. But, in sharp contrast to the Colombian upstarts from Medellín, Suárez and other traffickers in Bolivia came from well-known, albeit not necessarily wealthy, families.

In 1980 Suárez had two principal objectives: to diversify his international alliances and break away from the Colombians; and to establish monopoly production and commercialization capabilities in Bolivia. As Suárez attempted to expand his operations and free himself from the Colombians, he discovered that to achieve any type of autonomy he would either have to buy or shoot his way out of his association with Medellín. According to secondary sources, in 1980, Suárez had a serious confrontation with the Colombians, who threatened him and demanded that he desist from attempting to expand his operations without their involvement.

Without political support and a great dose of coercive capacity, Suárez realized he would also face a tremendous confrontation not only with small-time suppliers of coca paste but with competing trafficking organizations that developed during the 1970s. Thus, to protect his operations and to launch his strategy, Suárez initially sought protection from the Bolivian military. The turmoil associated with the transition to democracy, however, made the military an unreliable ally. But officers in the military had a very good recommendation: they suggested that Suárez contact Klaus Altman, better known as Klaus Barbie, the infamous Butcher of Lyon. Altman/Barbie arrived in Bolivia in the early 1950s, placed there with the assistance of U.S. intelligence agencies. Barbie was granted Bolivian citizenship under his mother's maiden name and he became a permanent intelligence consultant for every Bolivian government from at least 1956.

Barbie also became a prominent business person with interests in Peru and elsewhere in the region and an important member of military schemes in the late 1960s, which included arms trafficking among other illicit activities. In short, in contacting Barbie, Suárez realized that he was also knocking on the doors of power. These would serve him well in achieving his two primary objectives of breaking with the Colombians and establishing a Bolivian monopoly.

With the transition to democracy looming, and with the real possibility that a left-of-center coalition could take office in 1980, Barbie and his Bolivian civilian and military friends became part of the plot to stop the democratization process dead in its tracks. The coup plotters feared most of all that the UDP, the center-left coalition that was about to win the elections, would not only prosecute General Hugo Banzer Suárez but also install a Communist government that would wipe out the Bolivian private sector.

Perhaps owing to Barbie's presence, Bolivia attracted a bizarre but sizable number of French, German, and Italian neo-Nazi elements. A few, such as Joachim Fiebelkorn and Pier Luigi Pagliai, were fugitives from European justice, while others were simply drawn by the mystique of working for Barbie. Barbie and Fiebelkorn became associates and, with the remaining neo-Nazis and a number of Bolivian foot soldiers, they established a large paramilitary group which at one point may have had as many as one hundred members and which called itself *los novios de la muerte*, or the bridegrooms of death.[12]

An important relationship between Barbie, Fiebelkorn, and Suárez developed. Suárez hired Fiebelkorn to establish a paramilitary group to protect his organization from the Colombians. The group included people like Manfred Kuhlman, a Rhodesian mercenary who entered Bolivia with Fiebelkorn; Hans Stellfeld, an ex-SS member and old friend of Barbie; Jean "Napoleon" Le Clerc, a Frenchman whose main job was to protect the air fleet of coke planes leaving from the Beni region by making sure that the Colombians paid the agreed-upon amount before leaving Bolivian soil. Le Clerc was once arrested, but instead of serving jail time, he was asked to work with the police.

Fiebelkorn claimed that there were always problems with the Colombians, so they established a defense system made up of "bazookas" that were lined up on the runway and used to shoot at the Colombian planes that failed to pay for the merchandise. More significantly, Fiebelkorn was the principal bodyguard for Suárez. Fiebelkorn was paid well; he achieved enough wealth to open up his own bar, which he called Bavaria, in Santa Cruz de la Sierra.

Fiebelkorn's group had a good deal of protection from the military at nearly every level. The Suárez organization was a perfect match for the criminal organizations working within the military. This linkage matured especially with the arrival of Colonel Luis Arce Gómez to the scene as the military government's minister of the interior. Arce was also known for owning a *taxi aereo* company that serviced the Beni region.[13]

Arce Gómez had been preparing for this day for a long time. In late 1979, as chief of the second department of the army, primarily an intelligence unit, he raided police and Ministry of the Interior files, transferring these to the army. These files provided valuable information on most known trafficking organizations and were to serve the government's purposes quite well. The Minister of the Interior compiled a list with 140 names of relatively small and medium-sized dealers.[14]

Roberto Suárez, among other narco-trafficking families, financed the 1980 coup; but he also lent the military around forty of his best men, including Fiebelkorn and other Germans, to help take Santa Cruz de la Sierra. The paramilitary unit, dubbed "Grupo Especial de Comando," faced little resistance and controlled the city very quickly.

At the outset of the García Meza government, Barbie called a meeting with the Germans (including Fiebelkorn) to discuss the commercialization of coca paste with Colonel Luis Arce Gómez, by then minister of the interior. Arce Gómez's list of 140 small fish was turned over to the *novios,* whose job was to force them into retirement. The strategy to eliminate the smaller and medium-sized traffickers served two purposes; it would be used to convince the United States that the government was seriously combating drug traffickers, and it would put the large ones on notice that the military government required a larger share of their profits. The message to Roberto Suárez was that the military government would provide his organization protection to establish a monopoly in exchange for a larger share of the profits.[15]

Barbie's men targeted competing smaller operators. As this strategy unfolded, money flowed in to the government and to Barbie's henchmen. Everything from cocaine to property was seized and turned over to the *novios* and to Arce Gómez. Arce Gómez's show continued; in November 1980 he announced that drug traffickers would face the death sentence.

Secretly, the G-2 army intelligence group Arce once commanded prepared a plan known as Plan 001-FRGE. Under this plan, it became clear that military intelligence entered into negotiations with the larger traffickers and designed a plan to produce cocaine and export it through the safest and most efficient channels. In exchange for government protection and the wiping out of the smaller competitors, the traffickers would pay a tax directly to the government.

As valuable as the *novios* became to the government, they also became a nuisance, especially in the Santa Cruz area where the official credentials issued to them by Barbie and Arce Gómez were used to carry out all types of abuses. Several retaliatory moves occurred. Hans Stellfeld appeared dead of gunshot wounds, while other Germans were simply forced to leave the country. While these individuals may have been an embarrassment to the military government, they were an asset to Arce Gómez, who took a cut from all business carried out by the *novios*. Those who refused to pay, paid with their lives.[16]

As the embarrassing situations escalated for the government, General García Meza ordered a crack down on the Fiebelkorn group in Santa Cruz. The attempt to bring this group into line was not very successful. A majority left Santa Cruz or went to La Paz, where the paramilitary group was still alive under the guidance of Italian terrorist Pier Luigi Pagliai.

At the same time, the government was attempting to stay in power despite an U.S.-led international boycott, the withdrawal of General Banzer's support, and the forced resignation of Arce Gómez.[17] Little is known about the impact of the government's crisis on its relations with Roberto Suárez. It could be said that the government's travails had no impact on the cocaine business; in fact, things were booming. In 1981, after the departure of Arce Gómez and replacement of García Meza with General Celso Torrelio, Suárez received an important boost with the arrival of his nephew Jorge "Techo de Paja" Roca Suárez from the United States. Techo de Paja had been living in the United States for a few years and brought with him an important list of contacts and injected a new vitality into the Santa Ana-based organization.

Democracy and the Santa Ana Cartel

In October 1982, Bolivia experienced a final transition to democracy. Hernán Siles Zuazo presided over a very weak and troubled coalition that failed to prevent the total collapse of the Bolivian economy and an even more serious institutional crisis. Under Siles and with U.S. support, the first police efforts to combat narcotics organizations were initiated with the creation of the Unidad Móvil de Patrullaje Rural (UMOPAR). Siles also established a special counternarcotics unit and named Rafael Otazo, a close personal friend, to head the new organization.

Siles Zuazo's government faced its most critical year in 1984 when in June a group of UMOPAR officers orchestrated the president's kidnapping. Embarrased U.S. officials falsely claimed that UMOPAR had not been trained by the United States and that it had had no knowledge of the kidnapping.[18] Reports of corruption in UMOPAR had already reached critical levels. Former air force major

Clarence Edgar Mervin, former director of the Air Force's Special Operations School who had supervised the training of the UMOPAR "Leopards," concluded after his stint in Bolivia that every officer in the unit was on the take.[19]

Siles, however, was responsible for finally ending the Barbie-Fiebelkorn paramilitary organization. In 1982, in joint operations with the French and Italian governments, Bolivian security forces not only arrested and shipped Barbie to a French prison but also shipped Pier Luigi Pagliai back to Rome.

The arrival of democracy and the ostensible threats posed by the new police unit to his operations did little to shake the foundations of the Santa Ana organization. As he had done with the military, Suárez simply sought a new arrangement. At one point Otazo met with Suárez, who allegedly offered to pay off Bolivia's foreign debt if his organization was left alone.[20] Suárez's main problem had to do with the nature of a completely unregulated industry. By 1983, he faced increasing competition not only from a number of organizations that flourished after the military government collapsed but also even from within his own family-based network. His nephew Techo de Paja had already branched out on his own and had bypassed Suárez's international contacts. More importantly, Suárez had failed to establish a monopoly under García Meza and was now facing significant challenges. By 1985, Roberto Suárez had all but handed the leadership of the Santa Ana cartel to Techo de Paja, who took the Bolivian TCO to another level.

Between 1982 and 1984, the Chapare became a territory completely under the control of trafficking organizations such as the Santa Ana cartel. In June 1984, the town of Shinahota, for example, was overrun with traffickers, addicts, and prostitutes. Police presence was rare and when it occurred, it was ineffective. Only the arrival of the military in August 1984 slowed the town a bit.

The Chapare was a crucial component of the Santa Ana-based Corporación. Coca fields provided several yearly crops that were used to produce *sulfato* or base in maceration pits spread throughout the Chapare and the Beni. A fleet of Cessnas used a network of clandestine airstrips and enabled the movement of the *sulfato* to processing labs operated by the cartel throughout the Beni and even in Brazilian territory.

The cartel headquarters in Santa Ana were manned by Techo de Paja, the Roberto Suárez clan, and at least two other prominent Bolivian drug barons named Winston Rodríguez and Hugo Rivero Villavicencio. The family network that linked these individuals was extensive, involving almost the entire Beni and large parts of Santa Cruz. The political network was equally impressive. In Bolivia, the Santa Ana cartel had inroads into the government, the military, and the police. In short, the transition to democracy had simply forced the organization to reaccommodate itself to the new realities.

The Santa Ana-based Corporación also benefited from the almost complete collapse of the Bolivian economy. In 1985, afflicted by an estimated 26,000-percent inflation rate, the collapse of the traditional tin-based economy, and a major drought in the highlands, the economy hit bottom. Attracted by stories of easy money, thousands of unemployed peasants, former miners, and others flooded into the Chapare, becoming an important labor force for the cocaine economy and for organizations such as the Santa Ana cartel.

This population became important not only as a large reserve labor force but also as a significant political tool. As thousands of families came to depend on the production of coca and *sulfato* to survive, they also formed unions and joined political parties to defend their right to grow coca. At the same time, however, they also became a permanent interest group unwittingly defending the interests of the Santa Ana cartel.[21] Unlike most TCOs elsewhere in Latin America, this organization benefited from social mobilization which, in some measure, protected it from law enforcement efforts.

The Corporación also understood that under the new rules of the democratic game, it could play an important role in helping significant contenders achieve office through campaign monetary and in-kind donations. During the 1985 general elections, Roberto Suárez claimed to have funded at least two of the top three parties. To make sure he had blackmail material, Suárez installed video cameras to record the presence of prominent politicians. Caught red-handed were Alfredo Arce Carpio, the chief of campaign for Acción Democrática y Nacionalista, General Banzer's party, and General Mario Vargas Salinas, who once served in Banzer's cabinet in the mid-1970s.[22]

Internationally, the Corporación became a full-scale transnational criminal organization. Apart from the already well-developed linkages in Colombia that Roberto Suárez had developed and Techo de Paja had deepened, the Santa Ana group developed an impressive array of contacts in Mexico and the United States. In 1985, the Santa Ana-based organization had contacts with officials in the Mexican Federal Police (MFJP) and even in the Mexican military, which provided protection to cocaine shipments. Once in Los Angeles, the smuggled cocaine was easily distributed with help from Techo de Paja's contacts.

The cartel's success was measured by the millions of dollars that Techo de Paja's mother and sister would carry back to Bolivia in suitcases. At least according to one DEA report in one year they were said to have transported up to US$60 million in suitcases.

The Demise of the Santa Ana Corporación

Roberto Suárez became a victim of his own success. In 1988, he was still the best-known trafficker and the myths about his wealth and the capacity of his organization far exceeded reality. In fact, Suárez had been left behind by the exploits of Techo de Paja and was living off the earnings from his glory years.

The April 1998 discovery of videotapes linking General Banzer's party to Roberto Suárez were the beginning of the end. In the scandal that followed, pictures showing Jaime Paz Zamora, the head of the MIR, also surfaced. Accusations against the ruling Movimiento Nacionalista Revolucionario (MNR) were not far behind. In one of the most bizarre events ever, Suárez called in to a television program hosted by Carlos Palenque, a popular talk show host with political aspirations. Suárez's son Roberto Jr. was one of the guests invited to discuss the narco-videos. Suárez denied he was the "King of Cocaine" and noted that the real king was the U.S. embassy and that then-president Víctor Paz Estenssoro was the viceroy. The next day, the government closed down Palenque's television and radio stations, inadvertently giving the man a platform to run for office and to found a political party that has become very significant. Less than two months later, law enforcement arrested Roberto Suárez in his Beni hacienda and flew him to jail in La Paz. In the meantime, the three political parties issued a declaration claiming that international drug-trafficking forces were threatening to undermine Bolivian democracy.[23]

Since his arrest in July 1988, Suárez has served most of his fifteen-year sentence in the cold altiplano. In 1990, his son Roberto Jr. was killed in a gun exchange with the Bolivian police. In 1995 Suárez was moved to Cochabamba, owing largely to health reasons. Recently, he was hospitalized for the fourth time for a serious heart ailment. He is presently back in a jail cell in his native Beni, where he will likely remain for the rest of his days. If he survives his jail term, the United States still has a request for his extradition.

Techo de Paja became a victim of his own greed. After forging a crucial alliance with Mexican traffickers, military, and police officials, he sent industrial shipments of cocaine into southern California. But he took one trip too many. In 1988, an undercover DEA operation netted the Mexican connection, and in 1990, Techo de Paja himself was arrested in San Diego. In a press conference Attorney General Richard Thornburgh described Techo as "the most significant narcotics trafficker in Bolivia. While many see him as a folk hero, his ruthless methods enabled him to cultivate and corrupt Bolivian officials in order to protect a narcotics trade that was both far-reaching and extremely deadly."[24]

Luis Arce Gómez was arrested in Argentina in the early 1980s; after serving one year in prison there, the Argentine courts rejected a U.S. extradition request. Arce Gómez lived underground in Argentina and Paraguay until December 1989, when he was arrested in a joint operation by Bolivian police and the DEA in the city of Santa Cruz de la Sierra, the old stomping grounds of the *novios de la muerte*. He was then taken to a runway in the department of Cochabamba, where he was placed on a DEA plane bound for Miami. Arce Gómez stood trial in Miami in December 1990 and January 1991 and was convicted of conspiring to export cocaine into the United States. He is currently serving a thirty-year sentence at the Memphis Federal Penitentiary.[25]

Finally, in July 1991, the last vestiges of the Santa Ana cartel were targeted in a U.S.-supported military operation called Safe Haven. While the operation was carried out with great fanfare, Hugo Rivero Villavicencio and Winston Rodríguez, the last of the prominent leaders of the cartel, were long gone. A few weeks later, however, the government of Jaime Paz Zamora (1989–1993) came up with a so-called Repentance Decree that enabled the entire Santa Ana clan to turn themselves in in exchange for lenient sentences. Between August and December 1991, seven of the Santa Ana bosses turned in were arrested. When all was said and done, Rivero and Rodríguez among others were sentenced to five years in a Bolivian prison; they were also promised no extradition to the United States.[26]

CONCLUSION

This chapter reveals at least four fundamental characteristics about Bolivia's role in the transnational narcotics world. First, like most criminal organizations, it was a family-based enterprise that spanned not only the extended Suárez clan in the Bolivian east but also included family members in the United States with well-developed networks in cities such as Miami and Los Angeles. At the same time, Suárez had very close ties with other prominent families who shared not only the same business interest but also, at the outset, a fundamentally conservative political agenda linked primarily to the Bolivian right. These tight-knit family organizations characterized most of the early enterprises. Interviews with Bolivian law enforcement officials in 1996 suggest, however, that contemporary criminal organizations are less family-based.

Second, as with other family-based trafficking organizations, the Suárez organization developed very early relations with the Bolivian armed forces and other security institutions. These relations not only included the standard corruption of minor officials involved in law enforcement but also reached into the upper echelons of both police and military institutions. The Suárez group established significant linkages, which spanned three decades, with these institutions. These ties were fundamentally important for the criminal organization's efforts both to achieve a monopoly over the drug industry in Bolivia and to insure protection from U.S.-promoted law enforcement efforts and from domestic and international competitors. At the same time, the security needs of TCOs such as this one required it to establish alternative arrangements with paramilitary groups such as the infamous *novios de la muerte*.

In the mid to late 1990s, linkages with security forces and the military continue although in contrast to those of the early 1980s, these are with corrupt officials and not with the institution as a whole. Nevertheless, on more than one ocassion in the past five years, significant members of the police forces have been accused of involvement with one trafficking group or another. Corruption of the FELCN in 1995, for example, produced yet another major overhaul in an attempt to weed out officials who were reportedly on the take. In short, drug-trafficking organizations cannot function effectively without suborning members of law enforcement and the armed forces. Only the range and depth of the linkages have changed since the early 1980s.

Third, drug-trafficking organizations such as the Suárez organization required a significant amount of political cover. Thus, while the Suárez group originated under the protection of right-wing military governments, it also penetrated the upper echelons of democratic administrations. In this sense, it was a pragmatic organization that accommodated quickly to the new democratic period that Bolivia initiated in 1982. If the numerous charges against the principal political parties are true, the TCOs flexibility became evident with its efforts to finance several presidential campaigns in 1985, 1987, and 1989. Suárez and others did not bet on a single candidate, but instead made sure that all likely winners got some contribution.

Bolivian TCOs required a broader-based source of support that transcended political parties, the armed forces, and police. While this statement is controversial, it is quite clear that organized coca growers who mobilized against government efforts to enforce eradication agreements with the United States unwittingly became members of the TCO-supporting coalition. This does not mean that peasant unions or their leadership were willing partners of the TCO; however, the fact remains that most of their crop, especially that grown in the Chapare, provided the basic raw material for the production of cocaine.

The transition to democracy in Bolivia may have also had the paradoxical effect of democratizing the structure of organized crime. As the military and police connections of the Suárez organization suffered important setbacks in the early 1980s, smaller and bolder competitors proliferated. In some measure, this proliferation increased the challenges for law enforcement and military institutions to combat drug trafficking. This essay reveals that Bolivia's TCOs have been able to restructure, retool, and accommodate to changing circumstances dictated by the changing nature of the marketplace, more effective law enforcement efforts, or transformations in the domestic political scene.

Fourth, the Suárez organization demonstrates that Bolivian TCOs developed stable, although not necessarily single, connections to international criminal networks. At its most influential period, in addition to its stable connections with Colombian organizations, the Santa Ana cartel controlled routes in Bolivia, Brazil, Panama, and Mexico, in addition to other routes through Argentina. In short, Bolivia was much more active in the production and export of cocaine hydrochloride than has been commonly asserted. As early as 1978, Bolivian organizations were able to deliver refined cocaine to distribution networks on both the East and West coasts of the United States.

It is also clear that the Santa Ana cartel developed an important laundering network that funneled cash back into the Bolivian economy. While this dimension is the least explored, the Bolivian banking industry, especially fly-by-night credit associations, became a fundamental part of the laundering schemes.[27] This chapter has not dealt with the money-laundering dimension of organized crime, and there are no works available on the topic. Nevertheless, law enforcement sources suggest that the Bolivian economy is replete with examples of laundering activities.

It is noteworthy that Bolivian TCOs received very little attention in the specialized literature and only a few journalists and former DEA agents have noted their size and significance. In a sense, this chapter suffers from the same defects; the Santa Ana cartel is the best known and therefore the easiest to write about. Its notoriety contributed to its downfall as perhaps the notoriety of Cali and Medellín led to their dismantlement. At the same time, however, it is important to note that Bolivian organized crime has been able to develop behind the protection of the attention given to larger enterprises in Colombia, Mexico, and elswhere.

Finally, an important comparative note must be made. Other equally significant organizations exist in Bolivia that are capable of moving large amounts of refined cocaine directly into Mexico and the United States. The most noteworthy case was that of Amado "Barbas Chocas" Pacheco, who for at least one decade smuggled cocaine into Mexico. Pacheco was arrested in September 1995 when his DC-6 loaded with 4.1 tons of cocaine was stopped at the Jorge Chavez airport in Lima, Peru. In contrast to the early days of the Suárez organization, which boasted that it could deliver 1,000 kilograms per month, the contemporary shipments are massive. Yet, little is known about these organizations outside of law enforcement circles.[28]

Current data on Bolivia (see Annex) suggests that despite increased law enforcement efforts on the part of the Bolivian and U.S. governments, criminal enterprises linked to the narcotics trade will not disappear. Law enforcement has been largely ineffective against organized criminal enterprises who have diversified their routes and expanded their strategic alliances throughout the hemisphere.

Bolivian trafficking routes have been identified in Argentina, Brazil, Peru, and Chile.

ANNEX

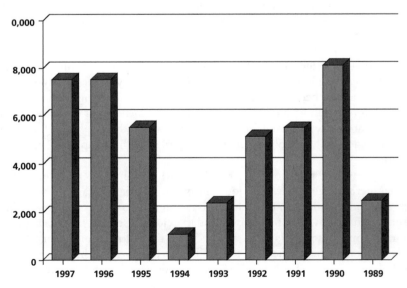

Figure 8.1   Coca Leaf Eradication
(1,000s of hectares)

Source: International Narcotics Control Strategy Report 1997.

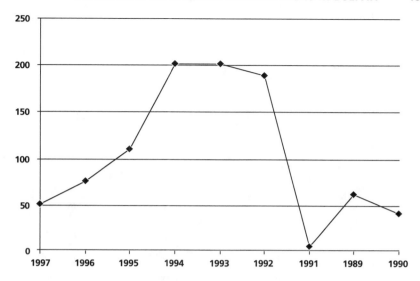

Figure 8.2   Coca Leaf Seizures (metric tons) 1989–1996

Source: International Narcotics Control Strategy Report 1997.

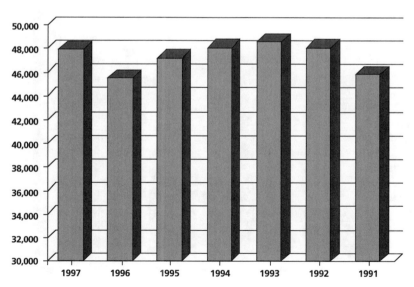

Figure 8.3   Bolivia: Coca Cultivation 1991–1996
(1,000s of hectares)

Source: International Narcotics Control Strategy Report 1997.

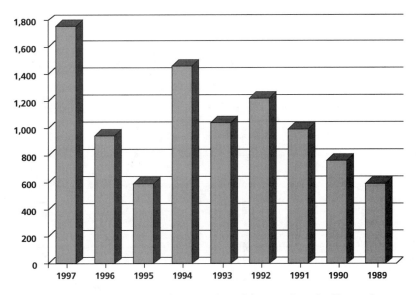

Figure 8.4   Arrests and Detentions (Drug-Related Offenses)

Source: International Narcotics Control Strategy Report 1997.

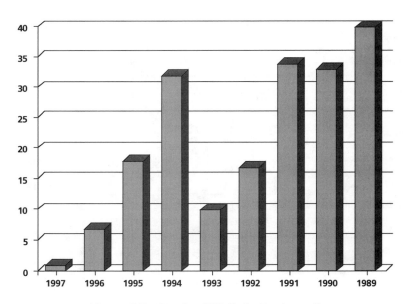

Figure 8.5   Cocaine HCL (Labs Destroyed)

Source: International Narcotics Control Strategy Report 1997;
Fuerza Especial de Lucha Contra el Narcotráfico 1998.

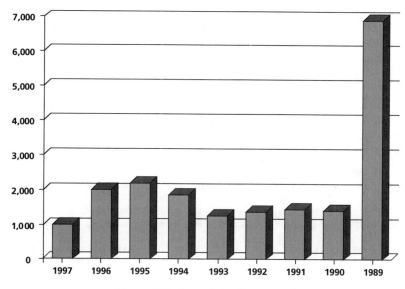

Figure 8.6   Base Labs Destroyed

Source: International Narcotics Control Strategy Report 1997;
Fuerza Especial de Lucha Contra el Narcotráfico 1998.

NOTES

1. According to one report, the first-known seized shipment of cocaine from Bolivia took place in 1940 when a customs agent discovered four cans full of cocaine ready to be shipped to Germany. At this time, clandestine cocaine labs were found in the city of La Paz. See William R. Mendoza, *Mercaderes de la muerte* (Buenos Aires: Marymar Ediciones, 1993).

2. House of Representatives, Select Committee on Narcotics Abuse and Control, International Narcotics Control Study Missions to Latin America and Jamaica (6–21 Aug. 1983), Hawaii, Hong Kong, Thailand, Burma, Pakistan, Turkey, and Italy (4–22 Jan. 1984).

3. Interviews with retired members of the Bolivian police who served during the MNR period.

4. See Mendoza, *Mercaderes*, p. 34–40 for a fascinating account of the linkages between Bolivian police forces and international traffickers. According to this account, when in the mid-1950s a major drug ring was busted, fifty individuals were arrested, including Argentines, Peruvians, Chileans, Spaniards, Greeks, Hungarians, Bolivians, and Germans.

5. These allegations have been discussed in a number of books by investigative journalists. Unfortunately, these accounts are replete with factual errors and with a great deal of uncorroborated speculation that detracts from the substance of the allegations. The worst examples can be found in Elaine Shannon, *Desperados: Latin Drug Lords, U.S. Lawmen, and the War America Can't Win* (New York: Viking, 1988) and Paul Eddy, Hugo Sabogal, and Sara Walden *Cocaine Wars* (New York: Norton, 1988).

6. See, for example, *Miami Herald*, 23 May 1980 for an account in the U.S. media.

A fascinating, detailed, albeit novelesque, summary of the operation can be found in Michael Levine, *The Great White Lie: The CIA and the Cocaine/Crack Epidemic* (New York: Thunder Mouth Press, 1993). This credible account claims that in 1979, Suárez's organization was already capable of delivering 1,000 kilograms of cocaine per month. The way in which DEA undercover agents infiltrated the organization with ease suggests that international strategic alliances are very footloose, constantly shaping and reshaping.

7. Interview by author with Roberto Suárez, La Paz, Bolivia. See also *Narcotráfico y política: militarismo y mafia en Bolivia* (Madrid: IEPALA, 1982); Mendoza, *Mercaderes*; Michael Levine, *Deep Cover* (New York: Delacorte Press, 1990); and Levine, *The Great White Lie*; Jonathan Kandell, *Passage through El Dorado: Travelling the World's Last Great Wilderness* (New York: Avon Books, 1984) for several accounts about the Suárez organization.

8. See, for example, James Dunkerley, *Rebellion in the Veins* (London: Verso, 1984).

9. Levine, *The Great White Lie*.

10. These events have been discussed in detail in James Malloy and Eduardo Gamarra, *Revolution and Reaction: Bolivia 1964–1985* (New Brunswick, NJ: Transaction Books, 1988).

11. While it is generally accepted that the coup was financed by Suárez and perhaps even other traffickers, there is debate over the motivations for the coup. International observers, especially the media and the U.S. government, insisted that the coup was because the traffickers had bought themselves a government to insure the flow of cocaine out of Bolivia. In my view, the coup had less to do with the interests of traffickers and more with an internal political situation motivated by the almost certain indictment of General Hugo Banzer Suárez by the National Congress. The Jul. 17 coup came two days after the National Congress voted to allow the incoming legislature the right to vote on an indictment of General Banzer and his supporters. Had the coup not occurred, a newly elected legislature, in which Banzer's opponents vastly outnumbered his party, would most likely have handed down an indictment. See my "Political Stability, Democratization and the Bolivian National Congress" (Ph.D. dissertation, University of Pittsburgh, 1987) and Raúl Barrios Morón, *Bolivia y estados unidos: democracia, derechos humanos y narcóticos, 1980–1982* (La Paz: FLACSO/HISBOL, 1989).

12. This account follows the fascinating work of Magnus Linklater, Isabel Hilton, and Neal Ascherson, *The Nazi Legacy: Klaus Barbie and the International Fascist Connection* (New York: Holt and Rinehart, 1984).

13. Allegedly, Arce Gómez's eight small taxi planes were also used for the transportation of cocaine. This section relies on personal notes taken at Luis Arce Gómez's trial in Miami December 1990 and January 1991, and an interview with Arce Gómez at the Metropolitan Center in Dade County, Florida on February 16, 1991. It also relies on a review of the transcripts of the trial, see *United States of America v. Luis Arce-Gómez*, defendant, United States District Court, Southern District of Florida, Jury Trial before the Honorable Jose A. Gonzalez, Jr.

14. Interview with Luis Arce Gómez, ibid.

15. The government's efforts to convince the U.S. of its commitment to stamping out drugs included the full-scale entry of the military into the Chapare. Arce Gómez claimed that the government's strategy of working with some traffickers mimicked DEA tactics of working with some to catch others. Testimony Miami, Florida, December 1990.

16. Arce Gómez used the *novios* to intimidate smaller traffickers into paying him large protection payments. Such was the case of Sonia and Walter Atalá, a husband-wife trafficking team that paid Arce Gómez $40,000 on one occasion. The Atalás went on to become key DEA informants in the U.S. trial of Arce Gómez.

17. Banzer was named ambassador to Argentina and at one point was a special envoy of

the government to the United States. Arce Gómez was first named commander of the military academy and then became military attache at the Bolivian embassy in Argentina.

18. The best account of the kidnapping can be found in Edgar Claure and Gary Prado Salmón, *Han secuestrado al presidente* (La Paz: Los Amigos del Libro, 1990).

19. For Merwin's account, consult David Kline, "How to Lose the Coke War," *Atlantic Monthly*, May 1987, 22–27.

20. The Otazo-Suárez meeting became one of the most significant scandals facing the Siles administration and led in some measure to the government's early withdrawal from office.

21. Few dispute the fact that coca grown in the Chapare is cultivated almost entirely for the cocaine economy. Still, it is politically unfeasible to attack the sole source of income for thousands of people.

22. The narco-videos, as they came to be known, proved numerous rumors about campaign financing. Few could explain how parties could spend lavishly on campaign paraphernalia, television spots, and expensive foreign pollsters in the middle of Bolivia's worst-ever economic crisis. Beginning with the 1985 election, trafficking organizations became an important source of campaign funding. The precedent it established proved devastating for other parties, such as the Movimiento de Izquierda Revolucionaria, which funded its municipal campaign in 1987 and its national run in 1989 with money and in-kind donations from Isaac "Oso" Chavarría, one of the most wanted drug barons in the country. Finally, in 1995 Miguel Angel Villavicencio, a Santa Ana cartel associate, claimed that Techo de Paja paid the Movimiento Nacionalista Revolucionario $2 million to fund its 1985 campaign. Villavicencio also claimed that Santa Ana paid $150,000 a month to Fernando Bartelemy, the minister of the interior, in 1987.

23. These events are discussed in Eduardo A. Gamarra, *Entre la droga y la democracia* (La Paz: ILDIS, 1994).

24. Press Release Office of the United States Attorney, Southern District of California, San Diego, California, 14 Dec. 1990. To convict Roca Suárez, the prosecution relied on the testimony of Miguel Ángel Villavicencio, a former Santa Ana cartel associate who was shot in 1986 under orders from Techo de Paja for refusing to pay a $250,000 debt. Villavicencio, who is paralyzed from the waist down as a result of the shooting, has been in the U.S. witness protection program since the 1990 trial.

25. Interview by author with Luis Arce Gómez, Metropolitan Correctional Institution, Dade Country Florida, 16 February 1991.

26. For a closer look at this period, see E. Gamarra, *Entre la droga y la democracia*.

27. Consult E. Gamarra, *Entre la Droga y la Democracia*, for an analysis of the credit unions in Cochabamba that were allegedly linked to Techo de Paja.

28. A history of Pacheco's organization is available in Gerard Irusta Medrano and Edwin Miranda, *De Huanchaca al narcoavión* (La Paz: Editorial Gráfica Latina, 1995).

SEMIORGANIZED INTERNATIONAL CRIME: DRUG TRAFFICKING IN MEXICO

9

Peter H. Smith

Organized international crime exerts its most powerful influence in Mexico through drug trafficking. Transnational syndicates and local organizations involved in the production, transportation, and distribution of illicit drugs have engaged in large-scale corruption of public officials, fostered waves of brutal violence, created nearly autonomous territorial fiefdoms, and openly flouted the rule of law. Soon after taking office in December 1994, President Ernesto Zedillo Ponce de León received an official report warning that "The power of the drug-trafficking organizations could lead to situations of ungovernability. . . . [T]he advance of drug-trafficking promotes impunity and uncertainty in [public] institutions, justifies violence, and increases intimidation of the authorities."[1] For all these reasons Zedillo, like his predecessors, has proclaimed that drug trafficking represents a paramount threat to Mexico's national security.

The narcotics trade also creates serious problems for Mexico's relationship with the United States. According to U.S. government data, there are roughly 13 million current users of illegal drugs in the United States, spending approximately $60 billion per year on this habit.[2] And it is estimated that Mexico now transports 50–60 percent of the cocaine that enters the United States, 20–30 percent of the heroin, and up to 80 percent of the imported marijuana. As a result, drugs and drug trafficking inevitably constitute a major issue in U.S.-Mexican relations.

How did this criminal activity develop? Where does it appear to be heading? What can law enforcement do? To examine these questions, I here explore four interrelated themes: first, the transformation of *narcotráfico* in Mexico from the late 1970s to the mid-1990s; second, the economic and political implications of drug trafficking within Mexico; third, the impact of the drug issue on U.S.-Mexican relations; and fourth, the range of policy options available to Mexico.[3]

DRUG TRAFFICKING IN MEXICO

Drug trafficking in Mexico has undergone fundamental change in recent years. From the 1930s through the 1970s, Mexico occupied a straightforward role in the international market, supplying some of the heroin and most of the marijuana imported into the United States. Both crops were raised by small-scale farmers in specific regions: opium poppies were cultivated in the north-central states of Sinaloa, Durango, and Chihuahua, and to a lesser extent in Sonora; cannabis (for marijuana) was grown throughout the country, not only throughout the northwest but also with notable concentrations in Michoacán, Jalisco, and Nayarit. During the 1950s and 1960s Mexico supplied as much as three-quarters of the U.S. market for marijuana and 10–15 percent of the demand for heroin; by the mid-1970s, after the rupture of the infamous "French connection" from Turkey through Marseilles to the United States in 1972, Mexico came to supply as much as 80 percent of the U.S. market for heroin.[4]

Throughout this period the processing and transportation of final products rested mainly in the hands of less than a dozen large and illegal organizations, although the marijuana industry was less centralized than the opium/heroin business. During the 1970s key organizations were identified with family names: Herrera, Aviles Pérez, Valenzuela, Araujo, Sicilia-Falcón. As a rule, these groups maintained close relations with local farmers, from whom they regularly purchased crops; they kept their headquarters in key production areas (Culiacán being one well-known site); and while they earned substantial profits, they did not expand their operations to reach new markets with new goods. They resorted to bribery and intimidation, of course, but mostly on the local and regional level, and they maintained relatively low political profiles.[5] While they exercised effective control over the Mexican narcotics trade, in other words, they were neither as powerful nor as internationally oriented as their Colombian counterparts.[6] They were local organizations dealing in locally-grown products.

In time, Mexican marijuana and opium became the targets of aggressive antidrug policies. In September 1969 the Nixon administration launched Operation Intercept, subjecting border crossings to intensive scrutiny and time-consuming harassment for nearly three weeks; after much frustration and scant seizures, the effort gave way to a face-saving Operation Cooperation the following month. It was in 1975 that, once again under pressure from the United States, the Mexican government initiated its Campaña Permanente against illicit drugs. Spearheaded by "Operation Condor," the Campaña launched a coordinated attack that focused on eradication of crops, interdiction of shipments, and disruption of commercial organizations. One particularly conspicuous element was collaboration with U.S. government agencies. Another was deployment of the Mexican army, which eventually devoted up to one-quarter of its personnel and resources to the antidrug campaign.[7]

The Campaña had remarkable results. Apparently as a consequence, Mexico's share of the U.S. marijuana market plunged from more than 75 percent in 1976 to 11 percent in 1979, 8 percent in 1980, and down as far as 4 percent in 1981. Similarly, the Mexican share of the heroin market dropped from 67 percent in 1976 to 25 percent in 1980. (This did not mean, of course, that American consumers were using less drugs. Instead, the vacuum in the marijuana market was quickly filled by growers in Jamaica and Colombia and within the United States, and stepped-up quantities of heroin came from Afghanistan, Iran, and Pakistan.) Eventually, Mexican entrepreneurs managed to recuperate a sizable portion of market share: by the mid-1980s Mexico was supplying around 30 percent of the marijuana consumed in the United States and about 40 percent of the heroin.

An unintended outcome of the Campaña was intensified concentration within the Mexican drug industry. While Operation Condor pushed some prominent traffickers out of the business—such as Pedro Aviles Pérez of Sinaloa—it also tended to strengthen the relative position of those who could survive. Stepped-up enforcement also encouraged the leaders of survivor groups to reorganize their enterprises, relying heavily on their comparative advantages: bribery and violence. (Probably the most notorious kingpin of this era was Miguel Angel Félix Gallardo, leader of the Guadalajara gang.)[8] As a result of this policy initiative, in other words, the Mexican drug industry came under the control of entrepreneurial organizations that were fewer in number, stronger in resources, and more dangerous to society and government.

Since the mid-1980s Mexico has held fairly steady positions in the international markets for marijuana and heroin.[9] But there also occurred a major change, which came about when *narcotraficantes* from Colombia began seeking new routes for shipping cocaine into the United States. As U.S. law enforcement agencies cracked down on shipments through the Caribbean and South Florida in the early to mid-1980s, Colombian entrepreneurs—especially leaders of the sophisticated Cali cartel—turned their attention toward Mexico. Initially, they ferried relatively modest shipments of cocaine in Cessnas or other small planes from Colombia to Mexico and then, with the aid of Mexican collaborators, sent them overland to the United States. In the early 1990s, as operations matured, Colombians began to fly their merchandise to central and southern Mexico in converted 727s and Caravelles capable of handling multiton loads; Mexican carriers would then take them north in trucks, small planes, and trains across the border to the United States, where operatives under the Colombians would break down the shipments for wholesale and retail distribution. Within the cocaine trade, Mexicans became classic "middlemen."

These joint ventures with Colombians had far-reaching consequences. First, Mexico became the primary transit route for cocaine entering the United States. As of 1989, the U.S. State Department estimated that 30 percent of U.S.-bound cocaine passed through Mexico; by 1992, the estimate surpassed 50 percent; for other years, the estimate has been as high as 75 to 80 percent. (It is most recently pegged at around 50–60 percent.)[10] Along parallel lines, seizures of cocaine in Mexico began a steep upward climb in 1985; they more than tripled between

1988 and 1990, and have remained at high levels ever since.[11] No matter what the indicator, one fact is inescapably clear: Mexico has become a major player in the international market for cocaine.

This development reshaped both the structure and the power of trafficking organizations. As indicated above, Mexico's traditional marketing groups maintained close ties with producers, operated at local levels, and maintained low political profiles. The increase in cocaine traffic changed this picture in far-reaching ways. Where the Colombians forged joint partnerships with existing groups, as in Guadalajara, it expanded and strengthened their economic base; and where the Colombians enticed other criminal organizations into the cocaine trade, as in the state of Tamaulipas, it led to the emergence of new contenders. Smuggling rings in Ciudad Juárez and Tamaulipas—virtually unknown in drug circles prior to the late 1980s—came to assume unprecedented importance. And when Mexican prosecutors cracked down on the Tamaulipas group, their efforts created new opportunities for their rivals in Ciudad Juárez, who quickly became the prime intermediaries along the market route from Colombia to the United States.[12] Second, the profitability of the cocaine business greatly augmented the economic resources of trafficking groups. According to Thomas A. Constantine, current head of the Drug Enforcement Administration, annual profits for Mexican *traficantes* now approach $7 billion; the Mexican attorney general's office has placed the figure as high as $30 billion per year. Third, the emphasis on cocaine has severed the long-standing relationship between farmers and distributors. Mexico's new traffickers therefore have less allegiance to local areas, less reason to concentrate their attention on the local scene. They are competing against each other for the same goods and the same market.

Ever the opportunists, Mexican traffickers have also turned toward the manufacture and distribution of methamphetamine, one of the fastest-growing markets in the United States. In the form of crystal or "speed," methamphetamine has gained notable popularity among U.S. middle-class, white-collar workers in their twenties and thirties. Once again, the syndicates have seized an opportunity: with the crackdown on methamphetamine laboratories in the United States, especially in Southern California, Mexicans have taken up the slack. As a result of increasing production and availability, the average price has dropped by 20 percent (from $50 per gram to $40 per gram). As DEA head Constantine once put it: "The Mexican traffickers who flooded the U.S. with marijuana and heroin in the 1970s and 1980s and cocaine in the 1990s threaten to overwhelm us with methamphetamine now." With regard to this class of drugs, Constantine added: "We believe that the major drug gangs operating out of Mexico pose the largest threat currently."[13]

HOW ORGANIZED IS ORGANIZED CRIME?

The acceleration of drug trafficking in Mexico raises basic questions about the level and nature of organization within the industry. This is not merely a matter of academic curiosity: it has policy implications. If drug operations in Mexico are highly and centrally organized, it should be (theoretically) possible to destroy them through decapitation, almost at a single stroke. If they are disaggregated and decentralized, however, this would call for a lengthy war of attrition.

It is clear that Mexican drug syndicates have continued to grow in prominence and power in recent years. The dismantling of Colombia's Cali group in 1995–1996 created new opportunities for Mexican traffickers, who began to develop their own wholesale and retail operations in the United States. Bypassing now-weakened Colombian operators, they also started forging direct links to coca leaf farmers and processing laboratories in Bolivia and Peru.

According to the DEA, there are now four major drug organizations in Mexico.[14] All deal in a variety of drugs, but they specialize as well. Two deal mainly in cocaine:

- The Carrillo Fuentes organization, based in Ciudad Juárez, principally engaged in the transshipment of cocaine from Colombia and other points in South America into the United States. With storage locations in Guadalajara, Hermosillo, and Torreón, this enterprise reportedly generates tens of millions of dollars in profits per week. It is also involved in heroin and marijuana trafficking. Top leader Amado Carrillo Fuentes (a.k.a. the "Lord of the Skies") unexpectedly died in July 1997 from postoperative complications after extensive plastic surgery undertaken to help elude law enforcement. Since then a violent power struggle has ensued—resulting in approximately 50 drug-related murders in the Juárez area alone.

- The Arellano Félix organization, based in Tijuana, led by three brothers: Ramón Eduardo, Javier, and Benjamín (chairman of the board), linked by family to legendary boss Miguel Angel Félix Gallardo. The Tijuana group deals in multiton quantities of cocaine and marijuana, as well as large quantities of heroin and methamphetamine. According to Constantine, "this organization is one of the most powerful, violent, and aggressive trafficking groups in the world. More than any other drug trafficking organization from Mexico, it extends its tentacles directly from high-echelon figures in the law enforcement and judicial systems in Mexico, to street-level individuals in the United States."[15]

One group specializes in marijuana:

- The Caro Quintero organization, based in Sonora, led by three brothers: Miguel, Jorge, and Genaro Caro Quintero (related by family to the notorious Rafael Caro Quintero, a leading kingpin of the 1980s, and also to Miguel Angel Félix Gallardo). This group specializes in the cultivation, production, and distribution of marijuana, and also transports and distributes cocaine and methamphetamine.

The fourth group concentrates on methamphetamine:

- The Amezcua group, operating out of Colima and Guadalajara, also led by three brothers—Jesús, Adán, and Luis Amezcua Contreras. This organization is thought by the DEA to be "probably the largest smuggler of ephedrine and clandestine producer of methamphetamine in the world today."[16]

There are half a dozen additional groups that play significant roles in the drug trade, and many other minor participants (perhaps a hundred or more). As a sign of rapid turnover, two organizations that stood near the top in 1995–1996 are virtually out of business as of 1998: the Tamaulipas syndicate, weakened by arrests of top leaders and by competition with the Juárez group, and the Sinaloa syndicate, diminished and defeated by the more powerful Tijuana group.[17]

What is the level of organization within the Mexican drug industry? And how might this compare with international organized crime elsewhere in the Americas? Analysis begins with definition. Organized (or not) in what sense? According to what criteria? To approach these questions, I here assess degrees and types of organization with regard to four key factors: internal (intramural) organization, turnover in personnel, level of collusion, and overall structure of the industry.

Internal Organization

The leading drug syndicates in Mexico are highly and efficiently organized. Often led by family members at the top, they involve hundreds of individuals with specialized roles—from security chiefs to hired guns to marketing agents, accountants, financial consultants, and money-laundering specialists. They make regular use of sophisticated technology, countersurveillance methods, and state-of-the-art communications devices. Supported by the lure of financial reward and the threat of physical punishment, internal discipline appears to be strong. These businesses are notably successful in achieving their principal goal—the accumulation of profits. It has been said, only half in jest, that they might represent some of the most efficient private enterprises anywhere within the Western Hemisphere.

Personnel

To put it euphemistically, there is a high rate of turnover, especially among upper echelons of the major syndicates. This is not due to natural causes. Leaders usually fade from view either because they are arrested or because they meet an untimely (usually violent) death. Such was the case of Rafael Muñoz Talavera, murdered in 1998 during a succession struggle over control of the Ciudad Juárez group, and of Amado Carrillo Fuentes, who died of postoperative shock in 1997. The top of the mountain turns out to be a dangerous place.

Precisely for this reason, leadership is frequently controlled by family relatives. This is true for all four of the uppermost organizations as of 1998—run by the brothers Carrillo Fuentes, Arellano Félix, Caro Quintero, and Amezcua Contreras. (It has been rumored that Amado Carrillo Fuentes's brother Vicente had assumed leadership of the Juárez syndicate by mid-1998.) Clearly, this conspicuous presence of family ties reflects the need for (and scarcity of) trust among institutional leaders. Even as big businesses, these remain family-led operations.

Degree of Collusion

Relations between the syndicates are more competitive than cooperative. In fact, the term "cartel"—commonly used for the Mexican groups—is a misnomer, and for that reason I avoid this label. To be sure, the most powerful Mexican syndicates form an oligopsony/oligopoly with regard to a significant share of world cocaine supplies. On occasion they also reach tacit agreement on market boundaries, particularly for transit corridors into the United States, usually as a result of a fragile truce among competing syndicates. Unlike classic "trusts" or "cartels," however, they do not engage in collusion to establish market prices—and they couldn't do so even if they tried, since they do not control sufficient market shares. Mexico produces less than 1.3 percent of the world's opium poppies and less than 30 percent of the international marijuana supply—not counting U.S. domestic production, which accounts for at least one-quarter of the marijuana actually consumed in the United States.[18] And while Mexico might have ferried as much as two-thirds of South America's cocaine exports in peak years, this was largely at the discretion of Colombian partners—who generally maintained control of U.S. retail markets, and who did not want to have their customers gouged for the sake of Mexican middlemen.

Although Peter Lupsha and others have spoken of a Mexican "federation" of drug lords,[19] there appears in the 1990s to be more rivalry than coordination among the syndicates. Competition among the top groups also appears to be more intense than in the early to mid-1980s. In the precocaine era, a prestigious figure such as Miguel Angel Félix Gallardo could function as a "godfather," adjudicating disputes and regulating market shares. This is no longer the case. Mexico's newly arrived *capos* have little connection with (or respect for) counterparts in other organizations—they are ruthless and relentless, and they readily resort to violence. After all, the stakes are now much higher than they were before.

Tension sometimes leads to bloodshed between members (or hit men) of the different gangs. On other occasions, kingpins entice (or wait for) Mexican and/or U.S. law enforcement agents to weaken rival gangs. Thus, when Mexican police finally managed to track down Joaquín Guzmán (El Chapo) of the once-prominent Sinaloa organization, then locked in a bitter struggle with the Tijuana group, the arrest "in effect turned the government into an enforcer for the Arellanos."[20]

Structure of the Industry

Throughout all this turbulence, there is considerable continuity in the structure of the industry. Since the mid-1980s, and perhaps before, the Mexican drug industry has consisted of three tiers:

- A top rung of three to five major organizations—these days, fully integrated operations with international contacts, networks, and markets;
- A middle layer of perhaps six to twenty mid-level organizations—smaller units that sometimes collaborate with the major firms, sometimes operate on their own, occasionally carving out subsidiary portions of the market for smuggling or wholesale distribution;
- A bottom layer of small but numerous units, perhaps with only a dozen operatives each, usually specializing in one specific part of the business or subcontracting their assets to larger organizations.[21]

Despite volatility in personnel and market share, this pyramidal structure has persisted over time. This may be due to several factors. First is market position: so long as cocaine is being transshipped from Colombia through Mexico to the United States, there will be need for internationally oriented syndicates. Second is inequality in resources: so long as law enforcement maintains pressure on drug traffickers, it will tend to weed out weaker groups and leave the stronger syndicates intact, through a quasi-Darwinian process of natural selection. Third is financial incentive: so long as profits remain enormous, larger organizations will attempt to eliminate smaller competitors and dominate the market. (Where levels of risk are lower and rates of return are more modest, as in the case of methamphetamine and marijuana, there is more room for the small-scale operators who cluster at the industry's bottom rung.)

For all these reasons, it seems appropriate to regard international crime in Mexico as "semiorganized." It is organized in some respects and not in others. What this means, in terms of policy, is that decapitation will not bring an end to trafficking or traffickers. For every top *capo* who is killed or put into jail, there is an eager and able lieutenant ready to fill the void. Unlike some terrorist organizations, drug syndicates are hydra-headed monsters.

IMPACTS IN MEXICO

In apparent contrast to the situation in Colombia, drug trafficking in Mexico has not (yet) led to structural distortions of the national economy. This is mainly a function of size. With a GDP of nearly $350 billion in 1997, the Mexican economy is four times larger than that of Colombia. Mexico's (legitimate) exports are more than seven times those of Colombia. As a matter of simple arithmetic, the relative impact of the cocaine trade—from Colombia through Mexico to the United States—is therefore likely to be a good deal smaller in Mexico. Gross revenues of $30 billion, with profits of $7 billion or so, would have one kind of impact in Colombia, another in Mexico.

By the same token, drug revenues in Mexico no doubt exert significant influence at the local level. Economic structures and environments in Tijuana and Guadalajara, host cities to major syndicates, have no doubt been affected and distorted by drug-related money. Production areas for cannabis and opium poppy are heavily dependent on illicit incomes. And though it is difficult to measure the precise impact of money laundering upon the national financial system, there is little question that Mexico's banking sector has been affected by drug and drug trafficking.

Official pronouncements tend to minimize the economic consequences of the narcotics trade in Mexico. A binational U.S.-Mexican "assessment" of the drug threat, released by the two governments with considerable fanfare in mid-1997, asserted (without supporting evidence) that the "impact [of drugs] on the domestic economy has not been important enough to be seen as an element which can disrupt its development." Continued the report:

> Drugs are produced mainly by taking advantage of the rural economy. The dire conditions in some rural parts of the country do not imply the drug cultivation is the only vehicle for economic development. It should be pointed out that the production of drugs in Mexico uses only about 50,000 hectares, so it is inappropriate to portray drug growing areas as single crop cultivation regions. To illustrate the dimension of the cultivation of drugs within the general framework of the farming sector, it is important to take into consideration that these fields represent an area less than 0.1 percent of the area planted with corn in 1995. On the other hand, the payment received by the farmer for producing marijuana and poppy has not produced higher incomes or improved the prevalent impoverished conditions.[22]

With all due respect, this is an evasive statement. It addresses only the production of agricultural goods, cannabis and opium poppies. It omits the smuggling of cocaine. It fails to mention methamphetamine. It ignores money laundering. It also generates public suspicion: if officials in both countries are willing to resort to such transparent manipulations, then there must be something to hide.

The truth is that we do not know. To the best of my knowledge, there have not yet appeared any serious, rigorous, and independent evaluations of the economic impact of drug trafficking in Mexico. (There is nothing to compare with Francisco Thoumi's work on Colombia, for instance, or with other studies on the Andes.)[23] To its credit, the 1997 binational report issued a call for research on this question: "To quantify the economic dimension of the drug trafficking problem in Mexico demands the development of systems and methodologies adapted to the different aspects of the problem. Its character as an illicit activity make[s] it impossible to see its real dimension. This problem may be the object of an exchange of experiences and cooperation between investigators in Mexico and the United States."[24] One can only hope this comes to pass.

The Political Context

Whatever its implications for the national economy, the transformation of the *narcotráfico* business in Mexico has coincided with long-term changes in the country's political system. From the late 1920s to the 1980s, an authoritarian regime marked by a close alliance between technocrats, politicians, and leaders of key groups—especially labor and the peasantry—successfully imposed social and political stability. These coalitions were frequently sealed in explicit compacts, or *pactos*, that achieved and implemented consensus on economic policy. Key decisions were made at the top, behind closed doors, as an official party (the Partido Revolucionario Institucional, or PRI) routinely and regularly triumphed in not-very-contested elections. Opposition voices were muted, the media conspired openly with the ruling establishment, instances of rebellion and protest were sparse. From the 1940s onward, even the armed forces accepted a civilian monopoly on the presidential office. Turbulent Mexico, land of the first major social revolution in the twentieth century, thus succumbed to forces of political domination. With traces of envy and admiration, the Peruvian novelist-politician Mario Vargas Llosa once christened Mexico's system as "the perfect dictatorship."

As far back as the 1970s, the dominant-party system began to undergo funda-mental rearrangements. First, the historic coalition started to weaken: the peas-antry no longer represented a significant resource; organized labor lost authority; and while small and medium business remained a fragile sector, large-scale busi-ness was accumulating power and independence from the government. Second, the party system shifted: though still strong, the PRI came to stand at the center of a three-party system, with the Partido de la Revolución Democrática (PRD) on the left and the Partido de Acción Nacional (PAN) on the right, both of which were attracting considerable support from the urban middle class. At the same time, traditional fiefdoms reemerged: old-time politicians (*dinosaurios*) found refuge in state governorships, for instance, and in niches within the party appa-ratus of the PRI.

Mexico has thus been undergoing several simultaneous and interrelated patterns of political transition. One is a process of liberalization and pluraliza-tion, as represented by the mid-1997 elections in which the PRI lost its historic majority in the Chamber of Deputies and the PRD won the mayorship of Mex-ico City. (Many analysts freely speak of Mexican "democracy" as a result, though I myself regard that label as misleading and premature.) A second process is ero-sion of institutional authority. There is less power at the center, even in the pres-idency, than there used to be. To be sure, Carlos Salinas de Gortari was able to exert authority in an exceptional way, partly through personal guile and partly as a result of his lifelong immersion in the system, but Ernesto Zedillo has neither the will, the resources, or the opportunity to demonstrate such strength. Power is no longer as concentrated or extensive as it was for many years. Third is what might be called the emergence of a "familial" crisis—the appearance of profound schisms within Mexico's political elite, once regarded as the "revolutionary family." For decades, the coherence (and internal discipline) of this ruling elite comprised an indispensable foundation of political stability. While there had been stresses and strains from the 1940s through the 1980s, and occasional cracks in the edifice of power (including the splitoff of the *corriente democrática* against the PRI in 1986), there was nothing that would compare with the fissures of the 1990s.

A central and spectacular scene in this drama has revolved around two pairs of brothers: Carlos Salinas de Gortari and his older brother, Raúl; and José Francisco Ruiz Massieu and his younger brother, Mario. Both families were longtime pillars of the Mexican establishment. José Francisco also married (and divorced) a sister of the Salinas brothers, eventually becoming secretary general of the PRI; leaving a political gathering in September 1994, he was assassinated in downtown Mexico City. His brother Mario, then assistant attorney general, was placed in charge of the investigation. Within a month Mario issued a statement suggesting that drug bosses might have ordered the murder, and that high-level politicians were in league with *narcotraficantes*. In late November, about a week before Salinas was to step down from the presidency, Mario publicly resigned from both his position and the PRI, accusing party leaders (but not Salinas) of conspiring to cover up the assassination. In February 1995 governmental authorities (presumably with Zedillo's permission) arrested Raúl Salinas in connection with the Ruiz Massieu assassination. Rumors immediately began to whisper that Carlos Salinas must have been involved in the plot, on the ground that Raúl would never have undertaken such a brazen scheme without his brother's approval. On March 1 the deputy attorney general accused Mario Ruiz Massieu of obstructing justice during the investigation of his brother's assassination. The next day, Carlos Salinas began a hunger strike in order to clear his reputation; Mario Ruiz Massieu left Mexico for the United States, where he was soon arrested (for carrying large amounts of undisclosed cash) while boarding a plane for Madrid. Carlos Salinas ended his hunger strike on March 4, after the Zedillo government released a mollifying statement, but soon left the country in disgrace. In January 1999 a Mexican magistrate stunned the nation by finding Raúl Salinas guilty of masterminding the murder of Ruiz Massieu. Lawyers immediately declared they would mount an appeal, and the saga was bound to continue.

The Salinas–Ruiz Massieu intrigues evoke images of Renaissance Italy under the Borgias, rather than a modernizing country of the late twentieth century, but they also contain profound political significance. They reveal a split within the ruling elite that has become more public and irreversible than at any time since the mid-1930s. They also indicate a breakdown in rules of civility. Even at the highest levels of the political establishment, violence and murder were coming to replace the once-prized arts of bargaining, negotiation, and co-optation.

Expansion of the Mexican drug trade has thus caught the nation's political system at a moment of exceptional vulnerability. The 1990s have been marked by disintegration, liberalization, incipient reconstitution—and pervasive uncertainty. In the short run, the process of "democratization" in Mexico has probably eased working conditions for the *traficantes*.

Enter Cocaine

One clear consequence of the drug trade has entailed an escalation of corruption. To be sure, Mexico has a long history of illicit enrichment, often tacitly accepted as a necessary evil, but the windfall of cocaine profits brought this practice to entirely unprecedented levels. With estimated annual gross revenues of $27–30 billion and about $7 billion in profits, according to some calculations, Mexico's *nouveaux riches* traffickers can afford to spend as much as $500 million per year on bribery—more than twice the total budget of the attorney general's office.[25] Shrewdly, and characteristically, they have disbursed these funds among: (a) top-level *políticos* who could provide protection, (b) heads of agencies engaged in antidrug activities, and (c) rank-and-file foot soldiers in Mexico's antidrug units. The most conspicuous case is, of course, that of General José de Jesús Gutiérrez Rebollo, the military general who was named head of the Instituto Nacional Contra las Drogas in late 1996 and charged with corruption in February 1997.

Discretion is part of the game. Since it could be dangerous to approach a sitting president of Mexico, drug representatives have made contacts not with chief executives themselves but with their relatives—specifically, Carlos Salinas's brother Raúl, accused by Swiss investigators of collaboration with drug traffickers, and Ernesto Zedillo's brother Rodolfo, who apparently ducked out of what would have been a joint venture with *traficantes*.[26] A notebook captured from Juan García Abrego at the time of his arrest revealed a progressive scale for bribes: $1 million for the head of the Federal Judicial Police, $500,000 to the forces' operations chief, and $100,000 to the federal police commander in the city of Matamoros. Payoffs are thus made at each level of enforcement—"the higher the position, the higher the payoff."[27] In effect, drug traffickers regard corruption as a kind of tax: a price of doing business, and a fairly modest one at that.

Critics often denounce corruption as a sign of amorality among Mexican authorities. But, as Peter Andreas has pointed out, the use of bribery reveals a need for bribery. Corruption is, he writes:

> [A] two-way relationship: it reflects the influence of drug smuggling over the state and the state's influence over drug smuggling—and greater drug control capacity has arguably only deepened this influence. Corruption involves not only penetration *of* the state but also penetration *by* the state. Drug smugglers must purchase an essential service monopolized by government officials: the non-enforcement of the law. Those in charge of enforcement must be bribed because they cannot be entirely bullied or bypassed.[28]

Contrary to orthodox wisdom, the existence of corruption implies that law enforcement in Mexico can be remarkably effective.

The more intensive the law enforcement effort, therefore, the more likely it is that corruption will occur. Broadly speaking, as Miguel Ruiz-Cabañas I. has pointed out, deployment of the federal police (and enlistment of the national army) in Mexico's Campaña Permanente merely exposed rank-and-file officers and soldiers to risks of corruption:

> [T]o the degree that drug traffic tends to generate corruption and violence wherever it operates . . . the Mexican police corps has been constantly exposed

to situations that encourage corruption. Some of these cases involve middle- to high-ranking officials. In my estimation, one of the most negative consequences brought on by the drug-trafficking problem has been to delay and hinder the much-needed professionalization of the Mexican police corps.[29]

Corruption thus tends to be systemic. From the standpoint of the traffickers, agencies and units engaged in the fight against drugs are highly attractive targets for payoffs: bribing the sheriff (and, if necessary, the entire posse) is likely to yield instant and substantial benefits.[30]

A second consequence of drug trafficking, especially the movement of cocaine, has been the escalation of violence. Much of this reflects tension and rivalry between opposing gangs: throughout the early 1990s, for instance, the Tijuana and Sinaloa groups were locked in a bitter struggle for control of the Pacific corridor. The increase in violence might also result from expansion in the economic stakes involved, as the dollar volume of Mexico's drug trade swelled rapidly in the late 1980s and early 1990s. It may in addition demonstrate the influence of Colombians, especially former associates of the rough-and-tumble Medellín cartel, which unleashed a civil war in their own country for several excruciating years. Further, the rise in violence may represent a response by traffickers to heightened law enforcement, which has multiplied the number of clashes and raids.

But whatever the cause, the effect has been to produce a string of high-level assassinations:

- A former state attorney general of Sinaloa, murdered while jogging in a Mexico City park;
- A Roman Catholic cardinal, Juan Jesús Posadas Ocampo, assassinated (either on purpose or as a result of mistaken identity) at the Guadalajara airport in May 1993;[31]
- A federal police commander, allegedly killed by fellow officers;
- The police chief of Tijuana, ambushed on a highway;
- A former state attorney general of the state of Jalisco, shot on his way to teach a class in law.

A new federal chief of police, appointed by Zedillo, was poisoned in his sleep and temporarily paralyzed as a result. In addition, there is widespread conjecture that the assassinations of Luis Donaldo Colosio (in March 1994) and of José Francisco Ruiz Massieu (in September 1994) were related to drug trafficking in one way or another.

Gangland-style killings have also swelled in scale and scope. As already reported, the death of Amado Carrillo Fuentes in mid-1997 unleashed a brutal war of succession in the Juárez area. The more than 50 victims include four doctors, two attorneys, one police commander, and one major trafficker (Rafael Muñoz Talavera); a machine-gun shooting at the Max Fin Restaurant in August 1997 claimed six known *traficantes* and two innocent bystanders. And in September 1998 gang rivalry provoked the slaughter of 19 men, women, and children near the port and tourist town of Ensenada in Baja California.

There have been other costs associated with drug trafficking and, especially, with antidrug policy. One has been the frequent, some would say systematic, violation of human rights. Particularly in the early 1990s, sweeps and crackdowns resulted in injury, death, and torture of hundreds of *campesinos*. Another has been the delegation of political power to Mexican armed forces: as part and parcel of the antidrug campaign, the military has become "the supreme authority" in such states as Sinaloa, Jalisco, Oaxaca, Chihuahua, and, more recently, much of Baja California.[32] Empowerment of the armed forces occurs at the direct expense of civilian authority.

A third broad consequence of expanded drug trafficking in Mexico is infringement on constitutional authority. This threat takes multiple forms. One is open defiance of the government, most spectacularly through assassination. Another comes from the replacement of de jure constitutional rule by de facto informal authority, especially in poppy-growing regions and in host cities for the top cartels; in such areas, drug kingpins wield supreme power. They rule their fiefdoms without regard to the national government, much in the manner of traditional *caciques* in eras past. Yet another kind of threat, perhaps the most effective and sinister of all, results from the entanglement of political leaders within the drug-trafficking network itself. The logic of the traffickers is disarmingly straightforward: if top-level politicians stand to benefit from *narcotráfico*, they will not take serious action against it. Such factors serve to emphasize Eduardo Valle Espinosa's observation about the *traficantes*: "They have been able to create a state within a state."[33] It is in this fundamental sense, of course, that the drug trade has come to represent a genuine threat to Mexico's national security.

Taken together, all these consequences for the political system—corruption, violence, abuse of power—have helped generate widespread skepticism within civil society about the Mexican regime and its leaders. As a result, Mexican citizens have often come to assume the worst—about the motivations, integrity, and capability of their political leaders. Such disbelief undercuts support for the country's weakening authoritarian system, and may hasten its collapse, but it does not necessarily create civic foundations for political democracy. All in all, the progressive alienation of Mexican society from its leadership represents an unnerving and potentially troublesome trend.

IMPLICATIONS FOR U.S.-MEXICAN RELATIONS

Not surprisingly, drug trafficking has had pernicious effects on U.S.-Mexican relations. Especially during election cycles, U.S. politicians have succumbed to the temptation of charging Mexico with responsibility for drug-related problems in American society: indeed, "Mexico-bashing" has become a lamentably predictable element in public discussions of narcotics throughout the United States. In contrast, Mexicans tend to focus on the presence of U.S. demand for illicit drugs. Well over a decade after the initial proclamation of the "war on drugs," they point out, some 13 million Americans continue to use illicit drugs of one type or another. The fundamental problem, according to this perspective, is not supply from Mexico; it is demand in the United States. The drug issue thus creates conditions and incentives for mutual recrimination.

Official policies exacerbate these tensions. According to public pronouncements, the overall purpose of U.S. policy is "to reduce illegal drug use and its consequences in America." For the United States, drug consumption represents a threat to public health, claiming nearly 15,000 lives per year; it spawns crime, including violent crime; it encourages delinquency and gang membership in inner-city ghettos; and in general, it imposes yearly "social costs" in the billions of dollars. To combat this situation the U.S. federal government has increased its annual antidrug budget from $4.7 billion in FY 1988 to $15.0 billion in FY 1997 (and a requested $17.1 billion for FY 1999). About one-third of these expenditures goes toward demand reduction, including prevention and treatment; fully two-thirds are dedicated to law enforcement, including interdiction and international programs designed to reduce foreign and domestic sources of supply.[34]

A defining feature of U.S. antidrug policy has been high-handedness. Ever since Ronald Reagan declared a "war on drugs" in the early 1980s (as did Richard Nixon in the late 1960s), Washington has resolutely attempted to reduce the importation of illicit drugs from foreign countries. Time and again, expert opinion has revealed the unworkability of this approach and called for emphasis upon the reduction of demand rather than supply (leaving aside the question of legalization, which raises a host of complex issues). Despite mounting expense (and increasing evidence of failure), the U.S. government has stoutly resisted such advice. The explanation for this stubbornness lies not so much in bureaucratic inertia as in the domestic political arena: in this era of public concern, no American president can afford to look "soft" on drug addicts, pushers, or traffickers.[35] Prospects for a major change in U.S. policy seem slim indeed.

These concerns have led U.S. authorities to take unilateral measures, rather than collaborate with Mexico. This, in turn, has exacerbated underlying frictions. One illustrative episode stemmed from the torture and murder of DEA agent Enrique Camarena in Guadalajara in 1985, apparently in response to a law-enforcement crackdown the previous year. To avenge Camarena's murder the U.S. government launched Operation Intercept II, partially closing the border for eight days in February 1985 and publicly announcing its displeasure with the slow pace of Mexico's investigation. As María Celia Toro has explained, "Operation Intercept II marked a turning point in terms of Mexico's understanding of the new U.S. policy on drugs ... and of its consequences for Mexico."[36] And as frustration mounted in Washington, the DEA initiated Operation Leyenda, a plan to arrest all those people (at least nineteen in all) believed to have participated in the Camarena episode. Leyenda involved the capture and kidnapping of two Mexican citizens—René Martín Verdugo-Urquídez (1986) and Humberto Alvarez Machaín (1990)—who were smuggled into the United States in order to face charges of complicity in the Camarena murder.

These abductions clearly violated longstanding interpretations of international law. The U.S. Supreme Court then stepped into the fray, ruling that unlawful searches and seizures in other countries—with or without the participation of U.S. government agents—did not necessarily lead to the loss of jurisdiction for U.S. courts. In sum, foreign nationals were not entitled to the constitutional rights enjoyed by U.S. citizens. Eventually, one U.S. judge found that the Verdugo kidnapping violated the U.S.-Mexican Extradition Treaty; another exonerated Alvarez Machaín for lack of evidence in 1993.

Not much was learned from this experience. In May 1998, American customs agents climaxed a three-year investigation by luring scores of mid-level Mexican bankers into the United States through a sting operation (nicknamed Casablanca) and arresting them on money-laundering charges. U.S. Treasury Secretary Robert Rubin exultantly declared that "Money laundering is the lifeblood of organized crime, and [this] action is a major step toward stopping that flow." Indictments were brought against three major Mexican institutions—Bancomer, Banco Serfin, and Confía—with the freezing or confiscation of accounts worth nearly $150 million. Attorney General Janet Reno attributed Casablanca's success to "one of the strongest partnerships in law enforcement history"—alluding to cooperation between Treasury, Customs, Justice, the DEA, and the Federal Reserve—but she failed to mention one key actor: the Mexican government, which was completely excluded from this secret operation. Notified only at the last minute, Mexican authorities were outraged by the deception and the lack of trust. "There are a lot of things that we have not accepted and that we are not going to accept," declared Foreign Minister Rosario Green. "We Mexicans are very jealous of our national sovereignty."[37]

Adding fuel to these fires has been the annual process of "certification," as mandated by a 1986 amendment to the Foreign Assistance Act, which conditions U.S. economic and military aid, votes in multilateral lending institutions, and trade preferences on "full cooperation" with the U.S. campaign against drug trafficking. According to this statute, the U.S. government assesses the antidrug efforts of those nations, around thirty or so, believed to be involved in the international narcotics business. Governments under review receive approval in the form of "certification," disapproval in the form of "decertification," or special dispensation because of "vital national interests of the United States." The statute thus created a situation in which the world's largest drug-consuming society took it upon itself to pass moral and political judgment on the effectiveness of antidrug efforts by other nations around the world.

Exasperated by the continuing flow of drugs (especially cocaine) from Mexico to the United States, American politicians—liberal and conservative alike—have routinely called for "decertification" of Mexico. Democratic Senator Dianne Feinstein of California has become particularly vocal and vituperative, sometimes joining with archconservative Senator Alfonse d'Amato of New York to issue supercilious pronouncements about Mexico's abundant imperfections.[38] Indeed, the annual review of certification has become a ritualistic occasion for Mexico-bashing in Congress and the media.

Bureaucratic intrigue has also affected the process. In early 1998, for example, the DEA sent crystal-clear signals opposing certification for Mexico. Officals expressed deep misgivings over Mexico's reluctance to extradite its citizens to the United States, over procedural constraints on DEA operatives in Mexico, and over the persistence of corruption. As time for the decision approached, one news leak reported that a confidential DEA document asserted that "the Government of Mexico has not accomplished its counter-narcotics goals or succeeded in cooperation with the United States Government. . . . The scope of Mexican drug trafficking has increased significantly, along with the attendant violence. The level of corruption in Mexico continues unabated." All in all, the document concluded, measures by Mexico have not produced "significant results."[39] In congressional testimony DEA administrator Constantine publicly emphasized the power and apparent impunity enjoyed by Mexican syndicates. In contrast to the DEA, the White House and the State Department favored certification for a variety of reasons—mostly unrelated to drugs, such as the need to support NAFTA—and there followed two days of often chaotic bureaucratic maneuvering.

In the end, the U.S. government certified Mexico in 1998 with only the faintest of praise:

Mexico made progress in its anti–drug effort in 1997 and cooperated well with the United States. Nevertheless, the problems that Mexico faces in countering powerful criminal organizations, and the persistent corrupting influence that they exert within the justice sector, cannot be minimized. There are also areas of bilateral cooperation which must be improved for the two governments to achieve greater success in attacking and dismantling the trans-border drug trafficking organizations. The U.S. is convinced, however, of the Zedillo Administration's firm intention to persist in its campaign against the drug cartels and its broad-sweeping reform effort. Through daily interaction between agencies of the two governments, formal discussions in the HLCG [High Level Contact Group] and other bilateral groups, as well as collaboration in multilateral fora, the two governments are finding increasingly productive ways to work together against the common threats our nations face.[40]

True to form, Senator Feinstein then presented a bill to withdraw certification for Mexico and lost by a vote of 54–46. This was a sobering outcome: it would have taken only a handful of votes for the Senate to reverse the decision.[41] Once again, and despite its best efforts, Mexico escaped by the skin of its teeth.[42]

WHAT CAN MEXICO DO?

The costs of drug trafficking are enormous for Mexico. During a period of delicate political transition, *narcotráfico* empowers criminal groups, threatens constitutional authority, and confounds the country's relationship with its powerful northern neighbor. Pressing questions now emerge: What can Mexico do? How can its government most effectively confront this particular branch of organized international crime?

To begin, it is necessary to understand Mexico's national interests. They are not the same as U.S. interests. Mexico does not, for example, have a major problem with illicit drug consumption. Although drug use is growing in some areas, especially along routes of transit, the domestic demand for illegal narcotics remains modest in scale (there is excessive use of inhalants, especially by street children, but that is another story).[43] In and of themselves, the production and distribution of illicit drugs do not pose serious threats to the health of Mexican society.

Instead, the most pressing concerns for Mexico are fundamentally political. As described by María Celia Toro, one is "to prevent drug traffickers from directly confronting state authority," to obstruct the formation of "states within the state," and to diminish the threats of violence and narcoterrorism. A second goal, "equally important," is "to prevent U.S. policy and judicial authorities from acting as a surrogate justice system in Mexico."[44] In other words, U.S. policy itself poses a significant danger to Mexican national interests.[45]

These two concerns converge on one practical goal: the reduction (or elimination) of Mexico's role in the transnational cocaine business. This would diminish the economic, political, and paramilitary power of the trafficking organizations. It might reduce the level of violence between competing groups. It would lower the level of threat to state authority (as many governments have found, it is easier to coexist with "organized" crime than with unorganized, disorganized, or semi-organized crime). And it would ease some tensions with the United States, where publicity has tended to focus more on cocaine than on other drugs.

Achievement of this goal would not eradicate drug trafficking from Mexico. Instead, it would reinstate the status quo ante: that is, the conditions of the early to mid-1980s, prior to the arrival of the Colombians. There would continue to be cultivation and distribution of cannabis and opium poppy, and probably some processing of methamphetamine. There would be money laundering as well, on a much-reduced scale. But there would be little if any transshipment of cocaine.

Nor would this solve the U.S. problem with drugs. On the contrary, the closure of trafficking routes in Mexico would almost certainly redirect them to some other location—back to the Caribbean, for instance, or possibly to Central America. U.S.-bound shipments of cocaine from South America would not be stopped: they would merely be rerouted.

Parenthetically, this same point applies to *all* drug production and trafficking in Mexico. Let us imagine a complete shutdown of the entire industry: cannabis, opium, methamphetamine, cocaine, whatever. This would presumably solve all of Mexico's current problems (although it would undoubtedly create some others). It would remove a constant thorn in the side of the U.S.-Mexican relationship. But it would have little effect, if any, on the U.S. problems of consumption and addiction. The drugs would simply come from some source other than Mexico.

In pursuit of its national interests, the Mexican government has developed (or should develop) policies to deal with three sets of issues: (1) threats to governability, (2) impingements on sovereignty by the United States, (3) transnational ties to South America. These are distinct problem-areas, but they are interrelated. Let us take each in turn.

Threats to Governability

Here lies the most basic threat to Mexico's national security. And it is on this front as well that Mexico has devoted enormous resources. About one-third of the military budget is devoted to antidrug operations, with more than 25,000 soldiers involved. Local and federal officials frequently mount intensified law-enforcement campaigns—usually at the cost of human lives. The goal is to harass the traffickers, bring them to heel, reduce their profits, and, if possible, put them in jail. During 1997 alone Mexico arrested nearly 11,000 individuals on drug-related charges, including some prominent traffickers (among them Oscar Malherbe de León, operations manager for the now defunct Tamaulipas group, and one of the Amezcua Contreras brothers).

Corruption remains a major challenge. This is not a question of morality; it is a matter of human nature and material incentives. (Overtures from traffickers often come as tenders of *plata o plomo*, money or bullets, so recipients sometimes accept bribes out of fear.) There are no easy solutions at hand. In theory, if not in practice, Mexico could double or triple public-sector salaries, though it is not clear what effect this might have. The government could also place guilty officials under arrest rather than relieving them of their duties, as now tends to be the case. And the judicial system could be strengthened, as President Zedillo has recognized.[46]

From the standpoint of this goal, however, it would *not* be helpful for Mexican authorities to escalate levels of paramilitary confrontation with drug organizations or to increase the role of the military in drug control efforts. These are already at maximum feasible limits. More confrontation will only lead to more corruption. More military deployments will only lead to more mayhem, violence, and abuse of human rights. On these fronts, Mexico is doing just about as much as it can.

Interference by the United States

Much of Mexico's antidrug policy has a dual purpose—to reduce the power of trafficking organizations and, at the same time, to deflect the wrath of the United States. This is sad but true. To deal with the overbearing presence of the United States, Mexico has employed a range of several tactics.

Appeasement

For one reason or another, Mexico has frequently capitulated—or appeared to capitulate—to U.S. demands. In search of an improved bilateral relationship (soon to include negotiation of NAFTA), Carlos Salinas enlisted Mexico in George Bush's militarized war on drugs; approved a joint program between the DEA and the Mexican attorney general's office called the Northern Border Response Force, which expanded the use of U.S. helicopters and radars along the U.S.-Mexican border; allowed the creation of a military intelligence unit within the U.S. embassy to investigate drug trafficking; and, most controversially, authorized American-piloted AWACS to fly over Mexican territory in order to monitor drug-trafficking activities. Similarly, Ernesto Zedillo authorized the deportation of Juan García Abrego, reputed leader of the Tamaulipas organization who (as a U.S. citizen) had recently made the FBI's 10 Most Wanted list. Zedillo has also expanded the role of the military, overseen the arrest of several well-known king-pins, and vowed to intensify campaigns against corruption.

Distraction

Some efforts appear to have cosmetic purposes—to make Mexico "look good" in the eyes of the United States rather than to make serious inroads on drug traf-ficking. Most transparent among these tactics are crop eradication figures, eagerly tracked by hawk-eyed U.S. functionaries. In 1997, for instance, Mexico claimed to have eradicated over 1,000 metric tons of marijuana (up 3 percent from the previous year) and 343 kilograms of methamphetamine (up 75 per-cent). Whether or not these initiatives had any appreciable effect on the price or availability of drugs is quite another matter. The point is that Mexico could demonstrate good-faith efforts to cooperate with U.S.-designed supply control strategies.

Noncompliance

Rather than publicly challenge the wisdom of U.S. policy, Mexican officials some-times hold their tongues—and silently fail to respond to Washington's demands. The most conspicuous illustration relates to extradition. As a matter of national custom and law, Mexican authorities are (understandably) reluctant to deport Mexican citizens for criminal proceedings in the United States. They tend not to do so. They tend not to talk about it either.

Protest

This tactic is employed with great judiciousness so as not to invite a backlash from the United States. It is most effective when there is disagreement within the U.S. government, so that one agency can be mobilized to denounce or disavow the actions of another. So when Foreign Minister Rosario Green voiced griev-ances over Operation Casablanca, she addressed them to Madeleine Albright, the U.S. Secretary of State, who was equally annoyed at being excluded from the loop herself. In turn, it was Albright's complaint that drew apologies to Mexico by shamefaced U.S. officials.

Encirclement

A traditional tool of Mexican diplomacy, this involves the use of multilateral fora to expound views, express concerns, acquire allies—and isolate the United States. This was done at drug summits in Vienna in 1988 and again at the United Nations in 1998. In this second meeting, called partly at Mexico's behest, Ernesto Zedillo could vent his outrage over Operation Casablanca. While the over-whelming share of demand for illicit drugs comes from "countries with the largest economic capacity," Zedillo pointedly declared:

[T]he human, social, and institutional costs in meeting such demands is paid for by the producing and transit countries. It is our men and women who die first in combatting drug trafficking. It is our communities that are first to suffer from violence, our institutions that are first to be undermined by corruption. It is our governments that are the first to have to shift valuable resources needed to fight poverty to serve as the first bulwark in this war.

With Bill Clinton sitting in the audience, it was clear that most world leaders concurred with Zedillo.[47] Thus, Mexico was able to outnumber and surround the United States.

Ties with South America

As stated above, removal of the cocaine trade from Mexico is (or should be) one of the country's highest operational priorities. Partly because of preoccupation with other issues, however, Mexican officials appear to have devoted less-than-sufficient attention to the disruption of links between Mexican gangs and cocaine traffickers from South America. Pursuit of this goal would entail a reallocation of resources. Instead of interdicting drug shipments from Mexico toward the United States, it might make more sense to interrupt shipments of cocaine from Colombia to Mexico. Instead of eradicating marijuana fields, it would seem more useful to destroy processing laboratories. And instead of jailing lower-level *traficantes*, it would be more productive to make serious inroads on money laundering. Of course, there is no guarantee of success, but initiatives of this kind would directly respond to a national need.

For all their variety and ingenuity, these policies have met with little success. Harassment of major trafficking groups has sometimes impeded operations and even helped drive some groups (as in Tamaulipas) out of business, but it has not altered the basic terms of confrontation between a beleaguered Mexican state and transnational organized crime; nor has it markedly enhanced prospects for governability. Similarly, tactical maneuvering to dilute or circumvent the power and pretentiousness of the United States has yielded ephemeral triumphs and short-term respites, but it has not affected the underlying asymmetry of the bilateral relationship. And while efforts to stanch the inflow of cocaine from Colombia might in principle reduce Mexico's role as a transit country, interdiction of drug shipments has generally shown itself to be an ineffective policy tool.

Ultimately, there may not be much that Mexico itself can do. The country's situation could improve as a result of two developments, neither one of which, however, is under Mexico's control. First, the United States could revise its drug policies in line with long-standing advice from experts who advocate a focus on demand reduction and prevention rather than supply control. This could have a major and positive effect on such countries as Mexico, though there is little indication that it is likely to occur. Second, Colombian traffickers could decide to abandon Mexico and reroute U.S.-bound cocaine through the Caribbean. There is preliminary evidence that this is beginning in fact to happen—due, in large part, to the greed and ruthlessness of Mexican drug lords.[48] If this process continues and accelerates, it could alleviate Mexico of problems stemming from the cocaine trade. Ironically, it is the drug barons themselves, not public officials or police authorities, who might well drive cocaine out of Mexico.

NOTES

I wish to thank María Celia Toro for her advice and encouragement.

1. Mark Fineman and Sebastian Rotella, "The Drug Web That Entangles Mexico," *Los Angeles Times*, 1 March 1996.

2. Office of National Drug Control Strategy, *The National Drug Control Strategy, 1998: A Ten Year Plan* (Washington, D.C.: The White House, 1998), 74–75. "Current" users are those who have taken drugs within the past 30 days. See also Peter Reuter, "Foreign Demand for Latin American Drugs: The USA and Europe" (Santa Monica: Drug Policy Research Center, RAND Corporation, 1998), RAND/RP–691.

3. Portions of this chapter are adapted from Peter H. Smith, "Drug Trafficking in Mexico," with "Comment" by María Celia Toro, in Barry P. Bosworth, Susan M. Collins, and Nora Claudia Lustig, eds., *Coming Together? Mexico-United States Relations* (Washington: Brookings Institution, 1997), 125–54.

4. Miguel Ruiz-Cabañas I., "Mexico's Changing Illicit Drug Supply Role," in Guadalupe González and Marta Tienda, eds., *The Drug Connection in U.S.–Mexican Relations* (La Jolla: Center for U.S.-Mexican Studies, University of California, San Diego, 1989), 48–50.

5. See José Luis Trueba Lara, *Política y narcopoder en México* (México: Editorial Planeta, 1995), 54–56; and Peter A. Lupsha, "Drug Lords and Narco-Corruption: The Players Change but the Game Continues," *Crime, Law and Social Change* 16 (1991): 41–58, esp. 44–48.

6. Peter A. Lupsha, "Drug Trafficking: Mexico and Colombia in Comparative Perspective," *Journal of International Affairs* 35, no. 1 (Spring/Summer 1981): 95–115, esp. 100–102.

7. Richard Craig, "Operation Condor: Mexico's Anti-Drug Campaign Enters a New Era," *Journal of Interamerican Studies and World Affairs* 22, no. 3 (August 1980): 345–63.

8. See María Celia Toro, *Mexico's "War" on Drugs: Causes and Consequences* (Boulder, CO: Lynne Rienner, 1995), 79–80, note 78; and Trueba Lara, *Política y narcopoder,* 56–60.

9. Quantitative measures are notoriously unreliable. The principal source of the most commonly cited data, the U.S. Department of State, stipulates that the numbers represent a "best effort" to capture dimensions of the drug trade, but concedes that "the picture is not as precise as we would like it to be. The numbers range from cultivation figures, relatively hard data derived by proven means, to crop production and drug yield estimates, softer figures where many more variables come into play. *We publish these numbers with an important caveat: the yield figures are potential, not actual numbers. Although they are useful for examining trends, they are only approximations. They should not be treated as hard data.*" Bureau of International Narcotics and Law Enforcement Affairs, *International Narcotics Control Strategy Report, March 1996* (Washington, D.C., 1996), 19. See also Peter Reuter, "The Mismeasurement of Illegal Drug Markets: The Implications of Its Irrelevance," in Susan Pozo, ed., *Exploring the Underground Economy* (Kalamazoo: Upjohn Institute, 1996), 63–80, esp. 66–69.

10. See U.S. State Department, Bureau of International Narcotics Matters, *International Narcotics Control Strategy Report, March 1989* (Washington, D.C., 1989), 92; *Interna-*

tional Narcotics Control Strategy Report, March 1992 (Washington, D.C., 1992), 167; Bureau of International Narcotics and Law Enforcement Affairs, *Strategy Report, March 1996*, 141; and Bureau of International Narcotcis and Law Enforcement Affairs, *International Narcotics Control Strategy Report, March 1998* (Washington, D.C., 1998), 154.

11. For slightly different data revealing the same basic trend, see Toro, *Mexico's "War,"* 33–34.
12. Andrew Reding, "The Rise and Fall of the Drug Cartels: With Colombia's Kingpins Nabbed, America Faces More Elusive Targets in Mexico," *Washington Post*, 17 Sept. 1995.
13. Sam Dillon, "Power in Drug Trade Shifts from Colombia to Mexico," *The Sacramento Bee*, 27 Dec. 1995.
14. See Thomas A. Constantine, "International Organized Crime Syndicates and Their Impact on the United States," DEA Congressional Testimony before the Senate Foreign Relations Committee, Subcommittee on the Western Hemisphere, Peace Corps, Narcotics, and Terrorism, 26 Feb. 1998, esp. 3–5.
15. Ibid., 4.
16. Ibid., 5.
17. For analysis of leading syndicates as of mid–1996, see Smith, "Drug Trafficking in Mexico," in Bosworth et al., *Coming Together?* 131–33, and also *United States/Mexico Binational Drug Threat Assessment* (Washington, D.C.: The White House, May 1997), 77–79.
18. Outdoor production is notably significant in the states of California, Hawaii, Kentucky, Tennessee, and New York; indoor production flourishes especially in California, Florida, Oregon, Washington, and Kentucky.
19. Peter A. Lupsha, presentation at conference on "The United States and Latin America: Reassessing the Relationship," University of California, San Diego, 16–18 May 1996.
20. Andrew A. Reding, "Political Corruption and Drug Trafficking in Mexico: Impunity for High-Level Officials Spurs Lawlessness and Growth of Drug Cartels," statement before hearing of Senate Committee on Foreign Relations, 8 Aug. 1995, 2.
21. It is impossible to gauge the total number of drug trafficking organizations with certainty. One source has estimated that there were "about 200" organizations active in the early 1990s, but criteria for this assessment are not clear—and things have no doubt changed since that time. Peter Reuter and David Ronfeldt, *Quest for Integrity: The Mexican-U.S. Drug Issue in the 1980s* (Santa Monica: RAND Corporation, 1992), RAND/N–3266–USDP, 15.
22. *Binational Assessment*, 96.
23. For example, see chapters 4–7 in Peter H. Smith, ed., *Drug Policy in the Americas* (Boulder, CO: Westview Press, 1992).
24. *Binational Assessment*, 96.
25. Fineman and Rotella, "Drug Web."
26. James F. Smith, "Cartel Tried to Infiltrate Top Ranks in Mexico," *Los Angeles Times*, 21 Mar. 1998.
27. Peter Andreas, "The Political Economy of Narco-Corruption in Mexico," *Current History* (April 1998): 163. See also Andreas, "Sovereigns and Smugglers: Enforcing the U.S.-Mexico Border in the Age of Economic Integration," Ph.D. dissertation, Cornell University (January 1999), esp. 123–41.
28. Andreas, "Political Economy," 161.
29. Miguel Ruiz-Cabañas I., "Mexico's Permanent Campaign: Costs, Benefits, Implications," in Smith, ed., *Drug Policy*, ch. 10, with quote on 158.
30. On corruption of the military, see Lupsha, "Drug Lords," 53–55.
31. Reding, "Political Corruption," 2–3.
32. Kate Doyle, "The Militarization of the Drug War in Mexico," *Current History* (February 1993): 83–88.

33. Eduardo Valle, *El segundo disparo: la narcodemocracia mexicana* (México: Oceano, 1995).
34. *The National Drug Control Strategy, 1998*, passim.
35. Mathea Falco, "U.S. Drug Policy: Addicted to Failure," *Foreign Policy* no. 102 (spring 1996): 120–33. See also Eva Bertram, Morris Blachman, Kenneth Sharpe, and Peter Andreas, *Drug War Politics: The Price of Denial* (Berkeley and Los Angeles: University of California Press, 1996).
36. Toro, *Mexico's "War,"* 63.
37. See Tim Golden, "U.S. Drug Sting Riles Mexico, Imperiling Future Cooperation," *New York Times*, 11 June 1998.
38. See Smith, "Drug Trafficking in Mexico," 144–45, for a description of the certification process in 1996.
39. Tim Golden, "U.S. Lauds Mexico on Drug Efforts, Countering D.E.A.," *New York Times*, 27 Feb. 1998.
40. *Strategy Report, March 1998*, xxvii.
41. Eric Schmitt, "Senate Fails to Reverse Ruling That Mexico Is Fighting Drugs," *New York Times*, 27 Mar. 1998.
42. See also Douglas Farah, "Despite Objections, Clinton Administration Certifies Mexico as Drug-Fighting Partner," *Washington Post*, 27 Feb. 1998, A–33.
43. María Elena Medina-Mora and María del Carmen Mariño, "Drug Abuse in Latin America," in Smith, ed., *Drug Policy*, ch. 3.
44. Toro, *Mexico's "War,"* 2. See also María Celia Toro, "The Internationalization of Police: The Case of the DEA in Mexico," paper presented at meeting of the International Studies Association, San Diego, California (16–20 April 1996).
45. "More than any other nation," William O. Walker III has said, "Mexico has been the object of coercive diplomacy by the United States." Walker, "International Collaboration in Historical Perspective," in Smith, ed., *Drug Policy,* 273.
46. For a recent review of Mexican antidrug policy, see *Strategy Report, March 1998*, 148–58.
47. Christopher S. Wren, "At Drug Summit, Clinton Asks Nations to Set Aside Blame," *New York Times*, 9 June 1998.
48. See Larry Rohter and Clifford Krauss, "Dominicans Allow Drugs Easy Sailing," *New York Times*, 10 May 1998; and Mireya Navarro, "Upgraded Drug Traffic Flourishes on Old Route," *New York Times*, 31 May 1998.

BAD BUSINESS: A COMMENTARY ON THE CRIMINOLOGY OF ORGANIZED CRIME IN THE UNITED STATES

10

Alan A. Block

> In his room, Latimer sat down by the window and gazed out across the black river to the lights which it reflected and the faint glow in the sky beyond the Louvre. His mind was haunted by the past, by the confession of Dhris, the Negro, and by the memories of Irana Preveza, by the tragedy of Bulic and by a tale of white crystals travelling west to Paris, bringing money to the fig-picker of Izmir. Three human beings had died horribly that Dimitrious might take his ease. If there were such a thing as Evil, then this man. . . .
>
> But it was useless to try to explain him in terms of Good and Evil. They were no more than baroque abstractions. Good Business and Bad Business were the elements of the new theology.
>
> —Eric Ambler, *A Coffin for Dimitrious*

INTRODUCTION

Up until quite recently the majority of American criminological studies of organized crime was fixated on defining the phenomenon without considering it as phenomena.[1] For decades mainstream organized crime research took its cue from government needs and perceptions, concentrating on Italian American criminals to the exclusion of other organized criminals. The prevailing paradigm was that they were organized crime, others were affiliates or associates of organized crime, or indeed something else. They were the mob or the "outfit" or the mafia or La Cosa Nostra. They controlled the most important illicit activities as well as non-Italian American criminals of significance. And to some extent, in the decades following WW II, that was true, and particularly in those American cities with a large Italian American population. The mob or La Cosa Nostra was deeply embedded in the politics of certain American cities and some states, and in trade unions such as the Teamsters, the East Coast longshoremen, and the building trades.[2] With access to union pension funds, mobsters and their friends in law, accounting, and politics had a field day in private real estate development.

To an apparently large but unmeasurable extent they also controlled public-sector construction.

In New York City, for example, where "public construction projects are multi-billion dollar spending programs,"[3] organized crime's control of construction unions and firms put, at a minimum, tens of millions of dollars a year into its pockets. There was nothing peculiarly American about this, however. An analogous situation took place in Palermo, Sicily, when the Italian government finally decided to pour money south into the Mezzogiorno. Writer Alexander Stille remarked that this produced "The Sack of Parlermo."[4] He wrote that from 1959 to 1964 about 60 percent of the building licenses in Palermo went to three mafia front men. The mafia building boom went on for decades and led Stille to conclude that the "story of mafia power in Palermo can be told in terms of real estate—block by block and building by building—a legacy that is reflected both in the cheap construction and infernal congestion of the 'new' city and the total degradation of the old."[5]

It is unexceptional to find organized criminals, no matter where, with strong ties to local, regional, and national politicians cornering state-generated capital. It is equally unexceptional to find that Italian American criminals have been very significant in a country of such size, racial, and ethnic diversity as the United States, for their postwar dominance in key American cities is a reflection of well-documented demographic factors and mobility patterns.[6]

The power of ethnic criminal organizations is always contingent upon a large population base whose patterns of social and geographic mobility reflect a strong adherence to working-class lifestyles and petty bourgeois capitalism. Italian Americans in New York predominated in the construction trades, worked as waterfront laborers, labored as garbage men, and came to control the unions representing these trades. Given that these unions were devoid of any transforming ideology, and that violence is a mainstay of working-class culture, it did not take much to zip to the top of these organizations. In addition, the vast bulk of this population emigrated from Southern Italy, where personal violence was endemic because public authority, which represented the interests of a tiny elite, was incompetent.[7] Civil society was embodied by a rigid and conservative church and absentee landowners. Living in agro-villages, working as landless laborers, the population turned resolutely inward, trusting few outside the boundaries of kith and kin. Italian Americans stayed in place, culturally and geographically, for a longer period of time than other European immigrant groups that journeyed to the United States around the same time.[8] Their zeal for security was reflected through the prism of past experience in which family and place took center stage and combined with a generalized suspicion of the outside and outsiders.[9]

Nothing lasts forever. Italian American neighborhoods in New York City have substantially declined—suburbanization and other forms of mobility have taken root. The patterns of working-class life have irrevocably changed. It is thus no wonder that numerous observers are of the opinion that New York's La Cosa Nostra generation of the 1980s was the last Italian American one to exert extraordinary criminal control.[10] It was inevitable that the criminals who control New York's streets and political capital would represent other ethnic populations.[11]

One illustration of this transformation became evident in the 1970s. For many years the most dynamic center of New York's heroin trade was in northeastern Manhattan, running on an east-west axis along 116th Street and a north-south one along Pleasant Avenue. Few without criminal business chose to linger around that intersection. The neighborhood that sat at the epicenter of heroin importation and wholesaling was known as East Harlem or Italian Harlem. It had housed the largest Italian American population in New York City, according to the WPA Guide to New York published in 1939. At that time there were about 150,000 persons in this one-square-mile area, making it "the most densely populated section of Manhattan and the largest colony of Italian Americans in the country."[12]

East Harlem drug traffickers were well known by the 1940s. The leading organized criminals then, and for many years to come, were Michael Coppola, Salvatore Santoro, Frank Livorsi, Joseph Gagliano, Joseph Vento, John Schillaci, John Ormento, and Dominick Petrelli. They and their associates managed a number of organized crime enterprises, including the traffic in heroin. For decades organized crime and heroin trafficking continued on in basically the same hands and out of the same locations. It was passed down from father to son, from uncle to nephew in all the old familiar places.

Although the rhythm of life had seemed immutable, by the mid-1960s East Harlem began to experience accelerating and dramatic population changes. In little more than a decade Italian East Harlem had just about disappeared. The resident population became almost completely African American and Hispanic. The very few remaining Italian American residents stayed for economic and religious reasons.[13]

The center of East Harlem's Catholicism was the church of Our Lady of Mount Carmel in which the Madonna of 115th Street reigned. As Robert Anthony Orsi wrote in his fine study *Faith and Community in Italian Harlem*, the Madonna's church had become the village church for the area, replacing the "scores of hometown saints that had once scattered the devotional energies" of the residents.[14] In April 1986, the church's front door was bolted shut, through there was still an entrance through the rectory on 116th Street. On the day of its close, there were but "two worshipers . . . in the church, both black" while "parked near the front door was a sedan with a cardboard decal reading EL BARRIO TAXI SERVICE."

As the ethnic and entrepreneurial bases of organized crime in the United States shifted, so too has the criminological focus. It is now absorbed with the "transnational" nature of criminal syndicates. Thus articles on themes such as "The Globalization of Criminology," "The Internationalization of Business Crime," "Transnational Narco-Corruption," "Security Foreign Policy and Transnational Organized Crime," and "Trafficking Drugs in the Global Village," are now more-or-less standard criminological fare.

Of course international organized crime has been around for about as long as professional criminals have carried out their activities across national borders. In

North America during the nineteenth century, gangs that rustled horses in Texas and sold them in Mexico were involved in international organized criminal activities. Bootleggers who moved product from Canada or Caribbean nations to the United States during Prohibition were international organized criminals. Certainly Congress and the supporters of Prohibition believed they were in a battle against international organized crime and funded their war accordingly.[15]

A glance at the history of organized criminal activities raises some questions for me about the origins of the new scholarship, for I find it difficult to see clearly what differentiates contemporary transnational organized crime from old-fashioned international organized crime. I suspect that behind this scholarship is a perception of increasing social vulnerability expressed in the conceptualization that transnational organized crime represents a threat to social and political life even in some of the world's most stable and prosperous nations. I am not convinced that it is driven simply by changes in criminal organization and behavior. It is, of course, possible that the new emphasis is simply the result of a shared belief that what happens in Hong Kong's underworld has salience in Amsterdam and Buenos Aires and Houston.

TRANSNATIONAL ORGANIZED CRIME AS A THREAT

The National Institute of Justice's (NIJ) recent "request for proposals" opens with the premise that "decreases [in] barriers of language, communication, information and technology transfer and mobility, and the ever increasing globalization of the economy," have led to the growth of "trans-national . . . organized, financial, sex-related, immigration, and computer crime."[16] It goes on to say that in 1995 President Clinton revealed "international anticrime initiatives designed to promote the security of citizens in all countries, to prevent and deter money laundering, entry and immigration of organized crime figures, and commercial and financial dealings of foreign narcotics traffickers." Important examples of crossborder organized crimes, according to the State Department, which are listed by the NIJ, are the illicit drug trade within the United States, supposedly generating between $50 and $100 billion a year, the illegal exportation of stolen cars from the United States to both Central America and Eastern Europe, illegal Chinese immigrant smuggling, and about $100 billion annually laundered through United States financial institutions.[17]

The NIJ's eagerness to underwrite large-scale research on various manifestations of transnational organized crime is a sure sign that this issue has taken center stage. There were earlier signs as well—the launching of the journal *Transnational Organized Crime* in 1995, and subsequently the journal *Trends in Organized Crime*. The rationale offered by the latter publication is the following:

> Organized crime is a threat to local, regional, and international security. It has grown in scale and scope to the point where it is now increasingly able to overwhelm the integrity of local institutions and national governments through corruption and intimidation. Criminal enterprises are generating and accu-

mulating financial and other assets on unprecedented levels that undermine the national economies of several countries. Anticipating the development of these organized criminal activities, and devising strategies to counter them, is becoming a priority for governments, business and educators in many parts of the world.[18]

This "statement of purpose," is the heart of the issue. Let us look at some of the proofs.

In their 1993 study, *International Organized Crime: Emerging Threat to US Security*,[19] Roy Godson and William J. Olson argue that organized crime threatens both U.S. interests abroad and the quality of life at home. On the first point they claim, "New international criminals and local organized crime damage major American interests abroad" by (1) undermining "democratic institutions in key areas of the world"; (2) eroding "US alliances and coalitions"; and (3) sometimes providing "infrastructure for military operations against US interests."[20] They provide no information on (2) and (3), however, and thus the threat they actually discuss comes down to the ability of international organized crime to sabotage "democratic institutions" in what the United States considers "key" areas of the world. They neither define "democratic institutions " nor "key areas." They do describe the Colombian drug cartels and note that Chinese Triads are particularly adept at smuggling illegal aliens into the United States.

THE CONFOUNDING ISSUE OF DRUGS

Concerning the second point, the quality of life in the United States, their primary focus is on what they call the "effects of drug trafficking."[21] To set this issue up, they select the following quote from the Uniform Crime Reports issued yearly by the Department of Justice on the level of crime and violence in the United States: "A murder every 21 minutes, a forcible rape every 5 minutes, a robbery every 46 seconds, a burglary every 10 seconds, and so on."[22] Of course, as they recognize, it is impossible "to distinguish with precision the effects of organized crime from other types of crime."[23] The appalling numbers of murders, rapes, robberies, and burglaries reveal nothing about organized crime and are thus presented for no apparent reason. In any case, the core of their argument is the social and economic costs of drug use. To establish drug use as a national security threat, they cite figures from drug deaths and emergency room visits, and the costs of AIDS. They wish to place the blame for all this on international drug cartels. They do not consider the quality of life, or, in fact, anything at all affecting the demand side of narcotic use in the United States.

In fact, drug consumption is a relatively minor public health problem. The costs stemming from cocaine or heroin addiction are minor compared to those associated with cancers caused by industrial pollution or heart disease stemming from obesity. They are more trivial still in relation to the public health costs of tobacco use. Tobacco, after all, has sickened and killed more people than all the illicit drugs ever consumed. Additionally, there is growing reason to believe that the major tobacco companies have been engaged in a long criminal conspiracy to hide their own documentation concerning addiction and the deleterious impact of smoking on health. There are truly serious public health problems and there are problems merely alleged to be. Drug consumption is an example of the latter.

While no government has much of an idea about the real size of drug markets, claims made and data published "suggest they are grossly overstated."[24] Economist Peter Reuter, an acknowledged expert on these matters, comments in a 1996 publication that the U.S. government has what appear to be reasonable estimates about "domestic expenditures," but "these coexist with an essentially madcap series of federal figures on international production and prices that make a mockery of the whole enterprise."[25] He concludes the figures are fictions or "rhetorical conveniences for official statements" used to drive the policy process.

There are serious appraisals connecting the traffic in narcotics to issues of national security, although they are quite different from Godson and Olson discuss. In 1993, Alain LaBrousse's Paris-based organization, Observatoire Geopolitique Des Drogues (OGD) published an initial study on this issue.[26] The OGD rated nations on a three-point scale: (1) narco-states, in which the highest political levels are clearly implicated in the traffic and/or the profits from the traffic; (2) states under the influence, in which some significant part of the political apparatus is implicated in the traffic; (3) and susceptible states, in which there is proof of numerous cases of drug corruption. At the highest rank were Peru, Panama, Pakistan, Surinam, Burma, Nigeria, Equitorial Guinea, and Morocco. In the second rank were Romania, Bulgaria, Croatia, Turkey, Georgia, Azerbaijan, Uzbekistan, Tadjikistan, Cambodia, Laos, Thailand, Mexico, the rest of Central America, Colombia, Equador, Venezuela, and Paraguay. The third rank is not exceptional, for almost every state has had numerous cases in which the drug police have proved susceptible to corruption. In short, the relationship between nation-state security and narcotics-driven corruption is primarily a Third-World problem.

NUCLEAR SMUGGLING, OR NOT?

Godson and Olson are not the only new criminologists to ring the alarm bell about transnational organized crime's threat to U.S. national security. Phil Williams, the editor of *Transnational Organized Crime*, has taken a similar position. But his focal point is the smuggling of nuclear/radioactive materials from the former Soviet States. He has warned "that trade in uranium and plutonium during the past five years has given smuggling unprecedented relevance to international security."[27] To counter the threat, he and a colleague recommend "systematic multinational measures be taken as soon as possible to inhibit theft at the source, to disrupt trafficking and to deter buyers." They also strongly recommend that "the U.S., Germany, Russia and other nations with an interest in the nuclear problem should set up a 'flying squad' with an investigative arm, facilities for counterterrorist and counterextortion actions and a disaster management team."[28]

This essay in question, published in the widely-read *Scientific American*, offered not a single example of transnational crime syndicates smuggling nuclear materials. There is a discussion of unsubstantiated rumors of such smuggling and fears expressed that it could happen, given the state of nuclear security in the former Soviet Union. In one real case of smuggling cited by Williams and Woessner, agents from the German federal intelligence organization (the BND) induced a Colombian dentist and two Spaniards to smuggle lithium and plutonium from Moscow to Munich. In their handful of other examples, the smugglers included the following: regular and secret police officers from a number of nations, engineers and businessmen, and an Italian magistrate who was supposed to be investigating clandestine nuclear trading.[29]

Other sources tell much the same story. The U.S. Department of Energy, for example, sent out a notice on "Red Mercury" in February 1992. It contained basically three propositions: (1) more than 25 attempts to sell the allegedly nuclear material "Red Mercury" have been made since the late 1970s; (2) the allegedly nuclear material "Red Mercury" does not exist; (3) "black marketeers" and "opportunists" are trying to run a scam.[30]

About eight months later, a news story reported that Germany's domestic investigative agency (BKA) was hard at work investigating smuggled Soviet nuclear material, including osmium, niobium, scandium, californium, cobalt, deuterium, cesium, strontium, natural uranium in the form of U308, and other equally frightening material. The culprits trying to deal some of the material were "maintenance personnel from two USSR fuel fabrication facilities, one near Moscow, the other in Ust-Kamenogorsk, Kazakhstan. The story also noted that "nuclear materials are being smuggled from Russia to Europe via the Soviet Army's air transport links." Some of the material ended up at the Soviet military command center in Wuendsdorf, near Berlin. However, the Germans did not want to make a fuss about this for fear it would delay the final pullout of Soviet forces in Germany. Of the cases investigated by the BKA, one-third were simply fraudulent. Some organized-crime involvement was found only in the cases of fraud.

What brought this activity about was, of course, the end of the cold war. Since then, both Russia and the United States "have been dumping strategic material inventories." Dealers were thus frantic to sell, as the market was saturated and prices had crashed.[31]

TRANSNATIONAL ORGANIZED COMPUTER CRIME

Other transnational organized crime hot spots mentioned by the NIJ are computers, sex-related ones, and illegal Chinese immigration to the United States. Computer crime is presumably on the rise, though it is not apparent what this sort of crime has to do with serious organized transnational crime. The computer is like any other form of new technology in which those with a criminal bent see the normal advantage of going high-tech. The automobile, the telephone, the pager, the cell phone, credit cards, phone cards, and so forth, have all been adopted by criminals for illicit businesses for precisely the same reasons anyone else has adopted them—ease of movement and communication. Perhaps the inclusion of computer crime on the NIJ's list has to do with criminals using the Internet to gull Americans into some financial fraud. This would then put the Internet browser into a position similar to folks gulled by the ubiquitous telephone "cold call" of fraudulent penny-stock operators. Victims of the latter have sent money to fraudsters for investments into such worthy endeavors as creating gold from special Costa Rican sand. For crime fighters, the Internet is a boon.

More likely, however, the transnational computer crime of interest to the NIJ has to do with the organized theft of computer components, especially speedy data-chomping chips. Common sense would indicate that this type of organized crime is a natural consequence of decentralized transnational manufacturing—a bit done in the United States, another bit in the Far East, and so forth—of exceptionally tiny material whose half-life at the top of the market is about six months. To some extent, the 1991 government hearings on Asian organized crime bear this out.

According to the U.S. Senate's Permanent Subcommittee on Investigations (PSI), computer chip theft "is especially attractive to Asian crime groups for several reasons."[32] The first reasons stated, interestingly enough, have nothing to do with national origins. PSI staff pointed out that it is very difficult to detect and prosecute this type of crime. Computer chips have no registration numbers. Also, fences will buy them for "80 percent of their value as opposed to 20 percent for items such as jewelry."[33] Both are perfectly understandable reasons for criminals, no matter what their racial or ethnic backgrounds are, to specialize in stealing chips. The issue of national origins becomes clear when the subcommittee remarked, "Asian crime groups are uniquely positioned for computer chip theft because many Asians work for computer chip manufacturers and because there are markets for the chip in Southeast Asia." This places the issue of Asian gangsters stealing computer chips into the same commonsense framework as the following: (1) Jewish American gangsters extorted from garment businesses in the 1920s that were overwhelmingly owned by Jewish Americans; (2) Black American gangsters have run policy operations in Harlem. Ethnic organized criminals attach themselves to the economic activities and interests of their ethnic group.

COMPUTERS AND INTERNATIONAL SECURITY

Finally, if the transnational issue driving serious computer crime is the organized theft of secret computer technology that enables, for example, the production of weapons of mass destruction, then it would appear the concern is misplaced. The U.S. Senate Subcommittee on International Security, Proliferation, and Federal Services in its report *The Proliferation Primer*, published in January 1998, holds that it is the relaxation of "control over the export of dual-use goods" by "several western nations, including the United States," that has allowed other nations "to acquire or improve weapons of mass destruction technology and missile delivery platforms."[34]

In a detailed examination of this issue, the subcommittee added the following:

During the Cold War the wisdom of not exporting militarily useful goods to America's enemies was commonly accepted in the United States. This policy extended not just to technologies and systems whose sole application is military—America's long-range ballistic missile manufacturers, for example, didn't try to sell these weapon platforms to the USSR—but also to the sale of "dual-use" goods, technologies having both military and civilian applications. Notwithstanding the natural tension in any free society between trade and export controls, the western export control regime COCOM (the "Coordinating Committee for Multilateral Export Controls") was a success.

Less than one year after entering office, President Clinton assured the Chairman and CEO of computer manufacturer Silicon Graphics, Edward McCracken, he was "currently engaged in seeking major reforms to COCOM, which should lead to significant liberalization of [export] controls on computers, machine tools, and telecommunications."

President Clinton's "major reform" to COCOM was its dissolution. COCOM died on March 31, 1994, over two years before the establishment, on July 12, 1996, of its successor, the Wassenaar Arrangement (short for the "Wassenaar Arrangement on Export Controls for Conventional Arms and Dual-Use Goods and Technologies"). Unlike its predecessor, Wassenaar allows each member to determine for itself whether to allow an export to proceed. No member can veto another's exports. Where COCOM consisted of consensus before the fact, Wassenaar consists of reports after the fact.

SEX-RELATED TRANSNATIONAL ORGANIZED CRIME

The reference to sex-related transnational organized crime in the NIJ proposal refers to either the traffic in women and/or to the manufacturing and distribution of child pornography. Both are noxious criminal enterprises that should draw the attention of law enforcement wherever they occur, but there is little reason to believe that much can be done to curb them transnationally.[35] In the United States the production of pornographic videos is now primarily an amateur undertaking, thanks to the video camera and VCR. It is thus much more difficult for law enforcement to locate the pornographers and their products. This is a far cry from the national distribution networks of the 1970s, when organized crime, through the Sovereign News Company in Cleveland, Peachtree National Distributors in Atlanta, and Star Distributing Ltd. in Manhattan, controlled most of the pornographic magazine and film distribution in the United States.[36]

Traite des Blanches

The modern apprehension over the traffic in women in the Western world goes back to the nineteenth century. Edward J. Bristow's *Prostitution and Prejudice: The Jewish Fight Against White Slavery, 1870–1939* is a first-rate account of an intriguing part of this history. During the period 1875 to 1914, Bristow notes, some traffickers specialized in moving Jewish women from Eastern Europe to brothels in Buenos Aires, Constantinople, and New York. Other traffickers moved them to the Rand (South Africa) and Manchuria. Still other networks of traffickers sent Italian and Greek women to the "voracious brothels of the Middle East and North Africa."[37]

Often enough in the United States, early discussions of "white slavery" were tied into a xenophobic horror of recent immigrants, although the term was first coined to describe factory workers in Europe and America prior to the 1880s.[38] There were four factors in the nineteenth century that combined to identify and fight against the traffic in women: "strong, widespread anti-Chinese immigration activity in America; Victorian morals in Europe and America; agitation over female rights in Europe and America; and purity movements in Europe and America."[39] Patricia Klausner's estimable dissertation, "The Politics of Massage Parlor Prostitution: The International Traffic in Women for Prostitution into New York City, 1970–1986," points out the thematic role xenophobia played, quoting from an influential essay written in 1910 by Ernest Bell:

> Unless we make energetic and successful war upon the red-light district, . . . we shall have Oriental brothel slavery thrust upon us . . . with all its unnatural and abnormal practices, established among us by French traders. Jew traders, too, will people our "levees" with Polish Jewesses and others who will make money for them. Shall we defend our American civilization, or lower our flag to the most despicable foreigners—French, Irish, Jews and Mongolians? . . . On both coasts and throughout all our cities, only an awakening of the whole Christian conscience and intelligence can save us from the importation of Parisian and Polish pollution, which is already corrupting the manhood and youth of every large city in the nation."[40]

Although it is often noted that the first U.S. law to affect "alien" prostitution was the "temporary Chinese Exclusion Act of May 6, 1882," which was reformulated in 1903 and 1907, the first federal law actually addressing the issue was enacted in 1875.[41] The 1882 law restricted the immigration of Chinese and prostitutes; in 1903 it "included persons who procure or attempt to bring in prostitutes, or women for the purpose of prostitution; and in 1907 it banned "Importers of alien females; those who attempt to import females, and holders or harborers of such females for the purpose of prostitution or any other immoral purpose.[42] One year after the passage of the 1882 law, the Women's Christian Temperance Union, which played a central role in "purity" campaigns, published a tract that boldly stated "there is an organized, systematized traffic in girls."[43] Heat over the issue was building.

In 1899 a conference was held in London to "share knowledge, strategies, and concerns about what was to become known as white slave traffic." At this meeting agreement was reached on a constitution for the International Bureau for the Suppression of Vice and Traffic in Girls and Women.[44] In the autumn of 1900, The Committee of Fifteen was formed in New York to battle the connection between political corruption and organized vice.[45] In 1902 the French government convened a Paris conference on the *traite des blanches*. Several documents were produced that mandated nations to "establish national authorities and a centralized agency" to collect information on the international traffic in females for the purpose of involuntary prostitution.[46] The United States did not attend.

A couple of decades later, the League of Nations funded a study of the traffic that by then originated in at least eight European countries and ended in Argentina, Brazil, Mexico, Panama, Uruguay, and the United States. There was also a side trade to North Africa, principally to Egypt. To facilitate the traffic, counterfeit passports, visas, and marriage certificates were used. In time, the United Nations and Interpol took up the issue. In 1975 Interpol reported to the UN on several trafficking patterns, including Argentine women exported to Puerto Rico, the Middle East, and European Mediterranean countries; a European regional market; networks moving European women to the Ivory Coast and Senegal; an East Asian market centered primarily in Thailand, secondarily in the Philippines, sending women to unidentified countries; and lastly a merging of several trafficking networks supplying the brothels of Lebanon and Kuwait.[47]

The traffic in women and illegal immigration have been inextricably linked since the nineteenth century. However, what has always driven illegal immigration are precisely the same issues driving legal immigration: some combination of poverty or limited economic opportunity at home; perceived real opportunity abroad; and middlemen able and more than willing to arrange for false papers and to advance money to the migrant. These are known in the literature on immigration as *push factors*. In the long history of both legal and illegal immigration to the United States, the desire for cheap labor by firms in the United States is known as the *pull factor*.

THE SIZE AND SCOPE OF ILLEGAL IMMIGRATION

The modern era of American immigration policy began with the passage of the 1965 Immigration and Naturalization Act, which "removed the quotas for immigrants based on national origins and replaced them with a preference system based primarily on family unification and, to a lesser extent, on occupational skills."[48] Those who took the most advantage of the change in U.S. policy were immigrants from Asian and Latin American countries. The National Research Council's Panel on the Demographic and Economic Impacts of Immigration estimated that the Asian population in the United States by the year 2050 will likely reach 8 percent of the population and the Hispanic, 25 percent. Out of the far greater pool of legal immigrants are the undocumented immigrants whose annual migration to the United States is calculated at around 200,000 to 300,000. On the sensitive issue of immigration and crime rates, the panel concluded the following: "Crime rates rose from 1960 until about 1990, and since then have declined; there is no obvious link with trends in immigration this period."

In 1996, the Immigration and Naturalization Service (INS) published its best estimate of the total illegal-alien resident population, which was about five million.[49] Eighty-three percent of this population resided in seven states: California led the way with two million (40 percent), followed by Texas with 700,000, New York with 540,000, Florida with 350,000, Illinois with 290,000, New Jersey with 135,000, and Arizona with 115,000. The INS also determined that more than 80 percent of the entire undocumented population is from Western Hemisphere countries. Mexico was the leading source country, with an estimated 150,000 undocumented immigrants arriving annually. Looking at the fifteen top source countries, only the Philippines and Poland were outside the Western Hemisphere, and Poland's contribution has declined by 25 percent since 1988. The only U.S. states with fewer than 1,000 undocumented workers are North and South Dakota.

SWEAT LABOR

Undocumented workers—illegal aliens—are almost always a population in some peril. Their most obvious hazard is capture, jail, and deportation. But the most insidious menace is exploitation in the workplace, and the worst of that takes place in the reborn sweatshops, firms supposedly outlawed through the efforts of Progressive-era reformers and garment unions, particularly the Amalgamated Clothing Workers of America and the International Ladies Garment Workers.[50] The General Accounting Office (GAO) reported that garment-manufacturing firms, restaurants, and meat-processing plants were home to more sweatshops than any other industries. A $45-billion industry with more than a million workers, garment manufacturing was the most culpable. The Inspections Division, Office of the Inspector General, Department of Justice, recently stated, "Illegal aliens are held in sweatshops under conditions of involuntary servitude."[51] It added that sweatshops evade taxes and breed money laundering, labor racketeering, drug trafficking, and extortion. There are around 22,000 contract cutting and sewing shops in the U.S., and the Department of Labor figures sweatshops make up from one-half to two-thirds of the total. In 1989, the GAO calculated that "4,500 of the 7,000 garment sewing shops in New York City were sweatshops," and reported in 1995 that "up to 4,500 of the 5,000 garment sewing shops in Los Angeles were sweatshops."[52]

Attention was first drawn to the garment sweatshops in late 1979 by New York State Senator Franz S. Leichter and his modest staff. Leichter's investigation revealed there were "several thousand garment factory sweatshops" located throughout New York.[53] He went on to chastise federal, state, and city agencies for ignoring wage and safety laws, and for doing nothing at all about sweatshop conditions. The guilty agencies included the Federal Occupational Safety and Health Administration, the Federal Employment Standard Division of the United States Labor Department, the New York State Attorney General's Office, the Fire Department, and the city's Buildings Department. Two years later, Leichter released a second report in which organized crime's control of the sweatshops was featured. The report found the following:

Through [organized crime's] use of their dominated garment trucking companies, they finance new shops, arrange for work for these shops, and transport
the finished garments from the shops to midtown warehouses. Through
inflated rates and other means, these trucking concerns rake in enormous profits. My conservative estimate of the "take" from trucking overcharges in Chinatown, alone, exceeds $9 million a year.[54]

Leichter also pointed out that ten years previously there were no more than
two hundred garment sweatshops, most concentrated in New York's Chinatown.
By 1980, these were joined by at least one hundred in sections of northern Manhattan, around five hundred in the South Bronx, and several hundreds more in
Queens and Brooklyn. Sweatshops were established "wherever concentrations of
undocumented aliens exist," Leichter commented.[55]

Garment factories had been bailing out of New York for decades, first to low-
wage meccas in the American South, and then abroad to even lower-wage nations
that, until quite recently, were part of what was admiringly called the Pacific Rim,
particularly Hong Kong and Taiwan. Some garment manufacturing had returned
to New York because wages in Rim states, though still low, started rising, and
transportation costs "skyrocketed making it even less attractive to send work
overseas."[56]

New York's new wave of immigration since the late 1960s, within which tens of
thousands of undocumented workers came in, was made up of Chinese and
Koreans, Central and South Americans, and migrants from Caribbean nations
such as the Dominican Republic. With city, state, and federal agencies caught in
the grip of misfeasance, and with organized labor already on its slide to irrelevance, sweat labor became standard. To keep undocumented workers in line, they
were threatened by employers with deportation.

Illicit labor operations in the New York area had still another contributing factor. Garment manufacturers, called "jobbers," as Senator Leichter's investigations
revealed, were, more often than not, financed and set up by organized crime,
which squeezed them dry. The jobbers, in turn, relentlessly squeezed the sweatshop operators, called "contractors," who solved their problems by ever more
fiercely victimizing the new undocumented immigrant workers.[57]

Every city that had significant garment manufacturing had sweatshop labor.
In 1990, Elizabeth McLean Petras determined that Philadelphia's new sweatshops
were unlicensed, illegal, off-the-books operations paying "no minimum wages,
unemployment insurance or health benefits, and ignor[ing] child labor laws or
overtime pay regulations."[58] Her primary concern was the exploitation of Asian
females who were working, in some cases, around seventeen hours a day, every
day of the week. In Philadelphia, by the late 1980s, there were possibly one thousand garment shops, most owned by Hong Kong Chinese who either were, or
were working with, Chinese-organized crime syndicates. These syndicates smuggled workers into the United States and then forced them to work for no wages
until they satisfied the costs of passage. Many were forced to live and eat some-

where in the bowels of the factory, and to sign agreements to have their room-and-board costs deducted from their wages, when and if they ever actually get paid. The workers were, as Petras said, "little more than indentured servants."[59]

New Jersey's garment manufacturing industry was much the same.[60] A 1991 New Jersey Commission of Investigation (COI) inquiry found equivalent methods of exploitation. Among the violations New Jersey investigators uncovered, were the hiding of illegal aliens, the failure to pay overtime or minimum wages, the use of child labor, and the failure either to carry workers' compensation insurance or to pay payroll taxes.[61] New Jersey investigators also commented on the hold organized crime had on the trucking of garments, picking up where Leichter's investigations had led a decade earlier. The COI reported that Thomas F. Gambino was "the single most powerful organized crime figure in garment trucking." He was the eldest son of the racketeer Carlo Gambino, and had married into the Lucchese family, another powerful Italian American crime syndicate. Gambino and two of his brothers, Joseph and Carl, controlled eight major trucking firms and three leasing firms: "In 1988, the 11 Gambino companies had total assets of $34.5 million and revenues of $41,261,931."[62]

New Jersey authorities also found that in the spring of 1989 Joseph Gambino and several associates, Ray Buttafusco, John DiSalvo, and Gary Chan, a "sewing contractor in New York's Chinatown," scouted Philadelphia's "Chinatown" district as part of an expansion plan. They never got very far in this move because federal authorities finally indicted and convicted the Gambinos on racketeering charges. However, one of their Philadelphia contacts was the "past president of the Philadelphia branch of the On Leong Tong," a primarily criminal organization that arrived in the United States in the nineteenth century.[63] Along with other Chinese American criminal organizations, the On Leong operated "opium, prostitution, and gambling dens,"[64] and worked, from time to time, cooperatively with non-Chinese American organized criminals.

The current relationships between Chinese racketeers from Hong Kong and Taiwan and U.S. garment manufacturing came about initially when U.S. garment manufacturing made its move to Asian nations. There local criminal entrepreneurs either bought the firms, became partners with U.S. owners, or created new firms. When garment businesses returned to the U.S., a significant number of them were in the hands of Asian gangsters who augmented the regular and booming supply of cheap labor by smuggling in thousands, perhaps tens of thousands, of illegal aliens.[65]

In the Los Angeles area, there are more than 100,000 garment workers, the vast majority of whom are undocumented. The single most deplorable example of involuntary servitude took place in El Monte, a city that straddles Interstate 10 just east of downtown Los Angeles and that has more than 100,000 residents. For somewhere between three and seven years, eighty undocumented Thais and almost as many undocumented Latinos lived liked slaves while laboring on garments in an El Monte sweatshop that was, in fact, a forced-labor compound. Sleeping on mattresses twenty-five to a small room, working from six in the morning until midnight or later, the El Monte compound was surrounded by both barbed and razor wire and watched over by a guard tower of sorts. Locked inside for years, several Thais managed to escape and reported their bondage to the Thai Consul in Los Angeles. Eventually law enforcement was notified. The sweatshop was put under surveillance for as long as three years. Finally, in August 1995, federal and state cops raided the site. Two years later, attorney Julie Su, representing the workers, announced a $2 million settlement had been reached with B.U.M. International, L. F. Sportswear, Mervyn's, and Montgomery Ward, companies that contracted with the sweatshop. In 1996, the sweatshop owners, seven Thai nationals, pleaded guilty to federal charges of harboring illegal aliens and involuntary servitude, what is commonly called *slave labor.*[66]

Garment manufacturing is only one of several industries that encourage illegal immigrants. Stephen J. Hedges, Dana Hawkins, and Penny Loeb, reporting for *U.S. News & World Report,* noted that "big American industries—construction companies, nurseries and fruit growers—rely on these workers."[67] But perhaps, they added, the most dependent areas of big businesses utilizing low-wage illegal immigrants are the United States meat and poultry companies. More than half of the beef and pork side is dominated by three companies: IBP, formerly Iowa Beef Processors, Cargill's Excel Corp., and Con-Agra's Monfort Inc. Concerning beef alone, these companies controlled around 80 percent of U.S. production. IBP, which earned a profit of $257 million in 1995, was the focus of special attention from *U.S. News.* The magazine reported that IBP (and the others) kept their labor costs down by hiring illegal immigrants from Mexico.[68]

In 1996, the INS estimated that at least 12,000 illegal immigrants were working in Iowa and Nebraska meatpacking plants. This may not seem like much in comparison with the garment industries in New York, Philadelphia, or Los Angeles. However, Nebraska's population is about equal to that of Brooklyn, while Iowa's is less than Philadelphia. Dominated by farming and agri-businesses, neither state is a mecca for post-1965 immigrants. In fact, the INS's state-by-state estimate of the illegal alien population indicates that meatpacking accounts for almost all of Iowa's and Nebraska's illegal aliens.

Meatpacking is likely the most dangerous industry in the United States—an astonishing "36 percent of workers . . . sustain serious injuries each year."[69] In 1990, an IBP official stated that one of their plants in Iowa had an 83 percent annual employee turnover. Because illegal immigrants are far less likely to report injuries, anthropologist Mark Grey, quoted in *U.S. News,* characterized meatpacking work as akin to "slave labor."[70] Reporter Dana Hawkins commented that in 1987, IBP was fined $2.59 million by OSHA for having kept two sets of employee injury logs.[71]

There was a "human pipeline" between a small, central Mexican town, Santa Rita, and an IBP plant in Storm Lake, Iowa, population around 9,000. "Many of the Santa Ritans" paid a professional smuggler to get them across the border, where they were picked up for the long ride to Storm Lake. "Once there, some workers said, they bought phony birth certificates from an IBP employee."[72]

Social Security numbers were purchased from "Chicanos in Texas and California," and were then sold to the illegal immigrants for $500. The man running the pipeline claimed IBP paid him $150 a head.

One last point about the illegal immigration scene: it now appears that another racket has been spawned. Ian Burrell of *The Independent* reports that Turkish immigration racketeers appear "to be targeting British and United States Asians because their passports are the most highly prized for use in smuggling people from the Middle East, North Africa and the Indian sub-continent into Europe." The British suspect that some proportion of the 174 British citizens that have disappeared in Turkey during the past ten years, have been murdered for their passports, which may now be worth around $10,000 on the illegal market.[73]

IMMIGRATION AND DRUGS: THAT QUEER LADDER OF SOCIAL MOBILITY

It was bad enough that many Dominican migrants to New York in the 1960s ended up in sweatshops; it was worse that in a relatively short period of time, perhaps half a decade, many found economic and social mobility in the narcotics trade. The rise of Dominican crime syndicates parallels their mass migration to the New York metropolitan area, where there are now approximately one million Dominicans, representing around 12.5 percent of their home country's population.[74] Currently the net outmigration rate in the Dominican Republic is 4.6 per 1,000, while the unemployment rate is about 30 percent and inflation, after economic reform significantly reduced it in 1994, averages around 12.5 percent.

These discouraging figures are in stark contrast to the amount of U.S. investment in the Dominican Republic, which has been extraordinary.[75] Between 1980 and 1992, the U.S. directed more than $840 million in aid to the Dominican Republic. The money was channeled through the U.S. Agency for International Development (USAID) and could not be used to fund either public health or education. In fact, 97 percent of USAID funding went to the private sector, which was allegedly going to provide sufficient wages to allow workers "to purchase the health care and education they wanted."[76] From 1980 through 1993, AID money created more than "150,000 maquiladora assembly jobs" that made products for the U.S. market.[77]

According to the National Labor Committee's "Special Investigation" concluded in November 1993 and titled *Free Trade's Hidden Secrets: Why We Are Losing Our Shirts*, here's how the system worked. In 1983, American Airlines, prompted by the Commerce Department, laid off scores of U.S. workers and moved certain jobs offshore to Barbados. Four years later American Airlines expanded to the Dominican Republic, setting up shop in the San Isidro free-trade zone, constructed with money from the World Bank and the InterAmerican Development Bank. Dominican workers earned around 50 cents an hour. From the Dominican Republic, it took dead aim at the United States. W. Patrick Griffith, president of American Airline's offshore data-entry operation, stated that American Airlines intended to attract "offshore a segment of the industry dominated by U.S. data-entry bureaus and corporate in house services...."

[It] aggressively pursued Fortune 500 companies, primarily in travel, utility, financial and health-care industries." American Airlines "now does data-entry work under long-term contract for two dozen major U.S. corporations." Griffith noted that the "average cost of doing data entry in the Caribbean is $0.60 per thousand key strokes, versus $1.75 in the U.S." From offshore they could and did underprice U.S. firms. American Airlines processes 40,000 medical claims a day under a contract from the Equicor Insurance Company, which is the Tennessee-based subsidiary of Cigna Insurance. The Commerce Department referred to this American Airlines operation as a "success story," although jobs that used to be in Tennessee are now in the Dominican Republic.

In 1986, the Commerce Department, helped by the Business Promotion Council, took Westinghouse offshore to the Dominican Republic. At that exact time Westinghouse announced that it was closing its Bryant Electric Plant in Bridgeport, Connecticut, which made circuit breakers, because of excess plant capacity. Westinghouse moved into the Itabo free-trade zone, in which there were no taxes, no regulations, no unions, and low wages. Apparently, however, the wages were not low enough, for they were slashed as U.S. investments poured in.

Westinghouse paid 52 cents an hour in the Dominican Republic. It also demanded overtime, most often without overtime pay, and discouraged its Dominican employees from going to night school by threatening to fire them. Westinghouse did not take kindly to Dominicans attempting to create unions either, firing anyone foolish enough to try and circulating "their names on a blacklist" to "other free zone companies." With all this USAID activity, the net results were not very encouraging if one were a citizen of the Dominican Republic. In the fast-growing free-trade zones, real wages actually went down over time by 46 percent, thus contributing to an increase in real poverty. It should also be noted that per-capita spending on health care and education in the Dominican Republic is the second lowest in the world.

Caught between the vicissitudes of sweat labor in New York and the quite awful conditions in the Dominican Republic, the turn to narcotics trafficking likely appeared a reasonable course to some Dominicans. As the Justice Department's inspector general said: sweatshops breed drug trafficking.

The contemporary Dominican involvement in narcotics began when Colombian drug bosses hired the Dominicans in New York as "couriers, street sellers and hit men."[78] With their retail business expanding, they slowly began to move into wholesaling. During the 1990s, as relations between Colombian syndicates and Mexican ones soured, the Dominicans were well placed to offer Colombians an alternative, less-expensive route into the United States.

Today, the DEA estimates that Dominican drug traffickers "transport as much as one-third of the approximately 300 metric tons of cocaine that enter the United States each year."[79] Thomas A. Constantine, the DEA administrator, testified that the leadership of these surging drug syndicates, both men and women, command the predominant forces at the wholesale level of narcotics (both cocaine and heroin) operations on the East Coast.

MONEY LAUNDERING

Money laundering, of course, is the process of changing illicitly acquired wealth into what appears to be licit. The processes or methodologies were developed for old-fashioned tax evasion quite some time ago. And it was six decades ago that they first became a public issue. In 1937, President Roosevelt received a report from Treasury Secretary Henry Morgenthau, Jr., on tax evasion. Roosevelt then sent the report to Congress with this message: "Efforts at avoidance and evasion of tax liability [are] so widespread and so amazing both in their boldness and their ingenuity that further action without delay seems imperative."[80] In response, the 75th Congress created the Joint Committee on Tax Evasion and Avoidance.

Treasury Secretary Morgenthau's alarming report to Roosevelt listed the major and unprecedented devices used to beat the income tax. Number one was the creation of "foreign personal holding corporations in The Bahamas, Panama, Newfoundland, and other places where taxes are low and corporation laws lax." Morgenthau pointed out the difficulty of gathering information on Bahamian companies (owned by Americans) that are "organized through foreign lawyers, with dummy incorporators and dummy directors, so that the names of the real parties in interest do not appear."[81]

In testimony before the joint committee, Morgenthau castigated the many "ingenious lawyers and accountants" who are very handsomely paid to construct immoral methods for their clients to avoid taxes. Thirty years after this first congressional hearing, an ingenious, handsomely paid attorney had this to say to IRS Special Agents attempting to untangle his enterprise:

> There is nothing more corrupting to our society than a system of taxation. I have no words strong enough to condemn the society in which we are living in terms of taxation. . . .
>
> He (the taxpayer) puts money in a Bahama central trust. Why in the Bahamas? There is no income tax or estate tax in the Bahamas. Why in a trust? A trust is like a corporation, a separate legal entity. This separate entity is a non-resident alien, and a non-resident alien can sell an asset in the United States with no tax. How delightful! Now, if that non-resident alien ties in with a distributing company in the Netherlands Antilles, which can earn interest in the United States without a tax under any circumstances, he has put together a perfect set-up. He takes losses and deductions in the United States and he takes gains and profits abroad, under a tax treaty.
>
> Do you think any Congress we have is going to change the laws that allow this? Let's not kid ourselves. With those savings, the rich of this country can afford to buy the entire Senate, if necessary.[82]

While there is no proof that it was necessary to buy the entire Senate to protect the methodology of tax evasion, it is certainly the case that high-level political corruption has smoothed the evader's path. Indeed, in the decade of the 1970s, the Intelligence Division (now called the Criminal Investigation Division) of the IRS was eviscerated by IRS leadership for looking too closely at Americans who constructed offshore tax evasion schemes.[83]

For the most part these days, only historically minded criminologists refer to money laundering in connection with such indigenous organized crime activities as the Teamsters Pension Fund and a substantial piece of the savings and loan debacle. Today drug syndicates are center stage and it is their money laundering that gets almost all of the attention. Over the course of the past fifteen or twenty years, drug racketeers have used U.S. banks[84] (some bought a few), New Jersey casinos and more recently Indian reservation casinos,[85] jewelry and gold exchanges, border states' *cambios,* firms of almost every description, virtually every Caribbean nations' banking establishment, Swiss banks, Austrian banks, Channel Island banks, banks in Cyprus and Hong Kong, banks in tiny and obscure Pacific Island nations, banks, in fact, just about everywhere.

And despite what some reformers have predicted about the coming demise of "confidential private banking," the most recent survey of confidential private banks by the *Financial Times* shows the industry is expanding. The reasons for this are the "rapid growth of entrepreneurial businesses, privatisation and stock market appreciation" that have contributed to "the accumulation of huge sums in the hands of a concentrated group of wealthy individuals." It is estimated by private bankers that this concentrated wealth, which is their "target market," is currently around $17 trillion. Most experts believe this pool will continue growing for many years at least twice as fast as the regular banking market.[86]

Sophisticated money launderers also work in derivatives, which include such esoteric items as "Repackaged Asset Vehicles" (RAVs) created by Morgan Stanley. A RAV, Frank Partnoy, author of *F.I.A.S.C.O.: Blood in the Water on Wall Street,* remarked, "was used to repackage existing securities [unmarketable Mexican governments bonds or 'Colombian deposit receipts'!] into new derivatives using various investment vehicles, including trusts and special companies." In the trade RAVS were often called "'black box' transactions, because you put securities into a trust or company—the so-called 'black box', and then magically the securities turn into derivatives." David Whitby, a retired British banker and head of the BCCI Private Study Group, has noted that BCCI and its commodities firm, Capcom, and arms/drugs dealers formed "special purpose" single-transaction companies, usually in the Netherlands Antilles or British Virgin Islands. Furthermore, he added, "If the money launderer/drugs dealer has a derivatives' team from a private bank fronting their trades then the funds can be passed through London/New York without detection."[87] Whitby concluded, sensibly enough, that "U.S. investment banks creating and selling derivatives don't give a shit whether their clients are crooks or just plain stupid corporations like Proctor & Gamble and Orange County—they are only interested in the bottom line."[88] On the same theme, Partnoy has written that simple black box transactions were commonplace; "almost every bank and major drug dealer used them, and business publications such as *The Economist* even advertised them."

Criminal entrepreneurship is relentless. One fairly recent drug-money-laundering investigation that had targeted a Panamanian citizen is a case in point. This particular criminal used nine major U.S. companies ranging from a national supermarket chain to a national discount chain to launder hundreds of millions of dollars in drug profits. He also owned or controlled a maritime company, a grain company, an investment company, an oil company, a trading company, and a construction company.[89] He is not unique.

CONCLUSION

It seems to me foolish to believe that drug production and consumption, money laundering, sophisticated financial crime, the theft of computer chips, the smuggling of aliens, and so forth, can be controlled by any nation, or indeed by the United Nations, and that collectively they are a new and unique threat to democratic life. Criminals, like most other people, respond to a set of conditions collectively called an *opportunity structure*. In the examples discussed above, these structures came from the demand for cheap labor, the high price paid for computer chips, the creation of a financial system that caters to tax evaders, and so on. Criminal syndicates large and small, loosely or tightly organized, supplying highly valued commodities obviously have found and will continue to find ways to satisfy demand.

NOTES

1. Some of this discussion is derived from a paper, "Svet vshuru nohama kriminologie organizovaneho zlocinu," I presented at a conference in Prague, The Czech Republic, Oct. 1995. The paper was subsequently published in the collection *Organizovvna Kriminalita v Ceske Republice a USA*, by the Institut pro kriminologii a socialni prevenci, Prague 1996.
2. See U.S. Senate, Committee on Governmental Affairs, Permanent Subcommittee on Investigations, *Oversight Inquiry of the Department of Labor's Investigation of the Teamsters Central States Pension Fund* (Washington, D.C.: Government Printing Office, 1981); United States District Court, Southern District of New York, United State of America, Plaintiff, against International Brotherhood of Teamsters, Chauffeurs, Warehousemen and Helpers of America, AFL/CIO, et al., Defendants, "Government's Memorandum of Law in Support of Its Motion For Preliminary Relief," 1988; New York State Commission of Investigation, "An Investigation Concerning Racketeer Activities in Connection with the Air Freight Industry in the New York Metropolitan Area," 1968; U.S. Senate, Permanent Subcommittee of Investigations, "Labor Racketeering Activities of Jack McCarthy and National Consultants Associated, Ltd.," 24 Apr. 1967; and Alan A. Block and Sean Patrick Griffin, "The Teamsters, The White House, The Labor Department: A Commentary on the Politics of Organized Crime," *Crime, Law and Social Change: An International Journal* 27, no. 1 (1997).
3. New York State Organized Crime Task Force, *Corruption and Racketeering in the New York City Construction Industry* (New York: New York University Press, 1990), 125.
4. Alexander Stille, *Excellent Cadavers: The Mafia and the Death of the First Italian Republic* (New York: Pantheon Books, 1995), 21.

5. Ibid., 22.
6. See Graziano Battistella, *Italian Americans in the 80s: A Sociodemographic Profile* (New York: Center for Migration Studies, 1989).
7. See Anton Blok, *The Mafia of a Sicilian Village, 1860–1960: A Study of Violent Peasant Entrepreneurs* (New York: Harper & Row, 1974); Pino Arlacchi, *Mafia Business: the Mafia Ethic and the Spirit of Capitalism* (London: Verso, 1986); Tribunale di Palermo, Ufficio Istruzione Dei Process Penali, "Mandato Dicattura," Palermo, Sicily, 29 Sept. 1984; and Alan A. Block and Bruce Bullington, "Thinking About Violence and Change in the Sicilian Mafia," *Violence, Aggression and Terrorism* (1987).
8. See Thomas Kessner, *The Golden Door: Italian and Jewish Immigrant Mobility in New York City* (New York: Oxford University Press, 1977); and the brilliant memoir by Marianna De Marco Torgovnick, *Crossing Ocean Parkway* (Chicago: University of Chicago Press, 1994).
9. See Jane Catherine Schneider, "Of Vigilance and Virgins: Honor, Shame and Access to Resources in Mediterranean Societies," *Ethnology* 10 (1971); and Danilo Dolci, *Sicilian Lives* (New York: Pantheon, 1981).
10. See James B. Jacobs with Christopher Panarella and Jay Worthington, *Busting the Mob: United States v. Cosa Nostra* (New York: New York University Press, 1994).
11. One of the boldest predictions of this transformation has been argued by Bruce J. Nicholl. He contends that "long before 1980, the ground was prepared for a blossoming of Chinese Organized Crime activity in the United States." In the ensuing years, entire Chinese criminal organizations were transferred to the U.S. "The result," he stated, "has been the virtual displacement of Traditional Organized Crime by the Chinese on the east coast of the United States and the establishment of the control of criminal activities on the west coast by Chinese Organized Crime groups and gangs." How the ground was prepared is not exactly clear, though it would appear to be the result of the growth of the Chinese population on both the East and West coasts. The criminological transformation is driven by large-scale Chinese immigration within which Chinese criminals have seen their opportunity and seized it. Bruce J. Nicholl, "Integration of International Organized Crime Activity" (unpublished paper presented at the National Strategy Information Center conference, "The Gray Area Phenomenon and Transnational Criminal Activity," (Washington, D.C., 4 Dec. 1992), 10.
12. Works Progress Administration, *Guide to New York* (New York: Random House, 1939), 269.
13. The Drug Enforcement Administration compiled a detailed report in December 1976 on drug traffickers active along Pleasant Avenue particularly a violent and unstable group called the Purple Gang. The DEA identified twenty individuals who were the original members of the Purple Gang brought up in the Pleasant Avenue/East Harlem neighborhood. By that time five had been murdered, two were in prison for murder, another on drug charges, another for assault, and two more were on parole for drug offenses and assault. One other Purple was a suspect in a murder investigation. That left only eight still hanging around, and they were under intensive DEA surveillance. Only two of the gang members still on the street remained in Manhattan, and just one of them in the old neighborhood. Four had moved to Yonkers, north of the Bronx, one to the Bronx, one to lavish quarters in Yorktown Heights, quite a bit to the north, and another to Lodi, New Jersey.

   In addition to the original twenty gangsters, the DEA identified 108 associates of the Purple Gang. Most of them were also from the Pleasant Avenue/East Harlem neighborhood, and most of them had also relocated. The locations of 102 heroin racketeers (including the few living original Purples) were pinpointed by the end of 1976. Forty-seven percent were in the Bronx; about 16 percent in Yonkers and nearby towns; around 5 percent had crossed the Hudson River and lived in towns such as Nyack, Nanuet, and Pearl River; and another 5 lived percent in New York State villages north of Westchester County. All told, 73 percent went north. Of the remainder, about 9 percent moved to the borough of Queens or to Long Island, and 10 percent lived in nearby New Jersey towns. That left only seven of the heroin racketeers still in Manhattan, not quite 7 percent, and only four of them in the old neighborhood. See, Drug Enforcement Administration, Department of Justice, Unified Intelligence Division, "The Purple Gang," File Number GF:C1–76–4167, 7 Dec. 1976.

14. Robert Anthony Orsi, *The Madonna of 115th Street: Faith and Community in Italian Harlem* (New Haven: Yale University Press, 1985).

15. The federal budget for prohibition enforcement grew by 1,134 percent from 1920 to 1930. The Prohibition Unit's own annual budget in 1926 was just shy of $12 million. In that same year the Coast Guard's antismuggling fleet of 300 vessels cost $15,519,427, which is more than $220 million in 1992 dollars. Philip Earle Metcalfe, "Lincoln C. Andrews and the Enforcement of National Prohibition, 1925 to 1927" (thesis, Portland State University, Department of History, 1998), 6.

16. U.S. Department of Justice, Office of Justice Programs, National Institute of Justice, "NIJ Request for Proposals for Comparative, Crossnational Crime Research Challenge Grants Solicitation," Apr. 1998, 1.

17. Ibid., 12.

18. "Statement of Purpose," *Trends in Organized Crime* 2, no. 3 (spring 1997), 1.

19. Roy Godson and William J. Olson, *International Organized Crime: Emerging Threat to US Security* (Washington, D.C.: National Strategy Information Center, Aug. 1993).

20. Ibid., i.

21. Ibid., ii.

22. Ibid., 35.

23. Ibid., 36.

24. Peter Reuter, "The Mismeasurement of Illegal Drug Markets," in *Exploring the Underground Economy: Studies of Illegal and Unreported Activity*, ed. Susan Pozo (Kalamazoo, Michigan: W. E. Upjohn Institute for Employment Research, 1966), 63.

25. Ibid.

26. Observatoire Geopolitique Des Drogues, *Etat des drogues: Drogue des etats* (Paris: Pluriel, 1994).

27. Phil Willams and Paul N. Woessner, "The Real Threat of Nuclear Smuggling," in *Scientific American* 274, no. 1 (January 1966), 40.

28. Ibid.

29. Ibid., 424

30. U.S. Department of Energy, "Red Mercury: Attempts to Sell Bogus Nuclear Material," Feb. 1992.

31. Mark Hibbs, "Smuggling of Soviet-Origin Material Is Escalating, Crime Agencies Say," *NuclearFuel*, 3 Sept. 1993, 3.

32. U.S. Senate, Committee on Governmental Affairs, Permanent Subcommittee on Investigations, *Hearing: Asian Organized Crime, Part II* (Washington, D.C.: Government Printing Office, 5 Nov. 1991), 30.

33. Ibid.

34. "U.S. Senate, Committee on Governmental Affairs, Subcommittee on International Security, Proliferation, and Federal Services, *The Proliferation Primer: A Majority Report* (Washington, D.C.: Government Printing Office, Jan. 1998), 37.

35. A contentious prosecution for distributing child pornography on the Internet took place in Germany this past May. The Munich district court convicted Felix Somm despite a "change of heart by the state prosecutor." Germany's technology minister, Juergen Ruettgers carefully stated that this prosecution must not interfere with "The development of the Internet in Germany. . . . This is about the jobs of the future." See "Internet Conviction Shocks Industry: A Former Compuserve Manager Was Convicted in Germany of Distributing Child Pornography and Other Illegal Material in Cyberspace," *The Orlando Sentinel*, 29 May 1998, A3.

36. Investigative Services Division, Metropolitan Police Department, Washington, D.C., "Organized Crime's Involvement in the Pornography Industry," Nov. 1978. This report was generated by federal, state and local law enforcement agencies in Arizona, California, Delaware, Washington, D.C., Florida, Georgia, Louisiana, Maryland, Massachusetts, Michigan, Minnesota, Missouri, New Hampshire, New Jersey, New York, North Carolina, Ohio, Pennsylvania, Virginia, and Washington. Also cooperating was the Royal Canadian Mounted Police. The material was analyzed and collated by the Organized Crime Branch, Metropolitan Police Department, Washington, D.C.

37. Edward J. Bristow, *Prostitution and Prejudice: The Jewish Fight Against White Slavery, 1870–1939* (New York: Schocken Books, 1983), 2.

38. Janet Eileen Mickish, "Legal Control of Socio-Sexual Relationships: Creation of the Mann White Slave Traffic Act of 1910" (Ph.D. dissertation, Southern Illinois University, Department of Sociology, 1980), 49.

39. Ibid., 72.

40. Patricia Robin Klausner, "The Politics of Massage Parlor Prostitution: The International Traffic in Women for Prostitution into New York City, 1970–1986" (Ph.D. dissertation, University of Delaware, Department of Sociology, 1987), 16. Also see Mickish, 57.

41. Ibid., 74.

42. Klausner, 19.

43. Mickish, 88.

44. Ibid., 155.

45. Ibid., 108.

46. Ibid., 156.

47. Klausner, 30–35.

48. James P. Smith and Barry Edmonston, eds., *The New Americans: Economic, Demographic, and Fiscal Effects of Immigration* (Washington, D.C.: National Academy Press, 1997), available at http://www.nap.edu. What follows is drawn from this source unless otherwise noted.

49. United States Immigration & Naturalization Service, "Illegal Alien Resident Population: Summary," found at http://www.ins.usdoj.gov/stats/illegalalien/indes.html.

50. The most significant event that led to sweatshop reform was the horrific fire at the Triangle Shirtwaist Company in New York in 1911. One hundred and forty-six perished. See Leon Stein, *The Triangle Fire* (New York: Carroll & Graf, 1962).

51. Department of Justice, Office of the Inspector General, Inspections Division, "Inspections Report," located at http://www.usdoj.gov/oig/i9608/i9608p1.htm.

52. Ibid.

53. See New York State Senator Franz S. Leichter, "Return of the Sweatshop, Part II," 26 Feb. 1981, in Alan A. Block, *The Business of Crime: A Documentary Study of Organized Crime in the American Economy*, by A. A. Block (Boulder: Westview Press, 1991), 91.

54. Ibid.

55. Ibid., 93.

56. Ibid., 92.

57. Ibid., 98.

58. Elizabeth McLean Petras, "Third World Workers in U.S. Cities: Asian Women in the Philadelphia Apparel and Textile Industry" (unpublished paper presented at the annual meeting of the American Sociological Association, 11–15 Aug. 1990), 1.

59. Ibid., 19.

60. State of New Jersey, Commission of Investigation, "The New Jersey Garment Industry," Apr. 1991, 2.

61. Ibid., 8.

62. Ibid., 27.

63. Jeffrey Scott McIllwain, "Organizing Crime in Chinatown: New York City's China-

town and the Social System of Organized Crime During the Progressive Era" (Ph.D. dissertation, the Pennsylvania State University, 1997), 193.

64. Senator Sam Nunn, "Opening Statement" *Hearings on Asians Organized Crime*, part ll, 5 Nov. 1991, 5.

65. Petras, "Third World," 11.

66. The "slave labor" simile, when it comes to the smuggling and exploitation of illegal immigrant workers, has taken root. During a hearing on immigrant smuggling, Congressman George Sangmeister said that "Aliens from the People's Republic of China are selling themselves into virtual slavery for a boat ride to the United States." See U.S. House of Representatives, Committee on the Judiciary, Subcommittee on International Law, Immigration, and Refugees, *Hearing: Alien Smuggling* (Washington, D.C.: Government Printing Office, 1993), 7. Similarly, the chief of the International Centre for Migration Policy Development in Vienna characterized immigrant smuggling as a "new form of slavery." See "The New Trade in Humans," *The Economist*, 5 Aug. 1995, 45. And in the magazine *Crime & Justice International*, published by the Office of International Justice at the University of Chicago, Tim Stone wrote that "Selling women into sexual slavery has become one of the fastest growing criminal enterprises on the international black market today, and since the fall of the USSR, Slavic women have become the most valuable commodities on this market." Tim Stone, "Slavic Women in Demand in Sex Slave Markets throughout World," *Crime & Justice International*, 14, no. 16 (May 1998): 7.

67. "Special Investigation: The New Jungle," *U.S. News & World Report* 121, no. 12 (23 Sept. 1996), 36.

68. According to the New Mexico Governor's Organized Crime Prevention Commission, Iowa Beef Processors was a "company which has been deeply involved with organized crime's monopolization of the New York City meat industry." In addition, the commission found Iowa Beef Processors worked with organized crime in a "labor leasing scheme." State of New Mexico, Governor's Organized Crime Prevention Commission, *1980 Annual Report*, Santa Fe, New Mexico, Dec. 1980, 11.

69. Ibid., 39.

70. Ibid., 37.

71. Ibid., 40.

72. Ibid., 41.

73. Ian Burrell, "British Asians Killed for Their Passports," *The Independent*, Monday 25 May 1998.

74. The population of the Dominican Republic can be found in the CIA's 1997 World Fact Book on the Internet.

75. The following material on the abuses of so-called "free trade," unless otherwise otherwise indicated, is from the National Labor Committee, *Free Trade's Hidden Secrets: Why We Are Losing Our Shirts, A Special Investigation: Summary*, Nov. 1993, and the full report written by Charles Kernaghan.

76. Ibid.

77. Appended to the National Labor Committee's study is a *partial* survey of the USAID-Funded Investment and Export Related Projects in the Dominican Republic beginning in 1980, totaling *$349,212,188*.

Project #5170190 Export and Investment Promotion (1985–1992)
Total Funding Planned $11,000,000.
    (USAID description: "Project to strengthen the Dominican Republic's Investment Promotion Council (IPC) as a mechanism to coordinate public and private efforts to increase investment and export opportunities. The project will improve the investment/export (I/E) climate, strengthen institutional support for I/E, and promote export business in key sectors. IPC will have these main roles: (1) to improve the Dominican I/E climate ... through changes in economic policy, tax

structure, and exchange rates and the development of incentives for both domestic and foreign investors; (2) to help public and private organizations involved in I/E services; and (3) to promote business opportunities, particularly in agribusiness and free zone manufacturing, by targeting key sectors in crucial foreign markets (mainly in the U.S.). While IPC will be the main exporting agency, several other private and public institutions—such as CEDOPEX, the American Chamber of Commerce, and the Association of Exporters (ADOEXPO)—will also be involved through contracts and subgrants in project implementation. TA and training will be provided to enable IPC and other organizations to: conduct policy analyses, seminars, and other activities to improve the policy climate; conduct investment and export promotion programs in foreign markets; contract for specialized assistance in locating and accelerating business networks; and provide services to existing Dominican businesses, export trading companies, and financial institutions so that joint ventures can be formulated and new markets developed. Also, an existing cooperative agreement with the Chicago Association of Commerce and Industry will be extended two years. IPC's Santo Domingo office will be expanded and a U.S. office will be established in the Dominican Embassy in Washington, DC with long term advisors on both sides."Amendment of 1/31/90 extends project two years to 12/31/92, refocusing it somewhat to emphasize areas of greatest success (investment promotion).")

Project #517 0263 Investment and Trade Expansion (1992–1995)
Total Funding Planned $30,000,000
(USAID description: "Program to provide balance of payments assistance and support for Government of the Dominican Republic's (GODR) efforts to stabilize macroeconomic financial structures and address critical sectoral bottlenecks that constrain the country's development. The foreign exchange provided will finance imports critical to the GODR's development strategy. The GODR will provide counterpart local currencies which will be jointly programmed by A.I.D. and the GODR to support priority social and economic development activities.")

Project #517 0171 Private Enterprise Development (1983–1985)
Total Funding Planned $218,000,000
(USAID description: "Program to provide balance of payments relief to the Government of the Dominican Republic (GODR) and to promote development of the private sector. The GODR will receive a loan of $41 million in Economic Support Fund (ESF) monies to import U.S. spare parts, capital goods, and industrial agricultural imports for the private sector. Equivalent counterpart funds will be targeted for private sector development in three areas: promotion of exports and agribusiness; institutional development and training; and investment in productive infrastructure needed for private sector expansion. Amendment of 9/29/83 increases loan-funded balance of payments support from the ESF by $8 million. Equivalent counterpart funds will be allocated to the private sector export expansion (including the development of free zone facilities) and for productive infrastructure needed to accelerate execution of IDB, IBRD, and A.I.D. projects aimed at private sector investment. Amendment 12/26/83 provides the GODR with a $40 million grant from ESF. . . . PAAD of 4/22/87 provides a $19.835 million grant for FY87 to provide balance of payments support. Dollar funds will be used for private sector imports of raw materials, spare parts, machinery and equipment; local currency will support free zone development.")

Project #517 0255 Economic Support Fund (1988)
Total Funding Planned $13,835,000
(USAID description: "Cash grant of $13.835 million from the Economic Support Fund to provide the Government of the Dominican Republic (GODR) with immediate balance of payments support. The GODR will deposit . . . the peso equiv-

alent of the dollar grant in the special account in the Central Bank for use in investments and development activities jointly agreed upon by GODR and A.I.D.")

Project #517 0252 Industrial Linkages (1989–1994)
Total Funding Planned $5,000,000

(USAID description: "Project to help local manufacturers in the Dominican Republic to increase their sales to manufacturers located in the Industrial Free Trade Zones (IFTZ), and eventually to other offshore markets. It will be implemented by the Association of Industries of the Dominican Republic (AI) and the Association of Dominican Free Trade Zones (ADOZONA), with help from an institutional contractor. Through the Investment Promotion Council or other channels, the project will pursue direct dialogue with the government. The project will also fund direct TA for local firms in such areas as production, quality control, packaging and marketing, and will sponsor a series of workshops on production issues.")

Project #517 0186 Agribusiness Promotion (1985–1992)
Total Funding Planned $24,500,000

(USAID description: "Project to provide credit and TA to new and expanding agribusiness in the Dominican Republic and to improve the mechanism and policy framework for promoting and financing agribusiness. The project will be implemented mainly by the Central Bank (FIDE) and the Dominican chapter of the privatesector Joint Agricultural Consultative Corporation (JACC/DR). JACC/DR will ... (1) help potential agribusiness investors analyze their credit needs and prepare feasibility and business plans; (2) conduct market and technical studies for clients and provide problem-related TA; (3) help potential foreign and domestic AB investors to conduct pre investment studies and develop investment strategies; and (4) work with other organizations to provide management training and to promote policies favorable to agribusiness.... A special fund (operated by the Development Bankers Association) will finance the feasibility studies and business plans mentioned above, while a grant to the Trade and Development Program will assist potential U.S. investors.")

Project #517 0188 Policy Analysis Training (1980–1984)
Total Funding Planned $5,170,188

(USAID description: "Project to train a cadre of economic and business sector analysts in the Dominican Republic. The private and public sectors of the Dominican Republic strongly support the Carribean Basin Initiative. As the Dominican Republic begins to articulate its new economic policies, it finds itself constrained by a critical shortage of trained, competent, and experienced senior economists, business analysts, and international development affairs specialists.... Further, foreign expertise is extremely expensive and sometimes not available when needed. There is, therefore, acceptance and recognition of the need to train a cadre of senior economic and business advisors who would recommend for the policy makers short- and long-term development strategies and their implementation schemes based on rigorous analyses.")

Project #517 0262 Public Policy Reform (1992–1996)
Total Funding Planned $6,000,000

(USAID description: "Project to develop strong support within the Dominican society and capacity within the Government of the Dominican Republic (GODR) for sustained implementation of internationally sanctioned economic policies and programs. First, it will encourage debate and discussion in the private sector by supporting private organizations that promote a market economy. Assistance will be provided through such activities as seminars, roundtable discussions, and special studies to aid groups with the sector, including importer, exporter, domestic manufacturer, and labor groups, to carry out dialogue with each other and the government. Second, the project will help the GODR analyze policy-level issues and design required reforms. Third the project will help the GODR design the institutional strengthening activities required to implement the selected policy reforms. To provide a forum for project implementation, the mission will propose the creation of a joint public/private council with representatives of the key government economic policy bodies, private business and community groups, and specialized nongovernmental organizations.")

Project #517 0237 Debt Conversion (1988–1992)
Total Funding Planned $3,500,000
(USAID description: "Project to generate increased private U.S. and domestic equity investment in the Dominican Republic by establishing a debt/equity conversion mechanism within the Central Bank (CB). While the project strategy focuses on CB institution building, a promotion campaign is also funded.... A promotional campaign will be implemented by the Investment Promotion Council to attract potential investors and creditors. The project is expected to generate as many as 30 debt/equity conversions, accounting for some $500 million in new investments.... A few of the debt/equity transactions will involve the transfer of GODR assets to investors, but most will involve the transfer of local currency. The GODR will provide the equivalent of at least U.S.$100 million to finance the conversions.")

Project #517 0216 Development Training (1986–1994)
Total Funding Planned $15,000,000
(USAID description: "Project to train professional managerial, and technical personnel in the Dominican Republic in priority, export oriented, private sector areas. The project ... will be implemented by the National Council of Businessmen (CNNR). The training will be tailored to specific job, enterprise, and for private sector needs. Group training programs will also be designed to respond to sector—or area—specific training needs. Partners of the Americas, under a subsequent agreement with CNNE, will arrange a tailored course of U.S. study and observational visits.... Amendment of 8/24/88 more than doubles project funding in order to expand training to cover needs not currently met by USAID/DR projects.

Project #517 0157 Corporate Management Training (1983–1991)
Total Funding Planned $6,500,000
(USAID description: "To offer graduate programs in business and public administration, to train public and private sector executives which will be assisted by an Advisory Council of key Dominican business leaders ... and housed in a new building funded under a separate A.I.D. loan.")

Project #517 0146 Training Advisory Center for Women (1980–1984)
Total Funding Planned $407,000
(USAID description: "Skills training and human development training programs to ensure that young women possess the skills to perform their jobs safely and efficiently while simultaneously carrying out their home responsibilities.")

Project #517 0236 Sugar Diversification (1987–1992)
Total Funding Planned $5,000,000
(USAID description: "Grant to the Dominican Republic's State Sugar Council (CEA) to implement a sugar diversification program. The project, to be implemented by CEA's Agroindustrial Operations Division (DACEA) will ... promote private investment in diversification projects.... Private investment will be promoted through a variety of activities, including visits to international trade shows and conferences, observational tours to other countries, in-country seminars, field trips for members of the press, radio and TV announcements, and the distribution of

brochures and other promotional materials. DACEA will also work closely with the Joint Agricultural Consultative Committee and the Investment Promotion Council to promote foreign investment in diversification.")

Note: All project description quotations are drawn from USAID program abstracts available on CD-ROM.

78. Clifford Krauss and Larry Rohter, "Dominican Drug Traffickers Tighten Grip on the Northeast," *New York Times*, 11 May 1998, 1, 16.
79. Ibid., 16.
80. Joint Committee on Tax Evasion and Avoidance, *Hearings: Part I* (Washington, D.C.: Government Printing Office, 1937), 2.
81. Ibid., 2–5.
82. Statement of Harry Margolis in Nicholas J. Bartolone, "Audit Division, Report of Visit," 6–11 Aug. 1973, 5.
83. See Alan A. Block, *Masters of Paradise: Organized Crime and the Internal Revenue Service in The Bahamas* (New Brunswick, NJ: Transaction Publishers, 1998), chaps. 8, 9.
84. See the *Frontline* production "Murder, Money & Mexico: The Rise and Fall of the Salinas Brothers—Family Tree: The Salinas—Citibank Affair," at http://www.pbs.org/wgbh/pages/frontline/mexico/family/citibankaffair.html.
85. See the series by Jeff Testerman and Brad Goldstein on Seminole Indian casinos, particulary "Banking on Full-Scale Casinos," and "Seminoles Gain Entry in Caribbean Casinos," in the *St. Petersburg Times*, Dec. 1997.
86. George Graham, "Covers Come Off the Wealth Business," *Financial Times*, 26 Nov. 1997.
87. On regulating derivatives, Gregory Millman points out that banks and trading houses "strenuously opposed legislation, as have most financial regulators." Gregory J. Millman, *The Vandals' Crown: How Rebel Currency Traders Overthrew the World's Central Banks* (New York: The Free Press, 1995), 270.
88. The creativeness of investment banks is dazzling. In addition to the RAV, for instance, Morgan Stanley created PLUS Notes, which stood for Peso Linked US Dollar Secured Notes—"Investors thought they were buying short-maturity AA-bonds in US dollars, whereas they were actually Mexican peso-backed inflation-linked derivatives issued by a Bermuda tax-advantaged company, unlisted on any exchange." See Frank Partnoy, FIASCO: Blood in the Water on Wall Street (New York: W. W. Norton and Company, October 1997).
89. Federal Bureau of Investigation, SA (C-9), "WF 13240 CW-D, Statistical Accomplishments," 25 Sept. 1990.

CONCLUSION
FIGHTING TRANSNATIONAL ORGANIZED CRIME:
MEASURES SHORT OF WAR

Tom Farer

TRANSNATIONAL ORGANIZED CRIME

On May 9, 1998, the *International Herald Tribune* published an article concerning the efforts of the European Union to secure U.S. government assistance in combating the smuggling of American cigarettes into various of the union's member states.[1] According to European law-enforcement officials, the world's largest tobacco companies—several of which are American based—have been selling billions of dollars of cigarettes each year into contraband pipelines. European concern sprang from three facets of the contraband phenomenon: in recent years its volume had tripled; the consequent tax losses had become considerable, estimated at $1.5 billion for 1997; and finally, it was believed that organized crime syndicates were running the smuggling operations, hence, they were enhancing the resources of already dangerous actors. American brands being prominent among those being smuggled, European investigators attempted unsuccessfully to secure from American tobacco companies the names of large-volume international customers.

R. J. Reynolds, the second-largest U.S. company, was the immediate target of the investigators' efforts. In one case actively under investigation, Spanish customs officials had detained a ship carrying eighty million cigarettes originally loaded by Reynolds onto two other ships in Charleston, South Carolina, and Savannah, Georgia, and sent to Greece. There they were transferred to the vessel belonging to the smuggling operation that carried them to Barcelona and their unintended rendezvous with the Spanish authorities. While denying any knowledge that the cigarettes would end up in the hands of smugglers, a Reynold's spokesman said that the shipments had been sold to a company with which it had a long-standing relationship. Revealing its name, the spokesman added, was not allowed by company policy. Among the company's long-standing relationships in Europe was one with a gentleman named Michael Haenggi, alleged by Spanish and Belgium investigators to have been the mastermind behind this particular operation. According to the article, he was one of Europe's biggest cigarette traders. He also appeared to be a man of rare openness in that the prior summer he had told the *New York Times* that (a) he had been a Reynolds customer for some fifteen years, and (b) that he had frequently been a supplier to persons smuggling cigarettes into Spain. Despite his winning candor, Reynolds, according to its spokesman, had decided to keep Mr. Haenggi as a customer.

If allegations of European investigators—that R. J. Reynolds regularly and knowingly introduces large quantities of its product into illicit distributional channels—prove to be true, then should one characterize the transactions as instances of transnational organized crime (TOC) and officials of the company as members of the international network of mafias, said by some officials and writers to constitute one, if not the gravest, threat to United States and, more generally, Western security? Certainly the effort to effect clandestine entry and to avoid excise payments—that is, smuggling—is a crime under Spanish law and, indeed, the law of most countries. Since it involves crossing boundaries, plainly it is transnational. The scope and complexity of the operations required repeatedly to effect illicit entry and to complete the distributional process would seem to satisfy any reasonable definition of *organized*. Ergo, this is at least a prima facie instance of transnational organized crime.[2]

One might, as R. J. Reynolds doubtless would, argue that as the original producer, it is insulated from a charge of coconspiracy to participate in TOC because it was indifferent to the distributional choices made by persons who purchased its products. Exculpating Reynolds on that ground would not, of course, be consistent with U.S. government views about culpability in connection with another line of addictive, mood-altering products, namely illegal drugs. For it would imply that those Colombian and other drug producers who move their product to Cuba, Mexico, the Dominican Republic, or even to the high seas off the U.S. coast, at which point title and control pass to buyers intending to distribute it in the United States, do not share criminal responsibility with their purchasers. Official Washington has been strongly inclined to impute criminal liability all the way back along the distributional path to just short of the impoverished campesinos toiling at the level of the raw crops. Surely that was the lesson of the arrest warrant served on General Noriega by an American expeditionary force.

In the area of transnational organized crime, scholarly and political discourse are jarringly different. The latter proceeds on the implicit assumption that there is a problem, a discrete, easily personified evil, recognizable to any fair-minded person, bereft of any social value, utterly disconnected from normal society, demanding eradication. The problem is a given; only the means to its solution is in doubt. For scholars, doubt settles first on the problem, or perhaps it would be more accurate to say on the political discourse that locates and isolates the problem in the maelstrom of quotidian life. In this, as in so many other matters of public policy, statements about problems are seen as contentious claims rather than the neutral registration of self-evident facts. Transnational organized crime, like terrorism (with which it is often associated[3]) is a label that, as a consequence of previous public discourse, has acquired the capacity to evoke fear and loathing. Therefore, by getting it attached to some person, institution, or transaction, one has normally succeeded in eliminating compromise and accommodation, or simply neglect, from the agenda of public-policy responses, leaving nothing but the rigorously punitive deployment of the state's police power.

Neither the *Tribune* in its headline nor Ray Bonner in his story invoked the label. They left the reader with a sense of possible impropriety, not organized crime. Implicitly and perhaps unconsciously, they drew a line and placed producers situated like Reynolds—and, indeed, cigarette smuggling in general—on one side. That is at least the most reasonable way of construing the story's statement that the report says organized crime syndicates are running the smuggling operations. By implication, Reynolds and possibly its alleged middleman, Mr. Haenggi, cannot be so described. In other words, the sheer fact of conscious and critical involvement in a smuggling chain operating on a large scale does not an international criminal make.

Why not? Because neither the service (that is, the movement of the cigarettes across the seas and the Spanish border) nor the product is what the common law calls *malum in se*, something deemed inherently and intolerably injurious to public health, safety, or morals?[4] (After all, Spain did not appear to object on the ground that untaxed and hence cheaper cigarettes fostered increased smoking and thereby multiplied tobacco-related illness in the country.) Whatever its other merits, that distinction cuts right across the list of TOC's heinous activities regularly cited by President Clinton, other officials, and most commentators, a list that includes unauthorized conventional arms transfers and facilitating the passage of undocumented immigrants.[5] Neither people nor weapons are inherently harmful; indeed, at least the former compares rather favorably in this regard with cigarettes. So one may reasonably presume that some other distinction shaped Mr. Bonner's discrimination between the alleged smuggling operation and TOC.

R. J. Reynolds is a business enterprise, that is, an organization persisting over time and functioning rationally within a market structure to produce goods and services at least theoretically for purposes of profit maximization. So are the Sicilian Cosa Nostra and the many other associations identified in popular and official discourse as the constituent elements of transnational organized crime. How, then, should one distinguish the legitimate from the criminal enterprise?

The latter is said to provide illicit goods and services or licit ones by illicit means. That proposition standing alone does not yield a very neat distinction. In an earlier era major American corporations conducted their labor relations by hiring thugs to break strikes and intimidate labor organizers,[6] that is, they provided licit goods (for example, cars) in part through the employment of outrageously illicit means. Well into the twentieth century, many trucking firms cooperated with mafia-dominated locals of the Teamsters in ways that violated the rights of workers set out in the National Labor Relations Act.[7] Since the adoption of the Sherman Anti-Trust Act, which includes criminal penalties, the Justice

Department has uncovered numerous conspiracies to restrain trade, some involving large and famous corporations. Students of transnational corporations believe that over the years many have manipulated the prices of intra-firm transfers of goods and services in order to evade the tax laws of jurisdictions in which they do business.[8] Even in the case of a corporation like the Ford Motor Company, which at one point employed criminals for the express purpose of violating the rights of its workers, was seen not as being itself among the country's criminal enterprises but simply as one utilizing their services.

Criminal organizations are also said to be characterized by their reliance on violence (or the threat thereof) and bribery. But Ford, like many other corporations faced with uncompliant labor, used violence. As for straightforward corruption, it was one of the ubiquitous features of the large-scale industrial capitalism that emerged after the American Civil War, hence the popular name for the early captains of industry: Robber Barons.[9] The finer distinction that seems to control perception, then, is the qualitative or quantitative extent of illicit means in proportion to an enterprise's entire business. In the collective unconscious where these distinctions grow, the test seems to be whether an enterprise can produce goods and services in licit markets without regular recourse to illicit means, particularly violence and bribery. Since it is primarily in cases where the enterprise's product is illegal that violence or bribery are essential to business, illicit means and ends have tended to coincide.[10]

Still, the distinction is less than categorical. The "clean-hands" investigation of political payoffs in Italy revealed a pattern of corruption so pervasive and profound that it seemed coterminous with the operation of certain major business enterprises. Companies that do a major proportion of their business in certain African and other Third-World countries must regard bribery as an ordinary and necessary cost of their operations, a practice tolerated if not encouraged by European governments with tax codes that treat bribes as legitimate business expenses. Drawing a clear and unmoving line between the licit and illicit can also seem difficult because criminals invest in legitimate enterprises, not always to advance their illicit operations, and because the law can change: Bootleggers of the Prohibition era, in its aftermath, became impeccably respectable manufacturers and distributors of alcoholic beverages.

The transformation of criminals into entrepreneurs by means of a change in the law and the possibility of being both simultaneously when, as in the case of gambling, the law may vary even in adjoining jurisdictions (a crook in the United States, Meyer Lansky, was a paladin of business development in Batista's Cuba), underscores a basic point about organized crime obscured by the rhetoric of political entrepreneurs but central to the perspectives scholars have brought to the study of criminal associations, namely that they are *businesses*, with all that implies in terms of means and motives. The R. J. Reynolds affair suggests a second basic point about organized crime: not only does it mirror legitimate enterprises in its search for the highest possible return on investment but also it frequently connects with them in ways that are not invariably predatory, that may indeed promote their common pursuit of profit.[11]

Organized Crime and the Licit Economy

The economist Tom Naylor has proposed thinking of organized crime's relationship to the wider economy in terms of three stages: the predatory, the parasitical, and the symbiotic.[12] These are not necessarily historical and may coexist; nevertheless, he argues, one will dominate within a given geographic or economic space. The relationship is *predatory* when the bulk of organized criminal activity consists of small, loosely associated gangs focused on producing quick, once-for-all returns at the expense of legitimate society. Typical activities are kidnapping, hijacking, bank robbery, and extortion. It is *parasitical* (perhaps more revealingly described as *parallel*) when criminals organize more elaborately and focus not on ripping off the public on a random basis, but rather on providing illegal goods and services in demand by otherwise legitimate members of society. And it is *symbiotic* when the central focus of criminal enterprise becomes the provision of legal goods and services in illegal ways. Among the examples he cites are toxic-waste disposal services for legitimate companies (that, of course, ignore cost-generating health and safety regulations), union busting, and money laundering through legitimate casino operations. Personally I find more useful a simple division between activities that do and activities that do not respond to demand emanating from respectable society. The former correspond to Naylor's predatory stage. Extortion, hijacking, theft, and so forth simply add to the costs of generating desired goods and services. The latter merge his second and third stages in light of the fact that in both of them the criminals respond to straight society's demands for goods, services, and cash.

Needs and desires related to cash as such—the desire of financial services institutions for more of it and of criminal organizations to launder the stuff (i.e., to remove traceable signs of its source)—organize a critical interface between the licit and illicit economies. Since for many years each new U.S. president has sought to trump his predecessor by declaring a new and better war on drugs, it is easy to lose track of its real duration. Actually, the war goes back to the Nixon era.[13] By the beginning of the 1970s, in other words, illegal drug imports and sales were already big business.

Though the resulting income only foreshadowed the hundred billion or more dollar industry to come, it is safe to assume an income stream at least in the low billions. Peanuts, albeit big ones, compared to the economy as a whole. But this was, if not the only then certainly the principal, economic sector that dealt in cash—more than cash, in bills of fairly small denomination.[14] So when bank officers, particularly in Florida, found not always mature much less impeccably dressed and coifed customers appearing with sackfuls of bills for deposit, even the lamest brain among them had to have guessed their provenance. Like the dog that did not bark in the famous Sherlock Holmes story, what is significant here is what did not happen, namely a flurry of calls to local narcotics squads. In short, the banks showed as little interest about where the cash came from as R. J. Reynolds apparently has about where its cigarettes go.

The stunning volume of cash set limits to the amount that could be accumulated in houses, storage lockers, mattresses, and other rudimentary depositories. Moreover, huge accumulations of cash could be used as circumstantial evidence of criminal activity and were vulnerable to robbery, theft, and confiscation by the authorities. Thus the authorities, on the one hand, had powerful incentives to follow the cash, while the perpetrators, on the other, had equally strong incentives to effect its metamorphosis into respectable assets. The sums involved guaranteed handsome returns for those who chose to facilitate its metamorphosis. Many so chose.

Faced with the failure of banks to voluntarily assist in identifying drug money,[15] the national government made it compulsory, imposing reporting requirements backed by the threat of large fines and incarceration.[16] Even then, even after the norm of cooperation had been formalized and criminalized, drug money continued washing into banks, while bank officers, when they complied at all, complied with the strict letter of the law. For instance, they did not turn away the swift little dodgers employed by drug gangs to race from bank to bank with deposits just short of the $10,000 reporting threshold.[17] Hefty fines and exemplary criminal prosecutions eventually fostered better branch-banking controls by home offices and cooled the acquisitive ardors of branch officers in drug country.

U.S. banks (or at least their U.S. branches) and the U.S.-based branches and offices of foreign banks may no longer be entry points for drug money seeking to lose itself in the global financial system. Presumably much more cash must leave in bulk; hardly a remarkable trick, despite its size, given the number of people, vehicles, and planes crossing U.S. borders openly, never mind clandestinely. But whether deposited here or abroad, it remains in danger because sheer deposit does not sever its tail. Enter the offshore financial system, the global archipelago of financial centers that provide a haven for those seeking protection from regulators, tax collectors, judges, and cops, principally in their home countries or countries where they generate a significant proportion of their income.[18] Two characteristics have distinguished the offshore centers: one is insulation from local taxation of wealth acquired abroad; the other is laws reinforcing the inclination of banks to shield their clients from inquiries about the sources of their wealth. Despite pressure from the United States and some other members of the Group of Seven (G–7) to increase transparency, about three-quarters of the havens still make it a criminal offense for bankers (or lawyers and accountants, for that matter) to cooperate with foreign governments by providing information concerning clients.[19] While shielding locally deposited wealth from the view of foreign investigators, many haven governments have made it a point to obscure their own view as well.[20]

The origins of the havens phenomenon were more or less respectable. They first began to acquire a profile in the global financial system by providing unregulated and untaxed sites for Eurodollar bank loans, that is, loans of dollars earned outside the United States, primarily in Europe not long after World War II. Since the dollar was the world's only reserve currency, the essential medium of global trade, its continual recirculation through the Eurodollar market served the general interest and the U.S. one as well. But almost from its inception, the offshore system also operated as a haven for hot money illegally fleeing taxes and currency controls in countries around the world and for the dirty money emanating from activities, such as drug dealing and prostitution, prohibited with varying degrees of sincerity in virtually all countries.

Along with secrecy, owners of hot or dirty money, like other rational economic actors, want security. So they naturally prefer countries with stable politics and currencies. Whether the stability is indigenous, as in the case of Switzerland and Miami, or externally guaranteed, as in the case of British overseas dependencies like the Cayman Islands, matters less, if at all. The result of this natural desire is that specks of land subject in fact, if not in convenient legal theory, to the control of Western capitalist democracies (for example, the Channel Islands) or profoundly vulnerable to economic sanction by the United States (for example, Panama), much less the Group of Seven acting together (for example, Cyprus, a venue favored by Russian mafias), have functioned as amiable laundries for organized crime.

Seeing the larger, enduring organized crime groups as in the first instance businesses—enterprises engaged in the production of goods and services in response to market signals and, to that end, employing, contracting, accumulating and investing profits, and doing all the things native to business organizations operating within the framework of the global capitalist economy—is essential to the design of relevant public policies. It is equally essential to grasp the ineluctable relationship between criminal organizations and the state.

Organized Crime and the State

By its regulations, exactions, and prohibitions, and also by its omissions, the state induces and shapes organized crime. Through its positive acts defining what is licit in connection with the production of goods and services, the state necessarily defines the economy's illicit spaces, that is, its forbidden products or means for producing them and disposing of the resulting revenues.[21] Organized crime consists in large measure of the persistent and purposeful associations of men and women who occupy those spaces. It is also conjured into being by the state's failure to act and its concomitant prohibition of private action with respect to matters essential for the efficient operation of a market economy, such as enforcing contracts or clarifying and enforcing title to property.[22] That is why organized crime thrives in a weak state. And where the state is weak but acts as if it were strong, spewing out laws and regulations purporting to regulate, inhibit, and tax private activity, the resulting disjunction between the state's claims and its means effects a metastasis of formally illicit activity that in varying degrees obscures the distinction between the underground and the normal economy. As Renn Lee points out in his overview of organized crime,[23] contemporary Russia unhappily illustrates that condition. Under the circumstances, claims that a state has been taken over by its mafias conceal more than they reveal about the subject's political economy.

The state can also affect the incidence of organized criminal activity through the nature of its economic, social, and political projects or its sheer existence as an object of hostility. As noted above, antistate groups may resort to common crimes to finance campaigns for radical social change, self-determination, or other political goals. When they were still a fringe organization on the Russian left, the Bolsheviks used "expropriations" (as they characterized them) to finance the movement. Joseph Stalin played a leading role in these financial excercises, including a huge haul in 1907 from the Tbilisi Georgia branch of the Russian Imperial Bank. In our own time, groups as diverse as the Nicaraguan Contras, the Tupac Amaru and the Shining Path insurgents in Peru, leftist guerrilla groups in Colombia, Chechen separatists in Russia, Kurdist nationalist organizations in Turkey, and the Shan separatists in Myanmar have to varying degrees relied financially on narcotics, gun running, extortion, and other illegal transactions. According to a Colombian government report, the combined revenues in 1997 of the two principal guerrilla groups (FARC and ELN) from kidnapping, extortion, and participation in the narcotics trade came to just under one billion dollars.[24]

TRANSNATIONAL ORGANIZED CRIME AND NATIONAL SECURITY

The Threats

It is not a great exaggeration to say that transnational organized crime has been joined with terrorism to fill the gap in rhetoric about national security left by the Soviet Union's disappearance from the historical stage. For what is rhetorical national security other than an enumeration of threats? And for political purposes, the best threats have a human face. Global warming and other *threats without threateners* (as Treverton puts it in chapter 2) are on various lists of national security concerns, but they hardly suffice when one wants to flush adrenaline through an audience. Senator John Kerry typified, rather than parodied, the "New Millennium" security rhetoric when he warned several years ago that organized crime would be the new Communism, the new monolithic threat.[25] This was not populist rhetoric calculated to stir hearts in the Davenport Kiwanis while leaving Washington policy wonks unmoved. The same sort of language circulates within the national security pundit community. For instance, in 1994 a well-connected Washington think tank, the Center for Strategic and International Studies, produced a study stirringly titled *Global Organized Crime: The New Evil Empire.*[26]

Traditionally, crime, including the transnational crime known as smuggling, has been seen as an essentially domestic matter, a perception expressed in the international law principle that the courts of one national jurisdiction will not enforce the penal laws of another.[27] To be sure, international law has facilitated cooperation in the suppression of crime, most notably through the institution of extradition, although many states have insisted on an exception in the case of their own citizens, thus largely limiting the extradition process to returning criminals to their own countries for crimes committed there. During the Prohibition era in the United States, when British ships loaded with scotch would hover in international waters off the U.S. coast awaiting the arrival of fast boats to haul their inebriants to shore, measures for facilitating preventive action appeared on the agenda of Anglo-American diplomacy. And very occasionally, certain activities have been deemed so generally subversive of national interests and values— piracy in the eighteenth century, to which the slave trade was gradually added in the nineteenth and, in the twentieth, attacks on diplomats and commercial aviation and the perpetration of genocide—that countries have agreed to relax in varying degrees the normal limits on national enforcement jurisdiction. But while it cannot be said that until very recently, the problem of crime was absolutely unknown to diplomacy, certainly it was known only very occasionally and then only slightly.

The American president is hardly alone in calling today for international cooperation in the suppression of organized crime. Within Europe, the German government has been urging the creation of a federal police organization modeled on the FBI.[28] And European Union members have been trying for more than a decade to elaborate common controls over the union's border, which will provide an adequate substitute for the national controls supposed to be foregone as part of the effort to forge a more integrated relationship.

If, in the form of smuggling (which remains its main activity), transnational organized crime has—like death and taxes—been with us practically forever, why has it suddenly bounded onto the stage of global security to be greeted as a great new threat to widely shared national interests? Skeptics, most clearly represented in this volume by Peter Andreas, think the answer lies less in the nature and consequences of TOC than in ourselves. *Ourselves* means the national security bureaucracies, including military and paramilitary forces, the semi-independent think tanks they nourish, and political leaders anxious both to defend security's share of the budget and to reaffirm the need for states and for leaders, i.e., themselves. In other words, having been deprived of the cold-war rationale for their raison d'etre, institutions abhorring a vacuum of need move to fill it, in this case by transforming a chronic problem of national police and customs officers into an international threat to basic interests of national security. The cold-war rhetoric of the anticrime chorus—New Evil Empire—and its frequent invocations of Soviet mafias as key actors in the burgeoning international conspiracy[29] only add to the skeptics' sense that this is a scam trying to exploit residual cold-war anxiety reflexes in the general public.

Several other features of the present scene foment skepticism. One is the misfit between transnational organized crime and certain of the specific dangers said to stem from its enhanced mobility, wealth, and coordination.

Computer Fraud

Rogue hackers have shown an unnerving capacity to penetrate restricted computer networks. With money increasingly a virtual commodity subject to movement and reallocation, and even extinction, at the click of a computer key[30] and whole logistical systems that support life in industrialized societies progressively more dependent on computer programs susceptible to unauthorized manipulation, hacking does pose the threat of immeasurable damage both to commercial and social life. But the danger is qualitative. The latent threateners are one or a handful of inspired rogues, not some vast criminal apparatus.[31] True, a mafia group could help by using bribery or violence to extract data-entry codes from employees of the target. But association, even brief contact, with the large criminal enterprises that will be targeted by police and intelligence agencies aggravates hackers' risks of exposure and threatens their independence. Perhaps that is one reason why, until now, none of the rogue hackers who have been identified appears to have any connection to organized criminal groups.

Financial Scams
They are another threat often incorporated into omnibus references to the TOC danger. As there is nothing new about smuggling, there is also nothing new about financial frauds on a grand scale; indeed they seem virtually coterminous with the evolution of capitalism and are mirrored in the works of such nineteenth-century chroniclers of society as Balzac and Trollope. A fraud forms the connective tissue of one of Trollope's last and most distinguished works, *The Way We Live Now*.[32] Given the much greater sophistication and education of people with money and the vastly denser web of legislative prohibitions and administrative surveillance that has developed in the past fifty years, and finally, given the availability of on- and offshore investment alternatives provided by large, enduring, and heavily capitalized financial institutions under regular scrutiny by public officials, one might suppose that the opportunities for financial scams are rather marginal to the great streams of investment surging across the globe.

Be that as it may, and quite apart from questions about the relative magnitude and incidence of recent instances of financial fraud, there is the question of whether the more recent ones of any consequence can be imputed plausibly to the kinds of criminal enterprises that occupy the attention of New-Evil-Empire theorists, enterprises engaged primarily in the production of illicit goods and services and ready to employ violence for their ends. No one claims, for instance, that mobsters founded the notorious Bank and Commerce Credit International (BCCI) that ultimately sank in a sea of debt. The bank doubtless serviced the mafias; it serviced anyone who would bring it money, including various national intelligence services. And it bought protective political support with gifts and payments, like any other company.[33] Robert Vesco, the flamboyant entrepreneur who simply looted the mutual fund empire founded by the pleasure-loving schoolteacher, Bernie Cornfeld, has never been alleged to be an instrument of the American Cosa Nostra or any of the other identifiable criminal enterprises. He was an enterprise all by himself.[34]

Italian organized crime groups appear to have had a hand in two of the major Western bank failures of the past several decades: those of the Franklin National Bank in New York and Banco Ambrosiana in Italy. But the list of relevant actors also included the Vatican Bank, Italian neofascists, and the assemblage of industrial, financial, political, and intelligence figures associated in the "Masonic Lodge" conspiracy whose ramifications may never become entirely clear.[35] In any event, far and away the most consequential bouillabaisse of gross financial *mal-* as well as *mis*feasance was the U.S. savings and loan fiasco, stemming not from the machinations of organized criminal groups but from nothing more insidious than common greed unleashed by an ideologically driven surrender of federal control and supervision.[36]

The activities most commonly attributed to transnational organized crime are drug production and distribution, illegal arms transfers, stealing and smuggling vehicles, and moving undocumented aliens (including prostitutes) across national frontiers. While here the overall fit between TOC and illicit and damaging activities is generally better, in the particular case of alien smuggling, it still droops noticeably.

Illegal Immigration
The small army of scholars who have studied immigration concur in attributing its illegal no less than its legal dimension to obvious push-pull factors.[37] Around most of the globe, simple poverty and absolute misery, joblessness and hopelessness, war and mere butchery and their camp follower, famine, push like Sisyphus. In the rich countries, all the reverse of those pushing factors pull with the aid of globe-spanning communications media dispensing images of affluence and easing contact between those who have already made the crossing and intimates left behind. The First-World private sector, strapped for cheap, disciplined, and tractable labor and also for engineers and technicians, lends a hand. The legitimate transportation infrastructure required by a world capitalist trading system provides the principal bridge. Liberalism provides the ideological artillery to assault legal and institutional barriers erected or maintained to assuage electorates still less committed than capitalist managers and liberal activists to a borderless world. With all these elements at work, with 60 percent unemployment among a bulging youth cohort in North Africa,[38] just a little sea away from Western Europe, and hardly better economic conditions among the tens of millions just a river trickle away from the United States, is there any aggravating role for organized crime to play?

The answer is a qualified yes. Electoral pressure even in the relatively more receptive United States has pushed the executive branch to display greater effort at controlling the country's southern border. It has deployed more personnel and built fences here and there.[39] While there is no evidence that these measures have reduced the overall flow of undocumented aliens, it has made the crossing harder. In the past most people waded across the Rio Grande or sprinted past immigration posts on the Pacific Coast. If guides were needed at all, they required few skills or organization, just a knowledge of the terrain. Increased policing has increased the required degree of skill and organization. According to law enforcement sources, the result is an increasing presence of organized criminal groups in the border-crossing operation for Latinos, whether from Mexico or further south. Organized criminals facilitate, but do not appear essential to, evasion of the still-flimsy human and material barriers thrown up by the U.S. Immigration and Naturalization Service during the past few years. And in the event that large crime groups come to dominate the border, they might conceivably reduce the freelance mayhem—rape, robbery, and murder—visited on the crossers by border predators. If the United States ended up with the same numbers of illegal entrants and less mayhem *and no increase in the number of dangerous criminals insinuated into the exodus,* then organized crime might even look like a slightly ameliorating factor.

But greater organization means, among other things, greater expense. Moreover, being businesses, organized criminal enterprises will look for ways to increase return on their investment. If they control the border-crossing service, then they will seek higher fees than those required in the past. Their clients, however, are unlikely to have additional means. How will this circle be squared?

The immigrants who have relied most heavily on criminal groups to arrange their passage are the Chinese. Aside from daunting geographic obstacles, Chinese immigrants have been unable to rely to the same extent as Latinos and Caribbean islanders on friends and relatives well established in the United States. Recent immigrants are the first wave following a long caesural caused by tough and enforced anti-Asian immigration laws in the United States, then the Pacific war, and thereafter totalitarian controls in China on movement in any direction. Compared to the circumstances facing Latin Americans, the obstacles are high, yet push and pull are extremely strong. Despite China's economic renaissance, per-capita income remains very low and most of the improvement has occurred in coastal areas. The relaxation of social controls has exposed high levels of underemployment and growing unemployment; more and more people are drifting without a safety net. With millions washing off the countryside to join the extant floating population of the un- or barely employed in coastal areas numbering about one hundred million or more,[40] emigration potential is high. Since employment prospects in other adjoining Asian countries are poor, at least for the immediate future, the United States has to be the leading target of opportunity.

Journalists report villages and families pooling their resources to send an advance guard.[41] As good profit maximizers, crime groups have not chosen to rely for their compensation simply on the funds emigrants could raise to purchase a complicated and miserable passage and fake documents. Some have paid enough—the going rate is at least $35,000[42]—to make them valuable goods. The many who cannot pay enough up front must contribute at the other end of the journey. To that end, the smuggling groups have resurrected the Western colonial tradition of indentured servitude. Immigrants have been herded into sweatshops and held in conditions approximating slavery. Los Angeles is the center of these operations.[43]

Even immigration advocates concede that there are limits to the number of migrants who can be humanely assimilated at any given moment. Push factors are multiplying in China and now in Asian countries that were until recently growing rapidly enough to absorb new worker cohorts. Chinese criminal organizations, working with Central American groups which appear well connected politically,[44] will inevitably play an essential role in the migrant flow from Asia.

That is one reason for some concern. A second is the incorporation of migrants into an underground economy controlled by such organizations alone or in partnership with complaisant entrepreneurs, an economy marked by brutal conditions and extremely low wages. Whatever the immediate economic effects on the wages and welfare rolls in affected areas, this development will yield a class of people who, once used up by their sweatshops, will be flung out into an alien society without immediate means for assimilation. So while freelancing, including overstaying student and tourist visas, is likely to remain the principal means for evading immigration restrictions in the United States and other developed countries, the organized piece of the action in this area bears watching, particularly if Western governments make freelancing more difficult by purposefully deploying additional resources both to block unauthorized entry and to expel illegal residents.

Whether organized evasion of immigration laws constitutes a threat to what ought to be described as the nation's security depends in part on one's preference among contending constructions of security. I will consider that definitional issue below. It is in any event noxious, particularly because it can involve postentry control of immigrants by illegal enterprises. To be sure, the immediate *economic* effects of indentured servitude are unclear. Sweatshops may produce goods that would otherwise gravitate to low-wage countries; in that event, they might not have a direct impact on job opportunities for the unskilled in the U.S. labor market. They might, however, have an indirect impact by in effect evading restrictions on textile imports from precisely those countries. Be that as it may, their treatment of workers violates our conceptions of fundamental decency. In addition, to the extent postentry control inhibits assimilation, it is bound to generate social costs. The immigration and the production side of the enterprise, moreover, encourages and finances the presence of Chinese organized crime groups with a strong base abroad. Whatever its potential magnitude, that is a development meriting at least a scintilla of concern.

Arms
Arms smuggling into the United States would seem at first glance to be entirely a foreign-policy concern in that domestic industry licitly produces sufficient hand guns and assault weapons to arm the entire population twice over. It would be like smuggling tea into China. Of course the issue is entirely different for the rest of the West, since the United States is almost alone in acting on the conviction that democracy and the general good require a population armed to the teeth. Still, even in the United States, there are some grounds for concern. Despite their latitudinarian view of most conventional weapons, Americans do draw the line at missiles, land mines, and mortars. The mere credible threat at two or three U.S. transportation hubs to use handheld surface-to-air missiles—weapons that now circulate in global arms bazaars—could cause barely imaginable havoc in the nation's air-traffic system. After the World Trade Center and Oklahoma bombings, politically motivated threats cannot help but seem plausible. There is no reason to dismiss commercial ones either, or to assume that criminals and ter-

rorists are not ready to deploy biological, chemical, and nuclear devices. The Aum Shinrikyo sect's nerve-gas attack in Tokyo's subways demonstrated the ease with which a determined group with moderate expertise can produce and deploy lethal chemical agents. Richard Preston, the well-regarded science writer, in his novel *The Cobra Incident* suggests how developments in biotechnology and the transnational proliferation of biotech companies open the door for very small-scale enterprises, operating under easily assumed legitimate cover, to produce biological agents with far greater lethality, agents that could be dispersed even by a single individual.[45]

Biological and chemical weapons can be homegrown. Because of apparently tight domestic controls, nuclear ones cannot. So a nuclear device or the critical means for assembling one would have to come from abroad. While nuclear materials have been leaking out of the former Soviet Union, thus far both sting operations stimulated by Western police agencies and operations uncovered by them have not implicated major crime groups.[46] But if it is predictive, all the past demonstrates is that to date, the risk/benefit ratio of nuclear smuggling has compared unfavorably with other options on the lavish buffet of opportunities for criminal enrichment. Whether that condition will persist is uncertain. Any person, group, or governing elite with considerable financial resources and a grudge against the United States could alter the ratio. Using TOC clandestine networks would facilitate evasion of U.S. intelligence and, more important, would help conceal the initiator's fingerprints, thus neutralizing the United States' principal defense against state terrorism: the threat of obliterating retaliation.

Transborder arms flows outside the United States are quite a different matter. The wash of arms around the world plainly contributes to the incidence and virulence of civil conflicts. Arguably, that is not a bad thing in every case. The arms bazaar gives citizens a means of resisting military dictatorships in countries like Nigeria. Had it been open in the early 1970s and had the great powers been neutral, the eastern part of Nigeria might today be the thriving country of Biafra. But death and destruction being the only certain result of civil armed conflict, and the political outcome so frequently disappointing even where the oppressed win, the collapse of cold-war constraints on the arms trade is nothing to celebrate.

Developed countries have taken the point and the United States has joined in very preliminary efforts to get a grip on conventional arms transfers.[47] But at this point the grip is palsied. State or private corporations in many developing as well as most of the developed countries now produce and market conventional arms. If all the world's mafias were suddenly to undergo a conversion experience and become Quakers, conventional arms would probably remain widely available. That said, TOC involvement in the arms trade can still make a malign difference. Clandestine sales and transportation networks help neutralize international sanctions.[48] The experience of cooperation in other ventures, easy communication, and tested logistics enable national crime groups to locate, purchase, and arrange shipment of ammunition (with today's rates of fire, enough is never stockpiled) and the more advanced weaponry like artillery, the larger mortars, and missiles—in short, matériel not available everywhere. Criminal organizations in countries where the desired weapons are stockpiled by national armed forces are best placed to suborn the relevant officials on behalf of foreign mafias. In addition, criminal networks provide a means for states to evade the censure and pressure that would come if they sold the weapons openly to rogue governments, rebels, or terrorist organizations.

Car Theft

While decidedly junior to prostitution, car theft is not new, having been on the scene since the inception of mass car consumption and thus long before TOC alarm bells began clanging. For decades it has been among the most common crimes, part of the meat and potatoes of local law enforcement but arousing federal concern as well because of its interstate aspects. According to U.S. insurance industry statistics, more than 1.5 million vehicles were stolen in 1994, a recent representative year; that translates into one theft nationally every twenty seconds. The cost to consumers (although not necessarily to the economy as a whole) increased from $3.2 billion in 1970 to $7.5 billion in 1994, in part because more cars were stolen, in part because they were more expensive, and in part because fewer were recovered.[49]

Decreasing recovery rates, from 84 percent in 1970 to 62 percent in 1994, are connected to a sharp increase in the organization of car theft. The average thief then was a teenage joyrider. Today's paradigm is a theft ring that makes recovery far more difficult because much of its business consists of exporting whole cars or chopping them up for their parts. According to *Consumer Research Magazine*, growth in the theft industry lies mainly in overseas markets both for parts and luxury cars, markets that have dramatically expanded with the collapse of the Soviet Union and the expansion of upper-middle groups in newly industrializing countries. The estimated value of stolen luxury car exports is estimated at over $1 billion, with five hundred or more cars slipping out of the country daily.

Without a huge increase in the export inspection force, the traffic will grow. At present, inspectors are able to examine only about 1 percent of vessels leaving the country's 300 ports. Incentives are high. A Mercedes-Benz SL600 that retails for $130,000 in a Los Angeles showroom might sell for $350,000 or more in some Asian black market, where luxury cars are unavailable or—at best—can be had only after a wait of months.[50]

Disagreeable? Yes. A scratch across the surface of the citizenry's sense of security? Yes. But as a threat to the general welfare—in comparison to AIDS, alcohol-related deaths, homelessness, teenage pregnancy, child abuse, and a number of other societal problems—it seems sort of puny.

Drugs

Except perhaps in the Soviet Union, drugs are TOC's preeminent source of income.[51] Above all in the Western Hemisphere they simply trivialize other criminal activities, whether in terms of the size of the income stream, the complexity of the enterprise, or its political and economic impacts.

Estimates of the amounts involved are no more than suggestive, as most experts admit. Writing in 1996, Mathea Falco, a former assistant secretary of state with departmental responsibility for the drug war, cited estimates of $180 to $300 billion as the trade's annual business value.[52] UN experts have spoken in terms of $100 to $400 billion.[53] Like so many iterations of the macrofigures, these do not specify whether they are based on street as distinguished from wholesale prices, that is the price paid by retailers in the target country to those smuggling organizations that do not themselves handle retail sales. Since retailers expand the product by mixing it with a variety of inexpensive licit additives (in trade idiom, "cutting") and then charge whatever semielastic market conditions allow, the wholesale-retail price gap is huge, with the latter being as much as ten times the former.[54] Renn Lee, a leading authority on the drug trade,[55] insists that while the street value of transactions may exceed $100 billion, much of it is spent locally, and that no more than $30 billion per year enters the international financial system. The estimated constant market for the principal hard drugs, cocaine and heroin persons who are more than occasional users—is six million, of which one to two million are classified as addicts needing daily fixes.[56]

After countless iterations of the drug trade's costs for U.S. society, completeness calls for no more than the briefest of summaries. To begin with, narcotics are seen as a prime generator of ordinary crimes—particularly robbery, burglary, and theft—executed to support an expensive habit. The trade seduces vast numbers of poor adolescents into the criminal life and therefore fills the nation's prisons to the point where the United States, with a total figure of some one million persons, now leads the world in the number of persons incarcerated per capita.[57] In 1993, drug offenders accounted for over 60 percent of the federal prison population.[58]

The drug problem aggravates race relations, since African Americans are grossly overrepresented in that population in part because of gross race-based disparity in arrest, conviction, and severity of punishment.[59] The result in one city: in Washington, D.C. on any given day, 42 percent of all black men between the ages of 18 and 35 are in prison, on probation or parole, out on bond, or sought by the police.[60] Rates of incarceration adversely influence family life, particularly in the African American community, and add to the disadvantages of African American job seekers. In all communities, but particularly among poor ethnic ones, the drug trade encourages the formation of gangs and triggers inter-gang violence.[61] In promoting common use of syringes, it contributes to the contagion of hepatitis and AIDS. Add in the costs of job absence and loss, of drug treatment and welfare for children of drug-disabled parents or who are born with their mother's addiction, of the incremental law enforcement resources—police, drug enforcement agents, judges, prosecutors, court officers, and courthouses—demanded by the war on drugs, of the military operations increasingly undertaken in support of interdiction campaigns, add also the costs of training antidrug forces in foreign countries and of encouraging crop substitution by peasant growers of coca, poppies, and hemp, and then, to the extent a monetary cost can be assigned to all of these evils (and even this list is not exhaustive), it amounts to many tens of billions annually. In terms of associated misery, degradation, and rage, the costs are countless.

That is the standard enumeration summoned to justify a war on the organizations that refine the raw materials, smuggle the finished product into the United States, participate to varying degrees in retail distribution, and launder the proceeds. Somewhat less frequently enumerated, certainly to the general public, are the reasons why this roll call of disasters does not evoke uniform support for a relentless war on the enterprise. Opponents of war rest their cases in part on the inverse of the proponents' premise; they contend, in other words, that most of the enumerated costs stem not from the trade but from the prohibition regime on behalf of which the war is fought.

The suppression effort and the attendant risk and complexities of production and distribution multiply the retail price by ten times or more over the one that would prevail under a legal regime similar to the one for alcohol. Decriminalization of heroin, cocaine, and marijuana sales to adults would force a precipitous price drop and a coincident fall in the incidence of trade-associated violence, since most participants could turn to the courts for the enforcement of contract, property, and territorial claims. Judicial relief would be barred only to the vastly reduced number operating in the underground market defined by the regulatory statutes. Under the public health paradigm associated with the move from a prohibition regime to one of regulation, the authorities would provide indigent users with clean syringes. Treatment would no longer be associated with arrest and incarceration. Finally, at the stroke of a pen, hundreds of thousands of prisoners would be freed, converted from criminals to citizens, leaving ample space for the long-term incarceration of violent offenders.

Opponents also believe that the war cannot be won, at least not by means consistent with a constitutional regime of ordered liberty, with an open economy, and with an allocation of public resources responsive to the overall national interest. It was after arriving reluctantly at precisely this conclusion that the conservative intellectual William F. Buckley shifted into the ranks of the opposition.[62] A comparison of trends in drug war expenditures with trends in the street price of cocaine and heroin supports the belief that under existing restraints, the war is unwinnable. Between 1978 and 1994, the federal law enforcement budget directed to drug suppression rose from about $1.5 to just under $8 billion per annum, more than a fivefold increase. In that same period the cocaine street price fell from a 1978 peak of $1600 per pure gram to just under $200, an eightfold decrease. For heroin the comparable fall was from about $5,000 to roughly $700, a decrease of merely 700 percent.[63]

This abject failure to execute the mission of drastically reducing the flow of hard drugs to street dealers (and thereby raising their price) by interdiction, either at the smuggling or wholesale stage, stems in part from the sheer length of U.S. borders and the absence of formidable natural obstacles to entry, in part from a commitment to and growing dependence on open borders for purposes of licit trade.[64] During the past few years the number of cargo containers entering the United States every year has hovered around the nine million mark. By one estimate, it would take more than 65 million agent days to inspect them all, at a probable cost of $27 billion a year (without calculating the added costs of disrupting international trade).[65] Containers are just one possible means of entry. At the present time, more than a half million airplanes, 175,000 ships and boats, 100 million automobiles, and 400 million people cross the United States's 12,000 miles of coastal and 7,500 miles of land borders annually. An average of twenty thousand trucks cross the U.S.-Mexican border *every day*.[66] And these figures do not include clandestine crossing by land, sea, and air. With prospective prices at the point of entry 900 percent above the costs of preparing product for export,[67] smugglers have the means and incentive to acquire sophisticated equipment to facilitate both surreptitious crossings and the concealment of narcotics in planes, ships, cars, trains, and trucks crossing openly. The primary Mexican narcotics exporters are thought to earn profits in the range of $7 billion per annum,[68] a level of profits that provides a wide margin for additional investment in corruption of border officials and sophisticated clandestine transportation arrangements.

Perceptions of the drug trade's impact on U.S. foreign-policy interests fracture along similar lines. As this volume's chapters on Mexico, the Caribbean, Colombia, and Bolivia elaborately document, the trade, in large measure by fueling violence and corruption and a gross and conspicuous decline in the state's relative power, has undermined democratic government and the rule of law, stripping prestige from state institutions (including the whole edifice of procedural justice), polluting the electoral well, discouraging foreign investment, multiplying disorganized social violence, and seducing lower-class youth away from traditional values by glorifying violence and intimidation as means to instant affluence. The effect on human rights has been equally nasty and equally at odds with often-declared foreign-policy goals of the United States.[69]

That these things have occurred coincident with the growth of the drug trade is a proposition beyond reasonable dispute. What does incur dissent is the often-conjoined proposition that the drug trade is their primal cause. Skeptics impute that role to demand, first in U.S. markets and now, increasingly, in Europe as well. And in a replay of the argument about cause and effect of domestic evils, they assign the principal secondary role to the war declared by the United States on the drug trade, together with its refusal to tolerate neutrality. Intense and perhaps uncontrollable demand in the United States for a forbidden product—the criminalization of vice—induced in Colombian society an ineluctable and hence entirely predictable response. The artificial multiplication of value resulting from the attempted suppression of market forces transformed small-time smuggling operations into financial giants.[70] It invested the drug cartels with means for mounting a powerful challenge to the regime if it proved intolerant.

Having in a meaningful sense created the cartels, the United States then forced Colombia's government to be intolerant, and thus triggered the conflict that mutilated the already feeble corpus of Colombian democracy. Swollen with income from the trade, leading narcotics enterprises effortlessly financed the campaign of assassination, terror, and corruption that swept over the country in the latter 1980s. The country lost half its by-no-means-undistinguished Supreme Court in a single day, lost its most popular presidential candidate from the traditional parties, *and* lost two consecutive and impressive presidential candidates of the reconciled left along with whole regiments of their colleagues, which was a terrible blow to the politics of ideological reconciliation. Ministers of justice fled or died, and ordinary trial court judges, the essential grunts of any national judiciary, took silver in return for not-guilty verdicts, lead in return for guilty ones, or went into exile, altogether leaving the criminal justice system in tatters. Police were slaughtered in droves. Villagers in the countryside were, and continue to be, ground to bits between the drug-financed paramilitaries (acting often with the support of the national armed forces) and the armed Marxist left.[71] As the armed assault on state institutions diminished, it was succeeded by waves of money flooding into the congressional and presidential electoral campaigns.

Since giving drugs a senior place on the list of public harms, Washington has exerted relentless pressure on Latin American governments to secure their support for a campaign of elimination against delinquent flora and fauna, somewhat softened in the case of the former and their cultivators by offers of aid to develop alternative crops. The United States has demanded liquidation of coca, marijuana, and poppy crops, effective control of chemicals used in processing, and destruction of facilities, either rigorous punishment or extradition of drug entrepreneurs, and confiscation of their assets. To those ends, it has offered to equip and train elite narcotics units in the various Andean police and armed forces, units that have often, thereafter, distinguished themselves less for their efficacy in destroying the trade than for violations of human rights. On behalf of its antidrug campaign, the United States threatens Latin American countries with loss of foreign assistance, active opposition to loans from the international financial institutions, and other economic sanctions for failure to be certified annually as a worthy ally in the drug wars.

Although Latin American notables have rarely challenged the goals of this war, they have frequently attacked its means, including what is widely perceived as insensitivity to context and costs and the humiliation of certification, with its unilateral and flagrantly inconsistent determinations of who has displayed good faith and sufficient effort.[72] Also seen as humiliating, if not positively dangerous to territorial integrity, are various sorts of U.S. transborder law enforcement activities. In May 1998, for instance, the Foreign Affairs Commission of the Mexican Congress announced that it had filed a formal protest with the U.S. government in connection with a successful money-laundering sting operation executed in part through the use of U.S. undercover agents inside Mexico. The Associated Press quoted Senator Eduardo Andrade of the ruling Institutional Revolutionary Party as saying that while "it is true that all Mexicans are against drug trafficking . . . we are also against foreign intervention and [referring to the sting] attempts to destabilize Mexican institutions . . . [through] the corrupting power of the government of the United States."[73]

In the frequent episodes of finger-pointing between Latin American governments, supported generally by informed opinion in their countries, and official

Washington, contention over immediate issues of policy has occurred against a background of hostile first principles mingling ethical and instrumental elements. North Americans bear the major responsibility, Latin Americans contend, because the problem starts with demand. Demand, Washington responds, is inconsequential without supply; hence, Latin Americans bear an equal or greater responsibility on that ground alone. In addition, demand is a domestic matter and therefore none of anyone else's business. Latin American contraband penetrating U.S. shores is a transnational phenomenon and therfore very much a legitimate issue of diplomacy.

Do these contending perceptions form a logically impenetrable circle? Or is there a reasonable way of breaking free and assessing primary blame? In postmodern consumption capitalism, demand is not necessarily prior to supply because suppliers have the knowledge and means to create demand for new products. Consumers have hardly finished substituting compact disks for cassettes when they are assaulted with claims about a still-superior intermediary between performers and their ears. This was not, however, true in the case of cocaine. Here sequence is demonstrable. Demand came first. Colombian traffickers responded, not really to the raw, autocthonous demand but to the market opportunity, that is, the potential superprofits stemming from the public policy of the United States. The decision of governmental bodies at the local, state, and national level in effect to prohibit satisfaction of the craving for drug-induced pleasure made the demand. The public institutions of Colombia, weak under the best of circumstances and virtually absent in many remote parts of the country, had nothing at all to do with the initial organization of supply. After the play of market forces had equipped suppliers for war, the country's elite did attempt to limit supply, and paid a price far, far in excess of anything suffered by their North American counterparts.

Even if one accepts the dubious claim that in criminalizing the drug vice, Americans were enforcing a universal, rather than parochial, sense of the intolerable, the United States still had options other than generating irresistible demand and then compelling foreign governments to launch self-destructive campaigns against the supply side. It might have focused exclusively on repressing demand, concentrating its resources on all end users, regardless of class, and imposing draconian punishment. Or it might have invested the resources it has employed to repress and interdict supply in a vast campaign of advertising and public education, supplemented with intensive therapy for all drug users. In the case of the mentally ill, hopeless, desperate, and disoriented persons who predominate among hard-core addicts, it might have combined therapy with education and counseling and/or financial support. Being a rich state and a strong one relative to those in Latin America—a presence in every corner of the land, still enjoying a considerable albeit declining measure of credibility and legitimacy, lavishly equipped with coherent organizations, and with experts in education, propaganda, therapy, and enforcement—the United States had the practical means to choose and make its choices effective. Latin American regimes did not.

Questions of responsibility are neither mere academic play nor electoral rhetoric. The collective national decision to make war against the transnational drug trade and in the process to impose harsh choices on Latin American and Caribbean states is not the outcome of an informed, deliberate calculation of costs and benefits either to the United States or other societies. As the former surgeon general, Joyce Elders, discovered when she initiated discussion of decriminalization, proposals to deliberate the costs and benefits of the drug war provoke hysteria, the rabid fury with which religious zealots greet blasphemy. Long unchallenged, the claimed necessity of treating the appetite for drug-induced pleasure as a morally subversive no less than materially destructive monster whose extermination is a universal duty has hardened into an article of faith.[74] To challenge it now in any of its parts, including the one equating neutrality with sin, one therefore needs a discourse combining moral claims with material interests. Questions of responsibility obviously fall into the moral realm.

To be sure, the narcotics wars in Latin America may not be imputable solely to U.S. policy. The British political economist Susan Strange argues that "[t]rouble only starts … when governments of states which have hitherto tolerated the coexistence of a rival non-state authority, perceive a significant shift in the balance of power threatening their own survival."[75] Italy, Strange's exemplary case, is clearly one where a part of the national elite resolved to end the mix of collusion and acquiescence that had marked regime policy for almost four decades after World War II. Whether, in the absence of U.S. pressure, this might ultimately have occurred in Colombia and Mexico is unknowable. Colombia, with its elites' strong self-conception as guardians of the rule of law and sharp class distinctions, was the more likely site of a self-motivated assault on the main trafficking organizations. Tension between leftist political leaders (hardly handmaidens of U.S. foreign-policy interests) and the cartels, culminating in the latter's assassination campaign, reinforces the impression that at some point, a political coalition bent on strengthening the Colombian state and modernizing the society would have found the cartels an intolerable obstacle to their project as long as, by the nature of their trade, paranoia made them employ violence and corruption at home as well as abroad. Whatever might have been, the historical record, reviewed here in the chapters on Colombia and especially Mexico, documents U.S. influence on the character, scope, and timing of the antitrafficker campaigns and certainly allows for the conclusion that in Mexico, at least, the war has accelerated political instability, further undermined an always-problematic rule of law, and helped insinuate lethal violence into the higher levels of politics and administration.

MORE THAN THE SUM OF ITS PARTS?

It is, I think, less the present dangers and harms *connected to particular lines of TOC enterprise* than the TOC phenomenon itself that justifies concern. Let me counterintuitively suppose, since one cannot know, that the value of TOC enterprises has increased only in proportion to the increase in the value of the aboveground global economy or the increase in the value of all goods and services traded across national frontiers. Would it follow logically that since the criminal economy's share of the global economy had remained constant, the TOC threat to the interests and values of the United States and the other capitalist democracies had also remained constant? Of course not.

To begin with, take the obvious point that economic power units convert, at contextually varying ratios, into political ones. Since government action in many fields affects profits, the imperative of profit maximization drives business enterprises to seek to influence governments, that is, drives them into politics, even if their owners and managers have absolutely no independent interest in public policy. As governments commit themselves to a reduced role in the economy, both domestically and with respect to the transnational movement of goods and services, they reduce the incentives for legitimate businesses to play a political role (although sunset industries in particular will go on attempting to alter that commitment in favor of protection). Incentives for illegitimate businesses will remain the same; for by definition government continues to have an impact upon them as a threat, if not an active adversary. The precariousness of its position gives criminal enterprise disproportionate incentives to spend money on politics. Less spending by licit enterprises, no sign of which is yet evident, would, of course, leverage criminal contributions.

Absolute increments of wealth can have transformative results even when they do not alter certain relational variables. In Mexico, for instance, the scale and character of drug-smuggling operations (marijuana and heroin) during the period of roughly 1930 to 1970 was such that the enterprises were local in character and outlook and marginal to the country's political system. Engorged in the 1980s on income earned in large part by moving Colombian cocaine into the United States and facing in the form of the United States' drug war a greater challenge to smuggling activity, by the 1990s the major organizations had become, through corruption and violence on a national scale, major political actors powerfully affecting Mexican society. Whether, in light of growth in the overall Mexican economy, they had increased their share of GNP was irrelevant to their enhanced power.

Step-level jumps in consequence are not simply a function of profits. A more complicated and dangerous environment coupled with prospects for enhanced income encourages expansion and consolidation, demands greater skills, and fosters sophistication. Experts on Russian organized crime report, for instance, that during the past decade since the collapse of the Soviet Union and the precipitous decline of state power and elan, an initial horde of criminal groups has sorted itself out into about eighty of real consequence.

Much more money and the changes that go with it alter perceptions in criminal organizations about how to relate to the state. Where the state appears incomparably more powerful, criminal organizations (as opposed to the flamboyant predator anxious for a Warholian fifteen minutes in the sun) will tend to maintain a low profile, will try not to be noticed or at least to be seen as more than a localized nuisance. When they have billions of dollars at their disposal (one authority, for instance, estimates Mexican mafia drug profits at $7 billion per annum) and have become impossible to overlook, they will look at the state and will see something rather less formidable than they may have thought when they shrank from its glance.

Particularly outside the advanced capitalist democracies, most of the state's functionaries are poorly paid, and in practically all countries the salaries of police and paramilitary forces at every level are at best modest. The state's income is now chronically insufficient to satisfy the demands of mobilized populations of avid consumers. Its legitimacy erodes in the face of an overall reduction in respect for authority. In a media-dominated age, money is the electoral nutrient of its leaders. So even where the political order has roots in the society, some decent achievements and popular icons, and sufficient coherence and competence to perform the essential tasks of government, it can look and often is permeable to influence and vulnerable to threats.

Fear that organized crime has passed or is in the process of making a step-level jump (of achieving what might be called *critical mass*) stems not just from its higher profile but from the circumstances, outlined just above, in which the profile appears. Profile alone would not be very suggestive: the Soviet peak made lesser hills look diminutive. Once it was gone, they had to appear larger. The passing of Soviet power and the attendant cold war produced huge changes in material circumstances, not simply their look. One was the debilitation of state power throughout the vast area of Asia and Eastern Europe controlled by communist regimes. In many of the former Warsaw Pact countries, certainly in Russia itself and most of Eastern Europe, internal security forces were downsized, demoralized, purged of experienced officers, and forced to operate under previously unknown legal constraints. Their dilapidation together with the defeat of their political masters had to have decimated their networks of informants who, in any society, cooperate with the police for reasons related to money, fear, or ideological conviction.

What remained of the internal security bureaucracy functioned within societies of exploding consumerism and, with the leap toward privatization of state property, extraordinary opportunities for self-enrichment. Privatization together with the erosion of means for imposing discipline in surviving state industry caused a contraction in state revenue. Most governments lacked the technical means and authority to compensate by increasing tax collection. Where the state no longer has the means or will to terrorize, taxation requires a high degree of voluntary compliance that requires the kind of civic culture incompatible with the long-repressed and so raw capitalist urges and the deep cynicism inherited from the suddenly terminated Communist epoch.

Compounding the new regime's problems in Russia was the history of collaboration between the previous state and groups of entrepreneurs organized largely along ethnic lines that had lubricated the impossibly rigid joints of the command economy through informal—theoretically illegal—intermediation among suppliers and consumers. Despite their symbiotic relationship to the state, the entrepreneurs had to live in a netherworld of formal illegality, subject, therefore, to arbitrary exactions from state authorities and even occasional exemplary punishment by zealots or cynics seeking to maintain the myth of state industrial competence. In other words, embedded in the new Russia were economic enterprises skilled at functioning outside the legal economy and habituated to a culture of corruption. Privatization and the country's enormous wealth in natural resources, together with the debilitation of the police and security services, offered a field littered with opportunity on which the mafias could batten. Insecurity among senior officials of the old regime and downsizing or the collapse of salaries in industry and government swelled their ranks. Plunder was not the only opportunity presented by a weak state and chaotic capitalist society. The latter required services—protection of property and contract rights—that the mafias were better equipped and organized than the state to provide.

The existence of well-organized and armed mafias has fostered collaboration among organized crime groups. Russia offered a potential new market for the products, particularly drugs, of their foreign counterparts. The Russian mafias offered a valuable partner who was, at the same time, difficult to avoid. Simple cost-benefit analysis argued strongly for cooperation. The Russians, moreover, had their own products, including arms, they could siphon out of their country's military-industrial complex. Collaboration was only one means for acquiring an overseas presence. In addition, particularly in the United States and Israel, they could build with ethnic partners who had begun emigrating as soon as Gorbachev's glasnost had opened the Soviet door.

The transformation of politics, economy, and society in the former Warsaw Pact countries is one contextual element favorable to the waxing of organized criminal enterprise. Another is China's increased openness and evolving shift to at least a quasi-capitalist economy. There too the collapse of ideological fervor and the parallel growth of consumerism spell vast new opportunities for organized crime in an area where some of the most powerful and best-organized groups, the so-called Triads, have their home base.

Developments in China and Russia can, however, be seen in part as representative of changes—mentioned earlier—that operate throughout the world: openness of borders; frenzied consumption; erosion of communitarian culture; reduced state authority; metastasis in the arms bazaar; extraordinary enhancement of transportation and media networks. *But what matters above all is what has* not *happened, namely the creation of an international regulatory and enforcement structure corresponding to the exponential increase in the number, complexity, organization, speed, and influence of transactions and organizations crossing state boundaries.*

That there are today more and more powerful criminal enterprises operating across frontiers is indisputable. Certain mafias now active internationally—clearly those in Italy, greater China[76] (the Triads), and Japan (the Yakuza)—first became powerful through their domestic activities. Perhaps the most powerful mafia in China before World War II, the Shanghai-based Green Gang, cooperated closely with Chiang Kai-Chek, leader of the Kuomintang, and played a major role in his 1927 decimation of hitherto allied communist cadres in Shanghai. After the Communist victory in 1949, many are believed to have escaped with him to Taiwan. Today they are reliably reported to have bastions both in Taiwan and Hong Kong. And, even before the latter's reversion last year, authorities in Beijing had openly referred to their existence and had indicated a readiness for accommodation.[77]

The symbiotic relationship between the Italian mafias, particularly those in Sicily, and an Italian state dominated by the Christian Democratic Party after World War II is notorious.[78] Accommodation certainly seems the word to describe state-gangster relations in Japan. For years, gangs have dominated construction laborers in Tokyo, roughly blocking union organizational efforts.[79] They have extorted money from major corporations with threats to disrupt annual meetings,[80] and have borrowed large amounts from private banks. According to credible reports, their refusals either to repay or to allow foreclosure on mortgaged buildings have complicated public and private efforts in Japan to rehabilitate the country's imploding financial systems.[81]

In the case of the most significant Latin American criminal organizations, the Colombian and Mexican drug exporters, the sequence of national power followed by transnational activity has been largely reversed. As cigarette smugglers into Colombia (and to a minor extent marijuana exporters), Colombian criminal enterprises were a nuisance. As cocaine exporters to a swelling American market, they quickly became a serious threat to the state. The Mexican case is slightly more complicated. Mexican enterprises began supplying narcotics to U.S. markets even before World War II. By 1970 they were their northern neighbor's main source of marijuana and a substantial secondary source of heroin. Nevertheless, they maintained a low profile and appear to have had little effect on national institutions. These characteristics began to alter when, in response to intense pressure from the United States, the Mexican Government deployed military forces against the producer/smugglers in a fierce campaign of eradication and suppression.

The campaign was initially successful. Mexican producers virtually disappeared from the American heroin market and lost their preeminence as marijuana suppliers (U.S. producers helped replace them). But the gangs' Darwinian struggle to survive left in place a smaller number of more effective groups whose chance came when Colombian cocaine cartels, facing increased difficulty in moving product through the Caribbean and Florida, decided to come up through the Mexican underbelly. To that end they struck deals with Mexican gangs who then assumed the task of moving the cocaine through Mexico and across the U.S. border. Soaring income from this role supplied the gangs with the means, while the risk of a renewed central government assault (fueled by U.S. pressure) provided ample motive to buy protection at the national level. Their success in penetrating the police, the armed forces, and to a degree still unclear, the political elite is now generally acknowledged.

Russia, as usual, falls into a category more or less its own. As in the case of Japan, consequential criminal enterprises evolved largely in response to opportunities within the domestic political economy. As in the case of Colombia, opportunities abroad, for instance to barter sophisticated weaponry for drugs and to launder money, increased their power. But as sources of power, the external is ineradicably entangled with the internal: the collapse of the Soviet state and the resulting legal chaos, unemployment, and debilitation of the security services. Internal developments have fed skilled personnel from the old military-industrial-security complex into the world of Russian criminal enterprise with results that American police officials find alarming. What makes the Russians so dangerous, according to a senior Russia expert with the Drug Enforcement Administration, "is that they are capable of so much; they are extremely sophisticated. We are talking [about] people with PhDs, former senior KGB agents with access to sophisticated weapons, people who have [already] laundered billions of dollars."[82]

PRIORITIZING THE THREAT

That changes in the absolute dimensions and the opportunity structure for international organized crime have an impact upon the welfare of the United States and other liberal democratic states is hard to contest. Less clear, however, is the priority that ought to be accorded to these developments—where, that is to say, they should be ranked on the agenda of national security concerns. At its core, this volume is an effort to understand more fully the relationship between TOC and national security (of the United States and other nations) and then, in light of that understanding, to identify an optimal policy response. Implicit in a high ranking would be a call for treating organized crime as more than crime, traditionally a local or at least domestic concern, a call for the deployment of all departments of the government, including the intelligence agencies, for an integrated assault, and a call as well for heightened action outside the frontiers of the United States.

Impelled by his mandate to assess the proper place for TOC on the U.S. national security agenda, Greg Treverton necessarily begins with the definitional issue and finds the country, indeed the world, in an historic transition from a state-oriented and organized political order to one in which borders are far less significant and economics rather than geopolitical power is the main driver of international politics. In the mental and material order that is disappearing—an order defined by struggles for power among sovereign states—security has referred (inevitably, he implies) to the nation's territorial integrity, economic well-being, or core institutions. So conceived, he says, TOC probably is not a serious threat. In the rapidly emerging order of the market state,

> national security is much harder to define. . . . For starters, it probably needs to refer to the security of people in a state or nation, not that *of* the state or nation. That makes the definition both more expansive and less. It is more expansive in that it drives the definition of security toward the everyday. It may be less in that to the extent that the institutions and icons of the nation-state are being threatened, those institutions and icons are already becoming devalued (though citizens may still cling to them).[83]

Those are nice starters. Do they, however, finish with a new definition appropriate to or imposed by the changed conditions of international society?

Shortly after the excerpt above, but without offering a full definition distinguishable from the traditional one, Treverton proposes four ways in which TOC might indeed threaten national security: by destabilizing friendly governments; by risking wider violence; by materially affecting the economic well-being of citizens; or by sharply offending cherished values. With the possible exception of the last one, that enumeration of interests falls within the bounds of traditional definitions and, at least since the time of Woodrow Wilson, even the defense of cherished values has been a staple of presidential iterations of the national interest. Is there a deep contradiction, then, in Treverton's thought or perhaps a powerful unresolved ambivalence? Is the old conception changing, or just loosening up a little?

What I think Treverton is trying to say is something along the following lines. For the several centuries preceding the present moment, that is, since sovereign states (territorially based and hierarchic political organizations recognizing no higher secular authority) became the constituent elements of world society and their interactions the stuff of diplomacy, national security concerns focused on territorial integrity and political independence. Economic well-being was important initially in relationship not to the happiness of individuals but rather to the power of the state, economic buoyancy being translatable through taxation into firepower. The French Revolution's conversion of subjects into citizens bonded by feelings of fraternity and the French state's consequent success in raising from its notionally empowered citizens huge armies with high elan inaugurated a new era. To maintain the vital emotional connection between the state and its citizens, the former had to articulate a direct connection between national security and individual well-being.

In large measure, however, this was accomplished by idealizing the nation, that is, imaginatively transforming the historically random assortment of people who happened to be living within one or another sovereign state into a unique primordial community[84] and demonizing other national communities and the state forms and machinery through which they acted, so that for a peasant in Alsace it would become a matter of the highest importance whether he paid over a portion of his meager livelihood to an emperor-dictator-parliament in Paris rather than to a Kaiser in Berlin. Since governing elites were largely successful in effecting the requisite change in consciousness while retaining their inherited view of international politics as a struggle for power, in Europe (where a delicate and shifting power balance prevailed and small states lacked effective guarantees) the operational substance of international politics did not alter. Governments could go on defining national security primarily in terms of territorial integrity and political independence (which might require the preemptive seizure of other people's territories) in the well-based expectation that they enjoyed the requisite popular agreement.

Things were a little different in the United States. In the first place, from an early point in its national history it was unusually free of serious threats to its territory or independence. It was protected initially by its oceans, its unruly sprawl, and British control of the seas that barred the great European armies from access to North America. After the Civil War, its size and industrial power combined with geography and the weakness of northern and southern neighbors to make the country unassailable. In the second place, elites no less than the generality of persons were socialized in a commercial rather than warrior culture. So, while ready to bristle at any sign of resistance to its impulse toward continental economic development, its elite were not inclined to invent threats simply in order to find occasions for the expression of martial valor. Thirdly, the national state apparatus had difficulty accumulating power in an egalitarian political environment marked from the beginning by distrust of national power, a widely dispersed population absorbed with local social and economic problems, constitutional constraints, and a powerful tendency toward populist self-assertion and citizen self-organization. In short, the objective and conditions discouraged an active foreign policy of any kind, much less one that would have attempted to pursue power rather than the quotidian economic well-being of the American electorate.

And they continued to do so well into the twentieth century, even after the integration of the national economy and the Great Depression of 1929 persuaded the electorate that active government at the national level was necessary for the protection of its economic interests. Even as Japan moved in the late 1930s to extend its control over great chunks of northeastern Asia, and Adolph Hitler maneuvered toward German hegemony in Europe, President Franklin Roosevelt could not rally popular support for building an armed forces capable of blocking these developments until the Japanese ignited national passions through their devastating assault on Pearl Harbor. The North Korean attack on South Korea in turn regalvanized support, after a brief dip following World War II, for a power-oriented national security policy, support which remained in place until the end of the cold war.

Treverton begins with the obvious fact that the dissolution of the Soviet Empire left the United States without an identifiable threat to American security defined in the terms of traditional great-power diplomacy. But that is not all that has changed. The collapse of Soviet power and Communism as an ideology removed the various material and psychological constraints on the globalization of postindustrial capitalism. In this new order of things, the era of the "market state," as Treventon calls it, the electorate, progressively less a community than a loosely connected agglomeration of little consumption units, devalues the state in general while demanding from it contributions to individual affluence, economic security, and a general sense of well-being that the individual sovereign state is progressively less able to supply on its own.

What do these changes imply for a functional definition of national security and for efforts to assess the national security significance of TOC? They imply, to begin with, that the national security agenda contains a multiplicity of concerns that don't submit to easy prioritization either by the public or the community of foreign-policy experts. Prioritizing is difficult for at least two reasons. One is the diversity of opinion, interest, and preference within a society no longer unified by the perception of a single grand threat to everyone's deepest interests. Another is the difficulty of coping with contemporary concerns: people invest in public policy when they feel not only that there is a problem but also that there is a solution. Governments do not invest in repelling (as distinguished from mitigating the impact of) El Niño. A third point I find in Treverton is the proposition that a useful definition must incorporate the altered state of public sentiment that now focuses far more, if not exclusively, on the day-to-day individual existence rather than the grand goals and anxieties of World War II and the cold war. And it must incorporate an appreciation of the diminished capacity of the state to deal with threats to interests and values of the electorate, in part because the threats are transnational and embedded to greater or lesser degrees in the activities of dispersed private groups on whom it is difficult and costly to focus the power capabilities of the United States.

Transnational organized crime, Treverton seems to be saying, will be a concern, probably a progressively greater one, because it does promise damage to various American interests and values. But, in that, the extent of the damage will be controversial, the means and costs of responding effectively unclear, and the resources available to respond in demand for other purposes. He believes that the country will probably end up treating TOC as more than a nuisance but less than a real threat to national security (in the sense, I assume, of a *collective* sense of what is vital to the community as a whole).

Can Treverton's prediction be reconciled with two facts: first, that opinion polls evidence the continuing prominence of drugs on the public's list of major problems facing the nation? Second, that in popular media culture and in U.S. government rhetoric and policy, TOC is regularly identified as the ultimate source of the problem? I think so. After all, public concern over drugs and the largely unchallenged war against foreign suppliers have been going on now for some two decades. The president and Congress compete to demonstrate commitment by throwing money at the same nostrums, such as increased border surveillance activities by military units and some ramp-up in the border patrol-coupled with minimum penalties for traffickers, and so on. The money thrown is in the billions, a large amount for certain purposes that lack political buzz, like rehabilitation programs for all identified addicts and support services for the thousands of mentally disturbed persons in the hard-core addict population, but stealthily small in relation to the entire national security budget, which for the military establishment alone (excluding most of the intelligence community) is about $270 billion.[85]

The billions that have been hurled at the problem have failed to force an increase in the price of cocaine and heroin; indeed, their price has fallen substantially during the past twenty years. And, since public expenditure coincides temporally with a perceived increase in the wealth, sophistication, and transnational coordination of organized crime groups, a cautious person might offer simply as an hypothesis that they have done nothing very obvious to alleviate the TOC threat. But failure—or, if that is too harsh a word, then say, "lack of success"—has

not shaken the conspiracy between the electorate and those it elects to go on acting as if the right policies were in place and success demands only a bit more
money and effort and an occasional exemplary kick in the pants of other governments so they too get on with the job.

Despite twenty years of failure, policy and politics in the realm of transnational organized crime and the drug trade (largely conflated in American political discourse, at least insofar as Latin America is concerned) have achieved a
comfortable equilibrium. From this phenomenon you could draw an inference
along the following lines. The voters and the sort of people who tend to get
elected these days share so deep-seated a revulsion to the appetite for narcotics
that they simply cannot contemplate any relaxation of the prohibition on their
use; they are indifferent to the consequences of a prohibition regime even if it
empowers criminal enterprises. At the same time they are unwilling to contemplate the draconian, intrusive, and possibly unconstitutional internal measures—
long prison terms and personal asset confiscation for mere users, death penalty
for sellers, virtually universal random drug testing, to name some—or militarized borders, assault by all means short of force on nontransparency of private
activities in offshore financial centers, and other measures that would powerfully
affect our relations with other countries and our place in the liberal international
trading regime. Just what kind of traumas would have to occur in order to shake
the prevailing equilibrium, to open the policy discourse, is not entirely clear.

One reason so much of the public rhetoric about organized crime sounds
empty and leads nowhere is the unexamined premise that the issue is a problem
of human agency and thus amenable at its core to definitive solution. In the case
of destructive phenomena of the natural world—hurricanes and earthquakes, for
example—the incapacity of public policy to get at the core problem, at the thing
itself, is so evident that normal political entrepreneurs see no advantage in claiming otherwise.[86] So debate focuses on how to minimize the damage resulting
from these unassuageable and amoral forces. Where, however, the destructive
phenomenon is attributable to human agency—where it has a face—political
rhetoric tends to shift abruptly from the mitigation of consequences to the liquidation of the cause. In other words, consequences stemming from human agents
are perceived to be contingent on the survival of the agents. Eliminate the agents,
it is assumed, and one eliminates the damage they cause, while simultaneously
advancing the retributive ends of the criminal law and, therefore, the collective
sense of living in a moral universe. As I noted above in relation to narcotics, it is
the perceived moral dimension of the problem—people are enriching themselves
by choosing to ignore the electorate's judgment about what goods and services
are inimical to the public good—that demands strategies addressed to the human
agents rather than the results of their acts.

But what if the condemned service is passionately desired by a large number
of consumers? Could it not be argued in such a case that demand is the deepest
cause and that it has some of the elemental power of a natural force? Narcotics
are such a case. So is the demand one finds in the former Soviet Union for the
protection of contract rights and problematical property interests.

WHAT IS TO BE DONE?

The outline of an operational plan for responding to the phenomenon of organized criminal groups operating across national frontiers will develop at the intersection of answers to the following questions. *First:* What is the problem? Should it be thought of primarily in terms of the major extant criminal organizations? Is it primarily what they do or what they might do if they survive and thrive? *Second:* What are U.S. goals in relation to the problem? To liquidate the major organizations? To impoverish and fragment them? To inhibit their growth in wealth and power? To reduce sharply their capacity to conduct their present businesses? To secure their assistance in coping with worse scourges? *Third:* What is the foreseeable price the American people will pay—in terms of financial and human resources, moral values, protection of other interests—in order to achieve each of the enumerated goals. *Fourth:* What are the chances of marshaling the requisite degree of support from the American public and from other states? And finally, *fifth:* assuming the maximum conceivable investment of human and material resources (taking into account expectations of the willingness of the public and other states to tolerate the needed investment and predictable losses), is it possible to solve the problem and, if so, for how long is it likely to stay solved?

Policy usually turns out to be residual—what is left after the disqualification of alternatives. Alternatives get disqualified in part through a comparative analysis. Political rhetoric is linear and fragmented, indifferent to economic laws. When it comes to things perceived as evil threats, politicians bark at them sequentially, promising a decisive response as if there were no trade-offs, as if all the nation's resources were available for deployment, as they are in times of general war. Then when the policy wonks lay out the real costs of *la guerre à outrance,* politicians quietly settle for limited engagement. Limits do, however, vary. Sometimes the variance depends largely on what can be sold in the competitive political marketplace. Sometimes it depends as well on deliberate estimates of the probable efficiency of investment: the law of diminishing returns sets in at different times for different problems and strategies.

Grand Strategies: *La Guerre À Outrance*

Paradoxically, a mind game paralleling the politician's rhetorical approach to threats is often an efficient means for cutting to the residual which, at the end of the day, becomes public policy. The game is played by treating a given threat as if it were grave enough to trivialize all others, so they become the equivalent of, say, illegal gambling during World War II, while the threat assumes the dimensions of a victory for America's wartime adversaries. With reference to transnational organized crime, then, one plays by treating as true the claim that it constitutes a threat to American interests not unlike that posed by the Soviet Union and worldwide Communism in the aftermath of World War II or Japan and Germany on the eve of the same war. Against such a threat Americans wage war, and when America wages war, it fights to win in the sense of arriving at a point where the threat has been eliminated. The object of the game is to identify the measures that will make that happen. What makes this game so useful is its capacity to reveal the plausibility and the price of liquidating the threat as conventional wisdom defines it. Hard-headed calculations of cost and obstacles to victory irrespective of cost can fuel reordering of priorities and redefinitions of threat.

Organized crime is a case in point. Define victory as the liquidation of every organization of any size that is currently operating across national frontiers and the ongoing preemptive repression of new ones. Define victory in those terms, and one insures defeat. Superprofits; an unmanageable demographic bulge in many less-developed countries; a plethora of very weak states enjoying the formal attributes of sovereignty; the acquisitive values of postindustrial capitalism and their universal dissemination by global media; the decline of alternative ideologies; economic dependence on easy movement of goods, services, and people across frontiers; technologically enhanced ease of cross-border operations and the weakness of interstate governance and policing mechanisms—in combination these facets of contemporary world society guarantee the regular reproduction of criminal enterprises. This being obvious, in order to make the mind game interesting, one needs to define victory no more grandly than the decimation of existing criminal organizations, the crippling of their networks and logistical systems, and continuing repression sufficient to prevent the restoration of TOC to its present level of participation in the global and certain national societies.

A One- or Two-Front War?

Victory thus redefined, how might the United States achieve it? First, one might fairly (but it appears futilely) contend, by radically redefining victory in another war, the one against drugs. Certainly in the Western Hemisphere, drug-trade superprofits, generated by the current prohibition regime operating in the context of intense demand, are the generative force behind big-time organized crime. They provide the means and the principal incentive for building powerful core organizations, elaborating transnational logistical systems, corrupting governments, and deploying private armies of assassins and thugs. Experts estimate drug-related income represents about two-thirds of money laundered annually around the world.[87] Since estimates of money laundered include income from activities (such as securities fraud and bribery of government officials by legitimate businesses) not normally associated with private criminal organizations, the portion of TOC income attributable to the drug trade is bound to be higher. No other criminal activity even approaches it.

The story of organized crime's penetration of the political and economic order in Mexico, Colombia, Bolivia, and the Caribbean is simultaneously a narrative of the drug trade's ramification during the past three decades. In a war of attrition against another state, one attempts to cut the enemy's access to the petroleum products on which its air and ground power depend. In a war against TOC, money is the analogue of fuel. Theoretically it is vulnerable to two strategies: price reduction and interdiction.

Prohibition being their elevator, prices would plummet in a largely free market. As noted earlier, production costs are minimal in relation to wholesale and retail prices. The consumer pays hugely for the costs and, primarily, for the risks associated with smuggling product into the United States and other countries.[88]

Legalization of sales to adults of cocaine, heroin, and marijuana—a regime of regulation comparable to the one now governing the sale of alcoholic beverages in the United States—would pull the plug on prices and therefore on TOC income. Given the extensive and widely scattered venues, including the United States, for producing the raw materials, today's leading producers could not hope to maintain prices by reducing supplies. The leading drug enterprises are not, in fact, cartels; they lack the defining market power. While the continued prohibition on sales to children and adolescents would sustain some sort of black market, it would generate a tiny fraction of today's TOC income. The preadult market would presumably be more price sensitive; it would be subjected by the state to an avalanche of counterconsumption advertising, which could be financed by a small percentage of the resources currently committed to generalized prohibition; liberated enforcement assets could be concentrated on a much narrower front, and traffickers would have far fewer resources to finance strategies of law enforcement avoidance, co-option, and neutralization.

A black market limited to preadults would also weaken trafficking operations by sharpening everywhere the stigma of acquiescence, much less collaboration. And that in turn would facilitate interdiction of income. A strategy of interdiction alone, executed through assaults on money laundering, has raised the costs to trafficking organizations but to nowhere near the point where returns on investment would make the risks unattractive or would force an increase in retail prices. In other words, it has failed. But, one might well argue, that is so because Americans have executed the strategy of interdiction within constraints indigenous to peacetime. Since the premise of this mind game is that Americans are willing to make war, failure to date has little predictive value. And that is true not merely of interdiction, but of the parallel contemporary effort to shut off supply at its source. It therefore follows that until one has considered the full range of measures that would become available in the context of war, one need not resign oneself to a Hobson's choice of either crippling TOC or maintaining the drug prohibition regime.

The object of war, Clausewitz writes, is to break the enemy's will, normally by engaging and destroying his armed forces. One does what is necessary to that end; one accepts only the restraints consistent with that end. National frontiers are not among them. So if the United States launched a general war against trafficking and/or organized criminal organizations, what would it actually do? What measures would be most likely to bring victory expeditiously?

A grand strategy infused by wartime insensitivity to constitutional restraints and costs other than casualties to U.S. troops would have many of the following elements. With or, if necessary, without the permission of the concerned national governments, Americans would launch ground and air assaults against crops and processing facilities identified by U.S. national intelligence resources. These assaults would lace poppy and coca fields with powerful herbicides or incinerate them with napalm. Perhaps, after one or two demonstrative incinerations, it would suffice to threaten, on the one hand, and, on the other, to offer compensation to peasants who agree to liquidate their crops. If traffickers concluded that the threat would be executed, then they would have no incentive to compel campesinos to resist.

Traditionally, control of borders and unique responsibility for internal security and policing have been core (arguably the core) constituents of both sovereignty in relation to the external world and internal perceptions of legitimacy. Hence governments that allow or are unable to resist armed intrusions by a foreign state are virtually certain to experience a collapse of internal prestige, a cataclysmic loss of authority; that is, the capacity to govern with the consent, if not active support, of the governed. When that happens, if a government survives at all, then it does so only by ruling through brute force. In other words, a strategy of bringing war to the source of the narcotics traffic is very likely to destroy elected governments in the target states and could well make those states temporarily ungovernable. The collapse of central authority in Mexico has such catastrophic implications for its northern neighbor that the United States could not contemplate measures threatening to cause such a collapse without being prepared to occupy the country for an indefinite period.

The Liquidation Strategy

Making war against the mafia organizations themselves poses much the same risks. If war it were, then Americans would not tolerate the restraints imposed by national sovereignty and domestic interests in the home countries of these organizations. Neither enforcement activities by foreign governments nor the practice of extradition have proven very satisfactory, at least from a U.S. point of view. In some countries, the constitution itself prohibits the extradition of citizens. In others, nationalist sensitivities are nearly as preclusive. Where legal and political restraints are not at present a decisive obstacle, the legal process can be slow and is vulnerable to corruption and intimidation. Meanwhile, the target can slip away to parts unknown.

Arrest and prosecution of mafia leaders in their home countries has not proven a very satisfactory alternative in the Western Hemisphere any more than in Japan, other parts of Asia, and Russia. Colombia has imprisoned drug cartel leaders under negotiated conditions that left them free to continue operating their businesses in circumstances of ostentatious personal comfort. In Caribbean islands, prosecution is rare, conviction rarer still. Even in Italy, a member of the capitalist democratic core group, the criminal justice system has only recently performed its notional tasks effectively.

Having determined to treat the mafias as intolerable threats to vital national interests, once Americans went to war, they would necessarily resort to more dramatic means. Crushing pressure on governments, such as the threat of comprehensive economic sanctions identical to the U.S. boycott of Cuba, might force them to enlist in the war. But the decision to serve in effect as an arm of the U.S. criminal justice system might have much the same delegitimating effects as the failure to protect the national territory hypothesized above, and thus reduce the governments' capacity not only to liquidate the mafias but also to govern in general. A general weakening of governmental authority coinciding with even a successful antimafias campaign would, assuming no change in the global structure of incentives for smuggling, leave the society vulnerable to rapid recovery and enhancement of criminal organizations.

Rather than leaning on the weak reed of national enforcement mechanisms, for fear of shattering them, the United States might take direct action, either by large-scale intrusion, as in Panama, or through lethal strikes against the homes and offices of persons believed to be mafia leaders. Since other societies are unlikely to share the U.S. claim that mafia activity justifies armed intervention, they would see the military strikes as acts of aggression violating the most important norms of the UN Charter and of global customary law. Elected governments would be under enormous pressure to respond belligerently—for instance by cutting diplomatic ties and confiscating the assets of U.S. investors. And one could expect a rallying of hemispheric governments into an anti-U.S. coalition. Nor in today's interconnected world would the reverberations be limited to the region. Condemnation would be global and Americans would undoubtedly be forced to veto a Security Council resolution under chapter VII of its charter condemning the U.S. action, forbidding its renewal, and demanding reparations. Widespread termination of security arrangements with the United States, including the sharing of national intelligence, would accompany formal condemnation. Cooperation in other areas is bound then to be gravely depleted.

Even the threat of economic sanctions to compel more forceful action by governments against persons thought to constitute the senior personnel of criminal organizations could damage U.S. economic interests. The objects of these sanction threats that are members of the World Trade Organization (WTO) would challenge their validity under WTO rules. Since the challenge would almost certainly be upheld, if the United States refused to accept the result and withdraw its threat, then it would precipitate a dialectic of retaliation that could poison the atmosphere and ravage the institutions of the global trading system.

Aside from its unintended but fairly predictable consequences, direct action might not achieve its goal of shattering organized crime. If the morphology of organized crime approximated what Tom Naylor calls the "Godfather Model," that is, a centrally ruled, hierarchically structured criminal conspiracy to control global markets for goods and services,[89] then direct action might seem rationally related to the goal of crippling the operational capacity of organized crime now and for some time to come. If the Godfather Model approximated reality, then it would seem to follow that by incapacitating the conspiracy's head (of, if you prefer, smashing its spine), consisting of a small number of people most of whom could be targeted by a concentration of national intelligence assets, one would destroy its coherence and leave its multiple limbs twitching aimlessly.

For better or worse, reality and the model do not closely coincide. In a paper on the policing and control of organized crime prepared for the British government, a leading U.K. authority, Professor Barry Rider of the University of Cambridge and the University of London, presents the following numeric account of essentially independent criminal organizations in the countries the most powerful groups call home: in Russia, more than 3,000; in Japan, more than 3,300 (the Yakuza); in Italy, more than 200 ("clans," he calls them) with roots variously in Sicily (the cinegenic mafia), Calabria (the Ndrangheta), and Naples (the Camorra).[90] Before their decapitation by the Colombian government (reportedly with the help of information provided by drug lords based in Cali), a handful of figures prominent in the Medellín-based drug enterprises were frequently referred to as a cartel. Journalists, undoubtedly relying on various official sources, often asserted that the cartel controlled some 80 percent of the cocaine trade. Yet their decimation appeared to cause hardly a ripple in the price of cocaine, and in the press, rather than concluding that it faced a market with many actual or latent producers and distributors, simply transferred the 80 percent figure to the so-called Cali group. The subsequent arrest of its senior figures also failed to achieve serious market disruption.

To be fair, the numbers and market history can be misleading. Mafia groups vary greatly in size and competence. In Russia, out of the several thousand gangs, perhaps 200 are enterprises marked by coherent hierarchy, endurance, strategic planning, and division of function.[91] Ganglets specializing in small-time extortion or highjacking are not an international threat, however much of a nuisance they are to entrepreneurs trying to function in the Russian environment. In Italy, the trials of the past decade exposed within the Sicilian mafia a coordinating hierarchy performing the functions of an underworld government. Naylor is clearly correct in rejecting the entrepreneurial model that depicts criminals as essentially highly individualistic entrepreneurs and criminal organizations as little more than informal trade associations or old-boys' networks united in a disdain for the normal niceties of business behavior. The trouble with this buoyant free-enterprise model, he argues persuasively, is its facile extension of free-market theory (with its assumptions of open competition among equals and the flow of free information) into the criminal economy, where the three Fs—force, fraud, and fealty—are prime determinants of the distribution of reward.[92]

Reality appears to fall somewhere between these two models. Among the hundreds and possibly thousands of ganglets worldwide that operate to some degree across national frontiers, it would appear that at least several dozen have the features enumerated just above that the words *organized* and *enterprise* call to mind. They know how to contact each other and they do collaborate opportunistically. By virtue of their number and hierarchic organization, they present a determinate number of targets susceptible to elimination by direct action. Looking only at the short term, it would not, then, be like swatting flies in a tropical garbage dump.

On the other hand, decapitation strategy is not without precedent. In Italy, the mass trials of the past few years have decimated the senior ranks of the Sicilian mafia. Decimation, together with suspension of the symbiotic relationship between dominant elements of the Italian political elite and the criminal organizations, has reduced their power at least to the point where the Italian government believes it can withdraw troops from Sicily and govern more or less normally with the aid of the police. But no one, absolutely no one believes that the Sicilian mafia or its Calabrian and Neapolitan counterparts (also stripped of the thick political insulation enjoyed for decades or more) has been wiped out. The Sicilian mafia came closest to its destruction during the two decades of fascist rule. Yet even Mussolini, employing authoritarian measures that a democratic state can rarely employ and never sustain, succeeded only in repressing, not eliminating, the organizations, and they quickly rehabilitated themselves in the benign climate of post-World War II Christian Democratic government.

Largely for the reasons enumerated earlier, the contemporary climate worldwide is considerably more propitious. The drug trade alone has shown itself insensitive to the incapacitation of supposedly major figures. Of course, in my hypothetical case, multiple organizations would be targeted simultaneously for execution or incarceration under severe conditions. I see no reason to doubt U.S. capability to cause much greater disruption than has been possible acting within the constraints of international and U.S. constitutional law. But I also see no reason to doubt the rapid reemergence of enterprises, summoned by market opportunities, as soon as the United States relaxes its war posture. Moreover, as I have already suggested, the damage inflicted on national political systems and international cooperation by wartime measures ought to facilitate not merely the renewal of organized criminal groups but also their growth to new heights. Furthermore, the United States could employ the methods of war only in the Caribbean and Latin America. The potential costs and consequences of overt, large-scale, direct action against mafia groups in China, Japan, Russia, or even Italy, initiated without the consent of the particular country's recognized government, are so clearly preclusive that incorporation of that scenario would destroy the mind game's heuristic value.

One can envision cases where threatened criminal organizations, perhaps in alliance with dissident political elites and/or kleptocratic military officers, pose a direct military challenge to the regime, threatening not merely its overthrow but also the physical liquidation of its leaders and their supporters, that is, of a whole political class. Something very much like this did occur in Bolivia and could occur in Colombia, Mexico, and other Latin American, and especially Caribbean countries. A regime in extremis might plausibly call on the United States for assistance in suppressing the hypothesized insurrection. Intervention at the invitation of a generally recognized government is by no means novel, is not clearly inconsistent with traditional notions of national sovereignty, and for that reason, would not necessarily threaten the norms and institutions of international cooperation. Nor, under the circumstances, should it have a severely detrimental impact on the authority of the imperiled regime. In addition, by virtue of acting in conjunction with a legitimate national government, the United States could more plausibly hope to effect changes in the legal and institutional conditions in the target society that encouraged the growth of powerful criminal organizations.

Going for the Money

The third arm of a war strategy would be aimed at the income of organized crime. Of course it is part of the contemporary policing effort, carried out, however, within the constraints of a peacetime regime. Thanks to reporting requirements backed by serious penalties, U.S. banks no longer have a drive-through window for large cash deposits of dubious provenance. Crackdowns on checking, cashing, and money-exchange operations have narrowed, if not entirely closed, the window of laundering opportunities they once generously provided. Energetic policing may have reduced the efficacy of other traditional laundering strategies, such as the large-scale purchase for export of high-cost items like luxury cars. As a result, criminal enterprises have been reduced to exporting cash in bulk, exploiting the same intensely used, lightly policed borders facilitating the import of forbidden product.

Once clear of U.S. customs, dirty money, like money in general, enjoys the benefits of a liberal international financial order. As Francisco Thoumi points out in chapter 6, drug money moved more readily into Colombia once the government responded to the demands of the global marketplace by reducing its controls on financial flows generally. What I would call second-order pressure on the world-girdling tax haven archipelago has induced varying degrees of cooperation from archipelago states. Under the umbrella of bilateral legal assistance agreements, a substantial number now allow U.S. investigators to pierce the veil of banking and corporate secrecy. For the most part, however, this is only in instances where the United States can offer substantial evidence that accounts are drug-tainted. Investigations of tax evasion (even if instituted as a different route for getting at organized crime figures), securities fraud, and other crimes still run headlong in most places into an impenetrable wall of state-protected secrecy.[93] Pressure from Washington combined with pressures from the respectable private sector, expressed in the form of an operational preference for untainted tax havens, has also helped to catalyze greater efforts within some archipelago states to block use of local financial institutions for laundering. But the cleansing of one opens the door for another eager to enter the tax haven market. Moreover, because cleansing is largely limited to drug traffickers and money easily traceable to trafficking organizations, even the sanitized states can function as comfort stations for tainted money and enterprises. The net result, at this point, is a rise in the cost of laundering, from perhaps fifteen percent to as much as a fifty percent discount, an amount prohibitive for most businesses but only an irritant for enterprises earning superprofits in clandestine markets.[94]

If the United States went to war against organized crime, it would demand expeditious access to bank and corporate records of any individuals or corporations it reasonably suspected to be engaged in fraud, racketeering, or any other sort of organized criminal enterprise, including every form of smuggling, not excluding cigarettes. Recalcitrant venues, whether independent states or proto-colonial appendages of European countries, would be subject to total economic blockades of the comprehensive sort the United States has imposed on Cuba for the past forty years. U.S. companies, including their foreign subsidiaries, would be barred from any financial contact with the target venues, and foreign financial institutions with branches or subsidiaries there would be barred from doing business in the United States. Washington would deny visas to residents of the recalcitrants and landing rights to airlines that flew them from whatever place. Coincidentally the U.S. would offer financial carrots in the form of direct payments (even, if it seemed efficient, to officials for their personal use), increased access to U.S. markets for manufactured goods, and so on.

At existing levels of concern about organized crime, the United States would have to anticipate a furious response from traditional allies, the U.K. government prominent among them, since its appendages both in the Caribbean and in waters adjacent to Britain are leading tax havens with a history of ferocious attachment to banking secrecy. The City of London itself is believed not to be overly fastidious about the origins of the vast financial flows that make it one of the two great financial capitals of the world. Furthermore, most advanced capitalist states have bitterly resisted the extraterritorial application of U.S. laws—for instance antitrust and securities legislation—as a matter of principle. Nevertheless, there has already been some initial movement in this direction. Presidential Decision Directive 42 (PDD–42), a classified executive order issued in 1995, directs the executive branch to identify the most egregious overseas sanctuaries for illegally obtained wealth and begin negotiations with these countries to end safe-haven status.[95]

One additional wartime thrust against the financial underbelly of organized crime would entail freezing bank and brokerage accounts and exclusion from all U.S. markets and from contact with U.S. corporations and financial institutions of individuals and companies believed to be associated with organized criminal enterprises. On a limited basis, one commensurate with limited or low-intensity general war, the Clinton administration has already moved on this front. In addition to calling for negotiations to end safe-haven status, PDD–42 orders steps requiring U.S. banks to freeze the assets of Colombian drug traffickers, their associates, and front companies, and states that the Secretary of the Treasury "shall prohibit any U.S. person from engaging in financial transactions or trade with those identified individuals or enterprises." According to the *Washington Post*, the Treasury Department's Office of Foreign Assets Control (OFAC) has already issued a list of eighty names, including four drug kingpins, forty-three associates, and thirty-three businesses.[96]

Grand Strategies: Low-Intensity Conflict

PDD–42 may signify readiness to move beyond treating transnational organized crime as a problem mainly of the U.S. criminal justice system, a problem to be dealt with through federal and state policing and low-pressure interstate cooperation. Action is beginning to creep toward a rendezvous with the rhetoric of national security. Vigorously enforced and expanded to countries other than Colombia, the directive's methods would be integral to a strategy located somewhere between the fading operational status quo and general war, a strategy usefully thought of as low-intensity conflict.

Premised on a sense of acute threat to fundamental interests, general war envisions a rapid return to the Eden of peace. Low-intensity conflict is a term more appropriate to engaging with a chronic threat to less-than-fundamental intersts, a hydra-headed enemy immune to termination by one heroic exercise of national will. The cold war fell somewhere in between, the perceived interests at risk being huge but the threat appearing permanent.

Low-intensity conflict could easily embrace all of the strategies I associated with the posture of general war, executed, however, with more restraint, more respect for unintended consequences, more sensitivity to international opinion. For instance, in seeking to impose transparency and rectitude on tax havens, it would be selective in its targets and comparatively restrained in defining the occasions and procedures for access to information about account holders and real beneficiaries of trusts and actual owners of corporations, and, in the face of unyielding recalcitrance, would calculate the breadth of its sanctions with an eye to the sensitivities of the British, French, and other important actors in the world financial order. Quite possibly, internal pressures from the U.S. citizens and corporations that make generous use of the tax havens, much of it probably licit, would in any event limit the understandable and legitimate impulse to pry them open.

Securing general support among the G–7 for a tougher line on dirty-money havens may well be possible. All of the European countries are concerned about organized crime. Moreover, forcing more transparency on financial havens serves a common concern about another beneficiary of the hot-money centers, namely international terrorist organizations. Concern will only grow in the wake of the U.S. embassy bombings in Africa and with growing anxiety about terrorist use of chemical and biological weapons. Within a three-month period, from June to August 1998, *The Economist*, that bellwether of advanced elite thought in the transatlantic community, published major stories focusing on prospective terrorist use of weapons of mass destruction.[97] And in a lead editorial during the same period,[98] it urged governments to agree on a set of universal antilaundering standards, in the same way that they hammered out minimum capital requirements for banks in the early 1990s. Countries that flouted such standards would be sent to quarantine, with punitive taxes on capital flows to and from them imposed by other financial centers.

Outside a general war frame of reference, direct military intervention would with rare exceptions be limited to cases of invitation from a recognized government. Arguably enjoying a general exemption from international law's nonintervention norm,[99] it would be easiest to defend both legally and politically where the invitation came from an elected government threatened by criminals acting alone or in conjunction with political dissidents or corrupted military factions. Moreover, by virtue of acting in conjunction with a legitimate national government, the U.S. could more plausibly hope to effect changes in the legal and institutional conditions in the target society which encouraged the growth of powerful criminal organizations.

The Relationship between the State and Criminal Organizations in Conditions of Low-Intensity Conflict

Almost all relationships, the most romantic and even in most instances the harshly antagonistic, lie somewhere between the poles of pure cooperation and normless conflict. Out of people's need for a degree of predictability in their lives and the habitual character of so much human behavior, expectations about positive acts and reciprocal constraints emerge in almost all sustained human and institutional interactions. And as they are confirmed by practice and become the organizing structures of individual and institutional life, they acquire a normative character, that is, a quality of oughtness. There were rules of the game in the cold war; for instance, after the missile crisis, both sides struggled mightily to avoid circumstances that could lead to a direct confrontation between Soviet and U.S. forces. And traditionally, there have been rules of the game, however thin and brittle, between the police and the organized underworld. The first *Godfather* movie exhibited one: that police were normally not legitimate targets for gangland attack, unless one became a corrupt participant in intramural mafia conflicts.

The relationship between uncorrupted police organizations and the criminal underworld is complicated. In theory the former is dedicated to the latter's elimination. However, while destruction of criminal enterprises is part of their mandate, honest no less than cynical police officials recognize the permanence of illicit commerce in a market economy with a democratic and constitutional political order and therefore the utility, if not the inevitability, of understandings, more or less tacit, about how the hunters will pursue and their notional prey defend themselves.

Beyond some small measure of mutual restraint, there will be at least brief moments of collaboration. In time of war, criminal organizations may assist in identifying enemy agents, as the mob-dominated longshoremen's union on the East Coast of the United States did during World War II.[100] In time of peace, they might join in the hunt for an unauthorized assassin of police officers lest the police take reprisals against the organization as a whole.

Political versus Commercial Criminal Organizations

Occasionally, individual and group enmity crescendos to a point of mutual incomprehension and a hatred so intense as to admit no limits. As in the case of the apocryphal scorpion who stings the frog ferrying him across a stream, killing is the nature of their relationship. Communal conflict may not begin at that point but often escalates there by virtue of reciprocated brutality. Ideological conflicts can be no less murderous, though usually not, these days, if the combatants are states; in part because the present state system frowns, as its predecessors did not, on the elimination of any state actors; in part because states form identifiable and in varying degrees vulnerable targets. But ideologically driven confrontations between a state and a nonstate actor slide toward the virulence of intercommunal war.

The nonstate actor usually has fewer and smaller resources than the state. Its strength lies in its elusiveness and its lack of constraint in the employment of the limited force at its disposal. Never having experienced the responsibility and sobering compromises attendant upon actually governing a territory, it can more easily sustain a murderous purity of aims. Moreover, nongovernmental institutions using extreme violence, that is, terrorist groups, almost invariably emerge from some terrible trauma that leaves in its wake a searing passion for revenge. To the governments and peoples on which it declares war, the group's qualities and operations elicit fear, contempt, and revulsion. And its uncompromising rhetoric—instinct in a movement that must galvanize acolytes for missions of great danger and goals with little immediate prospect of fulfilment—no less than its behavior and puniness, discourages its opponents from even contemplating negotiation about ends or means.

Official discourse by U.S. government officials sometimes conflates and often pairs terrorism and organized crime, so that they appear either as two sides of the same coin or threats of equal virulence. But are they? Certainly there is ample evidence in recent experience that commercially as well as politically motivated groups will employ terror against state and society on behalf of organizational goals. Led by the sociopath, Pablo Escobar, the Medellín drug mafias ripped at the roots of Colombian democracy with a multiyear campaign of bombings and assassinations that reached into the highest levels of national politics. (Ironically, however, the goal of their declared "absolute and total war" against the Colombian state was to acquire the status of political criminals and thereby to qualify for a government amnesty.[101]) The Sicilian mafia gunned down a general and his wife, blew up the state's leading antimafia prosecutors, and bombed a priceless part of Italy's artistic heritage. And even when they target only private individuals, such as entrepreneurs in Russia who refuse offers of protection, mafias can cripple the state by driving out capital and discouraging enterprise. So one cannot categorically distinguish the two sorts of criminal enterprises on the basis either of their impact on political order or their readiness to use violence indiscriminately and/or against state officials.

Still, the difference in their purposes would appear to make violent political groups even more threatening to a democratic state and liberal society in a majority of concrete instances. The liberal-democratic state is not merely compatible with purely commercial criminal organizations, it offers the ideal setting in which to conduct illicit business. While the liberal-democratic state's character inhibits a lethal, no-holds-barred assault on organized crime, its relatively open borders and markets facilitate criminal enterprise. Hence assaults against the state directly or through terrorization of the general society are rational, in the case of mature criminal organizations, only as instruments of self-defense in the face of a threat to survival. Casual recourse to terror simply as a means of augmenting profits and reducing the normal risks of conviction and imprisonment will inevitably drive the state to make war on the organization, as ultimately occurred in Colombia.

Virtually by definition, the liberal-democratic state, *as constituted in particular cases*, is *incompatible* with the purposes of groups that assault it violently. For it is the perceived inability to achieve their ends through democratic avenues that inclines politically motivated groups toward terrorist means calculated, not always wisely, to price the electorate's extant policy preferences out of the market. The group may spring from a despised minority effectively excluded from majority electoral coalitions. It may act in the name of societies and peoples outside the target state yet powerfully affected by its policies. Whatever their origins, such groups demand wrenching and costly changes in the policies of the target state, changes generally seen by its elite and electorate as hugely costly in moral or material terms. In this important respect, then, they differ from most criminal organizations, since the latter usually seek no more than a certain degree of tolerance, that is, restraint in the measures the state employs to enforce its prohibitions.

If the suggested distinction—a priori in tone but rooted in contemporary experience—is persuasive, then it argues against a facile equation of international crime and international terrorism. If the U.S. missile attacks on installations in Sudan and Afghanistan (believed to be controlled by the Saudi terrorist Osama Bin Laden) is a mere prologue, then we can now anticipate increasing recourse by strong states to direct cross-border attacks on terrorist groups carried out with the frank purpose of annihilation, as well as still more intense pressure on states where terrorist leaders take refuge to imprison or extradite them, at a minimum. In other words, at least in relationship to certain politically motivated nongovernmental organizations, the U.S. has followed the Israeli position, implemented over several decades, of treating the conflictual relationship as one justifying the methods of general war. If for national security accounting one equates political and commercial criminal organizations, then the logic of that choice calls for waging general war against the latter as well.

Whether that would be a wise posture is a matter subject to considerable doubt. Confronting criminal organizations with the threat of sudden assault by land or air on their homes and enterprises or even with arrest, trial by summary procedures, and life imprisonment would remove all incentives for restraint on their part. As I noted earlier, assault on the very fabric of the states and societies that nurture them is irrational behavior for criminal enterprises, as long as they are not threatened with extinction. Once so threatened, they may be as ready as the most virulent clandestine political organizations to use any means, including biological, chemical, and nuclear weapons, that promise to deter. And they are almost surely better financed for that purpose. With a fortune estimated at $250 million, Osama Bin Laden is able by himself to maintain a complex network of businesses and intelligence and training facilities able to mount dangerous attacks on U.S. citizens and government installations. Compared to the income of drug businesses alone—$7 billion a year estimated for the Mexican cartels—Bin

Laden's capital just does not seem like a lot of money. Moreover, large-scale smuggling operations being at the core of its business, organized crime presumably has a far more elaborate and refined clandestine logistics establishment than any terrorist organization is likely to match. It could, therefore, prove a still more formidable foe to the United States and other states should they choose *la guerre à outrance*. On the other hand, it could prove a useful collaborator in operations against politically driven groups, particularly in gathering intelligence about their efforts to move operatives and to secure and deploy weapons. Conversely, it could multiply the danger to Western interests if pushed into collaboration with such groups for purposes of collective self-defense.

I am speaking here only about a general policy orientation, knowing from experience that in the day-to-day life of governments, such orientations tend to govern quotidian policy to the detriment of nuanced appreciation of particular instances in which policy must be applied. It is not my intention to endorse a policy of unrestrained and mindless violence against every illicit political enterprise that directly or indirectly challenges U.S. policy preferences. Force is an instrument of, not an alternative to, politics. Every organization that uses force against civilian or nonmilitary governmental installations or against democratic governments is not by virtue of that tactic irreconcilably hostile to Western interests. The African National Congress during its struggle against apartheid rule in South Africa is only one case in point. I was only warning against the reflexive extrapolation of a general war posture from the antiterrorist campaign to the struggle with organized crime *in cases where it is easy to distinguish the two from each other.* As I noted earlier, organizations with ostensible political goals not infreqently support them through mainstream criminal enterprise. On the other hand, a criminal enterprise that begins with commercial goals alone may, like the Medellín cartel, incorporate political goals for the purposes of self-defense. Moreover, organizations with different goals may cooperate for reasons of efficiency, much less survival where the state simultaneously attacks them.

A prudent government will be cautious about employing either the rhetoric or the means of general war in dealing with illicit enterprises irrespective of their goals. Violence will remain a necessary instrument in the armory of public policy, but one that almost always has costly side effects and not only unintended but wholly unforeseen consequences. So like extraterritorial application of national law and other unilateral measures, it needs to be applied with circumspection and only after the careful appreciation of costs and benefits in concrete circumstances.

Certainly at this historical moment of feverish and legitimate concern about political terrorism, the United States is far more disposed to make real war on clandestine *political* opponents than on *kleptocratic* ones. That disposition is likely to obscure opportunities for the reconciliation of ends and hence for peace. With respect to mafias, peace is unattainable, since by their nature, by their very definition, they are opponents of society's chosen policies. They do the forbidden. If they did something else, then they would not be criminal. It is their ends no less than their means that are inimical to the public interest. Violent political groups use forbidden and often heinous means, but not necessarily to intolerable ends. Zionists of the Zabotinsky persuasion used terror tactics to achieve an independent Jewish state. Terror tactics were not unknown to the followers of the genuinely saintly Nelson Mandela as they struggled against the obscenity of apartheid. Even where political ends are morally problematical, as in the case of the IRA campaign in Northern Ireland, their very character as political ends may open the way to compromise.

Conciliating violent political enterprises does not necessarily require the abdication of values and interests. Conciliating mafias always does, for what they seek is not a reconceptualization of the public interest, that is, the formal legalization of their trades, but a change in the enforcement of those interests. Legalization could put them out of business, for in the world of licit business, the comparative advantage of criminal enterprises—their facility in using force and fraud and their propensity to ferocious reciprocal fealty—is inoperative. *The nub of the matter, then, is that iron responses to violent NGOs of all types and character, responses premised on a Manichean perception of them, are no substitute for case-specific strategic judgments.*

That is not a formula for pacifism. Low-intensity conflict is still conflict and may require the threat or application of force. In the Caribbean, for instance, it is not difficult to envision the takeover of one or more island governments by criminal organizations. As it is, many governments show signs of deep penetration by or an independent taste for wholesale collaboration with drug lords. If governments, albeit elected, are unwilling or unable to prevent their territory from serving as an entrepot and laundering center for operations profoundly detrimental to licit global financial systems or the public health and safety of citizens in other countries, then "sovereignty" is not a bar to defensive measures by the affected states. Ideally they would be executed within the framework of a League of Democratic States formed by the Caribbean regimes and the United States together with Canada, France, the Netherlands, and the United Kingdom, the other countries with strong Caribbean connections.[102]

If, as I and many others believe, the supply of drugs has the ineluctable quality of an oceanic tide, then the problem is primarily one of demand, and if the other transnational services and products of organized crime—vehicles, migrants, prostitutes, and so forth—are malignant but not lethal, then on what grounds should Americans fight even a low-intensity conflict? Why not just go on with the classical game of cops and robbers, perhaps even seeing mafiosi in most countries as upwardly mobile elites who, as they become secure through the investment of laundered funds in licit enterprises, will gradually be assimilated into the established order, assuming they live that long? Why invest heavily in combating those who will ultimately join, rather than overturn, legitimate society?

The reasons for an affirmative answer run along the following lines. These are not classical times. For the reasons I sketched earlier, including, on the one hand, unparalleled ease (in the economic, psychological, and technological, not simply in the political sense) of movement across frontiers and, on the other, a lag in the evolution of transnational regulatory and policing mechanisms, both ease and lag occurring in the context of a ubiquitous postideological ethos of atomized consumption, organized crime enjoys unparalleled opportunities for expansion and cross-national cooperation. Without an extraordinary response from concerned governments led by the United States, criminal enterprises will enjoy progressively more stable, extensive, and sophisticated infrastructures for moving money, people, and commodities anywhere in the world.

As core enterprises themselves become more stable and protected by the influence stemming from great wealth and lethality, they will, following organizational logic, engage in long-range strategic planning, which must include self-defense among its subjects. Planning for self-defense leads to measures of preemption and deterrence. Preemption could be implemented by a variety of means damaging to liberal-democratic political orders: the systematic corruption and inculpation of senior officials and political leaders; assassination of politicians who resist an informal policy of tolerance for illicit enterprise; and the actual seizure of state power through tractable agents. The very effort to preempt, much less permit, its successful execution, would hollow out democratic institutions; the wide cynicism it would induce would, ironically, facilitate the subsequent seizure of power by persons and parties committed to the ruthless restoration of order by any means. Deterrence will ultimately encourage acquisition of biological, chemical, and even nuclear weapons, although mafias will continue to have more disincentives than terrorists with respect to their use.

Where, if anywhere, mafia chiefs evolve into respectable bourgeois gentlefolk, they will be able, like those with wealth acquired (one way or another) many generations earlier, to rely for self-defense principally on the state and will share in the general interest of preserving the state's ability to act effectively. But is such evolution likely to occur in many cases or in time periods relevant to national strategic planning? Certainly as long as the narcotics prohibition regime is in place, the illicit sector will continue to offer hyperprofits unavailable in the licit one. In addition, the type of person initially attracted to and successful in areas of business marked by secrecy and a readiness for violence is less likely than the average person to resist the centripetal pull of hyperprofits. He or she, moreover, may reasonably conclude that operating exclusively in the licit economy will be difficult because it will not reward what has hitherto been an integral part of their comparative advantage, namely an aptitude for corruption and violence.

Let us suppose that some capos opt for the straight life. They will not take with them the entire establishment of their organizations. Lesser figures will want to acquire the wealth that enabled those at the very top to make the move to respectability. This is not mere speculation. Contemporary experience does not encourage confidence in the assimilationist scenario. The Italian clans have amassed great wealth since World War II. And they formed until recently so close and symbiotic a relationship with Italy's anti-Communist regime as to be virtually a part of the country's effective government, at least in the southern part of the country. Yet they remained apart, engaged in political and economic projects incompatible with a market-driven capitalist economy and a liberal-democratic state. They remained violent bands committed to extortionate profits and the unrestrained delivery of goods and services whatever their consequences for the general welfare of Italian society.

Low-intensity conflict is not business as usual. It calls for tough decisions. If Washington is serious, then it must seek to dam the river of money flowing to organized crime, above all from the traffic in narcotics. That means elimination of the monopoly given to organized crime by the current prohibition regime. It means concerted, harsh action against the respectable corporations and lawyers, bankers, and accountants who regularly provide goods or services to criminal enterprise. It means forcing on the world's financial centers and institutions a level of transparency, self-policing, and cooperation with the public authorities of responsible states calculated to disturb not only core participants in international organized crime but also all those who seek, even in the most advanced liberal-democratic states, to conceal their transactions from governments regulators and tax collectors.

A call to face tough issues and, implicitly, to show some toughness in resolving them is not a coded appeal for aggressive unilateralism. It is extraordinarily unlikely that the United States, acting alone, could impose much higher standards of diligence and cooperation on leading financial centers. It will be hard enough for the leading economic powers, acting together, to impose on private financial institutions and the governments of hot-money havens the reporting systems and other measures required to expose the movements of funds generated by illicit operations. Aggressive unilateralism in other areas—for instance, securing jurisdiction over suspected criminals by kidnapping rather than attempting to extradite them, or threatening economic sanctions against traditionally friendly governments deemed insufficiently energetic or severe in confronting organize crime—is also calculated to miss its mark while impeding cooperation across a wide range of other national security issues.

As the United States wages low-intensity conflict with organized crime, its officials need to recall that a major cause for the concerns fueling their efforts is the discrepancy between transnational opportunities for the feloniously inclined and transnational structures of supervision and enforcement. Cops are cooperating more across borders but within the constraints of a system still structured by notions of national sovereignty conceived in the vastly different circumstances of the seventeenth century. Building the institutional structures that will enable cops to keep pace with agile and cosmopolitan criminal enterprise demands more than architectural ingenuity on the part of the United States and other countries. It also demands the practice of cooperation.

Cooperation in interstate relations requires the superpower to accept results in some individual cases that appear to it, but not to its collaborators, as suboptimal. If transnational organized crime presented an acute threat to fundamental interests, if it were closely analogous to the Soviet threat of the cold-war era, then there would be a case for the attitudes and methods of general war. War, with its lethal quotidian risks, must sharply discount the longer term. So it is not the natural friend of restraint on behalf of institutions yet to be.

But even in wartime, wise leaders sometimes take the longer view, offering to compromise immediate objectives for longer-term gains, because they know that victory is only the prelude to new risks and opportunities. And the United States is not at war, nor should it contemplate war with a problem that is chronic rather than acute, more than a nuisance but less than a threat to fundamental interests. Transnational organized crime is but one of the challenges faced by the capitalist democracies in a time of uncertainty and in the place where all peoples live: East of Eden.

NOTES

1. Raymond Bonner, "EU Seeks U.S. Help Against Cigarette Traffic," *New York Times Service*, 9 May 1998, 3.
2. In its reported insouciance about the channels through which its product moves to market, R. J. Reynolds enjoys no peculiar distinction. According to one report, the value of the combined cigarette exports of all the major tobacco companies to the island nation of Aruba, a traditional beachhead for cigarette smuggling into the northern rim of South America, is about four times the minicountry's gross domestic product. If that is true even to a rough order of magnitude, then assuming every man, woman, and child resident of Aruba and all of its tourists chain-smoke twenty-four hours a day from every available bodily orifice, a considerable residue of imported cigarettes still would be available for undocumented exports.
3. See, for one of a thousand instances, Max G. Manwaring, "Security of the Western Hemisphere: International Terrorism and Organized Crime," in *Strategic Forum*, National Defense University, Institute for National Strategic Studies, no. 137, Apr. 1988.
4. By not seeking to outlaw smoking, governments implicitly maintain that while tobacco is inherently injurious, it is not intolerably so.
5. See for example, Louis Freeh's Keynote Address at the Center for Strategic and International Studies Conference on Global Organized Crime in Frank J. Cillufo and Linnea P. Raine, eds., *Global Organized Crime: The New Evil Empire*, (Washington, DC: CSIS, 1996), 1–14.
6. See for example, Henry Freidman and Sander Meredeen, *The Dynamics of Industrial Conflict* (London: Croom Helm, 1980).
7. For detailed histories of the Teamsters, see Steven Brill, *The Teamsters* (New York: Simon & Schuster, 1978). For an insider perspective, also see Allen Friedman and Ted Schwartz, *Power and Greed: Inside the Teamsters Empire of Corruption* (New York: Franklin Watts, 1989).
8. See generally Roger Y. W. Tang, *Transfer Pricing in the 1900s: Tax and Management Perspectives* (London/Westport: Quorum Books, 1993) and *Tax Aspects of Transfer Pricing Within Multinational Enterprises: The U.S. Proposed Regulations* (Paris: OECD, 1993).
9. See generally Matthew Josephson, *Robber Barons: The Great American Capitalists, 1861–1901* (New York: Harcourt, Brace & Co., 1934).
10. Compare the definition of organized crime by an expert on its Russian manifestation, Anatoli Volubuev: "[As it appears in Russia, organized crime is] a negative social phenomenon, characterized by the unification of a criminal group on a regional or national basis with a division on hierarchical levels and selections of leaders, having organizational, administrative and ideological functions; use of corruption, attracting into criminal activities state officials (including law enforcement officials) for maintaining security for the participants; . . . monopolization and widening of spheres of illegal activity with the goal of achieving maximum material

income while maintaining maximum protection of the highest echelons from prosecution." (quoted in Frederico Varese, "Is Sicily the Future of Russia? Private Protection and the Rise of the Russian Mafia," *Archives Européennes de Sociologie* 35, no. 2 (1994): 224, fn. 4.

11. Profits may not be the only or even the primary goal of organizations engaged in drug production and distribution, kidnapping, bank robbery, and other "common crimes." Antistate groups seeking change through violence quite commonly use crime to finance their activities. See the discussion of political versus commercial organized crime in the final section of this chapter.

12. R. T. Naylor, "From Cold War to Crime War: The Search for a New National Security Threat," *Transnational Organized Crime* 1, no. 4 (Winter) 1995.

13. One of its earliest moves was an attempt to galvanize a Mexican war on drugs. The most conspicuous means chosen for that end was the initiation of comprehensive inspection for every vehicle seeking to cross into the United States. The resulting paralysis was such that after some days of chest thumping, the White House dropped the de facto blockade. Perhaps what really moved Nixon was an epiphanal appreciation of the way in which U.S. vulnerability to a tidal wave of immigrants fleeing any breakdown in the Mexican political order had stood the old power relationship on its head.

14. Of cash much can and has been said, including that in large quantities it is very heavy and space-consuming. Jack Blum's story (see Chapter 3) of the drug dealer who packed a whole house with it captures a sense of the dimensions.

15. See R. T. Naylor, *Hot Money and the Politics of Debt* (New York: Linden Press, Simon & Schuster, 1987), 288.

16. Ibid.

17. The Bank Secrecy Act of 1970 stipulates that all transaction above $10,000 must be reported.

18. See the discussion in chapter 3, as well as Mark Hampton, *The Offshore Interface: Tax Havens in the Global Economy* (New York: St. Martin's Press, 1996).

19. Ibid., 14.

20. See for example, Ingo Walter's commentary about Panama, in *Secret Money: The World of International Financial Secrecy* (Lexington, MA: Lexington Books, 1985), 116.

21. Compare Peter Andreas's analysis in chapter 4 of this volume.

22. The point is central to the work of one of the most distinguished analysts of the Mafia phenomenon in Italy, Diego Gambetta; see *The Mafia: The Business of Private Protection* (Cambridge: Harvard University Press, 1993).

23. See chapter 1.

24. The report is cited in Marina Cristina Caballero, "La guerilla billionaria," *Cambio*, 16 July 1998, 28.

25. Quoted in R. T. Naylor, "From Cold War to Crime War: The Search for a New National Security Threat," *Transnational Organized Crime* 1 no. 4 (Winter 1995) 37.

26. Linnea P. Raine and Frank J. Cillufo, eds., Center for Strategic and International Studies (Washington, D.C. 1995).

27. See *Restatement of the Law, Third: The Foreign Relations Law of the United States* (Washington, D.C.: American Law Institute, 1984) sections 421–23, 304–19, vol. II.

28. See generally, Joel S. Solomon, "Forming a More Secure Union: The Growing Problem of Organized Crime in Europe as a Challenge to National Sovereignty," *Dickinson Journal of International Law* 13 (Spring) 1995.

29. See Claire Sterling, *Thieves' World* (New York: 1994).

30. See Stephen Kobrin, "Electronic Cash and the End of National Markets," *Foreign Policy*, Summer 1997.

31. See for example, the discussion about "hacking" at the Center for Strategic and International Conference on Global Organized Crime in Frank J. Cillufo and Linnea

P. Raine, eds., *Global Organized Crime: The New Evil Empire* (Washington, D.C.: SIS, 1996), 37–59.

32. Anthony Trollope, *The Way We Live Now*, introduction by Robert Tracy (Indianapolis: Bobbs-Merrill, 1974). The original was published in 1874.

33. For a full discussion of the BCCI, see Mark Potts, Nicholas Kochan, and Robert Whittington, *Dirty Money: BCCI: The Inside Story of the World's Sleaziest Bank* (Washington, D.C.: National Press Books, 1992).

34. For an extensive description of Robert Vesco and Bernie Cornfield's activities and exploits, see generally Naylor, *Hot Money*, p. 40 et seq., fn. 15 above.

35. See generally, Naylor, fn. 15.

36. See generally, Kitty Calavita, Henry N. Pontell, and Robert H. Tillman, *Big Money Crime* (Berkeley: University of California Press, 1997); but cf. *The S&L Insurance Mess: How Did It Happen?* Edward J. Kane (Washington, DC: The Urban Institute Press, 1989).

37. See, for example, Myron Weiner, *The Global Migration Crisis: Challenge to States and to Human Rights* (New York: Harper Collins, 1995).

38. Paul Kennedy, *Preparing for the Twenty-First Century* (New York: Random House, 1993) 275.

39. *Washington Post*, 12 Jan. 1996, A 23.

40. See "Can China Reform Its Economy?" *Business Week* 29 Sept. 1997; "Communist China's Dilemma: Labor Strife," *Washington Post*, 11 Sept. 1997; and Jonathan Mirsky, "Democratic Vistas," *New York Review of Books*, 45, no. 13.

41. See Douglas Farah, "A Free-Trade Zone in the Traffice of Humans," *Washington Post*, 23 Oct. 1995, A1.

42. Ibid.

43. See discussion in chapter 10 of this volume.

44. Farah reports: "Senior Honduran immigration officials said that at least 20,000 naturalization cards, used to obtain Honduran passports and residency cards, were printed outside normal channels and sold during the administration of former President Rafael Callejas. Honduran and U.S. officials familiar with the case said the cards were sold for between $25,000 and $50,000 a piece to Chinese smuggling organizations in Hong Kong, netting an estimated $625,000. No one has been arrested or charged for the fraudulent sales." Ibid. Presumably the Chinese were willing to pay the high price because passports and other documents can be reused.

45. See also "The New Terrorism," *The Economist*, 15 Aug. 1998, 17–19.

46. See discussion in chapter 2.

47. Although the U.S. Congress mandated the creation of the Presidential Advisory Board on Arms Proliferation Policy in 1994, and 33 countries signed the Wassenaar Arrangement for Export Controls for Conventional Arms on 12 July 1996, neither effort has yielded significant results. See William W. Keller and Janne E. Nolan, "The Arms Trade: Business as Usual?" *Foreign Policy* 109 (winter 1997).

48. The case of Yugoslavia is only the most obvious. See "The Covert Arms Trade: The Second Oldest Profession," *The Economist*, 12 Feb. 1994.

49. For statistics on car theft, see Kevin Blake, "What You Should Know About Car Theft," *Consumer Research Magazine*, Oct. 1995.

50. John Howard, "Stolen Luxury Cars Leaving U.S. in Droves," *Minneapolis Star Tribune*, 4 July 1998, 1.

51. *The Economist* cites drug money, at $400 billion a year, as three-fourths of all laundered money. "Dirty Money," 26 Jul. 1997.

52. Mathea Falco, "U.S. Drug Policy: Addicted to Failure," *Foreign Policy* no. 102, 131.

53. Raphael Perl, "NAFTA: Implications for Illicit Drug Supply to the U.S.," *CRS Report to Congress*, 11 Nov. 1993, 2.

54. *National Review*, 12 Feb. 1996, 44.

55. See Patrick Clawson and Rensselaer W. Lee III, *The Andean Cocaine Industry* (New York: St. Martin's Press, 1996).
56. *National Review*, 12 Feb. 1996, 44.
57. Ibid.
58. See Eva Bertram, Morris Blackman, Kenneth Sharpe, and Peter Andreas, *Drug War Politics: The Price of Denial* (Berkeley and Los Angeles: University of California Press, 1996), 39.
59. There is a huge disparity between the punishment for those convicted of possessing or selling crack cocaine, who are generally black, and those dealing (at the retail level) in powder cocaine, who are generally white. Possession of five grams of crack brings a mandatory five-year federal prison term, while possession of the same amount of powder cocaine draws a one-year sentence. In 1995, President Bill Clinton aligned himself with congressional Republicans, who rejected recommendations by the U.S. Sentencing Commission to lower the prison terms for offenses involving crack cocaine to make them the same as offenses involving powder cocaine. See Ann Delroy, "Clinton Retains Tough Law on Crack Cocaine," *Washington Post*, 31 Oct. 1995, A.
60. See Bertram et al., 39.
61. *The Economist*, 4 Nov. 1995, 33.
62. *National Review*, 12 Feb. 1996, 35.
63. See Bertram et al., 264–70.
64. See generally Peter Andreas's chapter in this volume.
65. See Bertram, et al., 20–21.
66. Ibid.
67. Id. at p. 20.
68. See Peter Smith's chapter 9 in this volume.
69. See for example "Bolivia: Human Rights Violations and the War on Drugs," *Human Rights Watch Americas* 7, no. 8, (July 1995).
70. See Francisco Thoumi's chapter 6 in this volume.
71. See generally, Juan Mendes, *La "Guerra" contra las drogas en Colombia: La olvidada tragedia de la violencia politica*, (Bogota, Colombia: Centro de Estudios Internacionales de la Universidad de los Andes, 1991).
72. The case most illustrative of arbitrary discrimination was the 1997 refusal to certify Colombia, despite its arrest of senior figures in the Cali group of traffickers, while recertifying Mexico despite evidence of collusion between traffickers and high levels of the police, armed forces, and political establishment and the manifestly increased role of the Mexican groups in exporting drugs to the United States.
73. John Rice, "Mexico Protests U.S. Role in Money-Laundering Probe," *Denver Post*, 22 May 1998, 5A.
74. See, for instance, D. Brian Boggess, "Exporting United States Drug Law," *Brigham Young University Law Review* 165 (1992). After asserting, without supporting evidence, that "legalization" would fuel an "inevitable enormous increase in drug use" that would in turn "lead to similar increases in drug-related and drug-affected crimes, accidents, and untreatable addiction." He writes that, in addition, "legalization implicitly admits a moral defeat" (188).
75. Susan Strange, *The Retreat of the State* (Cambridge: Cambridge University Press, 1996) 120.
76. Hong Kong and Taiwan together with the mainland.
77. See generally Frederic Dannen, "Partners in Crime," *New Republic*, 14 & 21 July 1997.
78. For detailed accounts, see, among others, Peter Robb, *Midnight in Sicily* (London: The Harvill Press, 1998).
79. See *Tokyo Business Today*, April 1994, 47.
80. *Tokyo Business Today*, Nov. 1993; also see David E. Kaplan, "Yakuza Inc.," *U.S. News*

and World Report, 13 April 1998, 40–47; and Bozono Shigeru, "Yakuza on the Defensive," *Japan Quarterly* 45, no. 1 (Jan.–Mar. 1998): 79–86.

81.   *Washington Post,* 15 Dec. 1995, A1
82.   Quoted in Douglas Farah, "Russian Mob, Drug Cartels Joining Forces," *Washington Post,* 29 July 1997, A1.
83.   See p. 50 in Gregory Treverton's chapter 2.
84.   See Benedict Anderson, *Imagined Communities: Reflections on the Origin and Spread of Nationalism* (London: Verso 1983).
85.   Budget of the United States Government, Fiscal Year 1999, 149–54 (online at: wais.access.gpo.gov).
86.   To the best of my knowledge, among practicing politicians only that distinguished graduate of Yale University, the Reverend Pat Robertson, sometime presidential candidate, has claimed any capacity to affect the underlying problem.
87.   *The Economist,* "Dirty Money," 27 July 1997.
88.   Actually the middle and upper-class consumer pays thrice: first for the product then through taxation, for the costs of the effort to prevent the product's sale, and finally, in the form of personal insecurity, for the crime induced by the escalation of price caused by the prohibition effort financed by the self-same consumer. However, he or she is at least able to share the latter two costs with nonconsumers, thus mitigating the triple taxation, as it were.
89.   Naylor fn. 12 supra, at 5.
90.   See generally Barry A. K. Rider, "The Policing and Control of Syndicated and Organized Crime Activity in Great Britain," Oct. 1995, Report to a Select Committee of Parliament.
91.   See Lee's discussion in chapter 1.
92.   Naylor, note 12 supra, 5.
93.   See generally, Ingo Walter, *Secret Money.* See also Ethan A. Nadelmann, "Unlaundering Dirty Money Abroad: U.S. Foreign Policy and Financial Secrecy Jurisdictions," *Inter-American Law Review* 33 (Fall 1986).
94.   See discussion of money laundering in chapter 3.
95.   *Washington Post,* 5 Nov. 1995, H2.
96.   Ibid.
97.   *Economist,* 6 Jun. 1998, 23; and 15 Aug. 1998, 17–19.
98.   *Economist,* 26 Jul. 1998.
99.   But see David Wippman, "Military Intervention, Regional Organizations, and Host-State Consent," *Duke Journal of Comparative and International Law* 7, no. 1 (Fall 1996).
100. Peter Reuter, "Decline of the American Mafia," *Public Interest,* summer 1995, 91.
101. A point suggested to me by Renn Lee, see chapter 4 of *The Andean Cocaine Industry,* fn. 55 supra.
102. Compare Tom Farer, "The United States as Guarantor of Democracy in the Caribbean Basin: Is There a Legal Way?" *Human Rights Quarterly* 10 (Spring 1988): 157. But see Wippman, fn. 99 supra.

CONTRIBUTORS

Peter Andreas is an Academy Scholar at the Weatherhead Center for International Affairs, Harvard University. In recent years he has held research fellowships from the Brookings Institution and the Social Science Research Council-MacArthur Foundation Program on International Peace and Security. His publications include *Drug War Politics: The Price of Denial* (coauthor) and *The Illicit Global Economy and State Power* (coeditor). Starting in the fall of 2000, he will be an assistant professor of political science at Reed College in Portland, Oregon. He has a B.A. from Swarthmore College and an M.A. and Ph.D. in political science from Cornell University.

Alan A. Block is a professor of Administration of Justice and the interim director of the Jewish Studies Program at Pennsylvania State University. He has written, edited, and coauthored nine books covering topics such as offshore money laundering, illicit toxic waste disposal, the organization of narcotics syndicates, and sophisticated financial crime. He is currently working on manuscripts dealing with National Intelligence Services and their propensity for organized criminal behavior, the origins of the Iran-Contra scandal, and organized crime syndicates composed of diverse "new" immigrants in the United States who are stealing fuel excise taxes. Professor Block holds a Ph.D. in History from the University of California, Los Angeles.

Jack A. Blum is a partner in Lobel, Novins & Lamont, a Washington, D.C. law firm. He is an expert on controlling government corruption, international financial crime, money laundering, international tax havens, and drug trafficking. As a senior investigator he has played a central role in uncovering some of the most significant international scandals of the past twenty years, including BCCI, General Noriega's drug trafficking, and Lockheed Aircraft's overseas bribes. He has been a consultant to the United Nations Centre on Transnational Corporations, the United Nations Drug Control Policy Centre, and a number of foreign governments. He is presently a senior editor of the journal *Crime Law and Social Change*, and a guest lecturer at the Foreign Service Institute. Mr. Blum received his J.D. from Columbia Law School.

Tom Farer is dean of the Graduate School of International Studies at Denver University. He has been president of the University of New Mexico and of the Inter-American Human Rights Commission of the Organization of American States. He has also served as legal consultant to the UN operation in Somalia, and special assistant to the General Counsel of the Defense Department and of the Assistant Secretary of State for Inter-American Affairs. He has taught law at Columbia, Harvard, Rutgers, Tulane, The American University, and the University of Nanterre, and international relations at Princeton and the Johns Hopkins School of Advanced International Affairs. He is the author and editor of 11 books and monographs including *Beyond Sovereignty* (1996) and *Warclouds on the Horn of Africa* (1979). Dean Farer holds a J.D. from Harvard Law School.

Eduardo A. Gamarra is the director of the Latin American and Caribbean Center and a professor in the department of political science at Florida International University. He is also the editor of *Hemisphere*, a magazine on Latin American and Caribbean affairs. Dr. Gamarra is the author, coauthor, and editor of several books including *Latin American Political Economy in the Age of Neoliberal Reform* (1994); *Democracy, Markets and Structural Reform in Latin America: Argentina, Bolivia, Brazil, Chile and Mexico* (1995); and *Entre la Droga y la Democracia* (1994). The author of over forty articles on Latin America, he has testified in the U.S. Congress on drug policy toward Latin America. Dr. Gamarra received his Ph.D. in political science from the University of Pittsburgh.

Elizabeth Joyce is a Senior Research Associate at the Institute for European-Latin American Relations (IRELA) in Madrid. She was recently Fulbright EU-US Senior Research Scholar at Georgetown University in Washington, D.C. She has also held senior editorial posts at Oxford Analytica and EFE, the Spanish news agency. She is the author of several monographs, articles, and book chapters on transnational crime and international drug policy, and on Europe's relations with the United States and Latin America. Her book, *Latin America and the Multinational Drug Trade* (1998), coedited with Carlos Malamud, was published last year. She is currently completing a book on multilateral drug cooperation in Latin America. Dr. Joyce holds a Ph.D. from Oxford University.

Rensselaer W. Lee III is president of Global Advisory Services, a McLean, Virginia-based consulting firm specializing in international political and security issues. He is also an associate scholar at the Foreign Policy Research Institute in Philadelphia. His research experience for U.S. government and private sector clients spans such topics as transnational crime, narcotics trafficking, terrorism and insurgency, the criminal-political nexus, and illegal proliferation of nuclear materials. His publications include *The White Labyrinth: Cocaine and Political*

Power (1989); *The Andean Cocaine Industry* (second edition, 1998), coauthored with Patrick Clawson; and *Smuggling Armageddon: The Nuclear Black Market in the Former Soviet Union and Europe* (1998). Dr. Lee received his Ph.D. from Stanford University in 1973.

Anthony P. Maingot is a professor of sociology at Florida International University. He is also adjunct senior associate of the North-South Center, the University of Miami. He has been an adjunct professor of Mexican and Caribbean Studies of the U.S. Air Force School of Special Operations since 1985. His most recent books include *Small Country Development and International Labor Flows: Experiences in the Caribbean* (1991) and *The United States and the Caribbean: Challenges of an Asymmetrical Relationship* (1994). He is founding editor of *Hemisphere*, and serves on the Editorial Boards of *International Migration* (Geneva), *Anuario Social y Político de FLACSO* (Costa Rica), and *Caribbean Affairs* (Trinidad). Dr. Maingot holds a Ph.D. from the University of Florida (Gainsville).

Peter H. Smith is a professor of political science, adjunct professor of history, adjunct professor of the Graduate School of International Relations and Pacific Studies, director of the Center for Iberian and Latin American Studies, and Simon Bolivar professor of Latin American Studies at the University of California at San Diego. His major publications include *Argentina and the Failure of Democracy: Conflict among Political Elites, 1904–1955* (1974) and *Labyrinths of Power: Political Recruitment in Twentieth-Century Mexico* (1979). He is coauthor of *Modern Latin America* (1984), now in its third edition (1992), and editor of *Drug Policy in the Americas* (1992) and *The Challenge of Integration: Europe and the Americas* (1993). Dr. Smith served as president of the Latin American Studies Association and codirector of the Bilateral Commission on the Future of United States-Mexican Relations and of the Inter-American Commission on Drug Policy. He received his Ph.D. at Columbia University.

Francisco E. Thoumi has worked at the Colombian Planning Department, the World Bank, and the Inter-American Development Bank. He has been a professor of economics at California State University-Chico and director of the Center for International Studies at the Universidad de los Andes. He has written extensively on the impact of illegal drugs in Colombia and other Andean countries. He is the author of *Political Economy and Illegal Drugs in Colombia* (1995) and *Las drogas ilícitas en Bolivia, Colombia, y Perú* (UNDP, forthcoming). He is also the editor of *Drogas ilícitas en Colombia* (1997) and *Drogas ilícitas en Bolivia* (UNDP, forthcoming). Dr. Thoumi holds an economics degree from the Universidad de los Andes, Bogotá, Colombia, and a Ph.D. from the University of Minnesota.

Gregory F. Treverton is director of RAND's International Security and Defense Policy Center, where he is responsible for work on regional issues, arms control and proliferation, force planning, and international economics. Previously, he was vice chairman of the National Intelligence Council, and senior fellow at the Council on Foreign Relations, where he directed the Europe-America Project and the Project on America's Role in a Changed World. He has also held positions at the International Institute for Strategic Studies in London and the Kennedy School of Government at Harvard University. His recent books include *America, Germany and the Future of Europe* (1992); *Rethinking America's Security*, coathored with Graham T. Allison (1992); and *Making American Foreign Policy* (1994). He received his Ph.D. in economics and politics from Harvard's Kennedy School of Government.

INDEX